MERCENARIES AND MISSIONARIES

Capitalism and Catholicism
in the Global South

Brandon Vaidyanathan

CORNELL UNIVERSITY PRESS   ITHACA AND LONDON

First published 2019 by Cornell University Press

Library of Congress Cataloging-in-Publication Data   ϡ

Names: Vaidyanathan, Brandon, author.
Title: Mercenaries and missionaries : capitalism and Catholicism in the global
    south / Brandon Vaidyanathan.
Description: Ithaca : Cornell University Press, 2019. | Includes bibliographical
    references and index.
Identifiers: LCCN 2018045105 (print) | LCCN 2018047141 (ebook) |
    ISBN 9781501736247 (pdf) | ISBN 9781501736254 (epub/mobi)
    | ISBN 9781501736223 | ISBN 9781501736223 (cloth) |
    ISBN 9781501736230 (pbk)
Subjects: LCSH: Professional employees—Religious life—India—Bangalore. |
    Professional employees—Religious life—United Arab Emirates—Dubai. |
    Catholics—Religious life—India—Bangalore. | Catholics—Religious life—
    United Arab Emirates—Dubai. | Religion in the workplace—India—Bangalore. |
    Religion in the workplace—United Arab Emirates—Dubai. | Consumption
    (Economics)—Moral and ethical aspects—India—Bangalore. | Consumption
    (Economics)—Moral and ethical aspects—United Arab Emirates—Dubai. |
    Capitalism—Religious aspects—Catholic Church. | Work—Religious aspects—
    Catholic Church.
Classification: LCC HD8038.I42 (ebook) | LCC HD8038.I42 B368 2019 (print) |
    DDC 331.7/1095357—dc23
LC record available at https://lccn.loc.gov/2018045105

MERCENARIES AND MISSIONARIES

for Claire

Contents

Acknowledgments   ix

Introduction   1

1. The Mercenary   28

2. The Missionary   67

3. Missionaries in a Mercenary World   103

4. Finding Escape Velocity   134

5. Belonging and Civic Commitment in the Neoliberal City   168

Conclusion   209

Appendix: *Methodology*   223

Notes   237

References   255

Index   273

Acknowledgments

This book would have been impossible without the help of many people, many more than I am able to name in these few pages. First, my sincere thanks to Christian Smith for his mentorship and persistent confidence in me and in this book from the very beginning, especially in my many moments of doubt. I am grateful to him and also to Lyn Spillman for patiently reading several drafts of these chapters and my grant applications, as well as for writing the numerous letters of recommendation needed to fund my research. I am also especially grateful to Omar Lizardo and Dave Sikkink for our many thought-provoking conversations and for their insightful comments. Many thanks to Elaine Howard Ecklund and David Johnson for their encouragement and immensely helpful feedback. I am deeply grateful to Jim Lance, my editor at Cornell University Press, and to the reviewers of this manuscript for their enthusiastic support.

Conversations with several scholars over the past few years produced many helpful insights that shaped this book. My sincere thanks to Scott Appleby, Carson Dutt, Phil Gorski, Brad Gregory, Vittorio Hosle, Mike and Ines Jindra, Mary-Ellen Konieczny, Alasdair Macintyre, Margarita Mooney, Ebrahim Moosa, Jim Nolan, Tim Rutzou, Jason Springs, Don Stelluto, and Robert Wuthnow.

I am also grateful to Robert Brenneman, Anne Snyder Brooks, and Daniel McInerny for their detailed feedback and editing advice on earlier versions of the manuscript, and to Gail Chalew for her excellent copyediting. Many friends and colleagues provided valuable insights and comments on my ideas and drafts; they include Jade Avelis, Cole Carnasecca, Austin Choi-Fitzpatrick, Kari Christoffersen, Hilary Davidson Green, Jeff Guhin, Trish Herzog, Jon Hill, Peter Mundey, Melissa Pirkey, Paul Radich, Dan Roloff, Katherine Sorrell, Ana Velitchkova, Adrian Walker, and Meredith Whitnah. My sincere thanks to you all!

Ideas underlying many of this book's themes were presented at various workshops and conferences, including the annual meetings of the American Sociological Association, the American Academy of Religion, the Academy of Management, and the Society for the Scientific Study of Religion. I am especially grateful for feedback received from the working group on the Research and Analysis in the Sociology of Religion and from the Culture Workshop at Notre Dame, the Social Science Research Council Dissertation Workshop, the Religion and Public Life Program at Rice University, and the Human Ecology Institute at Catholic University of America.

Writing this book would have been impossible without the generous support of the Graduate School, the Institute for the Study of the Liberal Arts, and the Kellogg Institute for International Studies at the University of Notre Dame, as well as the Society for the Social Scientific Study of Religion. Sincere thanks to Stephen Keck and the Department of International Studies at the American University of Sharjah for hosting me as a visiting scholar. Thanks also to the Miranda and Avallone families for hosting me in Dubai, to the Driessens for their hospitality in Doha, to the Ahmed family for their hospitality in Kuwait, and to Michael and Kishore for providing me office space and finding me an apartment in Rome.

My sincere thanks to many friends for their invaluable companionship, which enabled me to sustain the energy and dedication needed to complete this book; they include Pietro Bocchia, the Buschbachers, Paolo Carozza, Carolyn Chau, Brandon Cook, Luigi Crema, Kim D'Souza, the Gardners, the Gianferraris, Maddi Giungi, the Michalska-Smiths, Josh Norcross, Fr. Robert Pelton, Pier Pigozzi, Alisha Ruiss, Vivek Trindade, and the Violettes.

Claire Vaidyanathan, my spouse and motivational guru, helped me think through every idea in this book and listened to more presentations and read more drafts than is good for anyone. Thank you so much for your continuing encouragement, inspiration, and love, without which this book would never have come to fruition. Irene, Marta, Mikey, and Frankie: thank you for accompanying me through this work, day in and day out—you have not known a world in which this project did not exist!—and for making it all worthwhile. My sincere thanks to my parents for putting up with this strange line of work, and especially to my brother Venky, without whose help my research in India would have been practically impossible. Heartfelt thanks also to the Petersons for all their support throughout the years.

Finally, my sincere gratitude to everyone who participated in the study, for inviting me into your lives and giving me your time, trust, and friendship. I have learned so much from you and hope that you find the results of the study interesting, if not useful.

MERCENARIES AND MISSIONARIES

Introduction

Most of us today are accustomed to living somewhat fragmented lives. We negotiate multiple and often competing demands on our energy, time, money, and sense of self. We experience our lives as being parceled out among many domains, each with its respective norms of what is appropriate or inappropriate, worthy or unworthy—and each staking rival claims to what we ought to value and how we ought to live. We find ourselves valorizing sacrificial commitments to one domain over the other: sometimes the personal over the professional and other times the reverse. The struggle is not simply about managing time; it is about maintaining a coherent sense of self and identity.[1]

Sociologists have long understood modernity as entailing such fragmentation—a differentiation of value spheres, as Max Weber called it.[2] But the relationship between these spheres is ever-changing and poses ever new challenges. In rapidly developing contexts such as emerging markets in the Global South, many people find themselves at the intersection of two kinds of forces: on the one hand, global flows of technology, capital, ideologies, and migration and, on the other, local cultural traditions and political institutions.[3] In such contexts, fragmentation is heightened by the intensive disruption and reinvention of routines, certainties, and identities. This book tries to understand what happens to people caught between the currents of global religion and global capitalism, who are straddling competing commitments to faith and work in such contexts, and what their stories might teach us about the cultural consequences of modernity.

Of Mercenaries and Missionaries

"In corporate industries, we're all mercenaries," laughed Ashwin Mathews.[4] "We work for the money. Honest—honest truth! I don't work for loyalty, right? I'm not loyal to the company. I work for the cash!"

I first met Ashwin in an old convent in the heart of Bangalore, where his prayer group met weekly. It was the last place I would expect to encounter a flock of self-proclaimed mercenaries. They are not the sort of mercenaries who fight and kill for money. Instead, they are part of a new breed of economic mercenaries engaged in a relentless, unabashed pursuit of upward mobility. These are young professionals, mostly in their thirties, climbing the corporate ladder in global firms such as IBM, Dell, HP, and Apple. Their ultramodern, glass-paneled, air-conditioned office buildings, nestled in pristine, sprawling campuses with gated security, stand in contrast to the dusty, noisy traffic of their surroundings in rapidly developing global cities. These professionals straddle Americanized or westernized workplaces and local, traditional family commitments. Their income far surpasses that of their parents at the same age. They spend lavishly on consumeristic pursuits, but manage to send remittances to families in their home towns; some even buy homes for their parents. They have done their parents proud, and their nations too: they are celebrated as drivers of progress, development, and modernity.

Ashwin, by day, works as a systems analyst for a U.S.-based tech giant. He has achieved the Indian middle-class dream of becoming an IT professional, the hero of the nation's new narrative of economic progress. Were he not already married, he would be eminently marriageable. He boasts an American—better, global—brand name on his resume, which pretty much guarantees him a position in the competitor firm to which he plans to eventually jump. Indeed, at the time of this writing, five years since I first interviewed him, he has switched firms twice and relocated to the United States. His work environment is intensely competitive: gossiping, brownnosing, backstabbing, and occasional sabotage are commonplace. Work as such holds little meaning for him; it is simply a means to more money and mobility.

On the weekends, Ashwin devotes most of his time to serving on the local leadership team of a Charismatic Catholic movement that originated in India and has now spread to more than twenty-five countries. The first time I attended a weekly meeting of one of their Bangalore groups, I encountered more than a dozen Indian IT professionals, with about an equal number of men and women, most of them single and in their late twenties and early thirties, sitting in a circle on plastic chairs in the foyer of the convent auditorium. One member of the group pulled out a guitar. Another passed around booklets of "praise and worship" songs written by U.S.- and U.K.-based contemporary Christian music artists, with titles such as "Shout to the Lord," "I Could Sing of Your Love Forever," and "Lord, You Have My Heart," all staples in professionals' prayer groups I visited in India and the Arabian Gulf. The music was fast-paced at first. The entire group was up on their feet, clapping, swaying, raising their arms, and following choreographed gestures for words such as "seek" and "heart." The tempo gradually slowed to create a more contemplative mood. The group members began to sit or kneel during the last song. Moments of quiet ensued. A couple of people prayed softly in tongues. A woman who had been moved to tears during the music began wiping her face and nose with a handkerchief. Soon all of those who were not already kneeling got onto their knees on the granite floor and pulled out their rosaries. The woman next to me noticed I did not have one and gave me the extra one she carried, and several people took turns leading the chain of *Our Fathers*, *Hail Marys*, and *Glory Bes*.

A stocky young man with a pencil-thin goatee and broad smile, who later introduced himself to me as Ashwin, then offered the group a "teaching." He pulled out his Android smartphone and began reading a passage from the Gospel. Most people followed along, from bibles that they had brought with them or their phones or by peering over their neighbors' shoulders. Following the reading— the passage about the miracle of the multiplication of the loaves and the fishes— Ashwin read an exegetical lesson that he found online, explaining how the miracle connects to the Eucharist; he then added his own reflections. He emphasized clinging to things of the Spirit more than to things that fill the belly, patting his own in self-deprecating humor.

Ashwin, like the other professionals I met in this group and in other church groups I visited in Bangalore and Dubai during my research, straddles disparate commitments to the realms of corporate life and religion. At work, he is a self-professed mercenary. He enjoys his job, but is resolved to go wherever the money is. He complains that he cannot trust his colleagues in the workplace: everyone is simply out to maximize his or her chances for promotion. So he avoids getting to know anyone too well, surmising that he too will be moving on soon enough anyway. When it comes to his church group, however, we see a different side of Ashwin. Like other leaders of prayer groups I encountered in India and the Arabian Gulf, he sees himself as a missionary, committed to loyal service to God and neighbor within a specific community: "This [prayer group] is my main mission, my ministry . . . . God is calling me to serve here . . . . I feel at home here." These are not missionaries in the traditional sense of going to the ends of the earth to proselytize; they see their mission as primarily to be a witness to those in their own churches who have not yet experienced God's healing power.

This book is a story about religion and capitalism in a rapidly globalizing world. Central to this story are two characters that have appeared quite recently on the global scene: the Mercenary and the Missionary. By "characters" I mean symbolic images that represent how people in particular social environments orient their lives.[5] Like stock characters in a play, these are recognizable models tied to particular social roles and contexts. For people in those roles and contexts, these models serve as templates for their personal conduct and for interpreting others' behaviors. They reflect distinct standards of worth, visions of the good, and behavioral expectations; they exemplify what it means to "play the game" well in a particular domain. Such characters serve as crucial reference points: even when people in these contexts distance themselves from such models, they recognize that they are breaking from the mold.

The character of the Mercenary governs global corporate workplaces and is steeped in cutthroat competition with colleagues who ought not to be trusted. Eschewing organizational loyalty, the Mercenary is not interested in maximizing company profits, but instead is oriented toward the relentless pursuit of individual mobility as measured in terms of salary and status. The Missionary, in contrast, is the orienting model in new religious communities generated by the global diffusion of evangelical and Pentecostal Christianity, which in the Catholic Church form an amalgam that I call Evangelical-Charismatic Catholicism. The Missionary seeks the transforming power of God in faith communities from which he or she seeks trust and healing. To be clear, I am not saying that these are the only orientations in these contexts: people certainly pursue belonging in corporations and chase after power and ambition in churches. What I am claiming is that these are the dominant orientations identified by people in these contexts.

The paradox, evident in Ashwin Mathews and many global professionals like him, is that the Mercenary and the Missionary are not different people. Rather they are conflicting orientations adopted by the *same persons*: people who often believe themselves to be living integrated lives. Such a paradox generates two questions that are the focus of this book:

> How and why do global professionals in emerging economies sustain starkly opposing moral orientations in the realms of work and religion?
> What consequences—both personal and social—does straddling these conflicting orientations produce in different sociopolitical contexts?

In answering these questions, I show how the distinct norms of the Mercenary and the Missionary are produced by powerful cultural mechanisms operating in global corporations and in globally diffusing Christian communities. In spite of their contradictions, however, these norms turn out to be symbiotic. An "apprehensive individualism" cultivated in the Mercenary workplace fuels the need for healing and meaning, which these professionals seek in church communities. Church groups cultivate a "therapeutic individualism" that rejuvenates members to return to face the cutthroat workplace. Work as such is meaningless to them, but the workplace becomes a mission field, providing numerous opportunities to symbolically integrate their faith. The professionals who live this symbiosis find new cultural capacities through which to navigate the challenges of corporate life, but without excelling at, transforming, or rejecting it. Local sociopolitical restrictions on minorities play a crucial role in shaping the lives of these professionals and the relationship between religion and capitalism in these contexts. As a result, the cultures of both workplaces and churches restrict possibilities for meaning, solidarity, and justice and reinforce a consumer citizenship among politically alienated middle classes in these cities. By uncovering the gains and losses that come with such symbiosis, this book provides new insights into the relationship between new forms of global religion and global capitalism.

How This Book Came About

My research questions emerged as I conducted twelve months of participant observation and two hundred interviews between 2010 and 2012, primarily in Bangalore, India, and Dubai, United Arab Emirates. The initial motivation for this research arose earlier, when I spent the spring of 2005 visiting my family and looking for work in both cities. I had been away from Dubai for five years and from Bangalore for nearly a decade, and I could not believe how much the cities had changed. None of the superlative architecture for which Dubai is now renowned was in place when I was a high school student there. And Bangalore had sprouted new glass-paneled office towers of multinational corporations, where the phenomenon of business process outsourcing (BPO) was being heralded as the key to India's future.

The more I learned about offshore call centers, the more I struggled to understand the cultural consequences of this form of global capitalism: Was this a new form of imperialism and colonization, with Indians toiling through the night, donning fake accents and identities to provide cheaper service to the West? Was the new economy having a corrosive effect on local cultures and traditions? There were certainly signs to suggest these sorts of changes were occurring, but the stories I was hearing were also positive; they were stories of newfound freedom, not only to pursue consumer lifestyles but also to fulfill traditional obligations such as supporting one's parents. As sociologists Luc Boltanski and Ève Chiapello have argued, new forms of capitalism, in order to generate a commitment from the actors who embrace their structures and values, need to be experienced by those actors as attractive and even liberating in some way.[6] While conducting research on call center workers for my master's thesis in 2007, I encountered, to my surprise, many employees for whom religion, rather than becoming a casualty of capitalism, played a vital role in motivating and sustaining their ability to work in these often difficult environments. My research taught me about the complexity of the relationship between modernity and tradition and, by extension, between capitalism and religion.

I decided to further investigate the relationship between religion and capitalism for my doctoral dissertation. I stayed in touch with several of the call center workers I had interviewed in Bangalore, who had begun climbing up the corporate ladder in multinational firms. In the meantime, conversations with old friends in Dubai in similar positions and companies started to suggest interesting similarities and differences with regard to the consequences of global capitalism. I then conducted exploratory research visits to Bangalore and Dubai for two months in 2010; these visits included in-person and focus-group interviews with professionals of diverse religious backgrounds. Deciding to narrow my focus to Catholicism to enable comparison of a single religious institution across the two cities, I returned in 2011–2012 to conduct the remainder of my research. My research for this book comprised participant observation in both religious and secular contexts: prayer group meetings, liturgical services, parish committee meetings, religious retreats, shopping malls, entertainment venues, workplaces, and industry association conferences. I conducted in-depth interviews with corporate professionals (both Catholic and non-Catholic), lay church leaders, and religious professionals, including local priests and bishops, and church officials at the Vatican. I describe my methodology in more detail in the appendix.

As my project took shape, a second, more personal reason motivated my work. It became clear to me that this tale of the Mercenary and the Missionary could very well have been my own. I grew up in these very environments and was on a similar trajectory. Like many of the people I interviewed in this study, I grew up a second-generation expat in the Arabian Gulf, shuttling back and forth between India and Gulf countries as my parents moved in and out of jobs. I also worked, and was being trained to work, in companies very similar to those of the Mercenaries I was studying. I frequented similar religious groups to the Missionaries I talk about in this book. But my subsequent immersion in very different environments disrupted old routines and led me to see what was once familiar, natural, and taken for granted as new and strange. The privilege and luxury of a liberal arts education taught me to ask questions that many of my friends, who either pursued technical degrees or began working right after high school, were not able to systematically ask: questions about the meanings of work, citizenship, the common good, and the role of social structures in shaping our lives.

I returned to these environments as both insider and outsider. This helped me ask new questions, see new connections, and identify blind spots ordinarily

inaccessible to someone completely immersed in these environments; in particular, my vantage point enabled me to find inconsistencies between Mercenary
and Missionary orientations. To be sure, my outsider perspective has not immu-
nized me from my own ethical inconsistencies, blind spots, and tendencies toward
mercenary and consumerist behavior. My intention in this book is not to pass
moral judgments on the people I studied, many of whom are now dear friends. Nor
is it to solve their problems, to which I do not see easy solutions. Rather, this book
is an exercise in "moral sociology": it is an attempt to describe the moral orientations that govern people's ideals, actions, and evaluations in different contexts; to
uncover the factors that sustain those orientations; and to analyze their personal
and social consequences.[7] My hope is that this descriptive and analytical work
can help illuminate problems and enable us to work towards solutions.

Contributions of This Study

This book is more than just a story about Asian Catholic professionals. By examining how these professionals negotiate the relationship between the Mercenary
and the Missionary, I develop new insights about why so many of us are able to
maintain conflicting commitments in disparate realms of life and how such processes are shaped by broader structural and contextual factors.

As Peter Berger has argued, modernity leads to a pluralism that amplifies the
range of choices open to human beings.[8] In rapidly developing postindustrial contexts, people confront a dizzying array of choices regarding work, lifestyle, and
religion. New forms of work in the global economy, as well as rapidly diffusing
forms of religion, such as Pentecostalism, have a highly individuating effect, dis-
connecting individuals from their taken-for-granted certainties, traditions, and
communities and giving them the opportunity to make new life choices and forge
new identities.[9] Making such choices also entails adopting new normative structures in those domains, learning new religious and secular discourses, and navigating the relationship between them. Not only is it cognitively difficult to integrate
these realms but also structural factors in one's social context shape the meanings and possibilities of integration.

In this book, I identify the key cultural mechanisms that sustain people's distinct normative orientations in different religious and secular domains, as well
as the gains and losses entailed by their efforts to navigate these realms. To do so,
I examine members of one religious institution, Roman Catholicism, who work
for global corporations in two rapidly developing cities: Bangalore and Dubai.
This approach allows me to study how new forms of global religion interact
with rapidly spreading forms of modern secularity, such as corporate life and

consumerism, outside the West. By looking at members of the new middle classes in India and the Arabian Gulf, this book provides an empirically informed account of what it is like, even outside the West, to live in what the philosopher Charles Taylor calls "a secular age": a pluralistic world in which religion has become one sphere of life among others and in which people spend most of their time in social realms whose internal workings do not require religious belief.

Existing studies in India and the Arabian Gulf on the consequences of global capitalism have largely overlooked the role of religion.[10] This oversight is a problem because corporate professionals are an increasingly important demographic in developing economies. Studies that examine them in isolation from their broader cultural contexts, in which religion plays an important role, leave us with an impoverished understanding of these actors and of their role in society.

My study of Christians as a minority population in both regions also helps me "provincialize" standard Western assumptions and models of these contexts; for instance, assumptions that Indian equals Hindu, Arab equals Muslim, non-Western equals "third world" or "undeveloped" or "traditional," or that citizenship is only about formal/legal belonging.[11] In the section "Religion and Capitalism" in this introduction, I provide more information about the particular contexts and cases I studied and why they are germane for our understanding of the relationship between religion and capitalism.

In chapters 1 and 2, I examine the factors that generate and sustain the starkly opposing moral orientations of the Mercenary in global corporations and the Missionary in Evangelical-Charismatic Catholic communities. In these chapters, I identify three cultural mechanisms that sustain each of these characters: (1) *narrative scripts* that guide people's evaluations and internal conversations about goals and strategies; (2) *mimesis,* or the largely inadvertent imitation of models, which generates similar dispositions among people within each realm; and (3) *habituation* or routinization of skills and practices, which creates a centripetal force to maintain consistency of dispositions. People's adherence to these representative characters is not primarily driven by their intentions to be good professionals or church leaders, but rather by cultural processes that tacitly shape their orientations and dispositions. This is why, in chapter 1, we find corporate HR directors oblivious to the irony of complaining about attrition in their firms while they themselves are plotting their next career jump.

Having outlined these two characters, I examine the interactions between Mercenary and Missionary orientations in people's lives: in their workplaces, lifestyles, and cities. Chapter 3 shows how and why the same person simultaneously participates in multiple modes of integrating and segmenting work and faith. Even if work as such remains inherently meaningless to these professionals, the workplace becomes a mission field, in which one's mission is to resist temptations to compromise one's faith. In practice, this means rejecting some of the means and strategies of the Mercenary while still adhering to the same ends. This chapter also shows how beliefs, skills, and habits cultivated in the Missionary realm prove to be both assets and liabilities for workplace performance. Both these professionals' successes and failures strengthen their commitments to their faith, while the therapeutic individualism of the Missionary realm enables them to return to the workplace rejuvenated to continue the struggle. The various possibilities for incorporating aspects of faith into the workplace allow professionals to see their professional and religious lives as integrated. But it also blinds them to significant structural and systemic constraints that limit the scope of integration.

Chapter 4 examines the lifestyles of corporate professionals in Bangalore and Dubai. It reveals how consumerism has become the default aspirational mode of belonging when one has been rendered voiceless. It also examines how difficult it is, given the strength of consumerism, for religion to become a dominant influence in the lives of these professionals, even those who aspire to be "missionaries." Here I identify the difficult conditions under which religion can generate "escape velocity" to foster an "exit" from the dominant patterns of consumerism.

Finally, in chapter 5, I turn to an examination of how churches mediate the relationship between professionals and their cities. I show how in rapidly globalizing cities, where people often feel alienated and disoriented, religious communities can provide not only a sense of belonging but also the means for professionals to give back to their communities. My findings, however, reveal a puzzle: Catholic professionals in Dubai, although expatriates in a nondemocratic nation, are more actively involved in poverty-alleviation efforts through the church than are their counterparts in Bangalore who are citizens in a democracy. I explain how distinct structural and historical factors in these two cities have led to these different outcomes. I also show how churches, in spite of providing a sense of home and a means of civic participation, reproduce alienating conceptions of civic worth that can perpetuate the very problems they are trying to address.

Studying the relationship between religion and capitalism in these contexts helps address a long-standing sociological question about the fate of religion in the modern world. This question is often framed as follows: Does "modernization" in the form of economic growth lead to secularization or religious decline, or can religion withstand the steamroller effect of capitalism?[12] I argue that framing this question in these terms is fundamentally wrong. Echoing Berger, I claim that modernity—and by extension, capitalism—does not necessitate secularization or religious decline, but rather a pluralism of religious and secular options. Religious decline is always a possible outcome, but so are various forms of religious resurgence and symbiosis.

In the contexts I studied, rapid economic development generates a weak symbiosis between global religion and global capitalism, in which the two largely support one another, often inadvertently. Each entity also generates mechanisms and processes that chafe against and inhibit the other, but such constraint is secondary. Both global capitalism and global religion thrive in these contexts: churches are packed and overflowing, and professionals play an active role in them; continuous migration feeds increased participation in corporate jobs and consumerist lifestyles; and the very same people inhabit and sustain the institutions of both religion and capitalism.

Some argue that economic development, by solving problems for which people traditionally sought solutions in religion (e.g., poverty and illness), produces existential security and thus weakens the need for religion.[13] But I demonstrate that global capitalism also generates new forms of existential *insecurity*, for which religion provides relief and refuge. In doing so, religion reinforces people's ability to participate in these new forms of capitalism, although not wholeheartedly. Religion serves this role not only for the poor, who tend to be the focus of studies of religion in developing societies, but also for upwardly mobile professionals.

The Mercenary and Missionary thus live a symbiotic relationship between an apprehensive individualism that emerges in corporate workplaces and a therapeutic individualism cultivated in church communities. This symbiosis ensures the persistence and importance of religion in "secularizing" contexts—but not without costs.

Background: Theories, Cases, and Context
Religion and Capitalism

The relationship between religion and capitalism was an animating concern for many classical sociologists. These scholars tended to see religion as a conservative social force that bolstered capitalism and assumed that the progress of capitalism—and modernity, more generally—would weaken religion.

Karl Marx, for instance, saw religion as a human creation and projection, a product of alienation and frustrated needs.[14] Religious consciousness would remain as long as capitalist structures perpetuated alienation.[15] But religion, in his estimation, was hardly a powerful force. He accorded it little importance, famously dismissing it as the "opium of the people": a tool for those who dominated society to keep in place illusions that would impede challenges to the existing order. This view is hardly irrelevant today. In chapter 5, for instance, we encounter a priest in Dubai who admits that the state only permitted the establishment of the church in the region as a means to prevent unrest and provide social control over migrant workers.

In Marx's view, capitalism's relationship to religion is essentially parasitic. Capitalism benefits from the support of religion, but at the same time "melts all that is solid into air and profanes all that is holy."[16] It does violence to religion and humanity alike, establishing itself as supreme with "godlike power."[17] Neglected from this view is any possibility that religion might serve as a source of resistance to capitalism.

While Marx saw religion as impotent, Max Weber viewed it as an important cultural force. In his analysis of the relationship between Protestantism and capitalism, he argued that religion was a crucial source of motivations and ideals that generated the dispositions central to modern capitalism.[18] Specifically, the unique ethic of Calvinism's "inner-worldly asceticism," developed through believers' attempts to validate their status as the elect, led them to engage in the methodical, systematic pursuit of profit as a calling, but to eschew its enjoyment through consumption. This fashioned the "spirit" of modern capitalism: the pursuit of profit as an end in itself. Weber was clear that Calvinism did not *cause* capitalism, nor was it simply a cover-up for "real" economic motives. Rather, it was a necessary-but-not-sufficient condition for the emergence of modern capitalism in the West.[19]

But in Weber's analysis, religion's role ends with providing the motivational underpinnings for a mechanism that in turn breaks free from its initial moorings and becomes self-sustaining. In his analysis of how the bureaucratic ethos of modern capitalism becomes divested of its initial status as vocation—"the Puritan *wanted to* be a person with a vocational calling; today we *are forced* to be"—he neglected to consider what role religion might *continue* to play in shaping capitalism.[20] In this book, I show how religion can provide cognitive capacities, practical skills, and even institutional supports that help sustain capitalism.

Weber largely came to be interpreted as a proponent of the classical model of secularization: the expectation that, with the advance of modernization, religious commitment would decline or become privatized, if not ultimately disappear.[21] However, this classical model of secularization proved to be problematic at both the theoretical and empirical levels.

At the theoretical core of the classical model of secularization is the concept of functional differentiation. This is the idea that modern societies are fragmented into autonomous domains; religion is no longer an overarching "sacred canopy," but simply one "value sphere" among others.[22] Weber understood value spheres as autonomous institutional orders oriented to distinct "ultimate" values—politics, the economy, religion, aesthetics, erotic love, and science—each with its own internally consistent logic. He saw these spheres as incommensurable, tending toward increasing autonomy, and coming into irreconcilable conflict with one another, producing clashes between rival gods.[23] Such clashes would put people in the inevitable position of having to subjectively commit themselves to one "god" or another.[24] Religion had an exceptional status among these spheres because of its unique totalizing tendency.[25] But having become simply one option among many, it was expected to lose its all-encompassing authority and to undergo perpetual challenge and weakening. Classical secularization theorists thus predicted that, through the process of modernization that accompanied the spread of capitalism, religion was fated to decline.

A number of empirical challenges disproved this prediction. Several countries saw the resurgence of new modes of public religion.[26] With events such as the Iranian Revolution and the rise of liberation theology in Latin America, religion began to be seen as a potential challenge to capitalism. In time, scholars began to point out numerous means through which religion was able to confront the dominant political-economic order, including through transcendent motivations, organizational resources, shared identities, social and geographic positioning, privileged legitimacy, and institutional self-interest.[27] Michael Budde, for instance, argued that the Catholic Church in the developing world would have an anticapitalist thrust.[28]

But religion in the late twentieth century would do more than just challenge capitalism. These decades would see—at least in the United States—a newly emerging role for religion and spirituality, in which they would be cast as vital supports for the functioning of capitalism itself. Weber could not have foreseen the explosion of interest in "spirituality in the workplace" and "faith at work" that has marked the past few decades. These movements arose in part from seeds of discontent sown by capitalism itself: repeated corporate scandals would produce handwringing about the need for "ethics and values"; the volatility of the new economy and the insecurity of the new psychological contract would produce anxiety and demoralization among employees.[29] Companies trying to increase innovation, productivity, and retention began to put emphasis on creating conditions for self-actualization and bringing the "whole person" to work. They started to offer not only yoga and meditation classes but also workplace chaplains.[30] Meanwhile, religious leaders—both clergy and laity—developed new theological discourses about the importance of supporting business as a praiseworthy vocation.[31] I say more about religion in the workplace in chapter 3, but let me emphasize here that this crucial way in which religion started to make its way into the workplace has remained largely neglected by sociologists.[32]

By now, it should be clear that Max Weber's central assumptions about value spheres—their requiring single organizing principles that necessarily come into conflict—are fundamentally untenable, at least as a basis for predicting the fate of religion in the modern world.[33] Not only are these assumptions theoretically problematic but they are also incapable of accounting for various empirical phenomena that shaped the role of religion in the past century, including forms of religious persistence and revival and religion's ability to both support and challenge secular spheres.[34] As Peter Berger, one of the foremost proponents of secularization theory, came to realize in his later years, modernity does not necessitate religious decline. What it does necessitate, instead, is pluralism: a differentiation and diffusion of multiple religious and secular domains.[35] There is no need to posit a priori an antagonism or clash between these realms. Such pluralism need not require a "weakening" (i.e., decline or privatization or generalization) of religion, although that might well occur. It might also result in relationships such as support, amplification, symbiosis, or mere coexistence between different aspects of religion and capitalism. Such relationships can also obtain at different levels of analysis: in microlevel interpersonal interactions as people try to integrate or segment their roles in different domains, in mesolevel interactions between religious and secular organizations, and in macrolevel interactions at national and global levels.

Undertaking such an analysis also requires examining the *mutual* relationship between religion and capitalism, in contrast to the one-directional approach of many classical studies. Attempts to recognize the mutual nature of this relationship have been rare. Notable exceptions are Liston Pope's analysis of the relationship between cotton mills and churches in a county in North Carolina[36] and works by Joseph Gusfield and Robert Booth Fowler that identify modes of symbiosis between religion and "modernity" and the "liberal order," respectively.[37] Building on such approaches, this book takes into consideration both sides of the relationship.

In this book, I empirically examine some of the most prominent forms of convergence in global religion and global capitalism: my focus is on members of a supposedly Western/global religion, working in Western/global corporations, consuming Western/global products, and living in global (and some might say westernized) cities. In fact, the next two chapters may read like a story about the Americanization of the world, depicting considerable uniformity across workplaces and churches. This narrative would resonate with various scholars' observations of "an emerging global culture" that is "heavily American both in origin and content," indicating that the world is becoming "a single cultural and social setting."[38] The similarity in orientations of the Mercenary and the Missionary across national contexts can suggest a convergence that is not only structural but is even cultural: at the level of meanings, values, and conceptions of the good. But it would be a mistake to conclude the story here. These convergent elements in fact interact very differently with local contextual elements in the two cities, as

I show later in this book. Global professionals in different geographical and political contexts might well share very similar moral orientations and visions of the good life. But these very same sets of ideals are differently supported by, and interact in different ways with, local contexts, forming hybrids or "multiple modernities."[39] Such differences in my cases become especially clear in chapter 5.

Since the range of phenomena encompassed by concepts such as "religion" and "capitalism" are too vast to be meaningfully examined in any one empirical study, I follow Joseph Gusfield's injunction to focus on specific cases as a starting point for investigating this relationship.[40] In the following sections, I provide a brief introduction to the cases and contexts I study and then provide additional relevant details in the chapters that follow.

Global Capitalism

This book is concerned with the dominant mode of global capitalism today, which is variously called neoliberal financial capitalism, finance-dominated capitalism, or simply neoliberalism.[41] This is a social structure, global in scope, the building blocks of which are private property, trade across international markets, employment contracts, and complex financial institutions.[42] This structure is distinct from other kinds of market economies or other "varieties of capitalism," such as coordinated market economies (CMEs) in northern Europe.[43] When I speak about "capitalism" in the contexts I study, it is to this specific form that I refer, not to market economies in general.

Neoliberal capitalism is not simply an economic system but also has important political and cultural dimensions. First and foremost it is, as David Harvey argues, "a theory of political economic practices that proposes that human well-being can best be advanced by liberating individual entrepreneurial freedoms and skills within an institutional framework characterized by strong private property rights, free markets, and free trade."[44] Pursuing this vision implies commitments on the part of the state; notably, policies that privilege free-market instruments and openness to global trade, as well as various forms of tax benefits and subsidies. As a logic of action, neoliberalism tends toward "the financialization of everything," as is evident in the commitment of states "to optimize the conditions for capital accumulation no matter what the consequences for employment or social well-being."[45] It also entails new cultural ideals and practices, such as new forms of individualism in people's aspirations for the good life, the idolization of entrepreneurs and professionals, and consumerism as a basis of worth and identity.[46] Leslie Sklair argues that three institutions—transnational corporations, the culture-ideology of consumerism, and the transnational capitalist class, which includes global professionals—sustain the global impact of neoliberalism.[47]

The model sketched here differs in many respects from the ideals to which its proponents aspire. Libertarian proponents, for instance, would insist on the rule of law and limited government (including the elimination of tax subsidies and various forms of cronyism) as necessary for the functioning of free markets, and they might reject consumerism altogether.[48] Sociologists and theologians who are proponents of "democratic capitalism" would insist on a pluralistic participatory democracy with well-developed moral virtues as necessary for the healthy functioning of free-market economies.[49] But my interest in this book is not to evaluate capitalism in its theoretical or ideal forms. Rather, it is to examine the logics, discourses, and behaviors of people who are shaped by this system as it actually functions.[50] Specifically, I look at the effects of the current global financial system on corporate cultures, consumer culture, and civic sensibilities in emerging economies. In doing so, I identify important challenges to the realization of its proponents' ideals.

The term "neoliberalism," unfortunately, has become a pejorative. Its overuse in the field of anthropology has led many scholars to call for a moratorium on it, arguing that it has become one of those concepts that explains everything and therefore nothing.[51] However, the term still has important analytical purchase, since it points to something more specific than capitalism. Following Thomas Hylland Eriksen, I argue that we still need the term to identify specific and distinguishable shifts in collective identification and subjectivity that accompany the global diffusion of this model of capitalism.[52]

As I show in this book, neoliberal contexts institutionally reinforce a very specific concept of the self: an autonomous, socially disembedded, maximally responsible individual. In workplaces, this model is evident in today's new psychological contract between employer and employee, in which the employee is expected to be entrepreneurial and take full responsibility and initiative, shouldering the complete burden for failure.[53] It is also manifested in the absence of collective bargaining and organizational loyalty from professionals' understandings of workplace norms.[54] Beyond the context of corporations, neoliberalism shapes new conceptions of civic worth, which both the state and its denizens do not measure in terms of participation in local communities or electoral politics; instead, one is a "worthy" member by virtue of one's economic contribution, especially as a consumer. Those found unworthy or undesirable according to these criteria—notably, the working classes and the poor—are thus excluded from new neoliberal public spaces in these cities, such as shopping malls.[55] In neoliberal cities that reinforce this self-conception, consumerism becomes the default mode of expressing civic worth. All this has important consequences for thinking about the scope conditions for identity and integration in postindustrial societies.

In practice, neoliberalism can look very different in different places. As anthropologist Ahmed Kanna argues, we need more research on how it is shaped by local contexts and meanings. In examining two neoliberal cities, this study reveals important differences between Dubai, the "city-corporation" with its iconic architecture and free-trade zones, and Bangalore, the so-called "back office of the world" and purported harbinger of global "flattening."[56] I show how religious communities in these cities are far from immune to neoliberal logics: they reflect but also challenge them in different ways. This book thus contributes to the incipient research on the relationship between neoliberalism and global religion.[57] My focus in these cities is on one central agent of this form of capitalism: the global corporate professional.

GLOBAL PROFESSIONALS

The central actors of the mode of capitalism I examine in this study are members of what scholars call the transnational professional class. This class is, as sociologist Smitha Radhakrishnan defines it, a distinct social stratum of *"professionals for whom the traversing of borders (or the possibility of doing so) is critical to their socialization, belief system, and expression of cultural belonging."*[58] Their beliefs and practices in various spheres of life—not only in the workplace but also in family, lifestyle, and religion—are shaped by their prospects of "globalized" career mobility. This mobility is not restricted to promotions within a single firm, but characterizes the trajectories they pursue across occupational sectors and even nations.[59] As members of the globalized new middle classes, they share similarities not simply at the level of occupation but also in their lifestyles and aspirations.[60]

I focus in this study on people working in transnational corporations who self-identify as professionals.[61] Because of the frequent appeal to the word "global" in their own self-understandings of the organizations they work for (and in the cultures of these organizations) and even of the cities they live in, I use the word "global" interchangeably with "transnational." My specific focus is on middle-management employees, mostly working in publicly traded Fortune 500 corporations based in the United States or Western Europe.[62] The people I study work in a range of occupations: accounting, consulting, engineering, marketing, finance, human resources, and general management.

Professionalism is now what sociologist John Meyer and colleagues call a global "cultural account"—a cultural model with widely shared assumptions and prescriptions about social actors and organizational forms—shaped crucially by the West, but spreading along with isomorphic structures such as transnational corporations.[63] Yet it is not purely homogeneous; it is inflected in particular ways by the contexts of new emerging markets. In these contexts, as we see in chapter 1, professionalism constitutes a moral ideal that stands for dignity, respect, discretion, and accountability, but at the same time is highly individualistic, bereft of any vision of the common good, and inhibits the voicing of grievances in any collective manner. I examine the paradoxes of such mercenary professionalism, as well as how the dispositions of professionals spill over into other aspects of life, including their involvement in religious institutions.

NEOLIBERAL CITIES

Bangalore and Dubai are ideal examples through which to highlight important similarities and differences in the effects of global capitalism. The two cities are situated in markedly different political regimes: Bangalore in secular, democratic, Hindu-majority India, and Dubai in the nondemocratic, professedly Islamic UAE. Yet, the central political projects in both cities are to promote neoliberalism and pursue leadership in the global market.[64] Both cities have undergone rapid economic growth over the past three decades, propelled primarily by global trade. They have both become iconic: Bangalore for its outsourcing, and Dubai for its being a shopper's paradise and also for its gaudy architecture. Both are now recognized as critical nodes in the global economy and have also marked the global social imaginary as epitomes of rapid globalization. Research also identifies similar social transformations in both cities: increasing individualism, consumerism, and socioeconomic inequalities, as well as the rise of a new transnational professional class.[65] As I argue in chapter 5, both cities share a similar neoliberal conception of civic worth, though refracted in different ways through their sociocultural particularities. Here I provide a brief introduction to the cities.

BANGALORE. Bengaluru, anglicized as Bangalore[66] and founded in 1537, is a relatively young city by Indian standards. In the decades after India's independence in 1947, Indian states and territories were reorganized along linguistic lines. The majority-Kannada-speaking region was renamed Karnataka in 1973, and Bangalore became its capital. Traditionally called the "garden city," Bangalore was seen as a retirees' paradise for much of the twentieth century. By the end of the century, it had become renowned nationally for its educational institutions, including prominent scientific institutes and engineering, medical, and business schools. But this rapid development carried costs of its own, evident in the city's new moniker of "garbage city."[67]

The pivotal year in this transformation was 1991, when India began moving along its path of neoliberal reform in response to an economic crisis precipitated by several decades of economic stagnation. Opening up to foreign investment and

FIGURE 0.1.   Standard markers of globalization, Bangalore.

multinational corporations enabled the boom in information technology (IT) and business process outsourcing industries, in which Bangalore played a key role, earning the city its reputation as the "Silicon Valley of India." With the rise of informational and communications technologies, Bangalore became a prime migration destination for job seekers in the technology industry. Concomitantly, it also drew many to the services sector (including hotels, cafés, retail outlets, and so on) and the construction sector that emerged in tandem with the growing real estate boom. While the IT sector generated middle-class migration into Bangalore, these other sectors catering to the new middle classes (evident in a steady growth in the number of shopping malls, retail outlets, cafés, restaurants, high-rise apartment complexes, and gated communities) brought in many migrants from the lower classes, mostly from villages and small towns in nearby states, but even from faraway states such as the conflict-torn northeast part of India.[68] The inability of these migrants to find or keep employment contributes significantly to poverty in Bangalore.

Many critics also argue that India's rising GDP and the boom in the IT and service sectors are misleading, since those positive impacts are restricted to the upper and middle classes, who constitute a minority of the country. The majority of the Indian population continues to remain uneducated and unemployed, and at this writing, more than 71 million Indians live below the poverty line.[69] Yet the costs of rapid economic development extend to the new elites as well. Research on middle-class professionals, for instance, tells a story of increased consumerism— not only in practice but also as an aspirational ideal and form of self-identification— as well as civic disengagement and the loss of traditional forms of sociality.[70]

DUBAI. The Arabian/Persian Gulf region, which comprises Bahrain, Kuwait, Oman, Qatar, Saudi Arabia, and the United Arab Emirates (UAE), is home to some of the fastest-developing cities in the world. Like most of its neighbors, Dubai, one of the seven city-states of the federation that is the UAE, is typically categorized as a "rentier state," which derives its income from renting resources (such as oil and gas), rather than from taxation and internal revenue sources.[71] Whether propelled predominantly by oil companies or free-trade zones (which are key to the economic success of relatively oil-deprived Dubai), the economy in many of these cities relies on a labor force of foreign guest workers, whose size often far surpasses that of the local population; for instance, an estimated 81 percent of the total population in the UAE and 75 percent in Qatar are foreign guest workers.[72] Dubai's development in particular is propelled by an almost exclusively foreign labor force that accounts for more than 95 percent of its working population; the majority of the foreign workers are South Asian, and most of them are Indian.[73]

Foreign workers depend on visas that have to be regularly renewed. Low-skilled workers in particular are subject to the *kafala* or sponsorship system, in which their visas are sponsored by local citizens. Many have likened this system to a form of slavery since employees are neither permitted to change jobs nor leave the country without the permission of sponsors, who are often capricious.[74] In recent decades, most Gulf countries have ruled out any possibility for foreigners to assimilate into the local population as citizens. This remains the case even for the many thousands of second- and third-generation expatriates born and raised in these cities that they have come to consider home. Since these cities also continue

FIGURE 0.2.   Burj Khalifa, Dubai. Photo by Marko Söönurm.

to see an influx of foreign workers, many of these regimes of "permanent impermanence" become extensions of people's national as well as religious cultures.[75]

As scholarship on the region has argued, the UAE, like most other Gulf states, is neither an autocracy nor democracy, but rather an "ethnocracy," ruled by an ethnic group. Anthropologist Ahn Longva calls it a "civic ethnocracy," in which the key defining feature of governance is "not race, language or religion but citizenship conceived in terms of shared descent."[76] This mode of ethnonationalism is preserved by the ruling family, which controls narratives of national history and identity. Strict boundaries are drawn around legal citizenship to preserve a notion of ethnic purity, a central concern given the ratio of foreigners to locals.[77] Until late 2011, even children of Emirati women married to foreigners were denied citizenship. Citizens also receive generous subsidies: financial stipends and free land, utilities, education, and health care.[78]

Dubai, with its city-as-corporation model, has established itself as the neoliberal paragon of the region.[79] Its current ruler, Sheikh Mohammed Al Maktoum, calls himself the "CEO of Dubai" and heads the ruling body, which is dubbed the "Executive Council." Dubai's growth strategy, in addition to building free-trade zones, was to finance through debt a series of massive and peculiar iconic building projects, including the world's tallest building, largest shopping mall, only seven-star hotel, and largest artificial private archipelago. Dubai's economy was propelled by a real estate boom that collapsed during the financial crisis of 2008. Nevertheless, the city has seen renewed economic growth since the Arab Spring, as businesses from more volatile cities have moved there.

Research on life in Dubai has shed considerable light on the increasing consumerism, individualism, and civic disconnect among its middle- and upper-class residents,[80] problems that have been identified in research on the urban middle class in India as well.[81] The city in addition has gained global infamy recently through exposés of the harsh and even abusive treatment of lower-class workers such as housemaids and laborers.[82] Despite these indisputable problems, I agree with anthropologist Neha Vora that privileging a labor-focused lens to study the Gulf, "focusing on human rights, coping strategies, remittances, or 'modern-day slavery,' for example," is counterproductive. This is because such an approach "effectively collapses migrant lives into economic terms and removes possibilities of community formation, political agency, cultural hybridity, emotional attachment, consumption, leisure activity, and other forms of belonging from South Asian experiences in the Gulf."[83] A consequence of this prevailing tendency is to reinforce the conflation of belonging with formal-legal citizenship. This implicitly denies to these foreign residents—whether we call them migrants, expats, or guest workers—the very possibility of belonging to places like Dubai even if they have spent their entire lives there, and even before understanding their own narratives of belonging.[84] In looking at the ordinary lives of ordinary people, I want to demystify Dubai's popular images, either as a "city of gold" or an "evil paradise" of neoliberalism.[85] The people I study are far from exotic: they are middle-class, churchgoing, corporate types who play an important role in sustaining the city.

In both Dubai and Bangalore, research has largely overlooked the role of religious institutions and communities in responding to the problems just identified.[86] Studies on the impact of neoliberalism, even those that consider the role of religion among professionals, have neglected the role of religious institutions.[87] In this book I examine one religious institution across the two cities: the Roman Catholic Church.

Global Religion

THE CONCEPT OF RELIGION

Since this is a book about religion and capitalism, let me clarify what I mean by religion. Some have criticized the concept of religion as ethnocentric and of limited applicability outside the West.[88] But to know what we are dealing with and to what phenomena or entities our claims can be generalized, we need at least a provisional definition of the concept.

For definitional purposes, I find Martin Riesebrodt's formulation generally helpful: "Religion is a complex of practices that are based on the premise of the existence of superhuman powers, whether personal or impersonal, that are generally invisible."[89] Secondary to this basic premise are the beliefs, doctrines, rituals, and organizational forms usually associated with the concept of religion. Christian Smith builds on this model to theorize religion as an emergent social structure.[90] What both approaches have in common is the understanding of religion as a social structure that is more than simply a "belief system." Religion is more than just a set of beliefs and values, and these beliefs are not always internally cohesive or congruent with members' actions.[91]

As social structures, religions have characteristic powers and causal capacities that are differently activated or inhibited by contextual factors. Such causal capacities include not only prescriptive teachings but also network ties, social capital, and legal codes.[92] The specific mechanisms through which the causal capacities of any particular religious institution are enacted vary depending on contextual factors. Countervailing mechanisms can operate simultaneously, which is why there can be no universal "covering law" that determines how religion operates in society, even with respect to capitalism.[93] Hence, in some cases religion becomes a force for maintaining the status quo or social order, while in other cases it is a "disruptive" force driving social change.[94] By the end of this book, it should become clear why the specific mode of symbiosis between religion and capitalism that we see in my cases obtains, in contrast to other contexts of Catholicism.

The people I study see themselves as belonging to a specific religious institution and identify themselves as religious. They understand religion as pertaining to specific superhuman entities: the triune God, angels, and so on. And in participating in this study, they understand my attempt to examine the role of religion in their lives as having to do with the relevance of these superhuman entities or of the beliefs, practices, and organizations centered on them. But religion in these contexts also plays various functional roles that are not unique to it: religion provides a sense of worth and identity, forms of solidarity, and social services, in ways that nonreligious institutions such as ethnic voluntary associations might do as well. I am as interested as much in religious institutions as sites for developing job-related social capital as for providing rituals for members to experience God.[95] I am neither trying to identify distinct mechanisms generated by "uniquely" religious properties of a religion nor to assess whether religious institutions are "better" than nonreligious organizations for the functions they serve. Rather, I am looking primarily at how religion operates—what it *does*, in the particular institutions and cities I examine here—whether or not these operations flow from intrinsically "religious" aspects of religions. Studying religion in this manner affords the possibility of analytically generalizing from this case to other religions and even to other realms of social life.

EVANGELICAL-CHARISMATIC CATHOLICISM

Roman Catholicism is a global religion, perhaps the oldest religious organization in the world. As sociologist Peggy Levitt notes, the Catholic Church itself can be seen as "a transnational corporation with discrete national units that function independently and as part of the larger operation at the same time."[96] In both Bangalore and Dubai, the Catholic Church, despite its minority status, is institutionally well established.

Bangalore has the third-largest Catholic population among Indian archdioceses, numbering around 400,000. Previous research suggests a prominent presence of Christians in specific sectors of the new economy, notably in call centers.[97] Yet the relationship between Christianity and capitalism in India remains unexplored. This is lamentable given the prominence of the Catholic Church in India, which runs numerous schools, hospitals, community colleges, universities, and other organizations—contributing both to the nurturing of the nation's elites and to addressing poverty and related social problems.

In Dubai, six miles from the world's tallest building, five miles from the world's largest shopping mall, and nineteen miles from the world's largest natural flower

FIGURE 0.3. Overflowing churches in Bangalore.

garden, lies what is believed to be the world's largest Catholic parish in terms of membership. This is because the UAE, while allowing the practice of foreign religions, constrains them to operate only in delimited spaces. The entire Catholic population of Dubai, estimated at more than 300,000, is composed of expatriates, since conversion from Islam is forbidden; all of its Catholics have to worship either at the main parish close to the city's downtown or in a smaller parish on the outskirts of the city. We see later how this arrangement generates unique challenges as parishioners negotiate the use of their limited space. The Arabian Gulf is also a unique context for Catholicism; as one bishop of the region put it, "This is the only place where the Catholic population exists for the sole purpose of making money."

   In both cities, Catholics are not only a minority but are also primarily migrants. Even in Bangalore, the Catholic population is composed predominantly of inter-

FIGURE 0.4.   Overflowing churches in Dubai.

nal migrants, originating from other parts of India, which contributes to ethnic violence even among Catholic clergy, as I discuss in chapter 5.[98] This book thus examines the relationship of religion to the economic migration resulting from and propelling global capitalism.

While Bangalore and Dubai have religiously diverse populations, social and political regulations in both cities govern minority religions such as Christianity. India professes to be a secular country espousing equal tolerance for all religions. But in recent decades, extremist Hindu nationalism has been a prominent force. Nationalist groups that subscribe to Hindutva ideology see India as a Hindu nation and Christianity as a foreign religion that must be expelled. Several states in India have passed anti-conversion laws, and fundamentalist groups have carried out forcible reconversions to Hinduism.[99] Minority religions such as Muslims, Christians, and even lower-caste Hindus have experienced discrimination and even violence in Bangalore.[100] Many Catholics I talked to in Bangalore, in spite of being Indian citizens, expressed a sense of feeling like second-class citizens. Because of the visibility of Catholic parishes and institutions, Catholic leaders felt especially vulnerable to the extremist attacks that occurred whenever Christian groups, especially foreign evangelical missionaries, engaged in proselytism. Catholic bishops have been outspoken in criticizing the state government for turning a blind eye to violent attacks on churches, staging public protests.[101]

While Christianity in Bangalore is subject to social regulation and at times persecution, in Dubai, it is not the object of persecution, but is strongly regulated by the government. Indeed, even a fundraiser that is not organized through state-sponsored charities technically requires prior permission from the Islamic Affairs and Charitable Activities Department of the government.[102] Recognizing the importance of religion for the foreigners who sustain their economies, most countries in the Gulf region—with the exception of Saudi Arabia—have granted foreigners freedom of worship. Foreign religions are allowed to express and practice their traditions within delimited spaces granted by the government. This makes possible a vibrant community life within these religious spaces that has largely been neglected by studies on the region. In spite of the religious tolerance in Dubai, however, church members told me that any perceived challenge to the state (e.g., criticizing the unjust treatment of laborers or domestic workers) could result in serious sanctions, including deportations or even the closing down of a parish. I discuss the church's relationship to the government in chapter 5.

In examining Catholicism among professionals in Bangalore and Dubai, I shed light on a peculiar hybrid that I call Evangelical-Charismatic Catholicism (ECC). This form emerges from the intersection of a number of globally diffusing and globally oriented groups and movements. ECC groups and members adhere to central tenets and creeds of the Catholic Church, including the sacraments, the church's teaching authority embodied in the hierarchy, and traditional devotions. They are also influenced by conservative American Catholic media such as *Catholic Answers* and the Eternal Word Television Network (EWTN). ECC groups bear the imprint of American evangelicalism in their focus on a "personal relationship with Jesus," "witnessing" and sharing their faith, frequent Bible reading, and contemporary Christian worship music. Most ECC groups are also either directly affiliated with or are outgrowths of the Catholic Charismatic Renewal, the Catholic branch of the global Pentecostal/charismatic movement. Thus, they often adhere to beliefs and practices common to Pentecostal/charismatic groups worldwide, which emphasize the power of the Holy Spirit in individuals' lives, as manifested through praying in tongues, prophesying, and miraculous healings. Yet these ECC groups, because of their embeddedness in the Catholic Church, largely do not share in the broader propensity of Pentecostal/charismatic groups for "prosperity theology": the belief that God rewards faithful believers with material prosperity.

Through the media they consume, the popular religious celebrities they follow—especially American prophets of positivity such as Joyce Meyer and Joel Osteen—and the international networks in which they participate, such groups generate a distinctive and recognizable form of religion that is rapidly spreading and shaping English-speaking Catholicism around the world. Because of the cultural and technological capital required to participate in this form of religion (e.g., English-language skills and Internet access), the majority of its adherents in the contexts I study are middle-class professionals. Studying similar kinds of religious groups provides a useful point of comparison between the two cities that would be difficult to achieve by studying the dominant religions in these contexts.

Professionals such as Ashwin Mathews inhabit the realms of global corporations and global Evangelical-Charismatic Catholicism in these neoliberal cities, negotiating the complex relationship between the Mercenary and the Missionary. This book tells the story of how and why they do so, what consequences result from their actions, and what it all means for how we understand the relationship between capitalism and religion more broadly.

THE MERCENARY

It took me nearly two hours in the characteristically noisy and dusty Tuesday after-noon traffic to travel twenty-five kilometers to David Menezes's office in Elec-tronics City. This aptly named suburb of Bangalore is home to one of India's largest industrial parks and to several global technology corporations, including MegaTech, where Menezes is the national HR director. Menezes recommended that I take the "luxury air-conditioned Volvo" bus from Bangalore's central bus station to get there, which would drop me off right at the gates of the company campus. But the route number he gave me must have changed since Menezes last rode the bus (if ever), because it would take a wild stretch of the imagination to call the bus I boarded "luxury." It did not even stop, but only slowed down as passengers embarked and disembarked. Swept up in the boarding crowd, I could not check to see if it was a Volvo, but it certainly was not air conditioned. I asked the despondent-looking driver if the bus went to Electronics City, and he grunted and waved me to the back. Every time I woke up after nodding off to sleep on the route, I would ask the conductor if we were close, and at one such moment, he gestured out the window nonchalantly to let me know that we had just passed the entrance to Electronics City on the other side of the highway. I scrambled out at the next stop and made my way across the busy highway to the main gates, where the guard on duty seemed surprised to see someone on foot and was unsure about how to get to MegaTech. I called Menezes to get my bearings straight and, in fifteen minutes, arrived at the MegaTech corporate campus.

Two guards sat within a booth at the campus's gate. One was on the phone. The other scrutinized my ID, called Menezes to confirm my legitimacy, and then asked me to write a set of details in a ledger: name, company, contact information, time of arrival, and so on. Just past the gate stood two other bored-looking guards. One told me to list the contents of my backpack in another ledger, while the other gingerly opened the bag, as though afraid to upset my laptop, and promptly closed it. Having passed the screening rituals, I was given a visitor badge and directed toward the main building within the lush, green campus. After I entered, one of the secretaries at the front desk called Menezes to let him know I had arrived. I sat down in a plush, modern lounge chair and did not have to wait long. Menezes emerged from the other end of the hallway with a confident stride: he looked the quintessential male IT professional, with his smartly combed hair, trimmed mustache, neatly pressed shirt and slacks, lanyard around the neck clipped to an official photo ID, and large smartphone clipped to the belt. He shook my hand warmly and led me to an area with a number of glass-paneled meeting rooms. He signed one out, and we sat on a pair of comfortable couches. He unclipped his phone, set it on the armrest, and glanced at it regularly during our conversation over the next couple of hours.

David Menezes exemplifies the Mercenary, the representative character of global corporate workplaces who is oriented toward the incessant pursuit of money and mobility. Today, Menezes is national HR director for India of one of the world's largest technology firms. But getting there was not easy. Menezes and his four siblings grew up in the city of Mangalore, around two hundred miles from Bangalore. They faced persistent economic hardship. Their father died when they were young, and Menezes recalled his mother "working from morning to night, wak[ing] up at 5 [a.m.] and sleep[ing] at 12 [a.m.]." "Work was worship for her," he explained. "She never had time to breathe, and she did that for forty years. So it was very, very, very, very difficult." An important determinant of his own career choices was to make enough money so that she could retire very comfortably and not have to face hardship again.

Early in his life, Menezes was motivated by a desire to help the poor. This led him to study social work at a prestigious Catholic college. But while working on his master's degree, it became clear to him that it would be a serious financial struggle to make ends meet, especially if he wanted a family. He recounted,

> Social work doesn't have money. At the end of the day, you want to live your life and you want to earn money, right? So social work doesn't have that. After doing the community social work, [his previous colleagues] have spent ten to fifteen years, they are getting 20–25,000 rupees [per month, about US $500 at the time]. I mean I pay a rent of more than that. So if I have to pay around 30,000 rupees rent per month, and then

you have to maintain a car and kids and all that, you need to have a disposable income, to live a lifestyle.

As a result, said Menezes, "I changed my mind." He switched to hotel management. Within a few years he had worked his way up to a senior managerial position in human resources at the Bangalore office of a world-renowned hotel chain. "I didn't know I would go so far," he beamed. Yet, in spite of his success in the hotel industry, Menezes felt restless. He did not think the industry paid enough. Looking around him at the economic boom in Bangalore, he started to make a "mental switch":

> I had to decide what I wanted: money in my pocket or suit on my body. If you had come to [my office at the hotel] now you would have met me in one of the five-star hotels. I would have come with a nice suit and a good tie and the receptionist would have escorted you to my office and I would have called a coffee on a speakerphone and a waiter would have come and served it to you and you would have felt, "Wow, he's a great guy!" But when I remove my pocket, I didn't have anything. So when you have seen that part of the world, you need to decide what you want: you want to make money or you want to live life?

Money, he stated without hesitation, was the principal factor driving his decisions to switch from the hotel industry to IT, and it continues to shape his priorities and goals in life. In the short term, his priority is "having a healthy bank balance. So, next five years, my bank balance should be such that even if I don't have a job I don't have to worry about it, I can manage easily." Money is also central to his long-term vision: "If I look at my peers from school and if you look at my standing in comparison to them, I am doing extremely well. Only problem is I pay a lot of taxes. So if I was working in Dubai or somewhere, I wouldn't have paid these taxes. That's the only pinch, if at all." I asked if he was considering moving to Dubai. "If I get a very good role, like a director role, where I am responsible for an organization, and I get good money, then I will switch," he replied almost immediately, suggesting that the thought had occurred to him before. "I can fly down [back to Bangalore] once a month or something. If I am earning that much money, doesn't matter."

Not much earlier in the same interview, Menezes had complained, as did most other HR executives I spoke to, that attrition was a serious scourge to the industry. He had even proffered a recipe to address the problem: "One, keep the employees happy; two, give them good salary; three, ensure that they grow. Then the attrition is less." He claimed his efforts successfully lowered attrition at Mega-Tech: "It has reduced drastically. Earlier, causes were very simple: you didn't have good engagement practices in place, career progression was not in place. Now, salary action has been taken." Evidently, he did not see the irony in his own willingness to switch jobs; nor would a salary increase be sufficient to persuade him to remain at MegaTech.

Keeping employees happy in these workplaces is difficult. As I discuss later in this chapter, these are environments of pervasive mistrust, where many learn the hard way to be wary of their colleagues who may at any moment throw them under the bus to advance their own careers. By the time professionals get to Menezes's level, they develop a thick skin and lose the palpable anxiety that many employees in earlier career stages expressed when talking to me about office politics. "At my level, I need to be smart enough; I can't blame anyone," shrugged Menezes. "Yes, you learn by mistakes and things like that. To trust certain people, tell them something, they go play around, *et cetera*—that's part of life, right? It's not so smooth." He admitted to having been betrayed by colleagues and, in response, has learned to keep his cards close to his chest and to play the game safe. The crucible of corporate life "teaches you—when to speak, what to speak, what not to speak."

Although comfortable in his current life situation, Menezes, like many of my respondents, articulated a consumerist vision of the ideal lifestyle to which he was aspiring. Few were as brazen (or perhaps honest) as he: "So, typically, I want to live in a big house with all facilities. Want a full-time servant; we're looking for another one; [the previous one] just left after many years. Dine out. Go to the best five-star hotels. Buy the best of clothes. Yeah, I mean, now, getting old, thinking of saving money as well" [*laughs*]. And what would a good and ultimately worthwhile life look like to him? "You need to be respected when you don't have a job and things like that," he explained. "You should have money to spend. You shouldn't have to think, 'If I had money I could have done this, if I had money I could have done that.'" A meaningful and worthwhile life for Menezes and many other professionals I met is a life that is free from the pervasive anxiety about money. Given the instability of a rapidly developing economy, such aspirations are far from uncommon.

Yet Menezes also identifies as a man of firm religious commitment. He is actively involved in his local Catholic parish as a member of his parish council and is the president of an ethnic association in the parish, for which he engages in charitable and fundraising work. Prayer plays a crucial part in his daily life. Menezes carries around a pocket-sized New Testament and prayer book and every morning spends a half hour praying. "I've been through many [difficult] incidents in life and I think only prayer has helped me get through all those and to keep me successful," he insisted. "I feel prayer has been responsible." His faith enables him to find a sense of peace, meaning, and solace; it is a source of support through the difficulties and stresses of life. It also supports his commitments to his family traditions and ethnic heritage and encourages him to use his corporate experience in service of others. Faith offers him a sense of meaning, purpose, and community that he neither finds nor seeks in the corporate world. It rejuvenates and recharges him so that he can cope better with the challenges of corporate life. In addition to these instrumental aspects of faith, his commitment to church puts him in regular contact with "workers, housewives, [and] very poor people" who serve in church with him. Yet, his religious involvement at most only chafes against the consumerist lifestyle to which he aspires: he seems unaware of any tension between the two. Indeed, his narrative betrays how income and mobility have become ends in themselves, so much so that he sees no problem with the prospect of relocating to Dubai and visiting his family "once a month or something."

In the remainder of this chapter, I focus on the realm of the global corporate workplace and the processes through which the inner logic of the Mercenary emerges and takes on a momentum of its own. I discuss the role of religion and life outside the workplace in later chapters.

For the sake of readability, I use the words "Mercenaries" and "Missionaries" as shorthand for the people who are governed by these norms. Yet these are only stock characters that are dominant in their domains; the actual people who inhabit those roles are complex human beings. Like all of us, they are not always consistent and certainly cannot be reduced to the orienting models that may guide their desires and actions, no matter how closely aligned their actions might be to these models when they are in the workplace.

The Professional as Mercenary

In global corporate workplaces inhabited by professionals like David Menezes, a distinct set of ideals, norms, expectations, and strategies is cultivated and reinforced. This blueprint of the Mercenary orients professionals both to the goals they must strive to achieve and the means by which to pursue them. It specifies the kind of self that a professional must be and the trajectory one feels one ought to pursue. It orients people in moral space and provides a basis against which they can measure their own and their colleagues' successes and failures. It thus constitutes a particular logic that shapes dispositions and actions in day-to-day work, providing the basis for professionals' workplaces and career strategies.

The Mercenary bears some resemblance to the pivotal character that scholars such as Alasdair MacIntyre and Robert Bellah identified in corporate workplaces in the 1980s: "the manager." Operating in the pressurized environment of the early postindustrial order and charged with the obligation to maximize profit,[1] this character had the fundamental task "to organize the human and non-human resources available to the organization . . . so as to improve its position in the marketplace."[2] Unlike the "manager" of yore, today's Mercenary is not primarily concerned with maximizing efficiency and corporate profit at any cost, except inasmuch as it maximizes his or her individual mobility.[3]

The character of the Mercenary is identifiable though the interactions, practices, and discourses prevalent in everyday life in workplaces of firms such as IBM, Dell, HP, Accenture, Tesco, and several other global corporations I visited in Bangalore and Dubai. Anil, an IT consultant I interviewed in Bangalore, described corporate life this way:

> All of us in the rat race are shoulder-to-shoulder with, you know, "Hey, what's happening with you, what's happening in your life?" And the conversation usually is around, "How many flats or condos or apartments do you own?" "What are the investments you make?" "What are the stocks that you are tracking?" "What's your next jump gonna be?" You usually orient your success around percentage of hikes you get every year. Salary-oriented. A lot of weightage to titles and designations.
>
> So those become the handles or levers for success that you see. "Are you a manager yet? Are you senior manager? Are you director? VP? AVP?" So those are badges or flags you wave. Of course salary's important. Flashier cars. Fancier houses. So that's usually the discussion that's there in corporate life.

These ends that Anil's colleagues articulate are shared, understandable, and seen as legitimate; their validity is rarely called into question.[4] The character of the Mercenary has its own internal logic, but the ends and goals within this are simply taken for granted, reflecting their successful and thorough institutionalization.[5]

The Mercenary embodies a distinctive vision of the good, which can be organized along several dimensions, as shown in Table 1.1. We can see here how the pursuit of mobility serves as an ordering principle, shaping judgments of good/bad, noble/vile, superior/inferior, and laudable/deplorable: what Charles Taylor calls "strong evaluations."[6] It is in this sense that it is a moral orientation. In what follows, I sketch out the contours of this moral outlook, using a framework adapted from Boltanski's and Thévenot's "economies of worth" model[7] to identify the various dimensions along which the apprehensive individualist pursuit of mobility unfolds. After doing so, I discuss how this peculiar model emerged in the current sociohistoric context and how it continues to be sustained.

TABLE 1.1. The Mercenary

Moral orientation	Apprehensive individualism
Basis of worth	Mobility: salary, career status, company brand name, employability
Trajectory	Rising up corporate ranks, switching to higher-paying positions
Demonstration of worth	Performance review, promotions, bonuses, company brand name, job title, office space, awards, conspicuous consumption
Peer base for comparison	Colleagues, competitors
Sources of knowledge	Management texts/gurus, business news, pop psychology, technical training, upgrading certifications, company gossip
Career ideal	Senior management
Strategies	Individual achievement, building coalitions, sycophancy, secrecy, negotiation, retooling, switching jobs, sabotage
Failure	Downsizing, demotion, being passed up for promotion, stagnation

For the Mercenary, the pursuit of career mobility is an obligation. One "should" pursue the job with the best salary package and ought not to "stagnate" in one company or position for too long. While the monetary benefits the Mercenary seeks are not necessarily atomistic—they are often oriented toward securing the well-being of family and kin—the moral orientation of the Mercenary is thus an *apprehensive individualism*, in which it is normative not to trust one's colleagues or organization. Furthermore, one thinks one ought to be distrustful and wary of colleagues. Acting otherwise is irresponsible, because it compromises one's move up the ranks.

Judgments of worth are made on the basis of indices of mobility: salary, position, corporate brand name, and so on. Individual priorities may vary to some degree: some may accord more weight to salary than to brand name, for instance. But there is a limited range of acceptable indicators of worth that are considered legitimate by fellow professionals. Appeals to alternative criteria, such as the quality of relationships in one's work environment or a sense of work as vocation, do not make sense within this logic.

Mercenary professionalism implies a trajectory of upward mobility, in which one rises in rank, climbing up the corporate ladder across multiple firms, to ultimately occupy a senior position. Note that this is not an upward trajectory within a single firm, in which one gradually gets promoted as seniority increases. In contrast, the Mercenary's pursuit of individual mobility requires regularly switching roles and firms, which prevents attachment to any one firm and explains the high attrition rates among professionals in both cities. The narrative of this trajectory differs considerably from the traditional workplace ideal that many professionals said characterized their parents' generation: work hard, be honest and loyal, and you will eventually retire comfortably. In the older model, mobility was understood to be a natural consequence of simple hard work; now, mobility needs much more strategizing, especially since seniority and loyalty are supposedly dead, and sticking to one company is a sign of stagnation.

While professionals rarely disclose their salaries to one another, there are numerous other means of signaling and demonstrating one's worth, including having an impressive job title or company brand name on one's business card, prime office space, awards for performance, and publicly announced promotions or bonuses. Regular performance reviews are key occasions for assessing such worth. One is constantly measuring oneself against colleagues in the same company, as well as the success and reputation of one's firm against its competitors. As Anil mentioned earlier, signaling worth through one's improved ability to consume— flashier cars, fancier houses—is also part of the norm.

The new ideal self in this context is "an individual constantly learning new skills, changing his or her 'knowledge basis,'" as sociologist Richard Sennett notes.[8] Management guru Peter Senge's ideal of the "learning organization"[9] is now instantiated in each individual professional, who perpetually reinvents him- or herself in the process of "creating You and Company" or becoming "the CEO of your own career."[10] The entrepreneurial self must pursue such continual retooling by not only being technically up to date but also by keeping up with the latest management gurus and pop-psychology wisdom: the aim is to keep coming up with new ways to repackage one's capacities and experiences into new contexts where one can gain better status or remuneration. Superiors and prospective employers especially value those who can keep ahead of the pack by constantly upgrading their skill sets and credentials. Note that this skill development is distinct from the pursuit of entrepreneurship as such, which can be a means of creatively solving problems and serving needs in the world; the entrepreneurialism of the Mercenary is oriented around the self and one's upward trajectory in the corporate world.

In addition to retooling and upgrading skills, there are other commonly used strategies for success. These include, on the one hand, the meritocratic pursuit of valued achievements (i.e., being able to demonstrate short-term results and productivity in terms of individual outcomes) and, on the other, skillful manipulation of relationships through coalitions, sycophancy, and even sabotage. Many of these professionals argue that promotions and such rewards should accrue on purely meritocratic grounds; nevertheless, the use of these "unfair" means is not only widespread but also considered legitimate within the "rules of the game," as we see later in this chapter. One is simply expected to know that being hired and promoted is not purely a result of merit. One is expected to understand that corporate life is unfair, that one ought to watch one's back, and that "politics" in the workplace should not be taken personally but is "just business." As Menezes re-signedly admitted, "That's part of life, right?" If success in a given company proves elusive, if one becomes a casualty of office politics, and especially if success within a particular firm is no longer as enticing as what a competitor has to offer, switching jobs becomes the best option. "Failure" for the Mercenary includes being downsized, demoted, passed up for promotions, or stagnating in one position or company.[11]

Mercenary professionalism amplifies the logic of mobility that Richard Sennett began to uncover in American firms in the late 1990s: "Failure to move is taken as a sign of failure, stability seeming almost a living death. The destination therefore matters less than the act of departure."[12] As one of Sennett's respondents told him, "When somebody tells me there's no future here, I ask what they want. They don't know; they tell me you shouldn't be stuck in one place."[13] The pervasive idea is that one needs to constantly move onward and upward.[14] The people I talked to assumed from the moment they joined a firm that they would be moving on, but not immediately: they need to give the impression that they are committed, that they are not going to get up and leave the next day, and that investing in them will not be a waste. A pattern of moving after spending less than a year or two in a company looks bad on a résumé, so one needs to stay on for three and, at most, five years. After that, it is understood that one has to jump. This is why professionals such as Ashwin Mathews, no matter how deeply committed they are to people in their lives *outside* the workplace, such as in their church communities, prefer *within* the workplace not to get to know colleagues too well. "Leaving the organization becomes that much more easier," he counseled, if you "don't become close" to people. The challenges of negotiating office politics and the inability to trust others contribute to such distancing.[15]

In addition to the sense of choice and imperative that professionals express in their decisions to move, there is also an element of personal rationalization in justifying to themselves and to others that they are acting of their own accord, rather than just being victims of circumstances. It is hard to deny, as Sennett notes, that "immense social and economic forces shape the insistence on departure: the disordering of institutions, the system of flexible production," and so on.[16] As I discuss later in this chapter, a feeling of detachment and being ever prepared to move on are understandable modes of self-protection in the face of fundamentally unstable and unreliable structures. Further, the "initial exhilaration" that comes with the decision to depart and move on to something new is always short-lived and constitutes a high that needs to be reexperienced, not simply because new experiences of work fall short of one's expectations but also because one has to perpetually start over, never knowing with any certainty where one stands in the system.[17]

The detachment that characterizes the Mercenary is echoed in theologian William Cavanaugh's analysis of contemporary consumerism, where what matters is not the purchased object itself (which gets discarded soon enough), but the *process* of continually acquiring something new.[18] One has to keep moving on; just as goods have to be relentlessly updated, one should not be stagnant or risk becoming obsolete. Thus, the relationship to the thing itself is not one of attachment but detachment.[19] It is not surprising, then, that Mercenary professionalism and consumerist lifestyles go hand in hand, reinforcing similar orientations, as we see in chapter 4.

This character of the Mercenary sketched here is hardly a naturally occurring social type. Rather, it is the product of particular sociohistoric conditions. What factors facilitate the emergence of this character in contemporary global corporations?

The Culture and Structure of Corporate Life

The dominant narrative used to explain the diffusion of global capitalism is a *structural* story. In this account, the proliferation of global corporations is presented as evidence that globalization fosters the "inevitable homogenization of economic and cultural practices, driven by competitiveness in a global market and by new technologies of communication."[20] Today's finance-dominated neoliberalism is seen as the reigning model of a post-traditional and postindustrial mode of capitalism.[21] It is based on shifts from mass production to mass consumption, from hierarchical to networked forms of capitalism,[22] and from the primacy of impersonal bureaucratic "rationalization" to the "subjectivization" evident in therapeutic human resources rhetoric of personal "fulfillment," "development," and "growth."[23] Relentless innovation at an accelerated pace has changed the nature of work, making it ever more complex and intangible.[24] These shifts accompanying the spread of transnational corporations are claimed to bring about a "flattening" of the world.[25]

Yet, despite the seeming homogenization, and the seeming recolonization of "periphery" or "semi-periphery" countries by Western transnational corporations, it is incorrect to see these developments as an inevitable evolution or a top-down assault. People on the ground—those who embrace these developments as attractive and worthy of support, as well as those who resist them as threats—are not merely puppets determined by social structures. Rather, they actively exercise interpretive agency. As sociologists Luc Boltanski and Ève Chiapello argue, new modes of capitalism require new modes of ideological appeal: they need to be seen and articulated as personally desirable and evaluated as indicators of improvement, progress, and liberation.[26] To neglect such aspects of interpretation and desirability—which also involve the reconstitution of narratives of what a better life for oneself and one's progeny should look like—is to succumb to an acultural and ahistorical account of these changes.[27]

Thus, in what follows, I connect a structural account of the constitutive tensions within new forms of capitalism to a cultural account of what these structures *mean* to the people who support and sustain them. Both dimensions are important in understanding how the Mercenary comes into being.

The Appeal of Global Corporations

In countries pursuing accelerated development, many factors foster the opening of doors to foreign companies. These include the perceived failures of past economic policies, new ideological commitments to the deregulation of markets as the sure road to prosperity, attempts of political parties or leaders to win the support of business constituents who stand to benefit from the new policies, and the ability to stoke nationalist sentiments by the promise of putting the country on the global map. But what features render jobs in these corporations attractive to the people who work there?

MONEY

The first factor mentioned by nearly everyone I talked to (whether employees and employers in these companies or educators in institutions that prepare people to work in the new economy) is money. These jobs often come with relatively high salaries,[28] topped with attractive benefits. These perks, such as housing allowances, company cars, health insurance, and food allowances, usually provide supports for more comfortable lifestyles. The study respondents who migrated to both cities often sought more money not only to meet their own needs but also to support their families, whether family members who migrated along with them or those who remained back home and depended on remittances.[29] Many respondents were able to use their earnings to buy homes for their parents and at an age at which their parents could not even dream of such financial stability.

MODERNITY

Given the rapid pace of development in the cities I studied, the very edifice of a global/multinational corporation can constitute an attractive incentive. Take for instance Julie, who calls herself "a hard-core Bangalorean," having been born and brought up in the city. In the summer after her final year of high school, she landed an interview with one of the first offshore call centers to be set up in the city. She remembered traveling several miles out of the city into a new tech park in the suburb of Whitefield for the interview. When she arrived at the building, it was still under construction, and yet she was awestruck by what she saw. The building was more than twelve stories high, with glass surfaces and spacious interiors in which each employee would even have his or her own cubicle—an exceptional ambience for India, she said, where "our idea of offices here is not too good; we have just tables and chairs. That's what we've seen so far, unless you've worked in a very good post!"

Banal though it seems, these tall glass-paneled towers play a powerful symbolic role in these new outposts of neoliberalism, signaling progress through architecture that might just as easily be visible in established "global cities" such as New York, London, or Tokyo. In both Dubai and Bangalore, as economic growth accelerated in the early years of the twenty-first century, these new office structures proliferated in new spaces distant from the rest of the city. These spaces take the form of enclaves, with names such as "Electronics City" (in Bangalore) or "Internet City" (in Dubai). These cities-within-a-city, the new habitat of the transnational corporate denizen—at least, during working hours—house offices of global firms such as Microsoft, Google, and Siemens (see Figure 1.1 for an example). Many characterized such spaces as an escape or refuge from the "third world," from the stark evidence of poverty and want and chaos in Bangalore or

FIGURE 1.1. Corporate campus in Bangalore. Photo by Bishnu Sarangi.

the barrenness and oppressive desert heat in Dubai, into plush, air-conditioned offices similar to those one might find anywhere in the West.

STATUS

Another strong draw is reputation. For many, a global brand name is a key criterion guiding their choice of employment. Tarun is one such example. Born in Bangalore, Tarun moved to the Arabian Gulf at the age of ten. He completed high school there and returned to Bangalore to pursue a business degree. He then earned an MBA in England and worked there for a year after graduation. Tarun then landed a job with an international technology firm in Dubai. Within a couple of years, he was promoted to business development manager. A year later, he returned to Bangalore to spend a few weeks with his newly retired parents. There he began to seriously consider the burgeoning opportunities in his hometown and decided to stay on, rather than return to Dubai.

Bangalore had become a global software giant, the national economy was booming, and it was now increasingly common for Indians who were educated and working overseas to return home. With his international background and experience in the technology industry, he saw this as "a brilliant move" for his career, and it took him little time to find a position in a famous global software giant that had recently started outsourcing some of its management functions to Bangalore. The company's name, he insisted, would be a definite asset to any résumé. Working there was an unprecedented opportunity to pursue a "world-class career" without having to leave India. After three years in this firm, he leveraged this experience to move on to a senior management position in the Bangalore office of another reputed American IT firm. Many of my respondents, like Tarun, not only aspire to careers in brand-name firms but also believe that settling for anything less than a "global brand name" would be "unworthy" in the reputation-based logic that governs their choices.[30]

Employment in global brand-name corporations is thus a status marker that allows people to signal that they have "arrived." It can even shape people's relationships outside the workplace. As Michelle, a marketing manager in Bangalore, explained, "Because first of all it's a brand name, and when you tell people, 'I work with GlobalTech,' it's like, 'Oh my God!' Like your eyes pop!" She gave the example of a friend who used to persistently belittle her, but once she told him that she had managed to get a job at GlobalTech, "[h]e had nothing to say after that! [*laughs*] . . . So people do have this sense of pride to say, 'Yeah, I work for GlobalTech!'"

Many thus are drawn to jobs in multinational firms because they constitute a key source of social mobility, not simply in terms of money but also of reputation. Reputational currency frees one from being bound to any particular reputational marker and allows one to pursue mobility by trading in such currency. It enables professionals to pursue positions with similar or higher status at firms with comparable reputations, either to obtain better salaries or perks or to avoid difficult bosses and colleagues in their current company.

Nearly all my respondents in both cities mentioned a further factor that they found especially attractive about global corporate workplaces: their "workplace culture." Often implicit in these declarations are distinctions from "local" or "traditional" companies that are talked about in terms intended to be derisive, such as "unprofessional," overly "formal," "disorganized," "autocratic," and "strict." In contrast, the new, desirable, attractive workplaces are imagined and described as "highly professional," "informal," and having "clear policies" and "flexible" work arrangements. One word emerged repeatedly in my interviews as the central defining characteristic of global corporate culture: "professionalism."

PROFESSIONALISM

Social scientists understand professions as occupational systems that make exclusive claims to expertise and jurisdiction over specific sets of tasks.[31] Medicine, law, and religion (i.e., members of the clergy or ministry) are considered the "classic" professions, though over the past century, the label of profession has expanded widely to include all sorts of occupational groupings.[32] "New professions," such as software work, lack standard features of established ones, such as licensing or formal codes of ethics, and, despite the white-collar setting, seem sociologically similar to more traditional technical work.[33] Yet employees in these sectors attach strong importance to self-identifying as professionals and to giving others the impression of being professionals, indicating that the title is a sought-after mark of social status and privilege. Identifying oneself as a professional is, for many, a way of affirming one's dignity and self-worth and the importance of one's activities. This is understandable in a context in which the tasks one performs can often be uninteresting, routine, and unchallenging and where the environment is often demeaning, stressful, and unwelcoming.

For the people I talked to, professionalism constitutes a set of ideals and practices pertaining to respect, merit, discretion, and accountability in the workplace. People used the term to talk about their relationship to tasks, as well as to people; they used it to refer both to what they expected of themselves and what they expected of others. As one Filipina professional in Dubai, Carol, said, "Professionalism is in your attitude at work. Even if you don't feel like working anymore, still you need to come [to work], because it is your job to do it, it is your task to do it. So finish it." In addition to identifying it as a personal attitude or disposition, respondents talked about professionalism as something that had to be embodied in codes and policies.

Many were drawn to global corporations precisely because they wanted to work in such an environment of professionalism. They contrasted it with what they considered "traditional" or "local" work environments and management styles, which they denounced as "unprofessional." Professionalism meant that managers should treat subordinates with respect and give them discretion and autonomy. Respondents who had previously worked in jobs in which they were constantly monitored and supervised—particularly sales and customer-service jobs— described these experiences as demeaning because they considered themselves professionals, and thought themselves therefore entitled to more autonomy.[34] Recognition of merit is another characteristic of my respondents' understanding of professionalism. Not that merit is always rewarded in practice; rather, it is appealed to as the principal criterion that *should* matter in the global corporation, rather than loyalty, seniority, and so on. Professionalism also meant accountability. Corruption served as a contrast to professionalism, and many pointed to examples of corruption in the form of managers pocketing money owed to employees, which they thought happened less frequently in global corporations than in local ones.

The pervasive preoccupation with professionalism is partly an attempt to safeguard basic interests and rights: being paid one's due salary on time, being respected, not being cheated, and so on. Many were frustrated when they discovered that these expectations were not met even in global corporations. It is crucial to note, however, that such frustrations find "voice" only in a very muted way, as a complaint in private contexts—or to the rare passing sociologist—but seldom publicly or overtly, and eschewing any collective, organized form that could actually give it traction.[35]

It is also important to note that the sense of solidarity that scholars in the West have identified among professionals is markedly absent among the self-proclaimed professionals I spoke to in my study.[36] I discuss later in this chapter how local contextual factors in Bangalore and Dubai play an important role in precipitating this absence of solidarity.

The myriad attractive features of these global corporate cultures—the factors that pull people to these environments—as well as their deficits and failures, result from a set of tensions built into the structure of neoliberal capitalism. I see these tensions as reflecting two central polarities of modernity: the first between rationalization and flexibilization and the second between collectivism and individualism. It is out of these tensions between control and autonomy that the Mercenary is born.[37]

Rationalization

By rationalization, I refer to the ongoing process by which instrumental rationality and the attempt to efficiently "master all things by calculation" comes to dominate the operation of complex institutions.[38] Its influence was prominent early in the twentieth century in F. W. Taylor's "scientific management" approach and the bureaucratic form that Max Weber described; these forms have since undergone considerable mutation to yield the present organizational forms that characterize "networked" or "flexible" capitalism. Two aspects of such rationalization shape the character of the Mercenary.

The first is perpetual reengineering. To please shareholders and to improve chances of firm survival in competitive markets, organizational leaders are under constant pressure to continually demonstrate vigilance, innovation, and dedication to efficiency. By the turn of the twenty-first century, the heightened need to be responsive to volatile investors and consumers produced the fad of "reengineering." Celebrated icons of this fix-it-before-it's-broke approach, such as "Neutron" Jack Welch of GE, were preaching and embodying a version of economist Joseph Schumpeter's "creative destruction" on steroids.[39] The "lean and mean" approach advocated by Welch and others was rapidly adopted and served to justify widespread downsizing and outsourcing in the pursuit of maximizing the short-term return on investment.

By 2006, even *Fortune* magazine declared this approach obsolete and unfit for the challenges of the new millennium, and Apple's Steve Jobs replaced Welch as the icon for the new capitalism.[40] But by then the damage was already done. The new "wisdom" had already spread to influence the habits and instincts of managers worldwide: older trends denounced in the "new rules" of management, such as the ranking of employees within corporate teams and regularly culling the bottom layer,[41] remain *de rigueur* in several subsidiaries of Fortune 500 companies in India and the Middle East, as many of my respondents attest. Structures and processes are constantly overhauled in their companies, and often neither the managers implementing these changes nor the subordinates affected by them understand the purpose of such changes. For instance, Carol in Dubai talked about an organizational restructuring that promoted several employees to the status of "managers," but with no clarity in either their responsibilities or the nature of the new reporting structures. "Before," she said with a laugh, "there used to be only three managers in the company, and now "there are so many managers, really! Even in the toilet maybe there is a manager!" Modes of rationalization are thus perpetuated through the isomorphic diffusion of these trends; that is, formal structures are imitated and adopted regardless of whether they serve any practical function.[42]

The logic of reengineering is evident in the continual reshuffling within companies and the pervasive threat of layoffs, which dampen employees' morale and weaken their commitment to their companies. As shareholders' perspectives become ever more focused on the short term, the prospect of building shareholder value over the long-term has become increasingly untenable.[43] At every level, then, commitment becomes fragile and short-lived. In such a context, it is no surprise that employees come to distrust their companies and learn to fend for themselves. As Mark D'Mello, a "People Development Manager" in the Bangalore office of a global IT giant, complained to me, "If the company cannot show loyalty to its people, then why should the people be loyal to the company?"

A second key aspect of rationalization is control without authority: the restructuring of organizations to give the impression of decentralization while masking modes of top-down domination.[44] Despite claims about how organizational structures have shifted from hierarchies to networks, where power is supposedly no longer concentrated at the top,[45] evidence suggests that "the institutional structure has become more convoluted, not simpler," and that "domination from the top is both strong and shapeless."[46] One manifestation of such power at the top is the constant shifting of jobs to whichever country is able to do the work at the cheapest cost. But these power imbalances do not render professionals passive in those contexts. Rather, they intensify pressures for survival within the organization, generating competition within and across branches, and even modes of resistance. These pressures in turn contribute to the mistrust that sustains the character of the Mercenary.

Consider one such example. Tarun in Bangalore told me about an incident that occurred in his firm: Indian employees were stealing sales commissions from their U.S. counterparts who actually had worked to create the deal. The practice was for employees who were working on a particular sale to get a percentage of the deals they closed. Some Indian employees, working while Americans slept, illegitimately picked up and closed deals that had been worked on by their U.S. colleagues the previous day, thus depriving those who had done the work from reaping the fruits of their labor. Though this was unethical, Tarun noted that "the management out here chooses to overlook it, primarily because they get paid on it as well." As a result, employees in the U.S. office, already enraged at Indians for "taking" their colleagues' jobs, began demanding stricter controls. The ripple effects adversely affected Tarun and his colleagues, who were consequently subjected to more scrutiny and bureaucratic controls. Tarun found it hypocritical that the very managers who were part of the problem were subjecting him to micromanagement: looking through his computer, tapping into his phone calls, and so on. Further, cost-cutting pressures on the Indian office increased, resulting in Tarun and his colleagues losing a fair bit of their compensation. "[I]f I don't get paid—and if the top management get paid in any which case—and if I don't get paid for having slogged on that, you know. . . . I don't want to work for a company that kind of cheats its employees," said Tarun. "And in sales, one of the few things that's important is the salesman's compensation; you take that away from him, or you strip him in half! Then why should I put in that effort?"

Early in the twentieth century, Max Weber expressed his fears that the rationalization accompanying modern capitalism would generate a "mechanized ossification," leaving society trapped in an "iron cage" or "steel-hard casing."[47] New modes of global control driven by reengineering processes evoke such fears. But there are fissures within the iron cage. Examples such as that described by Tarun reveal gaps and cracks in the system that local employees can exploit. Local managers also exploit structural rationalization to their advantage. "It's a joke, you know?" said Tarun. "When it suits their needs, they [blame] the Americans, . . . 'This is what the American [policy] is, this is how we're going to do it.' . . . [But] they just implement their own stupid policies!" These "stupid policies" he decried included various forms of "bureaucratic red tape" put into place in the Indian office, such as additional reporting protocols and channels that he knew did not exist in the parent company's offices. These protocols gave local directors more control over subordinates. In this manner, Tarun complained, they adopted the "worst practices" of East and West. Similar complaints were echoed by respondents in Dubai as well.

Despite their deterministic and sinister aspects, rationalized modes of control have their advantages. In fact, it is their very "impersonal" and "procedural" nature that employees consider to be safeguards not only of their dignity as professionals but also of key elements of their survival. Maryann, a Filipina marketing manager in Dubai, told me about an incident in which this strict impersonal adherence to policies and procedures preserved her job. She had been baited by a colleague who took something she said in an email and used it to misrepresent her to her managers, in an attempt to get her fired. Maryann claimed that the HR department "investigated properly without taking any sides or making biased decisions." She was initially concerned that she would not receive fair treatment because she was Filipino and the HR manager and the colleague who had complained against her were both Indians. "But instead of taking the side of their co-national," she said, the HR person supported her. The claimant, meanwhile, elevated the case to the HR department in the head office in Singapore, which conducted an investigation. Finally, the company concluded that Maryann was in the right and had behaved "in the most professional way." She said it was a fair process in which her company did not take sides but resolved the matter by strictly adhering to policies. Such policies are the cornerstone of formal trust, which becomes paramount in these workplaces in the absence of informal trust, which I discuss next. The differences in the accounts of Tarun and Mary-ann reveal the positive and negative outcomes of rationalization and why bu-reaucratic policies can be both enabling and constraining, both appealing and frustrating to Mercenary professionals.

Flexibilization

A paradoxical contrast with the rigid determinism of rationalization is what I call flexibilization.[48] By this, I refer to organizations' claims that their rules and en-vironments are adaptable and responsive to employees' needs.[49] While ratio-nalization valorizes structure and control, flexibilization celebrates autonomy, agency, empowerment, and discretion. Listen to the enthusiasm of Eric, a man-ager at a global technology firm in Bangalore, when describing his company:

> They give you a long leash in terms of the goals you can set, how long you can work. It's up to you! If you wanna screw up, it's your choice. If you don't perform, it's your fault. But they're not going to beat you up about it. Being a multinational technology company, there are a lot of protocols in place which make it easier for employees to come in and start working. The fact that you can hang out and have a beer with your boss is fantastic. I'm happy here. . . . It allows you to dream big and to achieve big goals. Because if you are treated small, then you think small and you act small; you're not going to feel empowered, entitled. So this allows you to feel empowered and entitled to achieve those big goals and set them for yourself. And this is encouraged. It's democratic!

This new "flexibility" thus brings with it a new sense of empowerment. But it also leaves employees to completely shoulder the blame for their inability to succeed. (In the next section, we see how incentive structures are set up such that someone always has to fail.)

One appealing aspect of this flexibility for most professionals is the informal-ity in global workplaces in contrast to local companies. For instance, many lead-ing technology firms do not require employees to wear formal attire to work. This was especially the case in companies that dealt primarily with customers outside their region or did not involve regular face-to-face contact with clients. By contrast, respondents noted that it would be unthinkable to show up to work in t-shirts and jeans in most locally run firms.[50] Global firms relax the expectation of formality in attire to create an informal environment that helps people feel relaxed and at home. In local companies, by contrast, the emphasis on formality is at times heightened to project a sense of legitimacy, which established for-eign brand names already have.

Other perks in many global workplaces include recreational facilities such as pool and ping-pong tables and gyms, as well as comfortable furniture such as bean bag chairs and couches to nap and lounge on. The underlying assumption is that such facilities will contribute to generating loyalty, creativity, and productivity.[51] Another aspect of informality is the practice of addressing superiors by their first names rather than formal titles such as "sir" or "madam," as is the norm in local firms. Informality is also understood as socializing outside the workplace, which also serves work-related ends such as "team building." In both cities, it was common for employees of global corporations to go out to bars or pubs during evenings and weekends with colleagues or to go on corporate "outings" to resorts and spas to celebrate the accomplishment of certain milestones and targets. In these efforts to make work more "fun," the tension between asceticism and hedonism, expressed in sociologist Daniel Bell's contrast between the delayed gratification expected in the rationalized workplace and the hedonistic "self-fulfillment" pursued outside the workplace, gets played out entirely within the realm of work.[52]

Overall, such informality in global corporations was characterized by my respondents as an improvement over local work environments with their formality and enforced rigid hierarchies. In Bangalore, this critique was applied by respondents to what they called "traditional" or "Indian" management,[53] and in Dubai it was applied to what people called "local" or "Arab" modes of management. In both cases the contrast was to "global" or "Western" management, which was understood to be less hierarchical, nonauthoritarian, nonracist, merit based, and, overall, more "professional."

A second feature that many find appealing is flexible time. Many professionals, such as Ashwin at CompuTech, expressed great enthusiasm that not only could they go to work in t-shirts and jeans, but they did not need to go into the office at all, but could work remotely:

> CompuTech is an awesome company to work for, because their work culture is pretty American. [Compared to] Indian companies like Wipro, Infosys and all that, in a way it's much more chilled out. . . . It's flexi-time! You can enter at any time in the office and come out anytime. . . . If I don't shave for two-three weeks, nobody cares. As long as you're delivering the stuff, they don't mind if you work from moon or Mars or anything. The whole of November and December I was working from home. So that way it's a very chilled-out place. If you have a family and kids, then you don't have to come to work at all, so for women it's awesome.[54]

I remarked that all that his company was doing for its employees sounded great. "They don't do it for charity," he laughed. He knew well that the company was saving money by not having to invest as much in office space or to spend as much on transportation costs and that it was not losing productivity during employees' traveling time, as most other companies that required employees to be physically present would. Still, he appreciated the fact that he could spare himself the nightmarish rush hour traffic by driving to and from work during off-peak hours.

A key claim about such new "flexible" arrangements is that lower-level units (whether subsidiaries or departments or teams) have greater freedom to use any means or method they see fit to achieve the targets set by the higher level. "This freedom is, however, specious," as Bennett Harrison argues.[55] Because of the anxiety generated by the loss of control over employees, many corporations put into place numerous new controls to continue to regulate this "flexible" work. People need to be accessible by phone or email around the clock, they need to use the company intranet (through which their work can be monitored), supervisors can open their emails, and so on. Thus, with flextime, employees may have control over "the location of labor," but not over "the labor process itself," in which they may remain perpetually subject to surveillance.[56]

Some of my respondents, however, like Ashwin, did insist that they had the freedom to work as and when they pleased, without any form of surveillance, as long as they got the job done. This was something they sincerely seemed to enjoy about working at their firms. Nevertheless, they knew well that it was not without cost. Greater "flexibility" meant a greater workload. "These perks come at a price," Tarun insisted. "They draw blood! . . . For every little benefit that they give you, they draw ten times out of it!" Another cost of such perks is usually a lower salary than they might get at other firms with a regular office schedule. Their appeal, thus, can be short-lived. Ashwin, who said he certainly enjoyed the benefits of "flexi-time," explained that since he got married and is starting to make decisions about children and other long-term planning, these benefits do not seem as appealing, and he is looking around for jobs that offer more money instead. Additionally, several respondents working flextime admitted that they were often irresponsible with their time and ended up panicking at the last minute about meeting deadlines. They had no prior training to help them remain accountable without constant surveillance. For this reason, when some of them assume management roles, they become less likely to encourage flextime among subordinates, being all too aware of opportunities for temptation and lack of productivity. Major corporations such as Yahoo! have started to withdraw this privilege as well.[57] The tension between rationalization and flexibilization thus tends to be resolved in the direction of the former. As we have seen, both processes are simultaneously enabling and constraining in different ways. But on the whole, a sense of structural constraint prevails, leaving employees wary of the system while also being drawn to it. The counterpart to these tensions at the structural level is a polarity at the cultural level between collectivism and individualism.

Collectivism

Collectivism in corporate culture is evident in the pervasive emphasis on teamwork and building "strong cultures." As did rationalist theories of management, this "culturalist" approach emerged as a fad among management practitioners, who were influenced by Japanese trends.[58] It is now part of conventional management wisdom that turbulent economic environments require sustained collective effort on the part of diverse work teams to generate creativity and innovation; therefore, organizations need to cultivate, in Rosabeth Moss Kanter's words, "collective pride and faith in people's talents, collaboration, and teamwork."[59]

These attempts to build strong cultures, as advocated by prominent management consultants and gurus, typically involved specifying sets of corporate "values" that would constitute the "core" or "bedrock" of an organization, which could be reflected in and reinforced through formal policies, informal norms, rituals, stories, and symbols and serve as a "glue" to bind people together around the common mission.[60] But by the mid-1990s, even Tom Peters, a pioneer in proclaiming the centrality of culture for "excellent" companies, complained that most of the money spent on "culture training" was a total waste.[61] Nevertheless, an interest in culture, values, and teamwork remains strong in global corporations.

Sociologists see this interest in culture as a counterpart to structural reengineering, but one with the serious potential for the manipulation of employees.[62] Gideon Kunda describes it as "normative control," which is "the attempt to elicit and direct the required efforts of members by controlling the underlying experiences, thoughts, and feelings that guide their actions."[63] Under this form of control, it is not coercion that drives people, but internal commitment and a strong and "deeper" sense of identification with the company goals. Through such culture-building efforts, Kunda argues, companies attempt to elicit high performance from employees while at the same time "provid[ing] them with 'the good life': a benign and supportive work environment that offers the opportunity for individual self-actualization."[64] The strategy is "to embed the rules, prescriptions and admonitions of the culture in the fabric of everyday life" in the workplace.[65] This is done through various means: stickers, memos, posters, documents, rituals, ceremonies, vision and mission statements, motivational speeches, and more. The aim of culture building is to create the postindustrial version of the "organization man"[66]: the dedicated corporate employee who feels a strong sense of loyalty, belonging, and commitment to the company.[67] For people whose hearts and minds are successfully captured by the organization, the distinction between self and company starts to collapse. Corporate values, including hard work and pride in the company's accomplishments, as one of Kunda's engineers claimed, "are what we represent. They are inside of us."[68]

Echoing precisely such a sentiment, Jackie, the senior HR director in Dubai of a major global soft drink company, proudly told me, "We're very big in values. It's drilled in the company: you have to do things the right way!" And in response to a recent company-wide survey in which employees complained that "we're not a fun company anymore" and that it had become "all about work, all about delivering numbers, delivering results," she and her team designed programs, including various company-sponsored activities for employees and their families, to cultivate a sense of fun, loyalty, and belonging:

> And we responded, big time! And now we do cooking classes for families for example. My son came, my husband came, I brought them along! We have yoga classes. The wives come and join for running. We have a trainer! We run with a group, and it's almost like a boot-camp! And it's paid for by the company. The cooking class is not cheap: it's 180 dirhams [U.S. $49] per person. The yoga class is 500 dirhams [U.S. $136] per person. The teacher comes on Saturdays. And it's open to the family. Our people told us, we responded. So that is actually our banner: "Your voice is heard!"

A common means of generating we-feeling and a sense of belonging is to organize work into teams. This too is linked to rationalization and the pursuit of efficiency: the volatility of the economy and intensity of competition provide the imperative for innovation and creativity that cross-functional teams are supposedly better at achieving than individuals working on their own. Teamwork is cultivated not simply in the workplace but also in frequent socializing outside work hours. This works best when it is not explicitly proclaimed as "team building." Girish in Bangalore, for instance, described what he considered one of his best experiences of corporate life, working for a U.K.-based firm in Bangalore:

> Everybody was just super-friendly. There was no kinda problem between each other. Every Friday night as soon as we finished work—we used to finish work one hour early—as soon as we finish work, the managers— all the senior managers—and everybody in the office would head straight to a pub. Or we would go to a manager's house, drink in his home, no worries.

It was a "very motivational" work philosophy, Girish explained. His experience reflects how companies attempt to generate loyalty and collective identity commitments through metaphors of "friends," "family," "team," and "community." Unfortunately for him, the branch turned out not to be profitable, and their managers closed up shop and returned to the United Kingdom within a year.

THE FAILURE OF NORMATIVE CONTROL

In spite of attempts to put into practice these mechanisms of normative control, skyrocketing attrition rates in corporations in both Bangalore and Dubai attest to a failure on the part of these efforts to generate collectivist cultures.[69] Even among companies considered the most sought-after global multinational corporations (MNCs), such as IBM, Microsoft, HP, or Oracle, whose HR executives strove to cultivate strong cultures, I found that many professionals adopted a Mercenary approach devoid of organizational loyalty.

To understand why such attempts at normative control fail, consider the case of Colin Perera, a middle manager in the Bangalore office of a leading U.S.-based technology consulting firm. As he stirred his sixth packet of sugar into his cappuccino (while I concealed my alarm), he confessed the disgust he feels in having to regularly participate in the "unfair" process of annual team evaluations, which invariably erodes any we-feeling that he tries to cultivate among the team during the year. "So every year when you have an appraisal, you represent your team," he explained. "And you know the inside story of what happens in an appraisal? There are a lot of under-the-table dealings which happen."

Colin described the appraisal process as a group of managers negotiating in a room. Each manager is responsible for a team of ten and has to place each team member into one of the following four categories: "significantly above peer group," "top of the peer group," "consistent with peer group," and "below peer group." The manager divides the team into these four "buckets," with no more than three members being placed in any one category. Once this is done, the managers collectively have to rank all employees, and again there are restrictions on how many can be put into each category. Each manager then tries to justify why his or her own employees deserve their particular placement. If others are not persuaded, the manager enters into negotiations: "Okay, so if you let my people be in the topmost things, then I will let your people be in the next-most one."

> So the people at the topmost get pushed down, and so on and so forth, and they fit into one of these buckets. And the bottommost bucket, if people go into it, they lose a lot of things: they lose their perks, . . . [their] bonus, they lose another thing called variable pay. So all they get is the basic pay. But somebody always has to be there in that category. It is a very disgusting and a very dirty kind of a thing, that way you'll find.

Colin recounted the case of an employee who was pushed to the bottom category two years in a row. During the third year, when he was once again being pushed into the bottom category, his supervisor fought hard to preserve a higher placement for him. Unfortunately, "there was nothing to distinguish him from the rest. So they had to find some . . . scapegoat to put in there. So that's how it happens." Eventually, his employee was fired.

The fates of these employees—their promotion, demotion, or termination—depend wholly on their supervisors' ability to negotiate in this "give-and-take system," as Colin put it. This competitive appraisal system structurally forces managers to regularly subvert their own efforts to generate camaraderie and team spirit among their subordinates. "So it is not a very fair system, right?" sighed Colin. "Nobody knows what happens."

Colin admitted that this process has been a source of much personal stress. At times, employees in his team who had objectively high performance scores were denied bonuses and promotions because Colin was unable to adequately fight for them. In response some took formal action against him with HR. Others ended up leaving the company altogether. Colin saw this system as fundamentally unjust: on the one hand, he had to cultivate commitment and loyalty among team members, but on the other hand, he had to rank them into winners and losers, pitting them in competition with one another. He knew the employees became wary of him and the company, and he felt disgusted by it. Yet he accepted it with a sense of resignation.

Such structures frustrate attempts at normative control. Many play along with the rituals and mantras designed to induce a collective spirit, but never fully buy into them. Inadvertently, what becomes normative is not loyalty, but disloyalty. Thus, in spite of managerial attempts at normative control, employees express a profound sense of ambivalence about their involvement in such "strong" cultures.[70] This ambivalence contributes to the failure of normative control. Unable to seriously trust or commit to teams and companies, employees become wary and distrustful of one another, looking out for opportunities to put others down, to climb up within the company, or to find greener pastures elsewhere. Despite corporate efforts to cultivate collectivism, professionals in emerging markets thus develop an apprehensive mode of individualism.

Apprehensive Individualism

Even though many professionals talk about workplace culture—its informality, after-hours socializing, celebrations, and so on—as an important part of what draws them to these workplaces, they are clear that their primary motivators are a combination of material and status benefits: salary, perks, company brand name, position, and so on. When I asked people what explained the high rates of attrition in their companies, the responses I received were similar to that of Donnie in Bangalore: "All my friends who have moved out of the company have moved out for the money. Work could also play a role, but finally it's been money."

Regardless of how much flexibility their job affords them or how much fun they have in their workplaces, most respondents admitted they were sooner or later going to pursue "better" opportunities in terms of salary or status. Not a single professional I talked to claimed that they were hoping to move to a company that had a stronger sense of community, or where they would get along better with colleagues, or where they felt a strong sense of belonging.

It is not simply that employees seek individual-level rewards. Incentive structures in these corporations militate against the very forms of collectivity they profess to encourage. Despite the requirement to work collectively in teams, reward structures are set up to encourage competition. Evaluations are primarily done at the individual level, and significant rewards such as promotions and sought-after opportunities (e.g., "onsite" or international placements) accrue primarily to high-performing individuals, not teams. Small bonuses and awards that are given to teams may provide short-term bursts of energy and incentive, but quickly lose their effect, especially when colleagues within teams realize they are competing against one another not only for substantial awards, but often for survival. Many managers and employees I spoke to described the evaluation system in their work teams as necessitating a ranking of employees, such as in Colin's case, which we saw in the previous section, which ensures that there are always individual winners and losers. In time, this structure generates resentment and mistrust among members. Why, one begins to ask, should I help my teammate succeed today if she could be ranked higher than me tomorrow, which could then get me fired?

Another aspect of this individualism has to do with ambition. People in this environment are out "to become somebody," to "not be an also-ran." They exhibit a sense of ambition and competitiveness that has been encouraged and cultivated throughout their lives: in their families, schooling, and colleges. Some would argue that this ambition and dedication are essential for survival and success in a developing economy. The people in my study are very much the product of such cultivation. They are well educated, and many are highly technically proficient. They have, throughout their lives, out-competed others. And having proven themselves as outstanding individuals in many arenas, they are now on the way to furthering their companies' aspirations for global market dominance.

Such ambition is similar to the "achievement ideology" highlighted in research on social class in America.[71] Echoed in a steady refrain throughout one's life— "Behave yourself, study hard, earn good grades, graduate with your class, go onto college, get a good job, and make a lot of money"—this ideology holds the promise that "diligent work [will] be rewarded with increased responsibilities, promotion, pay rises."[72] Its adherents are led to believe that equal opportunity and merit-based rewards abound. By implication, therefore, failure becomes solely the individual's responsibility, signaling that one has not worked hard enough to develop the required competence, skills, or initiative or the dispositions and attitudes required for success. Even those who in these corporate settings assume the roles of mentors or coaches see it as their primary role to foster this sense of initiative and responsibility. They genuinely believe that people will only be successful if they develop this sense of individual responsibility for their own successes and failures. "Attitude is everything" is the key mantra in this mode of individualism, enshrined ubiquitously in motivational posters and stickers around workplaces.

The sense of transience in work environments in both cities also militates against the development of any serious sense of belonging, loyalty, or collective spirit. "There's a high turnover in Dubai in the workplace, so your friends constantly keep changing," Gemima explained. She did not know a single person in her workplace who had been with her throughout her seven years in the company. Most of her colleagues had been there for less than five years. "I haven't actually found a friend or colleague with whom I can trust and share things," she admitted. Similarly, Donnie in Bangalore, who had been at his firm, a highly reputable Fortune 100 company, for ten years, told me that staying as long as he did was "unusual. Especially so long with this company, it's unusual." All his colleagues from his early years in the company had long since moved on and wondered why he had not. Many others described their work environment as marked by high turnover. People typically kept to themselves, despite having to work in team projects; that made it easier to move on as they eventually would. Wariness, detachment, and superficiality have become defining characteristics of workplace relationships in the new economy.[73]

Learning to Mistrust

Formal trust is maintained through formal agreements; as long as these agreements are honored, the parties see each other as trustworthy. Informal trust, however, "is a matter of knowing on whom you can rely, especially when a group is under pressure: who will go to pieces, who will rise to the occasion."[74] The aspects of individualism described here—the pursuit of individual material and status rewards, the individualized evaluation and incentive systems in corporations, the competitive ambition nurtured by the achievement ideology, and the imperative for moral responsibility to succeed in this regard—all work against the development of such informal trust. In addition, informal trust requires time to develop and mature, time that is lacking in these transient work teams and organizations with high attrition.

Mistrust is expressed in myriad ways in corporate workplaces.[75] Despite the valorization of meritocracy, people are constantly on the lookout for shortcuts, such as opportunities to ingratiate themselves to managers and get ahead of their colleagues. People in this environment thus often hold their cards close to their chest, afraid to reveal anything that could be used by opportunistic colleagues or could make them vulnerable. The palpable sense of suspicion and mistrust that Ajay voiced was expressed consistently by most of my respondents in both cities:

> I don't trust anybody that I work with. Because you never know what will happen. See, I don't want to fail, and I also don't want others to fail me. . . . Just to be on the safe side, I go do my job and hi and bye to everybody and just two-three jokes to everyone. He laughs, I laugh, then we go.

Learning to mistrust is seen as a mark of prudence and maturity. Martina, an HR manager with a global consulting firm based in Bangalore, spoke at length about how she had to learn the hard way that it was naïve to trust colleagues in the workplace. She talked mainly about her experience of working at MegaTech, an American tech firm, and how that experience shattered her assumptions about meritocracy and fairness in transnational corporations:

> When I joined the workforce, I believed that everyone is honest. And I believed that if you do your work well, you will get rewarded; if you don't do your work well you don't get rewarded. . . . But I learned the very hard way through experience, when it happened to me personally, after about five or six years. I learned that there was a lot that was going on behind my back. And that's when I learned that that is reality.

In "reality," her colleagues turned out to be very different from the initial impression they gave her. She started work there expecting professionalism. She thought that in a "major global MNC," of all places, you should be able to "just trust your colleagues; if they say that they're doing this, you just trust that they're doing it." It simply did not occur to her "that they will go behind your back and try to promote their candidate," or that they would spy on her work or acquire details about her salary or other personal information to further their own mobility in the company. "And this has happened big time, and I've learned it from my own experience." A colleague lied about her to her superiors behind her back, and as a result, she was overlooked for a promotion she rightly deserved.

I asked her why she thought people would act that way toward her. "Because they feel threatened," she replied. She saw them as constantly asking themselves, "Is there someone else who is also aiming for the same position that I am? Where is so-and-so going? . . . I am on a mission to become a senior VP or director, is there anyone else who is coming in my way?" But she recognized that their striving was not simply about work and career, but about improving their lot in life generally. "Many employees are coming from a lower-middle-class or lower-class background financially," she explained. "So everyone wants to come up in life. Everyone wants themselves to have a good life [and] they want their kids to have a good life." Ajay in Bangalore, when complaining about his managers who had pocketed his commissions, similarly expressed sympathy for these people: "What to do? He also has a family to support."

In addition to reducing trust in the workplace, such experiences take an emotional toll on people. When I asked Martina how she was affected by what happened to her, she admitted, "I think I did become bitter, to be frank, for a long time after that." She since moved on to another company and told me that the experience served a purpose in enabling her to develop a disposition more suitable to managing life in the workplace. She has learned to be "more alert" and "less foolish," which is to say, less trusting of others.

It is not just the "losers" in this environment who voice such mistrust and isolation. Even those who are highly successful, who may never have experienced such betrayal, and who may even be aware that they are being supported and groomed for more important roles in the company, still reserve for themselves the right to abandon their commitment to the company. And keeping oneself disconnected from others, keeping relationships in the workplace superficial, can help that process. As Donnie in Bangalore said, "As a person, I myself do not get into really kind of building the relationship in the sense of getting into details and all that. I kind of keep myself to my work." Like many others I talked to, he expressed this desire to maintain boundaries between personal and work friends as a matter of principle.[76] Donnie made it clear that his mistrust of people—including his unwillingness to share knowledge and information with colleagues—was not because of any betrayal he has experienced at the hands of bosses:

> My relationship to my managers has been good. I mean they consider me as a top performer, and whenever there is [sic] opportunities they send me onsite, which not everybody in the team gets. There are sixty in the team, and less than ten get to travel. So that way I'm at the top. I'm taken care of really well.

Nevertheless, he was not willing to take chances. Despite his success, Donnie acted in ways that revealed that he really did not trust people around him: "As a person what I've felt is that sharing knowledge, you really need to share. But there are times that you feel you want to hold that back." He admitted that he often "held back" because he feared that sharing his knowledge might allow colleagues around him to come to "know more and increase [their] knowledge base and go ahead of you." Mistrust and personal distancing, then, are not simply prerogatives of those who experience betrayal or failure in the workplace. Other "successful" professionals such as Ashwin voiced similar comments about the nature of their relationships with members of their work teams, with whom they had to spend most of their days: "Relationship-wise, you do your stuff and go back. It's not very personal as such. . . . People are not [the] friendly-friendly kind. Professional."

Professionals in this environment by and large are constantly watchful of one another, trying to interpret threats and opportunities in the ways in which their colleagues, superiors, and subordinates treat them. Past performance and seniority come to count for little and are even devalued by people espousing the need to succeed purely on the merit of present performance. Such performance is supposed to depend on teamwork and collaboration, but is usually evaluated on an individual basis, guaranteeing there will be losers no matter how "objectively" well one performs. Further, the criteria for such evaluations are not made transparently available to everyone in the team, allowing managers to play favorites and encouraging employees to turn into sycophants. What matters at the end of the day is perceived performance. Superiors in such a short-term performance-driven context develop "very short memories." As a result, as Sennett explains, one is "always starting over," and such continual exposure to risk with no proportional reward can "eat away at [one's] sense of character."[77]

Yet, as much as all these tensions may eat away at people, they do not seem to drive them to despair. Rather than being overwhelmed or submerged, people learn to swim in these waters. And in adapting, they become attuned to what it takes to survive and even succeed in these environments. Without necessarily consciously trying to do so, they develop a sense for the norms, roles, expectations, logics, and dispositions required to play the game, which together constitute the character of the Mercenary.

Sustaining Apprehensive Individualism

While the dual tensions of rationalization-flexibilization and individualism-collectivism generate the Mercenary, three cultural mechanisms work together to sustain this character: narrative scripts, mimesis, and habituation.

The orienting model of the Mercenary itself provides narrative scripts: pervasive injunctions, directives, assertions, and statements about the kind of self that one ought to become to survive and thrive in this environment. Here are some examples—some are direct quotations, some are paraphrases—provided by my respondents in Bangalore and Dubai:

"I'm in it for the cash; I don't care about loyalty to the company."

"Are you senior manager yet?"

"I'm not really getting the salary and perks I deserve here. I need to start looking out for better opportunities."

"I've been here ten years already, and that's way too long for anyone to be at a company!"

"I don't have a choice. I may not agree with it, but I need to do it to get that promotion."

"What matters at the end of the day is to become more promotable, more employable."

"You should always keep an eye on the market. You never know when things here will start going downhill."

"You can't trust anybody here; each one is simply trying to get ahead."

"I'd better tell the boss before [colleague] does; otherwise, she'll get credit for it."

"Her performance review was much better than mine; I've got to make sure I outperform her next time. Make sure you're in [the boss's] good books; otherwise, your evaluations will suffer."

The mechanisms that cultivate Mercenary professionalism are distinct from those that shape the forms of normative control that I discussed earlier. The scripts that drive normative control attempt to cultivate we-feeling and a sense of pride in and loyalty toward the company. The narrative scripts of the Mercenary, by contrast, are starkly individualistic. Normative control aims at producing an "organization man" or getting employees to buy into the "member role" or company spirit or to commit fully to the corporate mission and vision.[78] But Mercenary professionalism is not a matter of a simple adherence to roles; rather, it is a fusion of role and personality.[79] As Ashok, one of my respondents in Bangalore insisted, "You cannot mask professionalism; you have to *be* professional!" This is certainly not unique to corporate professionals; we see such fusion in other professions such as soldiers and doctors.[80] But if there is a form of control that generates such fusion or becoming, it cannot be imposed from the top, nor can it be as transparent (and thereby subject to cynicism, distancing, and parody) as normative control. Rather, the form of control is *mimetic*: it is based on imitation that is often unintentional. As theologian John Knapp notes, "Individuals at work tend to adopt the habits and attitudes of the group without recognizing the subtle coercion and pressures that cause them to do so."[81]

French literary critic René Girard's theory of mimesis provides insights that can help us understand this process.[82] First, Girard argues that the desire for any object is always borrowed from and mediated by an "other" who desires the same object.

The implication is that positions and promotions are not simply desired for the material rewards that they bestow, but for the sense of "being" that the aspirant feels she lacks herself but that the other person possesses: one seeks a greater sense of fullness or worth.[83] Thus, objects once obtained only yield disenchantment, until we find the next object that promises the sense of fullness we see in its possessor.

Second, the scarcity of desired objects gives rise to mimetic rivalry. We see the effect of this in teams in which everyone has to work together to deliver results, is vying for top slots, and is striving to not be eliminated—even though only some of the employees will be promoted. The rivalry that Girard claims is bound to result is rife in these workplaces. This contributes to the pervasive mistrust of colleagues in corporate contexts, no matter how "friendly" one's interactions with them are. "You're friends at work but you just stay as 'work friends,'" as Nikhila put it. "I just leave them where they are; I don't make them part of my friends' circle. They're just office colleagues and that's how I look at them. That's the best way to be, trust me!" She was wary because of the likelihood that most of her colleagues would be opportunistic and could use anything they inadvertently said or did to their advantage and to her detriment:

> They're gonna go back and crib [i.e., complain] to my team leader saying: this is what she did, she was on the phone to someone, she was telling someone she likes them, lalala . . . it gets reported! It's like a soap opera; it's terrible! It's like *The Bold and the Beautiful* with all the rivalry!

Rivalry is furthered when the "model" being imitated actively desires the object as well and puts up resistance to the competitor.[84] The rivalry that results is not only for positions and awards in workplaces but also for other desired symbols of greater "being" that circulate in conversations among peers. As Anil in Bangalore said, constant gossip about "how many flats or condos or apartments" one owns, or where one is aspiring to "jump" to next, whether one's colleagues have become "senior manager, . . . director, VP, AVP," or the types of cars or watches one owns fuels this ongoing comparison and rivalry. Thus, such narrative scripts and their implicit conceptions of selfhood—what it is good or worthy for me to be and what I must become (and concomitantly, what kind of self it is unworthy or bad to be)—are also objects of mimesis that exacerbate the sense of competition in the workplace.

Acquisitive desire and rivalry generate a mimetic contagion, as rivals become more and more alike. "The atmosphere in the workplace will be absorbed by you," insisted Terence, a Filipino in Dubai, admitting to his own mistrust of others at work and to having somehow become someone he did not set out to be. "You will be like them also!" This mimetic unrest tends toward violence and finds resolution only in the selection and expulsion of a "scapegoat," which allows the restoration of order, but often only temporarily, by "purging the community" of someone who is seen to "undermine" it.[85] Victims are usually those who adhere least to or are the furthest from the shared norms: in our case, those who least fit the Mercenary type or those who are unable to play the game well. The tensions within Colin Perera's team of subordinates, for instance, abate when the evaluations declare who is ranked at the bottom (and as he explained, the ranking system ensures that someone is always at the bottom), revealing who needs to be reprimanded and possibly terminated. Bureaucracy and organizational structures play a vital role in containing the "violence" in this context,[86] sometimes in paradoxical ways. For instance, managers and decision makers who have to fire the scapegoat can do so while portraying themselves as powerless in the face of external rules and pressures.[87] Colin expressed such a sense of helplessness when talking about the process through which a colleague's subordinate was terminated: "There was nothing to distinguish him from the rest . . . . They had to find some . . . scapegoat to put in there." That is simply "how it happens"; that is just how the game is played, and the ones who eliminate the scapegoat are simply carrying out the sacrifice required by the system to maintain order.

In addition to narrative scripts and mimetic contagion, the simple force of routine and habit over time generates consistent and predictable dispositions: a professional *habitus*, to use sociologist Pierre Bourdieu's term.[88] It is the sustained *practice* of professional life that, in combination with the processes described earlier, generates the Mercenary professional as a more or less consistent self with a keen sense of the "field" in which to play the game, equipped with skills and capacities to varying degrees, as well as the knowledge of the "correctness" of practices required therein. These resulting dispositions are not the direct result of formal training or rules or of explicit programming through normative control, but rather are habits, skills, and dispositions that are picked up and developed inadvertently through practice and become self-sustaining as people gain competence in navigating the field. As philosopher Robert Solomon notes, the corporate workplace thus cultivates "characteristic ambitions, aspirations, and expectations."[89] It is through a process of habituation and routinization that one picks up the skills to manipulate or to avoid being manipulated. One has to "learn through mistakes," as Menezes said, to mistrust colleagues or how to "manage" one's superiors and subordinates alike, until these dispositions become second nature and instinctive.

Thus, narrative scripts provide the deliberative and reflexive aspect, while mimesis and habituation provide the nondeliberative and interactional elements of the process that sustains the Mercenary. Together with the broader structural and cultural tensions I discussed earlier, these mechanisms generate the apprehensive individualism and the taken-for-granted nature of the goals of individual mobility that would have been unimaginable a few decades ago.

Failed Solidarity: The Effects of Local Contexts

For the most part, the processes discussed in this chapter operate almost identically in Bangalore and Dubai. Indeed, with the predominance of South Asians in Dubai, it was often difficult, when I visited some of these offices, to tell that I was not in India. But local contextual factors certainly play a role in shaping the apprehensive individualism and informal trust within workplaces.

A common complaint by Dubai respondents was racial discrimination in the workplace. In Dubai, as in the rest of the Gulf, the labor market tends to be segmented by nationality, and most respondents reported the same hierarchy that has been identified in other studies.[90] Top managers tend to be Gulf Arabs or Caucasians from North America, Europe, and Australia; engineers tend to be non-Gulf Arabs (e.g., Egyptians or Lebanese); accountants tend to be Indians; and sales and customer service staff tend to be Filipinos. These divisions help sustain stereotypes that in turn produce resentment and mistrust. In addition, nationality-based differences in pay are built into the wage structure and generate further resentment. This was often voiced in interviews I conducted with South Asians and Filipinos in Dubai, most of whom are paid lower wages than coworkers at the same level who simply happen to have a higher-status passport. "For the same position as me, these guys [referring to European colleagues] get paid three, four times [as much]," said Charles, a Sri Lankan finance manager, echoing the claims of many others.[91] Charles might be exaggerating, but data certainly confirm the nationality-based salary differences. According to the 2017 Gulf Business salary survey, the average monthly salary for an Asian finance manager in the UAE was USD 7,371, compared to USD 10,322 for a Western expat in the same position.[92] I describe in detail these forms of stratification in chapter 5.

Such discrimination was manifested not simply in pay and perks but also in position. For instance, Cyril, a senior operations manager, claimed that his Indian nationality was a ceiling that prevented advancement to a higher post, because his organization did not want nonwhites or non-Gulf Arabs in figurehead positions. "Dirty, blatant racism," said Cyril, bitterly denouncing it, but added that he could do no better at any other company. Nearly everyone I talked to claimed that they had simply learned to cope with the racism and not think about it. For instance, Noel described his experience at his consulting firm: "I deal with top management at the CXO level people in every single project. It's a bit difficult in the first meeting when you start talking and people have already judged you before you open your mouth based on a prejudice rather than your experience and what you know." He claimed that he has learned to overcome this challenge over the years. At meetings with new clients, he anticipates that they are not going to take him seriously at first, so he keeps quiet until a problem emerges to which he can provide a solution: "The first time I step in is when I'm directly addressed or when there's a problem I can directly solve. I don't waste time on niceties."

Discrimination is not simply practiced by Western expats and Gulf Arabs toward South Asians but is also rife among Indians and even between Indians and Filipinos. "Indians are the most racist people in the world" was a common statement I heard from Indians in both Bangalore and Dubai, referring to discrimination between Indians of different ethnolinguistic backgrounds. Filipinos also sometimes complained about discrimination from Indians. Certainly not all my Filipino respondents would have been forthcoming with me about this because of my Indian ethnicity, but some perceived me primarily as an American and so were honest enough to express this feeling. Terence, for instance, talked about how he was "much happier" in his second job in Dubai, in a German-owned company, since his managers were "much better" than the Indian bosses in his previous company. He apologized at this point, with nervous laughter, but I assured him I was not offended. "It's very difficult to deal with them," he said, referring to Indians, "because they came here first, before the Filipino," and as a result, "they want to give positions only to their people." The problem was not simply that they discriminated against him when it came to promotions but also that they seemed incompetent. "I am not boasting or being racist, but it's very different when you compare their work to back in the Philippines." He insisted that one Filipino could do the work of "three to four Indians," because the former knew how to multitask whereas Indians apparently did not. He said you could encounter Filipinos everywhere in malls or other service-related work in Dubai and see that "they know hard work," because "we're used to that kind of work." In comparison, he found his Indian colleagues "very relaxed, very slow." Such sorts of stereotypes were bandied about by several people of diverse ethnic and national backgrounds, attributing the perceived flaws of other groups to ethnic or national differences.

In Bangalore, while there is no counterpart to the pay ceilings or explicit wage discrimination based on ethnicity found in Dubai, there are other forms of ethnolinguistic discrimination that many respondents complained about. They cited examples of what they called "groupism" or "communalism," in which managers would favor employees belonging to their own ethnic backgrounds. These employees would thus have a cultural advantage over colleagues of other ethnic groups, simply by virtue of sharing the same background, language, and tastes of these managers. Ashwin, for instance, gave his current team as an example:

> Most of the people are from Andhra Pradesh [a neighboring state]. They have their own clique; they are more like a coterie. They don't talk to

others [in the team]. Whenever two of them are there, they always speak in Telugu [the state language of Andhra Pradesh]. Other people, what I see is, they start speaking in Hindi or something, so that the other guys will also understand. Whereas these guys prefer to speak in their language. So already you are cut off from them, right? So that way, relationship is not there.

Richard, another manager in Bangalore, talked about how, at his firm, they "are discouraged from talking in our vernacular, so it doesn't happen much. But I see people huddled together from time to time. I have seen it often." Nevertheless, he thought that this tendency is less pronounced in global IT firms than in local companies. Even within ethnicity-based coteries, however, it is not the case that people strongly trust one another. Carol, a Filipina junior sales manager in Dubai, talked about her disillusionment at not finding the sense of community she expected in the workplace, given that most employees were from the Philippines:

> I don't want to say bad thing[s] about my company, but, [despite] the fact that we are all employee[s], we are all getting paid, we're working in one company, sometimes they are acting differently from what—you cannot even trust people in your same nationality! Even Filipino[s] I cannot trust anymore!

I asked her why. "If they see something bad about you, they will definitely tell the manager," she replied, indicating that her colleagues were liable to use anything she said or did to get her into trouble. When I asked her what they sought to gain by such behavior, she said, "Of course, they will be beautiful in the eye [of the manager]." Her account of snitching and sycophancy in her firm was nearly identical to that of Nikhila in Bangalore, discussed earlier.

Despite the pervasive mistrust, employees, in appealing to professionalism, voice the belief that they have a basic dignity that needs to be respected by superiors: they want to be treated with respect rather than abused, they want to be paid for their work and in a timely manner, they want their experiences of injustice to be addressed, and so on.[93] But theirs is a severely muted voice that seldom finds any public expression in the contexts I study and is certainly not a collective one. Thus, despite the potential for solidarity built into these appeals for professionalism, in practice it remains dormant. The reasons for this are different in Dubai and Bangalore.

For Dubai, the reason is straightforward: associations that engage in collective bargaining, such as trade unions, are prohibited by law; this is also a key factor that draws businesses to the region. There were rumors in the media in 2006 that the UAE was considering allowing trade unions,[94] but such talk quickly fizzled. Since

2007, construction workers, predominantly of Indian and Bangladeshi origin, have periodically engaged in strikes, but these have been quickly disrupted and end with the deportation of organizers and participants. While these incidents mostly involved unskilled laborers, they reinforce the conviction among skilled professionals that there is no place in this environment for any mode of collective bargaining that threatens the sovereignty of employers.[95]

In Bangalore, the story is more complicated. While as citizens in a democracy, white-collar professionals certainly can avail themselves of a greater degree of freedom of association, they have little sense of collective identification. As individuals, they identify as professionals, but they share no collective we-feeling. Attempts at collective mobilization in sectors of the new economy have had little success, primarily because of the dominance of the kind of individualism described here: the low level of informal trust, the transient nature of these workplaces, and the unwillingness to jeopardize the normative ideal of mercenary professionalism—mobility.[96] Most professionals in this context are unwilling to commit long term to *any* organization, because doing so could cramp their occupational mobility. They are reluctant to be bound to *any* organization by ties of old-fashioned loyalty. Collective bargaining solutions, particularly those that would result in union members having to commit to staying at a company for a certain length of time, would impinge on the mobility that the Mercenary values above all. For the Mercenary, jobs, companies, and even unions are mere stepping-stones along an independent career trajectory. The great value placed on mobility also helps makes sense of the high rates of attrition in corporate sectors that managers like Menezes complained to me about. The combination of the new spirit of individualism, the low level of informal trust in workplaces, and the industry structure—with its abundance of new job opportunities and the low cost of switching—constitutes a formidable obstacle not only to unionization, but to organizational commitment in general.

Conclusion

The character of the Mercenary does not simply represent the banal pursuit of money and status, but constitutes a distinctive normative vision. It offers what Charles Taylor calls "strong evaluations" or qualitative judgments of worth and thus shapes the kind of person one thinks one ought to become.[97] One *ought to* constantly look out for a better-paying job, *ought not to* "stagnate" in a particular company or position, and certainly one *ought not to* trust others in the workplace, who can compromise one's mobility because they are trying to maximize their own opportunities. This vision is a kind of utilitarian individualism that pursues economic mobility as an ethical imperative.[98] Mobility has become a criterion of worth, a way for people to provide, as Robert Wuthnow puts it, "a legitimate account of themselves—to friends and family, coworkers, and themselves."[99]

There is certainly an element of self-justification involved here. At least when it comes to some of the strategies of the Mercenary, many professionals admit it is a "dirty game." But they tell themselves this is just the way it is. What strengthens their ability to justify their pursuit is that upward mobility comes with benefits for the community that matters most to them: their families and kin. This mode of individualism is not atomistic. Nevertheless, it is an *apprehensive* individualism, in which it is unwise to trust one's colleagues and foolish to be loyal to one's organization. Inward-facing and self-protective, this logic is the very opposite of the cooperative, communal ideal of the corporation put forward by conservative thinkers like Michael Novak.[100]

Is this loss of organizational trust and loyalty really a problem? Is it really worth bemoaning that such belonging and commitment are seldom found in the global corporate workplace?

To assess whether the present state indeed represents a decline, we can scroll back only a few decades, where we would have heard a somewhat different description of corporate professionals: "They are not workers, nor are they the white collar people, in the usual, clerk sense of the word. These people only work for The Organization. The ones I am talking about *belong* to it as well. They are the ones of our middle class who left home, spiritually as well as physically, to take the vows of organization life, and it is they who are the mind and soul of our great self-perpetuating institutions."[101]

That is how William H. Whyte described the "Organization Man" of his day: the conformist caught in the iron cage. This was a character committed to company but not to community or place, living in the stifling "self-imposed isolation" of suburbia. Whyte's source of optimism was the possibility of "individualism within organizational life."[102] The individualism of the Mercenary professional may not have been what Whyte had in mind, but his aspiration reveals a dark side of corporate loyalty that Richard Sennett's seeming nostalgia overlooks. From the standpoint of Whyte's critique of the "Organization Man," it is difficult to see today's Mercenary as much of a "corrosion."

The Mercenary professional I study differs in two important respects from Sennett's account of the "ironic man" of the "new capitalism." First, the perpetual uncertainty, mobility, and retooling that are bemoaned by Sennett's respondents are now embraced as normal in new outposts of neoliberalism. Second, this professional is not, as Sennett suggests, simply a tragic figure devoid of the possibility of a coherent narrative. There is more to people's narratives than their workplace careers; their broader trajectories are embedded in and sustained by factors extrinsic to the workplace. Their ideals and visions of fullness and the good life extend beyond the workplace into realms where they may even be capable of deep commitments.

Consider once again David Menezes, whom we met at the beginning of this chapter. His pursuit of monetary success and comfort is not simply the result of greed and hedonism, but is in large part motivated by family commitments and difficult economic circumstances. Menezes sees himself as a family man deeply committed to his wife, three children, and his ailing mother and to securing a future for his progeny that is free of the hardships he endured in his early life. Most professionals I talked to in Bangalore and Dubai articulated similar commitments. Menezes and most other professionals I studied also identify as deeply religious, with enduring commitments to their church communities (despite their purported willingness to relocate for a higher salary and perks). For such professionals, the workplace may be a realm from which informal trust and long-term commitment are excluded. But this does not mean they do not find and cultivate these needs elsewhere. The workplace, for them, is simply not an appropriate arena in which to pursue them; instead, it is a place where their survival enables them to sustain other spheres of life to which meaning and belonging are relegated. It is a public secular sphere, in which the only legitimate pursuits are amoral and neutral, however fanciful we may judge such claims to be: it is distinct from other realms of life, such as religious communities, which are seen as appropriate loci of belonging and commitment.

To be clear, the many forms of alienation in these environments, the pervasive mistrust, the practices and discourses that convey to people that they do not matter and that they are disposable and dispensable, and the anxieties and health problems that such a climate generates, cannot be condoned simply because people may find meaning and commitment elsewhere. These are toxic environments. Sennett is thus right to recognize them as causing a "corrosion of character." They are corrosive of the virtues needed for the flourishing of any organization, let alone a capitalist economy.[103]

Yet, it is important to recognize that the existential insecurities cultivated in these workplaces do not exist independently of the modes of meaning and belonging that professionals find in other venues, such as in religious institutions. As we see in the next chapter, ECC church groups provide many of these professionals with therapeutic relief from the wounds of corporate life. They reinforce professionals' ability not only to sustain their participation in the realm of the Mercenary—by recasting the workplace as a mission field—but also to tolerate its systemic injustices. Let us turn to examine how those who live as Mercenaries in the corporate jungle inhabit the realm of religion as Missionaries.

THE MISSIONARY

One morning in 2006, a week after being promoted to marketing manager, Randall Fonseca and his wife, Nina, were driving to work. Their brand-new SUV, a splurge purchase to celebrate Randall's new status, sped onto the Garhoud Bridge over Dubai Creek. It was 7 a.m., and traffic was flowing smoothly. They cruised steadily at 100 kilometers per hour, flanked by cars, buses, and motorbikes.

What happened next took only an instant, but the event continues to replay in Randall's mind today in slow motion: "I see the mini-bus's hazards on and breaking. And there was a big bus and I couldn't see what was happening on the other side." During our interview, Randall leaned forward onto the table to describe the traffic placement with his hands:

> I see one Pathan [i.e., an Afghani or Pakistani male][1] crossing the road [on foot]. This is my lane. He is coming. The [motorbike in the next lane] is just stopping and turning. If I turn, I hit the bike; he hits the bus. If I don't turn, I hit the Pathan. And if I turn left, I'm hitting another car! I just braked. I can still remember the Pathan. He just did this to cover his head.

Randall brought up one hand to cover his face to demonstrate this action and continued,

> He hit the side of my car, dented my door. My mirror breaks. Swirling around my car, he falls down behind. I said, "If I have not killed him,

the guy behind must have knocked his brains out." Because over there, you don't stop. It's just a free flow of vehicles.

My wife is howling in the car, because she is freaked out. The only thought that comes to my mind is: blood money. Because in this country, that's the thing is, whether you are right or wrong, if you bang someone on the road, you pay. And I'm behind bars. I'm telling her, "I'm not going to jail! It's not my fault!" Because you can't cross on that road [i.e., it's illegal]. But the law over here says it's different. If you bang somebody, he dies, you go [to jail], whether you are right or wrong.

Randall pulled over by a gas station on the side of the road. He double-parked and stepped out of his car and looked around. "My worst horror—I get out of the car and I cannot see the guy anywhere!" He stood frozen, baffled. He remembered the surreal feeling of calling the police and telling them, "I knocked somebody on the road on this highway. I can't find him. I don't know where the body is." An ambulance pulled up shortly. "He comes around and says, 'Where's the body?' 'I don't know.' He couldn't find the body." The ambulance left to continue the search. Suddenly, Randall spotted something on the other side of the highway. Straining his eyes, he saw what appeared to be a person sitting down. A mixture of shock, relief, and rage propelled him to cross the highway himself.

After my accident, a week later, they put up barricades. So you can't cross over [now]. But I saw someone sitting there and thought it must have been the guy. So I crossed the road, with so much of difficulty—because you can't cross with that traffic! And this guy was managing to cross the road! I was boiling with anger. "Couldn't you see where you were walking? Why were you crossing this road?"

He just stands up and says, "No, I was walking and I didn't. I just wanted to go to the Pakistani consulate." He just kept saying, "I just want to go to the Pakistani consulate, I just want to go to the Pakistani consulate." He was fine—there was nothing wrong with him!

The ambulance came and they did his [blood] pressure and they did the tests and everything. His pressure was a bit high because of the impact from the bang. My car was pretty badly damaged, it was 20,000 dirhams of damage on the car [approximately US $5450 at the time]—it was a new car. And all he broke was a nail, and his cell phone. That was all he broke. There was nothing else broken on his body. Not a scratch on him, nothing!

The next step was to go to the police station. The officer told him, "It's not your fault, but whatever he asks for, you'll have to give." Randall by this point was resigned to his fate and prepared for the worst. The police asked the man what he wanted from Randall. The man replied, "Nothing, I don't want anything. I just want to go to the Pakistani consulate." The police were surprised and asked him repeatedly if he was sure he did not want any money. "Because if I had to pay him, I had to pay him in front of them," Randall explained. But the man insisted that he did not want any money.

> I'm like wondering: what in God's name is happening over here? I knocked down the guy; there's nothing wrong with him, my heartbeat is faster than his heartbeat, all he's done is broken a nail! There's a blood-stain on my window which till date doesn't go. It's still—I've tried washing it, I've given up washing on it because I know it's there for another purpose altogether. That's all that's broken was his nail. And there's that one blood spot. That's it!

As they left the station, Randall told the man he would take him to the Pakistani consulate the next morning. He bought him a new cell phone and offered him money, 500 dirhams, which the man finally accepted with great reluctance. In the morning, Randall bought him breakfast at a Pakistani restaurant before dropping him off at the Pakistani consulate. Randall never found out why the man wanted to go there.

> I believe that was an encounter for me that I need to slow down and realize things that are around me. For me to understand that life is not in my control. For me, I was the maker of my destiny. And someone was just plonking me and saying, "Take it easy, dude!" Because with that impact—21,800 dirhams was the impact on the car—I thought he was dead! I mean you bang anybody at the speed of 60 and 70—I know a friend of mine who banged a guy at 30, he fell off, he hit his head at the wrong place and on the spot he died. And you hear about a lot of these deaths and all that. I don't know for the life of me how—it's something I can't understand. I can't explain it till date how that man survived!

Randall barely slept for several nights after the incident. He was so disturbed by what had happened that he could not focus and so took a few days off from work. "Everybody said it's a miracle that you are not in jail; it's a miracle, it's this and that," he said. A Pentecostal colleague who moonlighted as a pastor was especially encouraging, urging Randall to recognize God's intervention in his life. "And I'm still trying to rationalize with my head," Randall recalled. "Is God part of this? Is God a concept? Did my intelligence make me brake and turn in the right direction at the right time? I was still trying to argue that thought in my mind."

Until that point, Randall was not by any stretch a religious man. He thought religion in general was "just a big hoax" and was especially cynical about the Catholic Church. As he saw it, "A priest molests kids; one priest and all the priests were same for me."

Randall was born and raised in Dubai, the son of expats from Goa in India. Like many other second-generation Catholics I talked to in Dubai, he was put off by what he saw as constant petty squabbling and hypocrisy among older church folk in the various ethnic communities in church. After completing high school in Dubai, he earned an undergraduate degree in India and returned to find a job at his current company in Dubai, which also helped finance his MBA degree in the United States. He met Nina at work, and they were married several years later. Nina, a devout Catholic, was "always into church," but Randall never understood why. All that began to change after the accident.

A few nights after the incident, as he tossed and turned in bed restlessly, he felt that "something was telling me that I need to do some digging." So he went and picked up one of his wife's religious books, "a Catholic question-and-answer book" written by Steve Ray, an American Catholic apologist with a sizable following among Catholics in Dubai and in India. "The first page I get was: 'Is holy communion the true body and blood of Christ?' It explained it, but I didn't understand a word." So he thought to himself, "Nah, let me go back to sleep." But an hour later, he was still just as restless and again felt something prodding him to continue his search. His wife had a jar of "Bible verses for the day" by her bedside, and he picked one from the jar. "It was Luke 5:4 I think: 'I have not come for the righteous but I have come for the sinner.' He reacted: "I am a sinner? What are you trying to tell me?" As much as he tried to evade them, the questions haunted him persistently. He decided that he had to come to some resolution and needed to systematically start researching Christianity:

> For me, logic matters hell of a lot. All the dots have to connect. I started reading and reading and reading and reading. I took a year and a half of only research, on two thousand years of Christ and the Bible and whatever I could get my hands on. You won't believe: Dubai Duty-free is where I found my hub, so to speak. I traveled quite a bit, and the Dubai Duty-free is the only place—it is technically Dubai, even though it is international waters—that sells Christian DVDs. I picked up my entire collection of Christian DVDs: Paul, Peter, two thousand years of Christian history, several series about Christianity. In some way I thought it was just there for me to pick up those series at that time! Anywhere in Dubai you can't get it. [A Protestant church in the city] tries to ship it across illegally but they don't have enough of a collection.

While conducting his research, he was continually surprised that he kept finding answers to his questions. "I'm trying to find something I can find fault—anything! Like communion doesn't work, or spirituality is not there, or transubstantiation doesn't happen; I was trying to pinpoint every error, trying to question everything. And I always got a damn answer." At a certain point, things started to coalesce for him. He went to confession for the first time in years, which he found "fulfilling," and then started attending every retreat that was being offered in the area.

> That first year after my conversion I went for around six retreats. People thought I was crazy because I'd never go for one—this was six different retreats! And at every retreat I thought it was specially meant for me, even though it was for kids. I thought it was specially meant for me because certain things they would say or something or the other that I would pick up. That just helped me [with] going deeper and deeper and deeper. And then my perspective changed completely.
>
> My wife was saying I was like a lunatic. I would read every day and every night; I'd sit up till three or four in the morning. Next morning I got work, [but] I would sleep for three hours and just catch up on reading. Go to work. And for my free time, I'd google and Internet and whatever and just try to gather as much information as possible and whatever, you know, just to figure out. I'd read anything weird that could not make sense—about saints, about stigmatas, about anything. And trying to find logic behind it.

During this time of searching, his research would satisfy him to a point and then generate further questions that would be satisfied in turn by further research, which would then generate additional questions, and so on. Eventually, he said, this process enabled him to overcome all his initial obstacles to Catholicism. He felt that he sufficiently understood all that he needed to know in order to profess belief in and commit himself to Christianity.

It was at that point, just about a year after the strange event, that he decided that it was time "to impart the faith." He wanted to give people "the opportunity that [he had] not had," due to a combination of incompetent religious teaching during his own childhood and his own decisions to avoid church, which he attributed to a lack of compelling role models. He became actively involved in teaching the catechism and joined the parish council. His friends' circle and activities changed to reflect his increasing commitment to church. Along with his wife, he started a weekly prayer group with friends who were also actively involved in leadership committees in the parish.

Randall articulates his main focus today as "reaching out to people who are not practicing their faith—people who come here for different purposes, like for boyfriends or girlfriends or for your friends—to give them an understanding that, yeah, you come here for whatever, but your focus should always be, when you are here, on something else, on something higher." Randall still maintains a successful corporate career. But over the past few years, he has come to dedicate all his free time to what he sees as his new calling: serving the church and its people. "This is my calling," he smiles as he leans back contentedly. "This is my mission." This chapter examines the processes that generate and sustain the character of the Missionary.

The Missionary

The Missionary is the representative character of the rapidly diffusing form of religion that I call Evangelical-Charismatic Catholicism. This character bears the imprint of diverse influences from Roman Catholicism, American evangelicalism, and Pentecostal/Charismatic Christianity (see Table 2.1).

Although the Missionary is committed to serving others in community, the moral orientation of this character—the set of norms and scripts this model subscribes to and perpetuates—is fundamentally individualistic, according primacy to the believer's personal relationship with God. Many thinkers have identified the prevalence of this individualism among evangelicals and Pentecostals.[2] As Peter Berger notes, this religious form is intensely "individuating": one's worth derives from an individual decision to accept Christ as Lord, rather than from family

TABLE 2.1. The Missionary

Moral orientation	Therapeutic individualism
Basis of worth	Personal relationship with Jesus, experiencing and communicating God's healing power
Trajectory	Woundedness to healing, vice to virtue, sin to holiness, self-centeredness to discipleship
Demonstration of worth	Experience of healing, use of correct jargon, Bible knowledge, moral coherence regarding salient issues (e.g., avoiding lying, cheating, and drinking), charismatic gifts, commitment to church community
Peer base for comparison	Other ECC members, group leaders, "full-timers"
Sources of knowledge	Religious texts (mainly the Bible), religious media (EWTN, Joel Osteen, Joyce Meyer, etc.), personal revelation
Lifestyle ideal	Missionary/"full-timer," consistent tithing, service to church
Strategies	Church group meetings, retreats, religious media consumption, prayer
Failure	Moral "backsliding," hiding one's faith, compromise of principles

or community or nation.[3] Similar to American evangelicals, the Missionary assumes an ontology of the individual as existing relatively independent of social institutions, possessing free will, and being morally responsible for his or her actions.[4] But the Missionary is also Catholic and recognizes the validity of the institutional hierarchy and of obedience to church authorities. While this tension is mostly resolved by interpreting these authorities as expressing the will of God, there are regular occasions of conflict between the decisions of church leadership and one's inner convictions of the promptings of the Holy Spirit.

In stark contrast to the apprehensive individualism of the Mercenary, the spaces inhabited by the Missionary foster what I call *therapeutic individualism*: a conviction that what God wants most of all is to heal and empower the individual believer through a deep, personal, intimate relationship. The Missionary's fundamental call, then, is to experience and proclaim such transformation. This perspective not only accords the highest moral priority to the individual's personal relationship with Jesus but also sees the quality of this relationship as being manifested in a person's healing. This healing sought is not only from physical ailments but also primarily from the emotional wounds and anxieties generated in other spheres of a Missionary's life.[5]

I use the term "therapeutic individualism" differently from other scholars.[6] I do not mean by it the kind of individualism that makes the individual the locus of moral authority.[7] In contrast to how Smith and Denton define the concept, the therapeutic individualism I identify is one in which "personal integration, subjective feeling, and self-improvement toward individual health and personal well-being" are indeed linked to, rather than severed from, "religious faith and self-discipline toward holiness or obedience."[8] The Missionary believes in objective moral rights and wrongs as determined by God. My use of the concept is also principally analytical rather than pejorative: indeed, I argue it is impossible to ignore the therapeutic dimension of Christian belief, given that the image of God as a healer is pervasive throughout the Old and New Testaments.[9] The question we need to explore here is what happens when this element of healing assumes primacy, to the exclusion of other elements.

The Missionary displays higher levels of religious activity than do the majority of Catholics in their cities. Indeed, part of the identity of these Missionaries lies in the distinction they draw between themselves and "ordinary Catholics," whom they see as simply following traditions and routines out of habit, rather than living a personal relationship with Jesus Christ. And it is to these ordinary Catholics that they direct their primary mission; proselytizing to non-Catholics occurs rarely, even though the ideal in their minds is the biblical injunction to proclaim the good news to the ends of the earth. For the character of the Missionary,

proclaiming the gospel means proclaiming as good news the possibility of healing and transformation through a personal relationship with Jesus.

The Missionary's sense of worth derives from a personal encounter and relationship with God, which needs to be instantiated through service and fidelity to
a particular faith community. Many ECC groups see the highest form of this ideal
as renouncing everything, even one's job and career, for the sake of the mission
of serving God. For some, this means becoming a missionary in the more traditional sense of the term and going on "mission trips" to serve rural communities
in India and Africa. For others, it means a more permanent commitment of becoming a "full-timer." Full-timers are people who dedicate their time entirely to
the service of the church, while relying for their livelihood entirely on providence—
which means relying on God to provide them with people to support them
financially. But most Missionaries do not personally feel called to become full-
timers, to make such a radical commitment; indeed, in Dubai, the option is
structurally rendered impossible by visa requirements, since laypersons cannot
be employed as religious workers. But it is the *ideal* of total commitment to God,
signified by dedication to one's community—the "spirit" of the full-timer, if you
will—that Missionaries share in common. The various ECC groups articulate this
commitment in different ways: some call it "service," others "mission," and still
others "ministry." The language of any particular ECC group reflects the degree
to which it is influenced by evangelical, Pentecostal/Charismatic, or traditional
Catholic sources. Some focus more on a "personal relationship with Jesus," others
on a "personal experience" of God or the Holy Spirit, yet others on "God's will,"
and some groups on a combination of these elements.

The narrative trajectory of the Missionary, in any case, is a path from vice to
virtue, from self-centeredness to God-centeredness, from woundedness to healing. The Missionary offers stories of transition from unbelief to belief, like Randall's
narrative, or from modes of sinfulness to the pursuit of sanctity. Some have
dramatic conversion stories; for instance, from being a heavy drinker or smoker
to quitting altogether. For most, the transitions are from a weak or apathetic faith
to greater trust in God, and from low to high self-esteem as their faith gives them
greater certainty of their self-worth.

ECC group members have various means of demonstrating their "fitness" for
belonging to the group. These include using the group's jargon, being able to re-
cite Bible verses, trying to adhere to the group's moral stances against practices
such as smoking or drinking, or displaying Charismatic gifts such as speaking in
tongues. What seems to be valued most, however, is the extent of one's commitment to the group, manifested in regularly attending all of its events and dedicating one's time to its activities. In addition to service to the group, members and
leaders also stress the importance of "witness": of coherently living out the teach-

FIGURE 2.1.   ECC group meeting in Bangalore.

ings of the group in other domains of life. The precise content of such "witness" is not consistent across groups. For some, it involves developing dispositions of kindness, humility, and other such virtues. For others, it has more to do with refraining from alcohol and smoking, and not compromising one's principles. In chapter 3, we see how this dimension of witness becomes the primary mode by which Missionaries see faith as shaping their working lives.

Growth or progress for the Missionary occurs through various means: attending the group's meetings regularly, participating in the larger parish by regularly attending mass (often more than once a week), attending spiritual retreats, consuming religious media endorsed by the group, and cultivating one's "inner life" through various practices: personal prayer, rosaries, Eucharistic adoration, and other devotions. Regular Bible reading and consumption of religious books, movies, YouTube videos, and blogs are means of growth. In addition to dedicating their time to the group, Missionaries also try to consistently give generously to the group and its causes: some groups ask their members to tithe, to give 10 percent of their income to the group. "Failure" for the Missionary means compromising the faith in any way, such as through "backsliding"—relapsing into habits one has forsaken—or denying one's Christian faith. Other members of these groups, especially leaders, become one's bases of comparison in assessing "success" or "failure."

Attending weekly liturgical services, which are obligatory for Catholics, are a non-negotiable requirement for the Missionary. In contrast to ordinary Catholics, whom they perceive as experiencing the mass as a depersonalizing routine, the Missionary carries the conviction that one receives the real presence of Christ in the Eucharist. But receiving communion is a bare minimum. The Missionary also regularly participates in groups and activities in church: principally by attending ECC prayer groups, but also by sitting on parish councils, teaching religious education, and providing other modes of voluntary service. Positions of responsibility in church that laypersons take on in both these cities (e.g., youth ministers, catechists, etc.) are entirely voluntary and unpaid.

Missionaries espouse commitments to Catholic teachings, principally the doctrines and beliefs espoused in the catechism. They admit that they may not completely understand these teachings and sometimes may not fully agree with them, but assent to them in spite of their questions. They emphasize obedience and docility as the required dispositions of a believer, holding in tension fidelity to God's "rightful authority" manifested through church leaders and faithfulness to the spontaneous promptings of the Holy Spirit. Reflecting an approach that sociologists Nancy Davis and Robert Robinson call "religious orthodoxy," they believe in moral absolutism and that the state should play a strong role in ensuring social welfare (though their groups usually say nothing about political or civic matters). Although they hold conservative stances on social issues such as abortion and premarital sex,[10] they do not personally identify as "conservative," but rather as "liberal"—some even claim to be "very liberal" on their Facebook profiles—since they understand conservative to mean being strict and old-fashioned, advocating sex segregation, imposing curfews, and so on, or they associate the term with right-wing fundamentalists.

In comparison to American Catholicism, there is relatively little discussion among Catholics in Bangalore and Dubai on hot-button issues prominent in the West, such as abortion, contraception, or gay rights, although they may occasionally serve as topics of a "teaching" session during a youth retreat, and some individual members keep track of developments on these issues through Western media. Missionaries are fundamentally apolitical. Their main concerns in their religious groups are with matters of spirituality. Talks given in the various group sessions I attended were on the following topics: the inner life, intimacy with God, humility, docility, obedience, sanctity and holiness, the Cross, how to read Scripture, forgiveness, discernment of God's will, conformity with God's will, the fatherhood of God, Christian leadership, the Holy Spirit, the power of praise, chastity, evils of pornography, evangelization, self-esteem, God's love, and true happiness. None of the leaders or members of these ECC groups had received formal academic training in theology, although some had attended short courses in catechism training and evangelical-influenced Bible schools.

None of the groups I observed (except for one French group in Dubai) discussed anything relating to Catholic perspectives on the dignity of work, migration, economic issues, the role of the Christian in society, social justice, the common good, or other such issues. This is not to say that individual members of these groups did not discuss such themes in other venues—they might share articles on Facebook about women's rights, for instance—but such discussions were fundamentally disconnected from the discourses cultivated in ECC groups. Also, although these groups may say little about social justice, as I show in chapter 5, many groups are engaged in some way in serving the needy. While Roman Catholicism has a rich body of doctrine addressing social, economic, and political issues—what is referred to as Catholic Social Teaching—such concerns are outside the radar of these groups. (Ironically, the only group I came across that took an interest in studying Catholic Social Teaching was a French Charismatic group in Dubai whose members remained largely aloof from the needy in the parish).

Further, despite the influence of Pentecostalism and of religious celebrities like Joel Osteen, the ECC groups as a whole are not sold on "prosperity theology": the idea that God necessarily blesses the faithful with material well-being. Some members certainly expressed an affinity for it, but the group leaders largely saw this ideology as a theological aberration.

The Missionary is thus a hybrid character generated by dual influences. Global factors include the rapidly diffusing Pentecostal/Charismatic and evangelical movements, as well as various structural and cultural elements of global Catholicism. They are also influenced by more local factors specific to the history and culture of individual parishes and to the cities of Bangalore and Dubai, which generate important differences between ECC groups in the two cities. I address some of these local factors in this chapter, and treat them in more detail in chapter 5. For now, I will focus primarily on the global influences on ECC groups and how they shape the character of the Missionary in similar ways in Bangalore and Dubai.

A Global Phenomenon

The Pentecostal/Charismatic movement is, as anthropologist Robert Hefner describes it, "an affectively expressive, effervescent Christianity that takes literally the wondrous miracles described in the New Testament's Acts of the Apostles (2:1–4), and proclaims their availability and importance for believers today."[11] It is the world's fastest-growing religious movement today, particularly in the Global South.[12] Estimates of the number of Pentecostal/Charismatic Christians worldwide range between 500 to 600 million, comprising more than one-quarter of the world's Christian population.[13] As Peter Berger argues, "Most of Christianity in the Global South is at least moderately 'Pentecostalized.'"[14]

The origins of Pentecostal/Charismatic Christianity are typically attributed to the Azusa Street Revival of 1906 in Los Angeles. Despite the dominant North

American influence on the movement, it should not be seen as a purely American innovation. Scholars identify the existence of a number of independent "proto-Pentecostal charismatic" movements dating back to 1860 in India, 1903 in Korea, 1904 in Wales, and 1907 in Chile.[15] In their narratives and self-understandings, Pentecostals trace their origins to the beginnings of the church in the New Testament, when the Holy Spirit descended on the apostles as described in the Acts of the Apostles. It is with reference to this event that they authenticate their identity and experience.

Pentecostalism is a heterogeneous movement, with no single "essence" or "normative archetype."[16] Theologian Allan Anderson offers a helpful classification of four distinct varieties of Pentecostalism: classical Pentecostals, older church Charismatics, older independent churches, and neo-Pentecostals.[17] The groups I study mostly fall into his second category: "Older Church Charismatics" comprise Charismatic movements within Anglican, Catholic, Orthodox, and other Mainline Protestant churches. These Charismatic groups remain embedded within their respective traditions and are shaped by them while also offering opportunities for ecumenical contact with other churches in the Pentecostal/Charismatic movement.

In spite of differences in doctrine and institutional structure, the diverse groups that comprise the Pentecostal/Charismatic movement share certain elements in common. First, they emphasize the believer's individual commitment to Jesus Christ through an initiating experience of being "born again" in a transformative experience, often called a "baptism in the Holy Spirit." Pentecostals, Charismatics, and evangelicals share in common the belief in Jesus Christ as the sole redeemer of a sinful humanity and in the necessity of a personal relationship with Jesus Christ as the basis of salvation. Indeed, the lines between global Pentecostalism and evangelicalism have become increasingly blurred, as evangelicals incorporate Pentecostal elements into their worship while Pentecostals incorporate many evangelical beliefs.[18]

A second central emphasis in the Pentecostal/Charismatic movement is a personal experience of the Holy Spirit. The effects of this experience are established through various "charisms" or spiritual gifts, notably, speaking in tongues, prophesying, and healings. The global movement shares not only the belief in the importance of such practices but also the physical embodiment of these practices. Such embodied practices include postures and gestures during prayer and in coordination during group interactions, such as when "catchers" break the fall of someone who is "slain in the Spirit" or who collapses under the purported influence of the Holy Spirit. For most members of Pentecostal/Charismatic groups, intense emotional and spiritual experiences take priority over doctrine or ritual (even though the Pentecostal experience itself is highly ritualized).[19] Recent survey research also suggests that speaking in tongues is far less common among Pentecostal/ Charismatic Christians than is the emphasis on healing.[20]

Research on the Pentecostal/Charismatic movement has focused on its economic and political impact. Early research on Pentecostalism characterized it as a religion of the poor.[21] Even now, the common perception is that its growth is primarily if not exclusively found among marginalized classes. Only recently has scholarship begun to acknowledge its growing prominence among upwardly mobile social classes: my research contributes to this effort.[22] Scholars identify in Pentecostalism a distinctive set of beliefs and habits that are useful for adaptation to global capitalism. Sociologist David Martin, for instance, argues that it provides support networks that foster economic activity, as well as "orderliness" that is congruent with factory work.[23] At the same time, he rejects any necessary connection between Pentecostalism and large-scale economic activity or prosperity.[24] In today's neoliberal capitalism, in contrast to industrial capitalism, "the ability to be punctual, regimented, and obedient" is much less important "than the capacity to be self-motivating, to control the work process without direct supervision, to be reflective and self-monitoring, and to manage interpersonal encounters skillfully."[25] Pentecostal/Charismatic Christianity supplies some of these "postindustrial virtues," as we see in the next chapter, where I examine how practices and dispositions cultivated in ECC groups spill over into the workplace. Its strands of "prosperity theology," while not prominent in the groups I studied, in other cases help justify the pursuit of wealth and even extravagant spending.[26]

But scholarship on Pentecostal/Charismatic movements is on the whole ambivalent about its effects on members' economic activity. On the one hand, Pentecostalism can nurture qualities of self-discipline, reliability, and trustworthiness among members, which are appealing to employers; on the other hand, it may lead people to compromise their earthly work for the sake of spiritual commitments.[27] My research in Bangalore and Dubai reveals a similar ambivalence. In this context, it is difficult to argue that Pentecostalism produces a modern-day "Protestant ethic" similar to that produced by the Calvinism studied by Max Weber.[28]

Nevertheless, I think it is correct to see the Pentecostal/Charismatic movement, as David Martin does, as "a cultural revolution, and one undertaken from below, with no political theory to guide it and no political ideology to promote."[29] The transformation it brings about may not always yield economic success, but it does result in visible changes in the behaviors of individuals, which affect their families and communities; for instance, it disrupts patterns of machismo, domestic violence, drug taking, and alcoholism.[30] These changes reflect the socially conservative nature of Pentecostalism, with its prohibitions on alcohol, gambling, premarital sex, smoking, and other vices. Such proscriptions were voiced by many of the people I studied.

Many have also commented on the apolitical nature of much of Pentecostalism, which distinguishes it from a number of other prominent religious movements such as liberation theology, evangelicalism, and even new Hindu and Islamist movements. As Robert Hefner argues, Pentecostal/Charismatic Christianity, for its adherents, "is first and foremost a matter of individual and local rebirth—ethical subject formation, not structural reform."[31] It has no clear political stances driven by doctrinal convictions. It is individualistic, but not atomistic; rather, it is consonant with participation in voluntary communities, which foster a strict separation of adherents from secular or pre-conversion communities and practices.[32] As Robbins notes, Pentecostal/Charismatic communities range in their political expression from being strongly authoritarian to participative, even serving as "a force for democratization."[33]

The largely apolitical nature of Pentecostal/Charismatic Christianity has drawn the ire of many critics. For instance, historian Paul Gifford complains that its focus on personal healing "diverts attention from social ills that are crying out for remedy" and that its focus on "personal morality" blinds it to systemic injustice.[34] Martin similarly notes that because of their focus on personal and small-group experiences, Pentecostals and Charismatics are uncomfortable thinking about "large-scale social mechanisms," especially those that are beyond the control of "individual moral action," leading them to have "a truncated understanding of the social world."[35] Yet, other scholars argue that, from its very origins, members of Pentecostalism were not disconnected from the material needs of their surrounding communities.[36] Miller and Yamamori, studying Pentecostal/Charismatic movements in twenty countries, document a variety of forms of social outreach, including the provision of food and shelter, disaster relief, education, counseling, medical assistance, economic development, and arts programs and involvement in developing public policy.[37] Nevertheless, even these scholars note that these programs focus more on individual needs, neglecting structural/political concerns. As we see in chapter 4 when we examine civic engagement, ECC groups in Bangalore and Dubai can be subject to the same criticisms.

But what has made this religious form a global force, so compelling to an ever-growing constituency around the world?

The Global Diffusion of Pentecostal/ Charismatic Christianity

A number of factors have facilitated the global diffusion of Pentecostal/Charismatic Christianity. First, contexts of relatively high religiosity seem particularly conducive to its taking root and spreading. Scholars note, for instance, how it has flourished in the United States and in many parts of the Global South, but not in

Western Europe or in secularist Latin American countries like Uruguay. In those latter contexts, as Robert Hefner argues, people may look to "secular liberalism, socialism, ethno-nationalism, consumerism, or expressive individualism to provide the terms of participation in a brave but disenchanted new world."[38] The high level of religiosity in India and the Arabian Gulf is one factor that helps explain the diffusion of the movement to these contexts.

A second conducive factor is the experience of marginalization within a religious context. As Hefner notes, those drawn to Pentecostalism often found themselves alienated in some way from established religious institutions and their leaders. They may see religious leaders as bedfellows with corrupt political and economic elites, as in several Latin American countries, or mostly as self-interested administrators lacking genuine spiritual commitment, which was the opinion of many Catholic Charismatic leaders I met in India. Such marginalization may be a necessary but not sufficient condition: a grievance that contributes to what social movement scholars call "mobilization potential."[39] To those who feel marginalized and disempowered by established religious institutions, Pentecostal/Charismatic groups offer lay leadership and opportunities for social status. The empowerment offered by these groups occurs not only at the social level; the individual believer is also empowered by the movement's emphasis on religious experience unmediated by a religious bureaucracy. Nevertheless, the Pentecostal/Charismatic movement is not immune to what sociologists call the routinization of charisma: bureaucratization and formal structuring eventually set in as organizations grow in size and leaders become vested in preserving their power and influence.[40] This tendency is found even in the ECC groups I studied, as we see in chapter 4.

A third factor is the anomie generated by the unsettling nature of rapid globalization. As religion scholar Donald Miller notes, migration and urbanization bring about a sense of "cultural dislocation," characterized by "heightened insecurity, growing detraditionalization, . . . and an explosion of new aspirational imaginaries."[41] The promises of Pentecostal/Charismatic Christianity—food for the hungry, healing for the sick, the possibility of dramatic transformation of one's life, and the gospel's promise of "abundant life"—find great resonance in these contexts for disoriented people who feel they have no life at all.[42] In rapidly globalizing cities such as Bangalore and Dubai, this holds true not only among those who are materially poor but also among those who are emotionally worn out by the anxieties generated by the new economy.

A fourth factor provides a market-based explanation for the success of the Pentecostal/Charismatic movements: they outperform the competition by offering superior products. These include "vibrant music, a compassionate community of caring people, visionary preaching, affirmation of one's dignity as a child of

God, and life-changing encounters with the sacred," as promoted by entrepreneurial and charismatic leaders.[43] In addition to the nature of the products they offer, these groups also benefit from the flexible structures and low barriers to entry in Pentecostalism: the lack of formal training or credentialing requirements makes it relatively easy to start new churches or prayer groups.

A fifth contributor to the diffusion of these groups is the ability of this form of religion to address everyday life problems: its ability to deal with crisis, misfortune, illness, and so on.[44] Pentecostal/Charismatic groups not only address existential problems but also serve as a form of moral community that is able to address difficulties within families, such as alcoholism, gambling, or domestic abuse.[45]

As anthropologist Joel Robbins notes, it is also important to explain why Pentecostal/Charismatic churches flourish in the "resource-poor conditions" in which they are growing. Why it is that their members are willing to invest not only significant amounts of time (by attending services and activities more than once a week) but also to donate significant proportions of their income, even in contexts of significant poverty? The answer lies in the ability of these groups to produce successful rituals characterized by what sociologist Randall Collins calls high "emotional energy."[46] Emotional energy, according to Collins, is a durable "feeling of confidence, elation, strength, enthusiasm, and initiative in taking action."[47] Pentecostal/Charismatic groups generate emotional energy by providing regular opportunities for members to participate fully in shared rituals, as well as ritual tools that can be used anywhere and by anyone. The success of Pentecostal rituals is partly evident in their recognizable similarity worldwide: "arms lifted in praise, hands laid on in healing, tongues speaking in prayer, voices lifted in song."[48] Pentecostal groups can garner high levels of commitment from their members because they offer frequent social occasions for the practice of successful interaction rituals that boost members' emotional energy. As Robbins argues, "it is the Pentecostal mastery of the technology of ritual production that makes these churches work."[49]

Finally, historical and institutional factors play a crucial role in shaping the movement's growth. The Pentecostal/Charismatic movement's diffusion into Roman Catholicism through the Catholic Charismatic Renewal (CCR) was paved by a number of institutional changes ushered in by the Second Vatican Council (1962–1965). Pope John XXIII, who invoked the global ecumenical council, intended it as an *aggiornamento*: an updating of the Catholic Church to the modern world, an opening of its windows to usher in the Holy Spirit. The Second Vatican Council's emphasis on the role of the Holy Spirit, its theological vision of the Church as "the People of God," its doctrinal developments on the importance of charisms and spiritual gifts, its emphasis on ecumenical dialogue with other Christian traditions, its new emphasis on the reading of Scripture, and its liturgical changes, including the adoption of the vernacular in place of Latin, all set the stage for the emergence of new movements.

The CCR began in 1967 at a weekend retreat in Duquesne University in the United States. Some of the retreat participants had recently attended an interdenominational Charismatic prayer meeting where they had received Charismatic gifts through a baptism in the Holy Spirit, and during the "Duquesne weekend," many other students underwent a similar experience.[50] The movement soon spread to the University of Notre Dame and elsewhere, gaining a following among educated, middle-class lay Catholics, as well as members of clergy and religious orders. By the time Belgian cardinal Leo Suenens encountered the rapidly growing movement during a visit to the United States in 1972, it had already begun to become institutionalized, developing into distinct communities with distinctive rituals and jargon. The two pillars of the initial Duquesne experience evolved into the standard means of initiation into the movement: first, an initiation course, formalized into a seven-week program called the Life in the Spirit Seminar, and second, the ritual of the baptism in the Holy Spirit, during which through the laying of hands, the "gifts of the Holy Spirit" are conferred on the newly initiated.[51] This represented a departure from the traditional Catholic teaching that the gifts of the Holy Spirit—wisdom, understanding, right judgment, courage, knowledge, reverence, and wonder/awe in the presence of God—are conferred during the rite of confirmation.[52] The CCR movement, while accepting this teaching, also emphasizes additional manifestations of the Holy Spirit, indicated in the New Testament, that remain dormant until believers experience the baptism in the Holy Spirit. These include speaking in tongues, interpreting tongues, prophesying, discerning spirits, bringing about healing, miracles, and specially revealed words of knowledge and wisdom.[53]

At the Vatican, Cardinal Suenens became one of CCR's foremost advocates, and support by Popes Paul VI and John Paul II enabled it to gain institutional legitimacy within the Catholic Church. Publications of books, lectures, and music by American clergy and prominent lay leaders and supported by Catholic publishing houses fostered CCR's rapid diffusion and consistency of expression in Catholic populations throughout the English-speaking world. It was through those publications that the CCR spread to Bangalore and Dubai, leading to the emergence of the groups I examine in this book.

Having examined Pentecostal/Charismatic Christianity and the CCR as global forces, I now turn to examine the other pole: the local contexts in which the ECC groups I study are embedded.

Local Contexts
Roman Catholicism in Bangalore and Dubai

The Catholic Church has had a long-standing presence in Bangalore, dating back to Jesuit missionary activity in the 1600s. The archdiocese currently is the third-largest one in India. It oversees more than 135 parishes, 80 schools, 30 colleges, and 40 hospitals and health centers. Many of these are run by religious orders, of which there are currently 505 communities representing 193 distinct congregations.[54] The Bangalore archdiocese has, since its inception, housed Catholics of diverse ethnic communities—Tamilians, Kannadigas, Mangaloreans, Goans, Malayalees, Bombayites, Anglo Indians, and more—which continue to maintain their linguistic and ethnic identities. Tamils have historically been the largest ethnic community among the city's Catholic population, resulting in conflicts that I discuss in chapter 5.

Accurate statistics on the city's Catholic population are unavailable. The archdiocese extends beyond the city limits, and the Catholic population of this jurisdiction has for several decades remained at between 1.5 to 2.5 percent of the population. (However, this figure is based on the number of baptisms only and is likely to be a serious underestimate since it neglects migration inflows.) Most of these Catholics live within the city limits. Bangalore has seen rapid population growth in recent decades, from around 1.7 million in 1971 to 9.6 million residents in 2011. Church officials I spoke to estimate the city's Catholic population as nearly 400,000 people.

All the countries of the Arabian Peninsula, with the exception of Saudi Arabia, have in the past few decades given foreigners freedom of worship in recognition of the importance of religion for the foreign workers who sustain their economies. Funding for the land and even sometimes for the construction and maintenance of Christian churches and Hindu temples is provided by the government. Foreigners are free to express their religious traditions within these delimited spaces and under certain conditions. While the space provided is often inadequate for the large size of the community, it nevertheless allows for a vibrant communal life, which has been neglected by studies on the region.

The presence of Christianity in the region predates Islam; archeologists recently uncovered a 1,400-year-old monastery in Abu Dhabi. But these early Christian communities disappeared during the first few centuries of Islam. More recently, the Catholic Church established an institutional presence in 1841 in Jeddah (Saudi Arabia), which was moved soon thereafter to Aden (Yemen). In 1889, the Apostolic Vicariate of Arabia was established to oversee the church's mission to its members in the region (mostly foreign nationals), and in 1971 its seat was moved to Abu Dhabi, the capital of the UAE. In Dubai, the Catholic Church was granted land to build a parish building and school in 1965. Both facilities were built to accommodate 2,000 persons each. Like Bangalore, Dubai has seen a rapid population boom in recent decades, increasing from 0.28 million in 1971 to 2 million inhabitants in 2011. The growing influx of Indians and recently Filipinos has contributed to turning its main Catholic church into what is believed to be the world's largest parish in terms of population, with an estimate of more than 300,000 Catholics in the city. In 2001, a second parish was opened in Jebel Ali, situated on the outskirts of Dubai on the road to Abu Dhabi. Given its distance from the city, its population remains relatively small.

Outside of regular liturgical celebrations, the most prominent form of activity in Catholic churches in India and the Arabian Gulf is in groups affiliated with (or at least influenced by) the Catholic Charismatic Renewal (CCR). The CCR spread to India in 1972 in Bombay and in 1976 to Bangalore, in both cases through a handful of lay professionals and Jesuit priests who had encountered either Pentecostals or Catholic Charismatics outside India. In Dubai, the first CCR group was started by an Indian professional who moved there from Bombay in 1978.

Consider how the CCR began in Bangalore. Fritz Mascarenhas, an Indian Merchant Navy officer from Bangalore, met a group of Pentecostals in Bombay and was initiated into the Charismatic experience through an experience of the baptism in the Holy Spirit. He then traveled to Japan where he "had a further experience through some beautiful American nondenominational full-Gospel Christians." These new spiritual experiences were especially powerful for Mascarenhas because, while growing up Catholic in Bangalore, as he described it,

> we had no concept of evangelization. We grew up in our Catholic schools, with non-Christians all around us, and it never dawned on me even for a moment that I had to tell them about Jesus! So with this experience in Japan, my spiritual eyes were opened to this reality that Jesus is the only savior.

Like most Charismatics I spoke to, he felt cheated by his experience of growing up in the Catholic Church, because he was never told about the possibility of an intimate relationship with Jesus. "No priest could tell me how to meet [him]; no nun could tell me how to meet [him]!" The Pentecostal experience, in contrast, "was so life-changing: Jesus came alive. Scriptures came alive. A thirst for prayer. A hunger for God." He then decided to "throw away [his] job and just go out and evangelize." The first Charismatic prayer meetings in the city were held at his home. His worried mother complained to the archbishop about her son, concerned that he was ruining his life. Mascarenhas was then called in to see him, and this is how he described the encounter with the archbishop:

He just asked me one question, "What's happened to you?" The next forty-five minutes I spoke to him and told him all that had happened. Finally when I ended, he said to me, "Son, I don't have this life that you have. Will you lay hands and pray for me for the Holy Spirit?" I was simply shocked. I couldn't believe the archbishop asking me to pray for him!

The archbishop had recently returned from the United States, where he had been deeply impressed with the CCR communities he encountered. He gave Mascarenhas his full support and blessing, encouraging him to work closely with a Jesuit priest who had also experienced the baptism in the Holy Spirit. This priest became the founder-director of an elite business school in the heart of the city, which gave the movement greater legitimacy. Charismatic groups soon proliferated in parishes and colleges in the city. Mascarenhas clearly believed that the success of CCR in the city was due in large part to the strong support of the archbishop and influential clergy: "Here in the Catholic Church, without the support of a priest and their encouragement, we laity couldn't do anything." The support of the bishop and influential Jesuits, he said, "opened all the doors for me!"

This story illustrates a number of themes that characterize the CCR worldwide: the global nature of the movement, the way in which its proponents see it as superior to yet fundamentally rooted in traditional Catholicism, and the role of both clergy and laity in propelling the movement's growth.

ECC Groups in Bangalore and Dubai

Catholic parishes in both cities house several dozen Charismatic or Charismatic-influenced groups. Corporate professionals who are actively involved in church are typically the leaders or prominent members of these groups. In both Dubai and Bangalore, the number of such groups and their membership have grown over time due to the steady influx of migrants.

The church-based groups attended by professionals in both these cities, with only a few exceptions, are either directly affiliated with or are offshoots of the Catholic Charismatic Renewal and operate in English. However, neither of the traditional initiation rituals of the CCR—the Life in the Spirit Seminars and the baptism in the Holy Spirit—was emphasized in the groups I studied. Most members, with the exception of those who were involved in the CCR in the 1980s or earlier, had not participated in them either.[55] See the appendix for information on the various groups I studied.

Meetings of these groups in both cities follow a similar format. They begin with fifteen to thirty minutes of "praise and worship" or contemporary worship music, a genre of contemporary Christian music characterized by a pop-rock, four-chord style, accompanied by a guitar or keyboard and sometimes bass and drums, with lyrics projected onto a screen in front of the congregation. Most groups I attended in both cities, English and Filipino alike, played the very same songs of American evangelical artists such as Matt Redman, Chris Tomlin, Michael W. Smith, and Don Moen.[56] Moen held well-attended concerts in both Dubai and Bangalore during the period of my research.

The four or five songs chosen for each meeting are played in a similar sequence, beginning with upbeat melodies and slowing down to something more emotive and reflective to help the audience become attuned to the promptings of the Holy Spirit and attentive to the teaching that is to come. Some of the longer-standing CCR groups with older members have a period of "praying in tongues," which is either more subdued or absent altogether in the younger ECC groups. All groups follow the music session with a Bible-based "teaching" by either one of the group leaders or a visitor, and these teachings I observed in the groups in both cities were on similar topics. Most teachings are aimed at cultivating practical changes in people's lives: increasing one's ability to practice virtues such as patience, humility, and gratitude; discerning God's will in daily life; and developing habits of prayer. Some attempt to elucidate concepts such as "God's love" or "the power of praise" and are aimed at helping people better understand the experiences that people in the group were having or were supposed to have.

Through these teachings and other activities, ECC groups strive to cultivate "discipleship": a new mode of thinking and acting in the world that results from deeper intimacy of the individual with God, mediated by the authority of the group. All these groups express alignment with the teaching authority of the Catholic Church, primarily by deference to local bishops and texts such as the catechism. Groups in both cities also share common jargon, particularly in their organizational structures. For instance, each group is run by a "core team"; "ministries" are subgroups in charge of particular activities such as music, drama, intercessory prayer, social programs, and outreach or service activities; "cell groups" are smaller groups within the large group in which members come together to share problems and support one another; and "resource persons" are leaders, often from other ECC groups in other churches and countries, who are called on to lead retreats. Most of these organizational similarities reflect the imprint of early organizational structures of the Catholic Charismatic Renewal, which have spread into offshoot groups that do not formally affiliate with the movement.

Despite the overall homogeneity of these Charismatic groups in both cities, individual group members hold different theological beliefs. A key source of these differences is the literature and media consumed by members. For some, the sources were prominent mainstream American Pentecostal/Charismatic celebrities such as Benny Hinn, Joyce Meyer, and Joel Osteen. Some respondents who followed those celebrities were inclined toward prosperity theology and typically rejected mainstream Catholic devotions and beliefs pertaining to Mary and the saints, preferring religious practices such as regular Bible reading instead. Some of them also attended non-Catholic Charismatic church services while continuing to identify primarily as Catholic. Others, however, appropriated only the "positive thinking" aspects of the messages of these celebrities, drawing from them a sense of self-confidence and a conviction that God wanted to bless them, though not necessarily with monetary wealth.

The majority of ECC members, however, regularly practice traditional Catholic devotions such as the rosary and Eucharistic adoration and integrate these with their Charismatic practices. For instance, some groups conduct healing services during Eucharistic adoration. Many groups are also influenced by new Catholic apologetics developed by former evangelicals such as Scott Hahn and Steve Ray and propagated through books and websites based mainly in the United States. The interest in such apologetics comes from the growing concern that "born again" churches are "sheep-stealing," as church leaders put it. That is, they prey on biblically illiterate Catholics and convince them that their faith is not biblically justifiable. ECC groups thus emphasize the importance for members of being able to understand why Catholicism is scripturally defensible.

Because of these different influences, authority can become a contested issue in many ECC groups. In most cases, members adhere to the injunctions of their leaders (either within the group or in the parish at large). But for some members, personal inspiration from the Holy Spirit is the primary criterion, even if it conflicts with the claims of group leaders or clergy. I witnessed such clashes occurring in both cities when church leaders forbade members to attend rallies conducted by the American televangelist Benny Hinn. Priests and ECC group leaders objected to his theology and sensationalist approach. Several members, however, saw this restriction as a violation of the inspiration of the Spirit and attended anyway. Those who obeyed accused those who attended of pride and bad discernment, as demonstrated through their disobedience. Such conflicts can lead to groups fracturing. In most ECC groups, I heard stories of former members who had broken away and either joined other groups or Protestant churches or sometimes started their own groups, because of disagreements with leaders. Some claim that God's will for a group is necessarily mediated by the "proper" authority (i.e., the parish priest). Still others depend on group consensus as an indicator of the inspiration of the Holy Spirit. There are also occasional conflicts between commitments to international CCR movements and to the local parish; for instance, when the international movement prefers a particular format or structure for an event, but the local parish priest wants to make changes. In most cases in both cities, members and leaders of these groups believed that the parish priest or the local bishop was the final authority. The pope, cardinals, and so on did not usually feature in their imaginary (although this has changed since the installation of Pope Francis and the positive global media attention he has received; many members share the pope's daily tweets, for instance).

While their focus is mostly local, there are particular occasions, such as pilgrimages, during which ECC group members gain a heightened sense of the church as a global community. The most notable of these is the World Youth Day events, which are large-scale international gatherings held every two to three years in a different country. Attending these events has a profound impact on participants. But due to the international travel entailed, attendance is very expensive, requiring extensive fundraising, and even then, only a limited number of participants from these groups are able to attend.

In addition to serving as sites in which to communicate and experience God's healing, a key function of these groups is to pray for one another's needs. Praying for healing becomes an occasion for members to integrate their needs across different realms of their lives: work, family, and spiritual. Table 2.2 provides an excerpt from a long prayer list compiled as an Excel spreadsheet, used by one of the predominantly Indian prayer groups in Dubai in its weekly intercessory prayer meetings. The types of requests and expressions of thanksgiving here illustrate the comingling of the arenas of religion and work in the context of neoliberal cities. They also underscore Martin Riesebrodt's argument for religion's critical role in solving practical problems, dealing with misfortune and crises, and providing the promise of fulfillment and fullness through access to superhuman powers.[57]

Becoming Involved in ECC Groups

In both Bangalore and Dubai, corporate professionals comprise a significant proportion of leaders and members in ECC groups. What leads them to become involved in these groups? In my interviews, their stories about how and why they came to become involved revealed two main paths: sudden conversions or gradual involvement. Through each of these routes, members found both an experience of God (e.g., falling in love with God or experiencing God's healing or intervention) and a strong sense of community.

Several leaders of ECC groups articulated narratives of sudden conversion experiences. Among older members and established leaders, the most common type of conversion story I heard in both cities was of their having been wild, nonreligious "party animals" in their youth; having gone to a religious meeting or

TABLE 2.2. Excerpt from prayer group spreadsheet

PRAYER REQUEST	DATE REQUESTED	DATE ANSWERED	CATEGORY OF REQUEST
Pray for my sister [X] as she is facing lot of financial issues and for abundant blessings on her family	28/4/2011		FAMILY
For [X] and his family. (The guy that is trying to sue my family for a large sum of money.)	1/11/2010		FAMILY
Wanting to be a family with the blessing of a Child	9/12/2011		FAMILY
Looking out for a new house	9/12/2011		FAMILY
Please pray for my family as the flat that we booked in India was supposed to be completed in 2008 but till now it has not been completed, pray for the tensions that we are undergoing due to this delay. Pray that the issue is resolved in his time.	10/9/2010		FAMILY
Has requested prayers for his back ache (his slip disc is aggravating)	28/4/2011		HEALTH
Pray for my brother [X] for his backache as he is suffereing a lot as well as my uncle whose kidneys have failed	28/4/2011		HEALTH
Pray for her anxiety attacks that she has been suffering from so that she is able to manage school and be fine at the new location	12/9/2011		HEALTH
Please pray for my friend [X] whose right vocal chords [sic] are paralysed due to a thyroid surgery a gone wrong, she is currently undergoing speech therapy.	10/17/2010		HEALTH
Pray for [X] who still struggles with cancer and is undergoing treatment, but he has personal issues that are inhibiting him from being open to healing	18/04/2011		HEALTH
Please pray for my ailing Father-in-law	4/9/2011		HEALTH
Please pray for me to find a better job	4/9/2011		JOB
Have started with my new job—need prayers for the probation period and to do well in the new job	28/4/2011		JOB
Looking out for a good job and for a good caretaker for her baby	12/9/2011		JOB
Pray for my intention to find a good job as per God's Holy Divine Will	28/4/2011		JOB
Please pray for my friend [X] as her dad has lost his job and she is working under her dad visa . . . and her sister is studying in [removed]. . . . so basically entire family will get effected . . . . .pls pray that [X]'s DAD gets an immediate job somewhere and he would be able to support his family	12/5/2011		JOB
Please pray that I may be able to handle the pressure at my work.	3/7/2011		JOB
Please pray for me and my brother to find better jobs	4/9/2011		JOB
Please pray for me to get a job at the earliest	4/9/2011		JOB

TABLE 2.2. (continued)

PRAYER REQUEST	DATE REQUESTED	DATE ANSWERED	CATEGORY OF REQUEST
Pray for me to get a job	30/01/11		JOB
I am grateful to God for this new job that I have. Please pray that I will be able to do well as the work environment is quite tough now.	9/5/2011		JOB
Pray for my intention of finding my soulmate that God has chosen	28/04/2011		MATRIMONY
Please pray for my brother [X] as he is seeking proposals to get married	9/5/2011		MATRIMONY
Please pray for my brother [X] and wife [Y] who are getting ready for their second baby	4/9/2011		FAMILY
For my friend [X] that her family growth in faith and that she have the strength of the Holy Spirit as she goes through trials and troubles	13/2/2012		SPIRITUAL
Pray that God gives me the wisdom and understanding to lead the Group and make the right decisions in life and live a life accepting HIS will. Strong in faith and be a witness	14/03/11		SPIRITUAL
Pray for my my parents and wife to increase in their faith in the Lord.	4/11/2011		SPIRITUAL
Please pray for me as I take up the one year commitments in [X], India as a full-timer	20/11/2010		SPIRITUAL
Pray that I may serve the Lord faithfully and never give in any temptations (Worldly Desires)	18/4/2011		SPIRITUAL
Please pray for my travel plans scheduled this month	4/9/2011		STUDIES
Please pray for my assignments that are due in October	4/9/2011		STUDIES
Pray for my daughter [X] as she is starting school	4/9/2011		STUDIES
Praise God for his wonderful blessing of a good job that I have got on 15/09/2011	4/9/2011	15/9/2011	THANKS-GIVING
Praise God as my UK travel was smooth and I'm back by the grace of God	4/9/2011	10/8/2011	THANKS-GIVING
Praise God as he is the provider of our new musical instruments which we have been desiring for some time now	4/9/2011	10/8/2011	THANKS-GIVING
Millions of thanks to our Lord who has removed all obstacles with regards to my work (Due to my pregnancy) as my Boss has confirmed that I can start work from this week onwards	9/12/2011	10/8/2011	THANKS-GIVING
Praise God as my uncle who had undergone a surgery for cancer is fine now and doing well	18/04/2011	10/8/2011	THANKS-GIVING
Praise God as the visa for my wife has been approved by my company	26/9/2011	10/11/2011	THANKS-GIVING
Praise God as we have received my Dad's passport after 4 months of long waiting	17/10/2011	1/11/2011	THANKS-GIVING

retreat for some reason; experiencing a "powerful" or "overwhelming" feeling during a time of prayer; and then never touching alcohol, cigarettes, and/or drugs since that moment. In these accounts, their behavioral transformation testified to the power of the Holy Spirit. The consistency of these narratives among older members suggests a scripting that develops over years of being immersed in these groups and adopting a hermeneutic of what is worthwhile. Sociologists David Snow and Richard Machalek argue that the ideologies, ideals, and registers of evaluations of the religious group "provide the basic algorithms upon which the convert constructs an 'appropriate' account of his or her conversion experience."[58] So it is not simply that long-term experience in the group alters converts' memories and interpretations; in addition, the initial exposure to these groups shapes members' ability to render an experience meaningful, as David Yamane claims.[59] Because I did not have access to the respondents' "experience" in real time, but only to retrospective narrative accounts, I was not able to study the actual experience so much as what made it meaningful to the convert. But arguably, what matters is not so much the initial experience, but the believer's response in faithfully obeying the promptings of God for the rest of his or her life.

In contrast to the stories told to me by older members, those that I heard from newer and younger members seldom conveyed examples of "cold turkey" conversions from vices. Rather, out-of-the-ordinary events that occurred suddenly, which they interpreted as divine interventions, disrupted people's lives and triggered a process of reorienting their lives around God. Randall's account at the beginning of this chapter is one such example. In Randall's case we can see how the structural conditions of the neoliberal city shaped his narrative. The influence of the political context is less obvious in Bangalore. There, I often came across accounts of miraculous physical healing. It is easy to be skeptical of such accounts, but they are certainly hard to explain when they are shared by non-Christians. Consider one such example.

Alok and Ashrita are a young couple I met in Bangalore at a couples' prayer group that was run by the Navjyothi community. In talking to them after the meeting, I learned that they were Hindu. Surprised, I asked them why they attended this meeting. They told me that they could not entirely explain it themselves. They had got married only a few months earlier. The day before they were to depart for their honeymoon, Ashrita had a fall and suffered a hairline fracture of her leg. A couple of days later, as she was sitting at home with her cast on, lamenting the unfortunate situation, a relative of hers told her about a retreat center where miraculous healings were taking place.[60] Since Ashrita thought she had nothing to lose, she and Alok decided to go to the center. While they were there, they attended a prayer service led by a priest, who at one point closed his eyes and stated that he saw someone with a broken leg being healed. Ashrita looked at Alok and said that she felt certain the priest was referring to her. They returned to their room at the retreat center and did what she considered the bravest thing she had ever done: they cut off her cast. The leg was completely healed, even though it was only a week since the doctors had clearly diagnosed the fracture and put a cast on it. A few weeks later, Alok moved to Bangalore to start his new job, still bewildered by what had happened to them. During his first week there working as a banquet manager, he met Wilfred, the leader of Navjyothi, who had come to the hall to plan his daughter's wedding reception. Wilfred happened to mention that he was a Catholic missionary, and Alok excitedly told him what had happened to them. Wilfred invited them to a meeting of the couples' group he was leading, and they have been part of the group ever since.

In addition to stories of physical healing, I also came across accounts of re-markable and inexplicable dreams: a few respondents in Bangalore claimed to have been called personally by Jesus or Mary to attend a Catholic event, as a result of which they became Catholic. On the whole, however, conversion from other religions to Catholicism was rare among my respondents. Most accounts of conversion I heard were from people who had grown up in Catholic homes and talked about returning to a dormant or lapsed faith, one that they had neglected if not rejected altogether.

While the experience of a miraculous conversion might help one acquire "star" status in the religious group, the more common experience of most people I talked to in these groups was that they had been consistently involved in church groups from a young age, increasing their involvement over the years. Their current higher degree of involvement might be seen as the result of a more gradual conversion, in contrast to the sudden conversions I described earlier.[61] These people had a combination of mixed motivations that over time cultivated habits and interests centered around the religious group. Preethi, a PR executive in Dubai, explained her trajectory thus:

> Growing up, I used to go to usual Sunday masses and catechism and everything. But I did have this sense of "I wanna have this friendship with God," you know? Your catechism teachers tried to tell you that: develop that friendship with God. But I guess, to be very honest, I had other in-tentions for going to church when I was growing up [laughs]. Growing up in a girls' school you didn't really have access to guys and stuff. Church was the only place where you got to see guys. So that did have a role to play. And then you get to a point where that's the motivating factor for you to go to church every time. So even after confirmation, I in-sisted I wanted to go back for youth classes and everything. And I'm one of those people who continued until 12th, whereas my brother stopped

after confirmation. Maybe it was because there were many guys I had a crush on [*laughs*]. I'd be embarrassed to tell my kids that.

But Preethi's motivations began to change after high school. She returned to India for college, where she came across "a good youth group; they were very close-knit and stuff. And I wanted to belong to something like that." She felt a strong sense of belonging to this community, and this, more than any attraction to particular individuals, sustained her commitment to the group. After college, when she returned to Dubai, she wanted a structure that could continue the experience that she had cherished in India. Coupled with the skills and practices she had cultivated over her years in youth groups, this yearning led her to take the initiative to start a young adults' prayer group in her parish.

Many, like Preethi, talked about how the desire to find a locus of belonging and community was a key factor in shaping their decision to join and remain committed to their religious groups. In many cases, people were referred to these groups by peers or family members. For people migrating to new cities, these groups also served as a locus of ethnic belonging, sustaining the language and traditions they were used to at home. Some French professionals talked about how moving to Dubai was a culture shock, where the pervasiveness of religion— mosques and burkas everywhere, as one noted—led them to question for the first time what their own tradition was and to find some means of rekindling their attachment to it within a community of similarly minded people.

Many Filipinos, such as Alonso and Terence, talked about not having been particularly interested in religion back home in the Philippines. However, after they moved to Dubai, they joined choirs, prayer groups and volunteer sodalities at church because doing so give them instant access to co-ethnics, a social life, and a support system to meet both pragmatic and spiritual needs.

Carol is one such example. She grew up Catholic in the Philippines, where she rarely attended church. Soon after she moved to Dubai, she separated from her husband when she discovered he had been cheating on her. At this point a friend invited her to an event held by the New Life community. She at first was concerned that it was a "born-again church," and she had heard negative things about these sorts of groups. After her friend assured her that it was "totally Catholic," she agreed to attend a meeting. It was held in someone's flat, and there were only ten people in the room. They were practicing "worship songs" and invited her to join them. Since she liked singing, she told me that she immediately felt "like I really belong[ed]." Because there were not many people in the room, she said there was "no other option," but for people to talk to each other and get to know one another. "You really feel like you're at home," she said. They sang songs that "really strike my heart," especially one called "Through It All." She sang its refrain: "I'll sing to you Lord / a hymn of love / for your faithfulness to me / I'm carried in everlasting arms / you'll never let me go / through it all."[62] At the time she was "broken-hearted," still very wounded by her ex-husband's infidelity, and was going through "the healing process."[63] "But when I joined the community, everything was gone," she claimed. "I divert[ed] everything to God." It was in that prayer group that Carol, for the first time in her adult life, opened her Bible. When she listened to the talks of the movement's founder, she said, they really "struck my heart": they finally made sense of the Catholic faith for her. She has felt a deep sense of belonging to the community for the past three years and is now active in its leadership.

Cultivating Therapeutic Individualism

Why are professionals in Bangalore and Dubai drawn to make serious commitments to these ECC groups? And how are they shaped by their participation in these groups?

Sociologist Christian Smith argues that, on an emotional and phenomenological level, believers experience the claims and promises of Christianity as a compelling response to a number of desires, interests, and needs. Specifically, Christianity assures them of "a universe that is not cold and empty"; it provides the "security, significance, and purpose" of "a meaningful life" and communicates to them the "unconditional love" of God. It gives them a means of addressing the "brokenness and darkness in the world" and their personal "guilt, regret, remorse, and shame"; it allows them to experience "freedom," "relief [and] release" by redressing their wrongs and failures, gives them transcendentally oriented "personal and collective worship experiences," orients them within clear "moral bearings," and enables them to find "social belonging in morally-significant communities."[64]

The ECC groups attended by professionals in Bangalore and Dubai provide those benefits to their members. They emphasize, through music, Scripture, and the content of their meetings, that, in the members' own words, "you are not alone"; "you are not abandoned—even if your mother forsakes you, God will never forsake you"; "you matter so much that Jesus died for you"; "you are meant for a great purpose"; "God has a plan for your life"; "you are called to great things"; "if you become who you are meant to be you will set the world on fire"; "you are loved unconditionally"; "you belong to God"; "your worth is infinite"; and "God does not make junk." These assurances shape people's narrative scripts in this realm. In contrast to the messages professionals hear and internalize in the workplace about how they need to be wary of others around them and keep seeking mobility, in the realm of the church they hear and internalize messages of trust and healing and injunctions to fidelity and commitment. In the respondents' own words:

> "My worth comes from God alone."
> "The most important thing is obedience to the will of God."
> "Do you have a personal relationship with Jesus?"
> "Jesus has to be Lord of all aspects of your life."
> "You have to embrace your cross and die to yourself."
> "I have to forgive even the people who have severely wronged me."

Affirmation of personal worth is a central theme across the meetings of these groups. Group leaders told me that this affirmation was important to them because many of their members had low self-esteem due to their upbringing or their experiences in their workplaces and cities. As one leader of the Salt and Light group in Dubai said, "These people are told all day that they are nothing—by their parents, their teachers, their bosses. Only the Lord can heal this wound of being unwanted." In a prayer meeting of this group that I attended in Dubai, participants were called to lay hands on one another and say, "You are precious in the eyes of the Lord." In one meeting of the New Life community I attended, we were all asked to introduce ourselves to the persons sitting to our right and left and then, calling them by name, to tell them, "You are a blessing." Such regular practices can communicate to people a sense of being precious, wanted, and chosen and blessed by God.

The groups' various teachings also emphasize themes of sin, confession, forgiveness, expunging guilt, and starting over: "Jesus makes all things new." Members are encouraged to participate in the sacrament of reconciliation or confession at church. In both cities, lines outside confessionals are consistently long and populated by people of diverse ages and social classes.

"Worship" in these groups, borrowing from the American evangelical/Pentecostal form, refers largely to a time of collective prayer facilitated by contemporary music. Members talk about the "powerful" music of these groups as being superior to the "old" or "boring" music of the Catholic liturgy, even though the liturgy itself is given considerable importance by the leaders and members of these groups. The lyrics either praise various attributes of God or have distinctly individualistic themes, emphasizing intimacy with God, the believer's desire for God, personal repentance of sin, and so on. These themes are also reinforced during the "teachings" offered in these groups.

The character of the Missionary is also sustained through ritual habits and practices endorsed by the group and through mimesis or inadvertent imitation. One of the curious things that struck me in several groups I attended was how some members imitated the expressions, tonal inflections, and bodily gestures of the leaders of their prayer groups, especially when they were instructing the group or talking about spiritual matters. As René Girard might say, they may have perceived a "lack of being," the fullness of which they saw in these leaders, and thus they inadvertently began to copy them. The members are likely not doing this consciously; they are not standing in front of the mirror on a regular basis trying to move their hands or heads in a certain way. This imitation reveals instead a mostly unconscious process through which they are trying to become the model or to gain access to the "mode of being" of the model, whether that is spiritual freedom or holiness or insight.

People do not consciously choose whether or not to participate in such mimesis. What they may be doing to some extent is choosing which models to imitate. Those who are trying to "imitate Christ" try to put themselves in contexts in which they are surrounded by particular "models." Those models need not be limited to other church members; they may rely on "models" who are not physically present; for instance, by reading about the lives and writings of the saints. The habitus of the Missionary self also depends on distinct kinds of "capital" for spiritual advancement, such as service, obedience, self-sacrifice, humility, modesty, purity, and sobriety. The decision of the Missionary professional not to go out drinking with his colleagues after work reflects his recognition that these contexts can lead him to become a kind of self that he does not want to be.

Belonging to these groups is in many ways a source of power for Missionaries. Principally, members gain access to a loving God, whom they learn to experience as capable of bringing healing and resolution to their problems and stressors, whether personal or professional. Through regular time spent in communal and personal prayer, they develop confidence that God hears and answers their prayers.[65] For many, this translated into a renewed sense of self-confidence and purpose. For instance, Ronald in Bangalore talked about how, having grown up in a working-class home, he felt ostracized from many of his peers in business school "in terms of not being able to adapt to, you know the very modern and classy people":

> There's a lot of difference—from a guy who wears a simple shirt and pants to a guy who wears a Levi's or branded jeans and t-shirt, it makes a difference. I have been through a lot of inferiority complex. And after I met Jesus, I have been able to overcome a lot of things like that. For me, Jesus has been a great source of strength.

Not only has he gained self-confidence—for instance, by being able to speak in public thanks to regular opportunities provided by his prayer group—but he also feels empowered to help others: "I feel there are so many people like that who are highly talented but are not able to express themselves. So I feel I must do something to bring a change in their lives as well."

Missionaries seek not only emotional but also physical healing. In many ECC groups, there are regular times for healing prayers, and healing sessions are a standard feature in Catholic Charismatic conferences. During these occasions, group leaders lay their hands on individual members in need of prayer, sometimes on the specific parts of their body that need healing. Sometimes they pray in tongues, but typically they pray in words requesting physical healing if the suffering was God's will and, if it was not, that the struggling individual be given the strength to carry on and offer up his or her pain. One prayer group meeting I attended in Dubai started with an activity in which participants were asked to pair up with the person sitting next to them and pray over each other for any ailments they were struggling with. The man sitting next to me had a shoulder injury and asked me to pray over him. My prayer did not cure him, but at the time I was undergoing physical therapy treatment for my own shoulder and was able to offer him some exercises. Nobody in that session experienced a miraculous healing (and nobody seemed discouraged by this either), although in my interviews I came across many who attested to the power of healing prayer. One incredulous man became a believer when, during a healing prayer session, he saw blisters on his hand disappear before his very eyes. Many ECC groups also organize healing masses, where in addition to the celebration of the Eucharist, the priest (often a visitor with special "gifts" of healing) would pray over the congregants.[66]

Members of ECC groups also talked about how their relationships had changed as a result of growing in their faith through their participation in these groups. Many discussed being able to forgive people who had hurt them and being less afraid of people, especially of their bosses at work. People talked about how their faith also pulled them out of their preoccupation with their own problems and helped them attend to the needs of others. ECC groups facilitate this process by providing not only discourses but also ritual activities. For instance, during one Lenten season, members of a prayer group in Dubai staged a reenactment of the Way of the Cross for the parish. This is a traditional devotional exercise in which participants contemplate the experience of Jesus Christ on the day of his crucifixion along fourteen stages or "stations." The second station depicts Jesus, after being condemned to death, beginning to carry his cross. After enacting this scene, the narrator shared the following reflection:

> You are overworked, sidelined, treated unfairly. Your cross overwhelms you. Jesus carries your cross with you. What are my crosses? Am I too fat or too thin? Do I lack finances? Am I unable to find employment?

In the fifth station, which is when Simon of Cyrene is brought in to help Jesus carry his cross, the narrator said, "You are trying to meet your family's financial demands, people's expectations of you, heavy work pressures. Heavy burdens. Am I willing to focus on my brother's needs in my time of need? Can I follow Christ in the midst of my business life?" Through such practices, ECC groups help members reflect on and connect their faith to various aspects of their lives.

The group experience of attunement to a common focus of attention and bodily co-presence also serves to generate what Randall Collins calls "emotional energy." For Collins, all human behavior is "emotional energy tropism": we are drawn to situations that increase emotional energy and are repelled by situations that decrease it.[67] When people assemble together around a mutual focus of attention and share a common mood, successful interaction rituals can be a key source of emotional energy. They not only amplify individuals' emotional energy but also generate group solidarity and charge the central symbols of the group with greater value, strengthening their power in individuals' lives even outside the context of the ritual. In contrast, unsuccessful rituals are characterized by "low level[s] of collective effervescence, the lack of momentary buzz," and thus they generate little emotional energy or group solidarity.[68] ECC groups provide regular occasions for successful rituals, bringing people together around ritually charged objects (for instance, the tabernacle in a chapel, where Catholics believe the actual body and blood of Jesus Christ are present), with music and teachings evoking emotions of passionate love, devotion, and surrender. Even physiologically, the bodily stances adopted by prayer group members often resemble "high-power poses" with arms outstretched in a V, which may empower people by increasing their sense of confidence.[69]

In spite of the emotional fervor that is found in these groups, it is misleading to characterize the prayer meetings of ECC groups as nothing more than an experience of collective effervescence. This is because members' experience in these groups is also one of deepening interiority, an inward turn away from others and the world. At times it is almost as if people compete to be more attuned to God than the others around them. Leaders encourage them to stay focused on the genuine peak experience of intimacy with, surrendering to, or communing with God: "don't look at others around you, just focus on Jesus in your heart"; "don't be distracted like others around you." Individual members are often lost in prayer, eyes closed, oblivious to others around them, and it is not clear that such an experience necessarily bonds them more deeply to others around them. That it may not is partly suggested by the fact that members who told me they felt shunned by the group and complained about cliques nevertheless continued to attend the meetings, because they believed that in the group meeting, they could have a powerful interior encounter with God. Inner experience, not community, takes primacy for the Missionary. And the aim of leaders is "to make Jesus present": "to give Jesus," as they say. The point of the group seems primarily to facilitate the individual's personal encounter with the divine physician, rather than creating group bonding or collective we-feeling or solidarity.

Unlike other forms of individualism, therapeutic individualism is not monadic but dyadic. Phenomenologically, for the Missionary, the key agent and initiator is God, not the choosing "I." The self experiences God, is pursued by God, seeks to follow the will of God, and strives to be in union with God. Therapeutic individualism does not necessarily imply a consumerist self that simply chooses what it finds pleasing; it is not the idiosyncratic "Sheilaism" that Bellah and colleagues talk about.[70] Rather, the Missionary claims that the one who acts is "no longer I but Christ"; one's choices are "from the Spirit." People say, "I felt God telling me," "the Lord led me to do this," "the Spirit clearly said, . . ." and so on. They see themselves not as freely choosing agents, but primarily as responders to something initiated by an Other. In conversations with me, some would claim that "this is something Westerners cannot understand," because it was a contradiction to the Western tendency to give primacy to autonomy and individual choice, which they saw as an inferior approach to life.

Individualism and Community

In the norms and narratives of the Missionary, all the "action" that happens seems to be exclusively between God and the individual. Nevertheless, many ECC members experience a strong sense of community. Among group members, a sense of mutual trust emerges as people find others who "really care about you as a person," as Shawn said. This helps many members overcome a sense of loneliness. The groups' regular social activities also emphasize a sense of family and belonging. Neil, a marketing manager in Dubai, expressed the acceptance and belonging he felt toward his group in an article in its newsletter:

> Ever since I have joined [the group], I have had the sense of belonging to something great. When I sing, I feel I'm doing a great job even if I don't have a good voice. No one criticizes you or reprimands you for having a below average appearance or voice, or the like. Although we are all from different parts of the world, and very few of us are related to each other, we are as strong as any family on earth. We are all different but there is one thing common to all of us—JESUS! . . . I joined as a youth looking for acceptance and I found it in more ways than one. I joined as someone looking for friends; instead I got a gigantic family!

What bonds them to each other is not so much the collective effervescence of praise and worship services. Rather, bonding is achieved through the various other practices and activities of the group as they share *life* together, beyond the confines of worship events: spending time with each other in sports, picnics, celebrations, and social activities such as movies and dining out. ECC groups create for members a climate of warmth and affection: members embrace each other, hold hands or lay hands on one another in prayer, affirm each other's strengths, celebrate important events together, welcome newcomers, and pray blessings for and share personal affirmations with those who leave. Attempts to create such a climate are often intentional; group leaders strategize how to help members experience God's healing touch.

One of my own fondest memories from my youth is from 1999, when I was leaving Dubai for Canada. The members of my church choir threw me a surprise farewell party during which they sat around me in a circle and each shared something personal about the difference I had made to their lives. I do not recall the specifics of what they said, but I do remember well the comforting sense of certainty it gave me that, wherever I would go, I had a community to which I felt I belonged and that deeply cared for me. Such attempts to cherish members and to communicate to them their value—while welcoming new members, celebrating birthdays and other special occasions, or sending members off along their journeys ahead—were common to these groups. One could, in such a context, make the theological claim that it is necessarily through specific persons, faces, and voices that one encounters the incarnate Christ, but no such claim is made here.

Admittedly the experience of these groups is not universally positive for members. The pervasive formation of cliques within prayer groups generated complaints of feeling left out. People also complained about leadership politics and struggles about authority and obedience that generated "drama" and rifts between people. I return to some of these problems in chapter 5. But on the whole, most members find ECC groups to be largely supportive. They feel that they are able to share their problems and difficulties and find solace and confidence when others pray with and for them. Thus, these groups are not merely sites of interaction rituals but also provide a meaningful sense of community and solidarity, in spite of the individualistic norms and language of the Missionary.

Conclusion

My focus in this chapter was on how ECC groups generate the common normative expectations embodied in the character of the Missionary. Although the norms, beliefs, and practices that orient the Missionary derive from both global and local factors, this chapter primarily examined those features of ECC groups that are common to Bangalore and Dubai alike. But as I discuss in more detail later, the local context plays an important role in shaping these groups. We see hints of its importance in Randall's story at the beginning of this chapter, which reveals how the local context can shape even the kinds of "miracles" people experience. Consider that the first thing to cross Randall's mind after he hit the man was the fear of "blood money"—having to satisfy the demands of the wounded party in accord with the local interpretation of Islamic law—and of being imprisoned for life, even though the accident was technically not his fault. In a different context, such as Bangalore, the very same accident would not have generated this particular kind of anxiety, and its resolution might not even have been interpreted by the driver involved as a miracle. Knowing the severity of the legal regime in Dubai, Randall saw his own life as, in a sense, having come to an end after he hit the man. And seeing him not only unhurt but also not interested in the blood money was not simply baffling to Randall: it was akin to a new lease on life, a death sentence lifted. Dubai is also a debtors' prison, where a bounced check could land someone in jail, and this regime again plays an important role in the religious conversion of a Filipino couple we meet later in this book. In Bangalore, as I mentioned earlier in this chapter, stories of conversion and miracles were narrated along very different lines, consisting mostly of physical healings and dreams or visions, in which the political regime seemed irrelevant or at least absent.[71] I return in chapter 5 to examine the ways in which the distinct social and political contexts in Bangalore and Dubai shape ECC groups and Catholicism more generally in these cities.

How does this character of the Missionary affect the lives of ECC group members in their workplaces? Recall that these workplaces are the domain of the Mercenary, a character oriented above all to pursuing socioeconomic mobility, that lives in perennial mistrust of others. These environments generate among professionals the sense of apprehensive individualism I described in chapter 1. Yet as we have seen, the very same professionals in their churches are governed by a starkly different moral orientation: that of the Missionary. The traditional doctrines of Catholicism, the evangelical insistence on a personal relationship with Jesus, and the emotional energy of Pentecostalism combine to generate a distinctive mode of therapeutic individualism in tightly knit ECC groups. While the habitat of the Mercenary leaves these professionals anxious, beaten down, and feeling like just another cog in the machine, the trust, healing, and sense of belonging they find in ECC groups empower them with a sense of self-worth and self-confidence, which they see as helping them survive and even thrive in their workplaces. But as we find in the next chapter, the Mercenary and the Missionary cannot live in perfect harmony.

MISSIONARIES IN A MERCENARY WORLD

Noel Thomas, like many Indian professionals I met in ECC prayer groups in Dubai, spent his childhood in different parts of India. He was born and raised in the south, then moved up north to pursue a degree at one of India's premier engineering colleges, and then returned south to complete an MBA at one of the world-renowned Indian Institutes of Management (IIM). In his final year, he was recruited by the Dubai office of an American management consulting firm. The firm was, as he put it, "not my top choice, not my bottom choice." He was initially unsure about whether to take the job, since people around him considered Dubai to be "a blue collar location," and he wondered whether it "might be a step down." He did not know any other IIM graduates who had taken jobs in Dubai. But the company held the promise of work opportunities with major players from industry and government, so he decided to try it out. He had a rough start and was especially taken aback by the racism pervasive in the city and in the Gulf in general. As I mentioned in chapter 1, he experienced such prejudice in his interactions with colleagues and clients, but, over time, learned to anticipate and deal with it. After nearly five years at the firm, he professed to be "quite happy for now." He told me that he saw his job as "getting paid to think for people who are too stupid to think." Once he started to feel that he was stagnating, he assured me he will start looking elsewhere. (Not long after this interview, he took up another position in Europe.)

Lijo George, a friend of Noel's who works in the same firm, was born in Dubai to parents from Kerala. After completing high school in Dubai, he returned to India for college where he trained as a computer programmer. During his studies there, he became actively involved with an ECC prayer group. After graduation, he started working as a programmer. Dissatisfied with his job and his prospects in Kerala, he made two visits to Dubai in search of work. He had no luck on his first trip, but on the second, he landed his present job, thanks in fact to Noel, whom he had met in his prayer group at church. In contrast to his more technical role in India, Lijo's new job entailed a management role. During his interview, he framed the leadership and organizational experience he gained from his church group in India as an asset that qualified him for this position and credited it for his success. Whereas in his previous job he was expected to work evenings and weekends on IT upgrades, in his current position, he had most evenings and weekends free and dedicated most of that time to his leadership role in his ECC church group.

Gemima, Lijo's wife, worked at the Dubai office of a major global bank. Like Noel, she grew up mostly in South India, moving back and forth between different states and cities. She moved to Dubai mainly to find a job that she could use as a stepping-stone on her way to Australia or the United Kingdom. "I didn't think this was 'the place to be' or anything," she said, referring to Dubai. Her aim, like most people who move to Dubai, was to "just make some money," tax free, and finding a job at a global brand-name firm seemed the perfect next step. She found work at a bank, but was frustrated with her job and was eagerly looking for an opportunity to quit and move on to something better. She described the work environment as competitive, racist, and overly demanding. In 2008, she found a job in the United Kingdom; however, before she left, she met Lijo in Dubai, fell in love, and decided to stay and get married. After the financial crisis that year, "when all the banks went apeshit," she stopped looking for work elsewhere because of "the insecurity about finding another job." In the past several years, especially because of the stressful work environment, she tried switching jobs a couple of times, but on each occasion received a promotion within the company that offered her a more lucrative deal.

Noel, Lijo, and Gemima are all active members of the same ECC group in Dubai. Each of them participates in activities of the group more than once a week: they attend a weekly meeting at church, a smaller prayer meeting at one of their homes, additional planning meetings to organize various activities, and various social events with members of the group. Yet, their understandings and expressions of the relationship between religion and work are far from homogeneous.

Lijo actively tries to integrate his faith with his work. For him, this primarily means "being a witness." In practice, this includes various acts of signaling, such as setting up his desktop screensaver to display Bible verses or telling colleagues about his church activities. However, he seldom talks to them about what he actually believes. His religious beliefs nevertheless influence how he performs work-related tasks and sometimes come into conflict with workplace norms. On such occasions, which I describe later in this chapter, he chooses to follow the demands of his faith expressed through his conscience, even if doing so generates difficulties at work.

Noel, in contrast, is uncomfortable displaying his faith in the workplace and actively tries to maintain a principled separation of the two realms. He does not see this as a compromise or a failure to integrate religion and work, but rather as showing due respect to what is appropriate for a professional. Noel also spends more time with his colleagues outside the workplace than Lijo does, during which time he engages in regular conversation about "personal" topics such as religion. While he does not believe in displaying his religious commitment through religious symbols like images or screensavers, he takes principled stances that distinguish him from others; in particular, not drinking alcohol during the numerous social events that his work as a management consultant entails. Abstaining from alcohol, smoking, swearing, and gossip are behaviors that nearly all of my ECC respondents in Bangalore and Dubai mentioned when talking about the relationship between religion and work. Noel also finds that his church commitments sometimes conflict with his work schedule. This conflict even led him to step down from a leadership role in his prayer group. Again, he does not see this as a compromise of his faith, but rather as being obedient to the will of God in respecting his duties as a professional.

Gemima sees the role of religion at work differently. For her, faith is primarily a psychological aid: it is a source of motivation that enables her to "maintain [her] sanity" in her routine dealings with difficult colleagues and customers. She also considers her workplace environment "hostile" to any discussion or expression of religion, because most of her colleagues are atheists. While she does not shy away from making her participation in church activities known to them, she prefers to live out her faith in the workplace not so much by talking or signaling, but rather by practicing habits and virtues consonant with her beliefs.

Joel, Lijo, and Gemima, like most professionals I talked to, are largely comfortable with the way they negotiate the relationship between faith and work. Some professionals, however, experience more overt forms of conflict, where the demands of faith clash with Mercenary norms and require a choice of one over the other. In still other cases, attempts at integration fail altogether. Nevertheless, on the whole, the professionals I interviewed believe they are doing a good job at integrating faith and work.

This chapter addresses how and when the beliefs, practices, and logics of the Missionary, cultivated in ECC groups, interact with the Mercenary norms of the corporate workplace. How do Missionaries navigate the Mercenary realm, given that (1) their religious beliefs make all-encompassing demands on them—"Jesus needs to be Lord of all or he is not Lord at all," as they put it; (2) their faith communities have little to say about work; and (3) the norms and structures of corporate life often pose challenges to living out their faith?

I found considerable variation in how individuals straddle the competing norms of the Mercenary and the Missionary. Members of the same religious groups, even those within the same household—indeed, even the same person in different situations—negotiate the relationship between faith and work very differently. In spite of idiosyncrasies, however, there is a clear pattern: even if work as such seems inherently meaningless to these professionals, the work*place* becomes a mission field, in which one's mission is to be a witness to one's faith. Being a witness, for them, does not mean proselytizing; rather, it is primarily about resisting temptations to compromise one's faith. In practice, it means rejecting some of the means and strategies of the Mercenary (e.g., lying, cheating, and gossiping) while still adhering to the same ends (i.e., maximizing mobility). Beliefs, skills, and habits cultivated in the Missionary realm often spill over into the workplace, proving to be both assets and liabilities for workplace performance. Both their successes and failures strengthen these professionals' commitments to their faith, while the therapeutic individualism of the Missionary realm enables them to return to the workplace rejuvenated to continue the struggle and to navigate the Mercenary realm without either transforming it or rejecting it.

Religion in the Workplace

The past few decades have seen a burgeoning interest in the topic of religion and spirituality in the workplace, expressed in popular articles and books for professionals and practitioners, books by religious leaders and theologians, and considerable scholarly research.[1] Numerous organizations and associations in the United States have also emerged around integrating "faith and work," which, as David Miller has documented, constitutes a significant and growing social movement.[2]

Several factors are responsible for this trend.[3] Corporate scandals in recent decades, such as the Enron fiasco, have led to an increased interest in business ethics.[4] A growing number of workplace initiatives are aimed at improving ethical standards, and ethics courses are increasingly required in business schools. Religion and spirituality have become part of this new conversation on ethics and values in business, with commentary produced by religious organizations and leaders.[5] Growing migration to the United States and Europe has generated increased attention to accommodating the increasing diversity in the ethnic, racial, religious, and cultural backgrounds of employees.[6] Multiculturalism has also shaped broader social trends in the West, spurring curiosity about and interest in Eastern philoso-phies, religions, and spiritual practices, such as yoga and meditation.[7]

A key factor that shapes the role of religion in the workplace is the changing nature of work itself. The increased anxieties, uncertainties, and demoralization among employees produced by trends such as reengineering contribute to strengthening the search for meaning and purpose in work, at least in the West.[8] The articulation of such needs is likely influenced by the growth of popular psychology: notions of "self-actualization" and of bringing the "whole person" into the workplace have become commonplace.[9] With professionals spending more of their waking hours at work, the workplace has become for many their primary source of community, replacing more traditional forms such as extended families or religious communities.[10] Thus, the depersonalized, anxiety-ridden workplace climate generated by the new economy has spurred the pursuit of higher-order needs of community, purpose, passion, and self-actualization at work, at least in the West. To survive in an increasingly competitive and volatile economy, many argue that it is necessary to replace older industrial, bureaucratic approaches and structures with new ways of harnessing employees' creativity in order to spur in-novation. Religion and spirituality in the workplace have thus become the new "cutting-edge panacea of the twenty-first century."[11]

A number of distinct research streams focus on the study of religion and of spirituality in the workplace. Research on religion in the workplace largely focuses on Christians, particularly evangelicals, and leaders at the top such as CEOs and entrepreneurs.[12] Some of the more prominent studies in this area categorize how people integrate religion into the workplace. For instance, Michael Lindsay and Bradley Smith, based on a national study of American evangelicals, propose a fourfold typology depending on whether the workplace is hostile or receptive to religion and whether the individual's expression is more overt or subdued: (1) the "pragmatic" type who attempts to witness to their faith in incremental ways, (2) the "circumspect" type focusing on "values" or inconspicuous practices such as silent prayer, (3) the "heroic" type compelled by convictions to express their faith in unreceptive environments, and (4) the "brazen" type who is more "in your face" and triumphalist.[13] David Miller suggests another typology that is not restricted to evangelicals or Christians: (1) the "ethics"-focused type concerned with matters of personal virtue, business ethics, and social and economic justice; (2) the "evangelism" type focused on overtly expressing faith in the workplace; (3) the "experience"-focused type, who adopts a more theological understanding of work, such as a vocation or search for meaning; and (4) the "enrichment" type, keen on practices such as prayer, meditation, and self-transformation.[14]

I found myself unable to satisfactorily use either of these categorizations when analyzing my data: nearly every individual I studied seemed to exhibit different integration "types" in different situations. This led me to recognize two problematic assumptions underlying those approaches: first, that people have internally coherent beliefs about what the relationship between faith and work should look like, and second, that they behave consistently in accord with these beliefs across different contexts and situations. Sociologist Mark Chaves calls this set of assumptions the "religious congruence fallacy."[15] Assuming such consistency between beliefs and actions blinds us to the differential effects of contexts and the pervasive inconsistency between people's professed beliefs and actions.

In contrast to the research on religion in the workplace, research on spirituality in the workplace focuses on defining and measuring workplace spirituality and its effects on corporate performance.[16] While the thrust of this discourse is predominantly positive—"spirituality may well be the ultimate competitive advantage," as Ian Mitroff and Elizabeth Denton assert[17]—there are also cautionary and critical voices. Some have decried the instrumentalization of spirituality for organizational ends, which reduces it to "a handmaid of corporate power,"[18] and others have noted how the enthusiastic proponents of workplace spirituality are oblivious to its potential for symbolic violence, cultish exploitation, and deeper normative control.[19]

With the diffusion of global capitalism, one might think that this interest in workplace spirituality would have also found momentum outside the West. But in the cities in which I conducted research in India and the Arabian Gulf, there seemed to be no comparable discussion of the topic. One explanation for this difference is the absence of the concern about church-state separation that underlies the discussion about religion in the workplace in the United States.[20] Religious expression, both in workplaces and public spaces more generally, is widely prevalent in the contexts I study. It is quite typical in corporate settings to see religious imagery displayed on people's workspaces, as well as dedicated religious spaces, such as prayer rooms for Muslims.

Yet these spaces also reflect "secularizing" tendencies such as the differentiation of spheres (work from home or church) and the separation of personal life from work, such that religion is relegated to the private sphere. Such privatization is evident in the discourse about professionalism, where there is a shared implicit expectation that work be treated as a separate realm, untainted by "personal" activities and concerns.[21] The workplaces I study are also pluralistic spaces, representing diverse ethnicities and religious traditions. Unlike the French model of laïcité, which excludes religious expression altogether from the public sphere, secularism in these contexts entails considerable tolerance for religious expression; indeed, there are limits to which religion can be excluded. In secular India, enforcing prohibitions on religious expression, particularly of Hinduism, would generate a social backlash. While the UAE is officially an Islamic country, its officials have expressed aspirations to a kind of secularism,[22] yet it would be un-thinkable for a Dubai office of a transnational corporation to prevent Muslim employees from fulfilling their prayer obligations during the day.

The tendency in corporate offices in these contexts is therefore to attempt to show tolerance and impartiality, primarily by allowing employees some freedom of expression in their workspaces (e.g., placing religious images on their desk or cubicle walls) and holding workplace celebrations of festivals of different reli-gions, such as Diwali, Eid, and Christmas. Christians in several global corporate offices also mentioned interdenominational prayer groups and Bible study groups that met outside of work hours, although members of such groups I spoke to complained that attendance levels were low, since it was difficult to find a time that worked for everyone. Overall, respondents cited such practices as evidence that there is no opposition to expressions of religion in the work-place. Nevertheless, some complained that these examples paid mainly lip service to tolerance, because their companies did not permit employees who actually celebrated those festivals to take those days off and spend time with their fami-lies then. Some Christians also were unable to obtain leave on Sundays to at-tend church. Overall, the dominant religious practices in these contexts (e.g., workplace prayer for Muslims or celebration of major Hindu festivals such as Diwali in Indian offices) seem to be permitted, even if they do not contribute to productivity.

While the formal emphasis is thus on accommodating religion in the workplace—mainly through celebrating religious festivals and allowing employ-ees to perform obligatory prayers—I also came across occasional "workplace spirituality" programs aimed at making work more meaningful and thus boost-ing productivity. A noteworthy phenomenon is the Art of Living (AOL) move-ment, an offshoot of the transcendental meditation movement founded in India by Sri Sri Ravi Shankar (not to be confused with the legendary sitar musician), which has spread around the world.[23] One of AOL's major initiatives is a stress management program based on a unique yogic breathing and meditation tech-nique. The organization promotes this program in corporate environments as a stress management workshop that encourages healthy lifestyles and improves interpersonal communication. The clientele includes major organizations such as the World Bank and Harvard Business School, as well as global corporations such as Coca Cola, Accenture, and Siemens.[24] Some of my respondents in both Dubai and Bangalore attended these sessions and claimed to find them helpful and interesting, but were not regularly committed to the practice. I also spoke with trainers from AOL who conduct these courses in corporations. From both sources, it became clear that while there is some interest in integrating meditation and spirituality into the workplace to improve concentration and productivity, reduce stress, and so on, there is very little sustained participation in those activities. Most people who participate try it once, out of curiosity, never to return.

In India, the occasional institutional efforts to integrate spirituality and work harness lessons from Hindu scriptures and mythology that are of relevance to leadership and productivity. For example, at the annual trade association meeting of the National Association of Software and Services Companies (NASSCOM) in 2010, one of the best-attended talks was by Devdutt Pattanaik, who was then "chief belief officer" of a major Indian retail corporation; his job was to create empowering rituals for employees and managers based on "essential" elements of Indian culture (i.e., traditional Hindu beliefs).[25] Except for such sporadic attempts, I found little discussion or institutionalized interest in integrating spirituality into the workplace. The majority of my respondents, as Roman Catholics, did not participate in such attempts, nor did Muslims I spoke to—likely because they did not share the essentialist and nationalist presuppositions of these initiatives. When I asked them if religion or spirituality played any role in their work lives, they usually did not invoke either concept, but spoke instead of the role of "faith," even though, as we see, many of their examples were not only about religious beliefs but also included practices, skills, and dispositions cultivated in religious contexts.

Let us turn now to examine what role religion plays for professionals like Noel, Lijo, and Gemima in the corporate workplace. What effects do the Mercenary norms and challenges of corporate workplaces have on those who aspire to coherently live out the ideals of the Missionary?

The Workplace as a Mission Field

For many recent Christian thinkers writing on faith and work, successful integration means seeing work as a vocation or divine calling.[26] The kind of integration these authors aspire to fuses the realms of faith and work, such that the requirements of one realm are identical to those of the other. In other words, one fulfills one's Christian vocation precisely through pursuing success in the business world. One's values, criteria of worth, and self-perceptions are experienced as identical in both religious and professional spheres, rather than as exclusive properties of either realm.[27]

This view was strikingly absent among the professionals I interviewed. A couple even laughed when I asked whether they saw their corporate jobs as a calling. For the Mercenary, work is simply a means to an end. At best, their job is where God had "put" them for the moment. Their calling was more to the workplace rather than to the work itself, as I discuss further.

The idea of work as a meaningful vocation emerged only among three professionals I talked to, all of whom had left the corporate world to start their own businesses. These entrepreneurs saw their business ventures, but not their corporate jobs, as divine callings. For example, Floyd, an Indian entrepreneur in Dubai, shared why he left a well-paying corporate job to start his own business in a completely different industry: he felt God was calling him to use his talent and creativity to make a difference in the world. He credited God with both his motivation to abandon a secure career and his success in his new venture:

> Now if money was the motivating factor, I would have continued in employment, right? Employment-wise, I had a situation that I couldn't have asked for any better. I was the number-two man in an organization in Dubai. An American company where I had an American secretary. Now how many Indians can boast of that position in Dubai, right? I had check-signing authority. . . . Virtually I was running the whole company. . . . And then I found this talent—this unique talent that God had given me—and I felt that I must use it, for bettering myself and for making the world a better place. Today as I look back on that, I feel that I have achieved that, and I can let it grow even more and make the world a better place by ensuring that my products . . . will help me make the world a better place.

But Floyd is a rare exception. Most of my respondents were not entrepreneurs and expressed a different sense of mission. Rather than understanding work as a vocation, they saw their mission or purpose in the corporate environment as being a witness.

Bearing Witness

If seeing work as vocation entails a fusion of the realms of faith and work, casting the workplace as a mission field means seeing these realms as distinct and one's own role as an emissary from one world to the other. The logic that these professionals shared was voiced best by Mona, an Indian administrator in Dubai: "Work is where God has placed me, and I have to be a testimony of God's presence there."

Such witnessing, or being "a testimony of God's presence" in the workplace, is largely implicit and discreet, rather than overt. Only on rare occasions did it mean inviting colleagues to one's church group or talking explicitly about one's faith. While the Missionary ideal is to proclaim the healing power of Jesus to all, it is important to be careful about public expressions of faith, both in Dubai—where proselytism by Christians could lead to imprisonment or deportation—and in Bangalore, where violence against Christians by extremist Hindu groups has been provoked by accusations that Catholics are engaging in proselytism. As a result, most respondents said they preferred not to talk about their faith and only selectively integrated it into the workplace in the practice of witnessing.

Let me provide an example of the exception before looking at the rule. Julie, an active leader in the Charismatic young adult group in her parish, worked as a training manager in a call center in Bangalore for a few years; there she saw her job as an opportunity to evangelize not simply colleagues but also customers. She proudly narrated an incident in which she shattered an American customer's stereotype of Indians and was able to share her faith with him. The man called about his mortgage, figured out he was speaking to someone from India, and started to needle her about her Western name: "How do you like your name? I mean, don't you feel bad about your fake name?" When she replied that Julie was her real name and that she was a Catholic, the skeptical customer started to interrogate her Christian beliefs. She elaborated,

> And I told him, "Listen, I know Jesus personally!" And he was very, very surprised. 'Cause their concept of India is cows, buffaloes, snakes, terrorists, everything not nice. And I told him how much of Jesus I know. And he was very, very zapped . . . . And he's like, "What?" [*laughs*]. I said, "Yeah, I have a prayer group that meets here every Saturday!" And he was very, very zapped! And especially just the privilege I got to introduce Jesus to someone in America who thinks that an Indian has no clue what Jesus is all about!

I share this example as a very rare case. Nearly all the respondents restricted explicit conversation about faith either to settings such as corporate prayer groups or to socializing outside the workplace.

Witnessing, as they understood it, mainly took two forms. The first mode had to do with signaling religious commitments. Even if people would not actively share their religious beliefs with colleagues, they should not hide the fact that they are Christian; doing so would mean being ashamed of Christ, a sign of failure for the Missionary. They would thus signal their religious commitments in numerous ways. In many workplaces in these cities, religious objects, such as religious posters, paintings, statues, or symbols, are commonly displayed, along with personal symbols such as family photos, comic strips, and so on; doing so is a way to bridge the realms of work and faith through material objects and symbols that render permeable the boundaries between the two realms.[28] Lijo in Dubai, as I mentioned at the beginning of this chapter, set up his desktop screensaver to display Bible verses, though he was uncomfortable with overt conversations about religion in the workplace. On the rare occasion that a colleague might pass by his desk and look at his computer when he was away, Lijo would have thus communicated that he is a Christian.

Another way of signaling commitment is through conversation. Most of my respondents did not actively make declarations of their religious beliefs, but nevertheless wanted to make it known that they were churchgoers and had commitments to church groups. We saw this with Gemima earlier in this chapter. Such signaling is not aimed at either persuading others or disposing them favorably toward one's religious beliefs; rather, its logic is one of (usually reticent) disclosure rather than proclamation. A case in point is Francesca, who at the time of our interview had been working for seven years as a business development manager in the Dubai office of a major European electronics firm. She also held a key international leadership role in a Filipino-origin Catholic Charismatic group. "In the beginning I wasn't really comfortable telling people that I'm so active in a Christian ministry," she admitted. It took her several years "to get to the place where it didn't matter what people think about [her]." While she did not feel comfortable being open with her colleagues about her active involvement in church, she also did not want to continue keeping her religious activity in the closet, "because this is such an important aspect of my life." It took her four years to be able to even admit to her colleagues that she was active in a church group. Indeed, she admitted that she still found it a struggle to talk about it. Having to explain one's religious commitment—its nature and meaning and importance—by translating it into secular language that is understandable by one's colleagues at work is challenging for Missionaries, who ideally want to proclaim their religious commitment.[29] Another relevant factor is the extent to which people perceive their workplaces as "safe spaces" that are receptive rather than hostile to self-disclosure about religion.[30] Yet even when such environments are perceived as unreceptive to religious expression, some Missionaries may still see these contexts as proving grounds in which to test their faith.

Yet another common mode of signaling is, for religious reasons, to avoid certain activities in social settings, such as drinking, smoking, cursing, and gossiping. Many ECC group members in both cities saw abstaining from alcohol as a key act of signaling their religious commitment to workplace colleagues, even though Catholicism has no prohibitions against drinking. When I asked them why they did not drink or how exactly their faith influenced their choice to not drink, they could not give me a clear answer. Some referred to a biblical injunction to avoid drunkenness and said that they simply preferred not to take a step that could potentially lead there. "See, I am not saying drinking as such is wrong," Colin said. "Getting drunk is. But you cannot get drunk unless you take the first drink, and I would rather not even do that." Colin admitted he had no problem drinking with his colleagues when he had lived in the United Kingdom a few years earlier, where that behavior was not a problem for his church community. Others similarly talked about refraining from gossip or from using foul language, even at the expense of ridicule by colleagues, as a means of signaling their religious commitment. Bridging religion and work thus seems to mean not only bringing religious meanings and logics into the workplace but also imbuing certain workplace activities with new meanings and drawing boundaries around them.

A particularly uncomfortable mode of signaling for many respondents was refusing to engage with religiously blessed objects shared by people of other faiths. This happened most frequently when Hindu colleagues distributed *prasad* (i.e., food blessed by deities) after returning from temples or pilgrimages. For some ECC members, refusing to eat this food was a source of some anxiety: on the one hand, the *prasad* was an offering sacrificed to deities they did not believe in, and they believed Scripture forbade them from accepting it. On the other hand, they did not want to offend their colleagues by refusing to partake of it. For some, refusing these objects was seen as a way to affirm their commitment to their God and to signal such commitment publicly, even if it meant being ostracized by colleagues. Yet they claimed they would try to do so delicately (or avoid the situation if possible), so as not to offend their Hindu colleagues.

In addition to signaling, a second mode of witnessing is more implicit: to simply communicate, through one's dispositions and interactions, that one is different. This "difference" was rooted in one's Christian commitment. Robert Rajan, a senior HR manager in a global manufacturing firm, explained it thus: "The Catholic Church does tell its members to go and spread the good news, but not in the way that Protestant churches would do it, where they would try and make every opportunity count to talk about the Gospel." He continued,

> For me personally, it's not been that way, you know, where I go and have a Bible next to me, and everyone who comes next to me, try and give them a sign that this is the way. That's not been my way. My way is just to be a person that people would like to look up to. People would like to have around. People would like to, you know, would love to learn something from, would love to come and share with you in case they have a problem. And I've found, in the worst of situations, I have found people coming to me, approaching me in the workplace, just because I was different. Very different in fact.

When I asked him what he meant by this difference, he replied, "No, it's just your way of life. It's happened over years. Years of trying to be different. It's like, you know, it's a practice. Like certain things become habits? Like that. There's certain choices you've made. And, you know, these are good choices, so you keep making those type of choices, and that becomes a way of life."

Robert's career began as a salesman. "It was a real all-out, cutthroat, dog-eat-dog environment, because everyone's running for targets, everyone's competing." At times he would be competing on even ground, but at other times, "you would find people going out of their way to undo you in something" or trying to get the better of you in front of the boss. He described these environments of low informal trust as continually providing "situations that test your faith, test your way of life, test your choices. Do you try to be someone's favorite? Do you try to take undue advantage of a situation? Do you try to corner a deal which is not yours? Do you try and get a deal which is not right, just to stay ahead of the curve?" Robert claimed that his experience in the corporate workplace tested and strengthened his faith "like a muscle," as he had to be a "different" sort of "presence" in the workplace. He claimed that his difference helped him get promotions and obtain financial success. In this way, he was able to attain the economic mobility of the Mercenary while adhering to the ideals of the Missionary. Several others similarly talked about the temptations of the workplace as providing an occasion to strengthen Christian virtues, particularly by not lying, cheating, stealing, or gossiping. But as I discuss further, avoiding such behaviors can entail costs and even failure.

Witnessing is facilitated by two other factors that shape the ways these professionals connect religion to work: the compatibility of religious values with those formally professed in the workplace, and the instrumentality of skills and habits cultivated in religious settings to achieving workplace success.

Compatibility

In discussing the role of religion in the workplace, many respondents talked about the compatibility of aspects of corporate culture with their faith, which they considered a form of integration of faith and work. They often discussed how the values formally espoused by their companies reflected and supported their "personal" and "moral" values. Jackie, a Filipina who was senior HR director of the Dubai office of a major global food and beverage company, claimed that her company espoused principles that were consonant with "not just my religious beliefs" but "also my values." For instance, in dealing with external vendors, her company prohibited its professionals from accepting gifts from suppliers: "We're not allowed to do that." She saw such practices as instances of corruption and so supported the company policy wholeheartedly. Like Jackie, many professionals believed that "good business" reflected not only their religious values but also moral values that people anywhere would espouse. Such values included fairness, discipline, hard work, and honesty: these were the sorts of values that were also associated with the norm of professionalism that many expected to be reflected in global corporations, as we saw in chapter 1.

When I asked my respondents whether any of their experiences in their Catholic upbringing or in Catholic institutions (schools or church groups) influenced their work, the notion of discipline usually arose first. Many of them credited their strict Catholic families and Catholic schools for having cultivated in them the value of discipline and order. Homilies in churches also often echoed themes of self-discipline, obedience, and perseverance in difficult situations. Respondents claimed that the resultant beliefs—that they should act in a disciplined manner, as well as their conception of themselves as disciplined people—served them well in their work lives, especially when having to endure long hours doing tasks that they did not want to do.[31]

Another example of compatibility was shared by Vinay, an engineer at an American firm in Bangalore, where employee performance evaluations entailed grading people on a 5×12 matrix, including components such as "leadership quality, the way you [act] with your team members, your learning capability . . . , how much of change you get in your team, how much of progress you show, how well is your result." He told me, "Based on these qualities, they rank you. So that way it is very professional." The comments he most often received on his performance appraisals were "your patience is very low; you should be more patient with people," and "you need to improve in your leadership qualities." In attempting to meet his company's criteria, Vinay believed that "Christian discipleship also falls into place, [because] they actually grade your patience, leadership qualities, and all those things. In that way, it is actually linked. But they don't quote it scripturally, they do it professionally."

Cherian, a prayer group leader in his church and a senior management executive in Dubai, claimed that "values like patience [and] humility" were both central to his day-to-day life in the workplace and enshrined in the new strategic plan he had recently launched. He was not *trying* to integrate religion into a secular realm; rather, he saw the internal values of the workplace as identical to those he would articulate in a religious setting. For most ECC professionals I talked to, the compatibility of formal beliefs in these ways was sufficient evidence that faith and work can be integrated—even if, as I show later, there is much more to the faith-work interaction than the compatibility of abstract values.

Instrumentality

The skills and habits cultivated in the Missionary realm can also be used instrumentally to one's advantage in the Mercenary workplace. For example, faith may serve as a coping mechanism in the face of difficult and stressful situations in the workplace.

Consider the experiences of Maryann and Carol, two Filipina professionals in Dubai who belonged to the same Catholic Charismatic movement. "I have to be honest," Maryann told me, "there are times I cry myself to sleep because of the stress and these kinds of intrigues and stuff [in the workplace]. . . . In my field, which is sales, it can be so stressful at times. You just wanna give up and go home, and you're like, 'What am I doing here?' One fine day, you wake up and [ask] 'Why the heck am I doing this job?'" It was primarily because of her prayer group that she was able to persevere: "It's our source of strength. Every Friday, you look forward to it." Carol similarly described her anticipation of the weekly prayer group meeting: "You're excited to come. . . . When you have one week full of stress or issues or whatever, at the back of your mind you know that Friday is there. You will be having the [prayer group meeting], you will be meeting your friends, you will be listening to the word of God, to [the founder's] talk. Then it rejuvenates you for the week ahead that you will be facing." One of their prayer group members regularly sent out Bible verses and reflections every day. Before she started her work day, Maryann prayed with these verses, saying that doing so made her "energized for the day" and helped her "become more patient in dealing with [her] customers."

Many respondents articulated how faith enabled them to persevere at work, providing a source of strength and even positivity in the face of challenges. A Spanish consultant, Juan, for instance, spoke of how, one morning, a particularly difficult client harshly reprimanded him in front of others in the office. A colleague later came up to him to commiserate: "Bad day, huh?" He responded, "No, not really. There is more to my day than this." His faith helped him maintain perspective on what is really important, particularly his family and spiritual commitments; to acknowledge the many positives and blessings of each day; and to be undeterred by difficult circumstances. If not for his faith, he insisted, he would have quit long ago.

Dianne, a PR manager in Bangalore, talked about using prayer to deal with stress at work:

> I always know that whenever I get anxious or stressed out, I realize at that point of time I'm not really surrendered to God. I'm taking the whole load on my shoulder and doing things my way. It helps at that point to just stop and say in my heart, "Lord you're here with me, you are my strength. I give this to you." I literally, like, see this big bag; I take it and say, "It's yours—you tell me what to do!" And then, you know, because of faith or because of grace, you immediately feel much lighter. You feel the stress go off. And you're not really bothered. Because you

know at the end of the day nobody can really fire you unless it's God's will for you to leave. And nobody can really retain you unless it's God's will for you to stay back, you know? So it works both ways. It's a practice of daily renewing your commitment to making him the Lord of your work life.

We see that it is not only that faith helps her manage stress but also that the workplace provides her a context outside typical religious settings in which she can regularly cultivate practices and habits—for instance, infusing religious logics that sacralize work and using particular spiritual techniques of imagination and attending to emotions—that reaffirm her religious commitments. Similarly, members of the Hindu Art of Living movement described meditation practices and breathing techniques they used during work to maintain their focus, let go of stress, and become more productive, echoing themes found in the literature in the West on spirituality in the workplace.[32]

Religion can also provide people with beliefs, skills, and capacities that are transferable to the workplace context. Respondents talked about ways in which the skills and capacities cultivated in religious settings were sources of competitive advantage at work. Vinay in Bangalore, for instance, talked about how his religious background gave him a practical edge over others, allowing him to integrate his faith in the workplace without explicitly "evangelizing." Religion equipped him with concrete skills transferable to the workplace context:

> The qualities I have learned, like submission and leadership qualities, they actually [give me an] edge. That is what I have observed. . . . My manager did come and tell me that you are one person who never gives up; you take the challenge and you do the challenge and you are there for the challenge. All this I got because of the way I was trained spiritually. I have twelve years of history being in the youth group. We have gone into different trainings of financial management, managing your work, managing your studies. So it really helped me to prioritize my work. That's really important in the work schedule, to prioritize the work. How to handle situations, actually, and how to escalate issues. . . . These are things that I have learned through my spiritual training. That is what I implement.

Vinay also mentioned attending leadership retreats through his church groups that taught him very practical techniques that were transferable to the workplace. He said he learned, for instance, to use a to-do list every day, for which he uses Windows 7 Post-its, "and I ensure I don't forget to do even a small job." The retreat taught him "to list down what you have to do and how to prioritize your work. . . . Now I can spend time in prayer, spend quality time at work. I finish eight hours of work in four hours."

In Dubai, members of a young adult group of Arab Catholics explicitly focus on cultivating professional skills. Rima, an active member of this group, credited the presentation skills she learned from her Arabic prayer group for her being hired at one of the top hotel chains in Dubai. Before her job interview began, she asked if she could deliver a short PowerPoint presentation that she had prepared about herself and why she believed she was the right candidate for her job. Her sales pitch, she believed, worked, because it allowed her to highlight her initiative and her positive qualities in ways not possible in a conventional interview.

Another mode of instrumentality is interpreting work-related events as miracles in which one's survival or success is owed to divine intervention. Some talked about getting a job itself as a miracle. This narrative was more pronounced among respondents in Dubai than in Bangalore, perhaps because there was a lot more at stake in the Gulf Arab city. The initial expense of obtaining the required visa, the limited time available to people while on their visas to find work, the expensive cost of living in the interim, and the difficulties of having to get a visa and returning to Dubai to search for work again if the initial search proved fruitless all contributed to generating a tense situation, which became a central focus of their prayers (and also those of their loved ones). Many saw the successful resolution of such a situation as a miracle—a sign that God wanted them to stay on and was rewarding their perseverance. Other "miracles," in addition to getting a job, included occasions in which people were "spared" from potential disasters.

In Bangalore too, many respondents talked about "miraculous" interventions of God in their work lives. Vivek, an accountant who worked for one of the Big Four accounting firms for several years before starting his own practice, talked about how, after losing a major client, he and his coworkers experienced a miracle that saved his business:

> Our finances monthly had dropped down by 85 percent. So unless I terminated my employees there was no way I could meet my budgets. There were three staff, and we just held hands around the table and just challenged God on one aspect. It was just a one-minute thing, we said, "Lord, we always believed we are your church, wherever we have gone. And you've always shown us victory and you have never let us down. So if today, and at any point of time, we lack finances, even to pay the salaries, God, it's not a shame for me; it's a shame for you. I know you will not let us down." And you will not believe it: from that very day, till today, we have been busy. So out of the blue, just, clients coming in, walking in: "Hey, we have been looking for your place last few days!"

Despite the instrumental aspects of such modes of overlap—the ways in which religion becomes an asset for their survival and success in the workplace—there is a sentiment in these accounts that the religious realm cannot simply be manipulated by people for their purposes. Its functioning remains elusive and catches them by surprise. The realm of work in these cases no longer remains a disenchanted sphere confined to its restrictive set of logics, but is re-enchanted, always pregnant with the possibility of divine intervention. Such intervention, however, is not always conducive to success in the workplace.

The Costs of Mission: Moral Conflict in the Workplace

In the attempt to bear witness to one's faith, religion can become an invasive force in the realm of work when the norms of the Mercenary clash with the demands of faith. While in Robert's case presented earlier, we saw it was possible to achieve financial mobility in spite of rejecting commonly used Mercenary strategies, there are many cases in which faith can become a liability instead.

Lijo, for instance, narrated an incident from his early days in the company when his boss insisted that Lijo and his team in the IT support center not respond to clients' emails for at least forty-eight hours, in order to give the impression that they were very busy. After complying with this order for a few weeks, Lijo said that his conscience began to trouble him; it became increasingly clear to him, he said, that "I should be faithful to God who gave me this job." As a result, he violated his boss's orders and began responding to emails as soon as he received them, which led to reprimands from his boss. Others similarly talked about how their conscience, shaped by their religious conditioning, bothered them when it came to other commonly accepted practices at work, such as overcharging the company for work-related expenses.

Such moral conflicts can sometimes force people to choose between faith and work. Ronald, now a finance manager working with a U.K.-based firm in Bangalore, talked about how his faith led him to quit his previous job at a leading bank in India. He explained why he was forced to quit this job:

> There were [a] lot of very challenging things. You had to say lies. . . . I was a manager, and I had to "buddy" with another manager to meet with high-net-worth customers. So when we would meet them, I would say the truth. I would say, "A particular investment would not fetch more than this." But I was not supposed to say that. I was supposed to say that it will fetch—it's a probability. But that probability has never been a

possibility in the last ten years at least [*laughs*]! So you were supposed to quote a probability and not a possibility.

So, coming from a finance background, after doing so much research, I felt what I was doing was an injustice to my career, injustice to what I believed in, injustice to the creator who touched my life. So I felt I needed to quit the job. And I did it, but again I had to go through a lot of persecution at home, because my parents were expecting me to take care of the family and things like that. And this was a highly paid job. But I had to quit that, just for Jesus.

Even the ability to make such difficult choices does not completely immunize professionals from the Mercenary logic. Later in the same interview, for instance, Ronald returned to the Mercenary mode and started talking about how success and failure at work were entirely a function of an individual's attitude: "I think it's your attitude that matters. If you have the right attitude, you can win anyone's heart." I asked if this was true at the banking job that he quit. "No!" he laughed in reply. "That's an organizational flaw. Sometimes the structure is wrong, the values they carry forward are wrong, and it cascades right to the lowest people in the organization."

Many also told me how they experienced moral conflicts when their faith began to influence their relationships with colleagues, superiors, and subordinates. Their accounts suggest a spillover of relational dynamics cultivated in religious settings into the workplace, which then chafe against the dominant Mercenary model at work. For instance, Ashwin in Bangalore talked about the role of faith in his workplace in this manner:

> ASHWIN: I try to be nice to people, though it's not always possible. But somehow that prick of conscience is always there right? Because if you're on a Sunday in a prayer meeting, then for the next five days you can't behave like Satan in office, right? Somewhere, not exactly like angel, but somewhere in between is possible. So faith does play an important role in my work, in dealing with people, how to deal with people.
>
> B. V.: Can you give me a specific example?
>
> ASHWIN: It helps me to give a benefit of doubt to other people. See, people talk behind the back of other people, right? . . . So when people talk behind backs, I try to avoid that. I made a conscious decision seven, eight months back not to do that, not to talk behind the backs of the people in my team.
>
> B. V.: So were you doing this before?

ASHWIN: I was, I was! In fact, I was doing it; I was also involved with it. But every time, there was a prick of conscience. . . . And I decided not to do it, and I decided to bring it on to everyone not to do that thing. Whenever you talk about a person, think that he is there, that's all.

I asked him what led him to eventually make the effort to change what had become a habit. "It was more of an inspiration," he said. "That prick of conscience was always there since I joined the project. But I avoided taking [a] decision." Eventually his conscience began bothering him considerably, and he felt as though God wanted him to stop participating in such gossip.

Dianne from Bangalore talked about how her faith compelled her to break away from the Mercenary norm of sycophancy. During her first several years on the job, she became adept at competing with her colleagues for the notice of superiors. The superficiality and anxieties of everyday interactions—sustaining "teamwork" while trying to ingratiate herself with her bosses and outdo her colleagues at the same time—started to take its toll on her. Dianne admitted,

I [got] into that mindset because everybody around me was doing it. It was basically put under this big terminology as "networking"—you gotta network!. . . . So that, you know, next time you need help, you go to this guy and say, "Hi boss, you know, I need another role," and the guy says, "Yeah, yeah, come, come, I'll help you." . . . What they say is: you can't survive unless you do that. And you start feeling very insecure.

I remember there was a time when I was really working hard, and I knew I had done [work] beyond my set boundaries, but [in my review] . . . I just got a normal "met expectations"—an average rating. And that really hit me, because I said, "Man, I bent backward for my manager and this is what I get!" And there was another guy who, I mean he did work, but he did a lot of this soft-skills thing, you know? He went and lunched with [the boss] and smoked with him and helped him to get a good venue to take the team out, got him discounted rates, blah blah blah. And he got some like fantastic rating. And I was like, "What am I doing here? Why am I working so hard?"

Then I insisted that if anybody wanted work from me, please mark my manager on it. And I marked my manager when I responded, so he knows what am I doing and all. And if I got any appreciation I used to forward it to him like a "fyi, did you know?" type. . . . And this went on for a while till I realized that, you know, I had become a slave to this mentality, and I was not working because I enjoyed the job that I was doing, but I was just getting by one day to the next. And after a while money also didn't make sense to me! And that's where my faith came into the picture.

I actually came to a point where I had to acknowledge that God was my provider. And my job, my boss, and all of it was given to me by him. So tomorrow if I'm going to lose it, it's because God wills it, and tomorrow if he gives me something better is because he wills it. So I just let go. And I stopped doing all of it. And I started doing things like if I could do it, I did it to the best of my ability; if I couldn't do it, I'd say, "I can't do it, do something else about it." I stopped keeping people in loop so that people knew what I was doing. I came to a point where when people did not thank me for stuff, it did not matter. So I got out of the mutual appreciation society sort of a club [*laughs*]. And so I'm much happier now.

But Dianne's eventual "happiness" came at a price. Refusing to ingratiate herself to a manager who was accustomed to sycophancy got her into trouble. She was denied promotions and even requests for leave when her mother was on her deathbed. Eventually, by what she considers a "miracle," she was able to transfer to a different department where she could work with a better manager.

In rare cases, faith commitments confront the heart of the Mercenary logic. Spiritual mentors play an important role here in prompting a reflexivity that allows these professionals to break from the Mercenary impulse to switch jobs for "obvious" reasons, such as for more money or simply because their colleagues were doing so. Donnie in Bangalore, for instance, has stayed on at his firm for ten years, which, he admitted, some of his colleagues find laughable. Yet whenever he thought of "moving jobs" like the rest of his Mercenary colleagues, his spiritual mentor would prompt him to examine his motivations and consider what God wanted:

What is the reason? Why am I doing it? I think faith also plays a role here. . . . First of all, what is the reason for switching? Is money the reason? If money is the reason, then being a Catholic, do I need to give that prominence? Or do I need to look at, what are the other things I get for staying on with the company? So that kind of thinking develops. But otherwise, it's money, and when money becomes the priority and you only live for money, I'd move to another company and get a hike, and whatever additional work I get I'm okay with it. And at the end of the day, how long will I stick on with that company? I mean, I can again move on and keep kind of hopping and get what I want. But I think that if you do take your faith seriously there is a lot more to that decision making.

Cherian in Dubai also talked about religion's role in leading him to stay on in his company. "I am involved in the ministry here," he said, referring to his leadership role in his prayer group. So whenever he is put in a position to have to decide "whether it is the right time to move now," he asked himself, "The ministry is in its particular stage or situation—should I move, should I not?" He decided to forgo several promotions that required extended travel and even a recent job offer where he would have been able to earn three times as much, "for the sake of the ministry." But Cherian did not make such decisions alone. Like many other committed members of his prayer group, he has a mentor who guides him in his decision making and whom he consults regularly. "I share with him what I am going through, the struggles I am going through," he explained. "He prays for me. If there is something that the Lord is speaking through him then he will let me know. Or sometimes he will give me opinions or suggestions." Relying on the guidance of this mentor and of his church group and family leads him to consider factors other than money, status, and mobility in making his decisions. Similarly, Vinay from a different ECC group in Bangalore talked about how religion played a role in preventing him from switching jobs:

> I did have plans of changing my job and such last December and Jan[uary]. I was in a state of confusion, just because I was thinking that the compensation I was getting is not enough for my work that I am doing. Because I gave huge profit to the company actually, as one person. Eighty percent of the profit that my team showed is my—one person's—work. So I was expecting my compensation to be proportionate. But that's not how it happened.

Instead of quitting impulsively as he initially wanted to, he talked to his spiritual director, an older layman who was one of the founders of the prayer group. This mentor in turn asked him, "Are you satisfied with what you are doing?" "Yes, I really enjoy what I am doing," Vinay replied. The mentor then asked, "Is this creating any problem for your commitment to God and your spiritual life?" Vinay replied that his company "was actually giving [him] all the time possible for [his] spiritual commitments." His mentor then counseled him: "Think about it. If you are having this, and you are only looking for money, then years down the lane, God will surely add money. So do not worry about the money." So after that, Vinay started praying, "God, show me signs that you actually want me to stay in the company." A few days later, his manager came up to him and asked how he was doing. Vinay replied that he was not happy, that he finished his eight hours of work in about four hours, and that he did not feel that he was working to his full potential. His manager agreed to give him more challenging work and also initiated Vinay's paperwork for a visa to the United States so that he could have the experience of working in a different sector of the company. "These were all signs for me to hold on to the job and be here. Now I don't have any doubts of staying back in the company. [As long as] my job is very interesting and challenging for me, I will stay."

These cases suggest that spiritual mentors can play an important role in cultivating the kind of reflexivity needed for professionals to break away from Mercenary norms and even challenge its taken-for-granted end of maximizing mobility. However, such cases were rare: most respondents did not have individual spiritual guides or directors and relied more on their ECC groups, where work-related decisions were not discussed. As a result, they remained oriented to the Mercenary norm.

Selective Witnessing: The Bounds of Integration

The mode of witnessing that these professionals engage in involves selectively disclosing or expressing their faith. But they also draw boundaries around what appropriate integration looks like. In spite of the various forms of overlap of religion and work described earlier, many of these professionals claimed they preferred to maintain boundaries between work and religion (and their private lives more generally). For example, Noel in Dubai articulated it in this way:

> I normally maintain a strict boundary between my personal life and my office life. So for example I use my office phone only for office things, nothing else. Even my faith and my Christian—not values but habits—I try to keep a distinction with it. So in the office for example, I wouldn't put a Christian screensaver on my computer, or I don't put Christian messages on my Facebook or on my Skype or Blackberry or whatever like that. So I keep that distinction. I don't know why, but somehow I think that in an office, you are there for working and you work, and once you come out of it, you can do whatever else you want.

Such professionals did not have a clear reason or justification for why such separation was important; they seemed to have been taught to think that it was "somehow" important, but could not articulate why. Nevertheless, they still engaged in forms of witnessing and signaling, such as making the sign of the cross before meals, telling colleagues that they attended church, or other forms of expression they deemed important in order not to compromise their faith.

In some cases, respondents seemed unable to see how religion could play any role at all in the workplace. This was especially the case for software programmers or engineers who worked either mostly on their own or in teams in which they claimed they did not experience any conflict, tensions, or ethical dilemmas. (This would change as soon as some of them moved into management roles.) In those settings, which reflect Stephen Jay Gould's notion of "nonoverlapping magisteria," work and religion are seen as disparate realms with their own internal autonomous governing logics.[33] Such separation is simply taken for granted. It was not that people espousing this view claimed that the spheres should not affect one another; rather, they could not even see how such an influence was even possible. When I asked if their religious beliefs affected their life in the workplace in any way, these respondents—again, many of whom would later talk about subtle modes of witnessing—would look genuinely puzzled. Consider the following replies, for instance:

> No, it doesn't affect it. Work is work and I don't see how my faith
>   could affect anything. (Charmaine, Dubai)
> I don't think my religious beliefs would change the way I work. It has
>   nothing to do with work and, above anything else, it's more of a
>   personal choice. It's not gonna shape the way I would work or
>   the way I would approach work. . . . It doesn't matter at work.
>   (Christopher, Bangalore)
> The way I work has nothing to do with my religious beliefs. I think it
>   has more to do with your personal beliefs, as a person. (Joanne,
>   Bangalore)

Such responses aptly illustrate Peter Berger's claim that religious believers who navigate contexts of secularity need to operate "as if God did not exist" at the level of task performance.[34] The "intrinsic package"—the particular discourses, skills, and habits intrinsic to their workplace tasks—is purely secular and identical to those of their non-Christian colleagues. Religion in this context becomes extrinsic, even if ultimately more important in the sense of giving meaning to their life.[35]

Others referred to structural constraints in corporations as making it impossible to meaningfully integrate faith and work. For instance, in chapter 1 we heard from Colin Perera in Bangalore, who had to cultivate trust and camaraderie among his team throughout the year, but eventually would have to rank them against each other and potentially fire the one at the bottom. "You tell me: how can I be a Christian here?" he complained.

Others, such as Michelle in Bangalore, felt that the demands of professional life sometimes oblige professionals to leave some (but not all) of their religious values at the office door. For instance, in her own work at a global internet corporation, she had to write ads for pornographic websites:

> We do work on porn sites. . . . And I mean it's against my religious views, because we don't believe that we should read this kind of thing. . . . But that didn't stop me. In fact when I went to my interview, my supervisor said, "You might have to work on porn, would you be okay with that?" And I said, "In today's world you have to be, because every second person is working on it." . . . Like, my religion, I have a strong belief, but in this kind of things . . . you can't be close-minded. So that definitely doesn't play a role in my professional life.

Michelle said she did not personally see pornography as a good thing; she claimed that it went against her beliefs about dignity. However, she interpreted her situation so that she saw the logics of work or business—whether for herself or the people creating or featured on those websites—as autonomous and so ought to be separated from religious or personal views.

In addition to drawing boundaries between work and religion as a matter of principle, professionals may separate the realms for pragmatic reasons. The low informal trust in these workplaces encouraged many of the people I talked to draw a firm boundary between work and matters of faith and religion. Again, we turn to Colin Perera in Bangalore, who described an incident in which he had to train a colleague who could potentially replace him:

> There was a guy who joined the project late. Both [of us] were at the same level. He was an associate manager, I was an associate manager, except he just got promoted; he was a recent promotee. So then the senior manager said [to me], "You have to go out and help this guy," and etc., etc. But the corporate world is not a world wherein you can say that things are fair and square, right? Everyone is measured by his or her contributions, right? And this guy was one guy who wanted to show that he was performing better than everyone else. And I started seeing that in him the minute he landed in. So obviously, when it came to kind of helping him out, I was also a bit reserved.

Colin was sure that if he did a good job in training this person, he would lose his own job. So he consciously made it a point to prevent his colleague's success. "I mean, you may be a Catholic, but at the same time you cannot let everybody walk over you, right?" he asked. "I mean then you're gone, right? And I cannot let that happen to me!"

Colin's manager had asked him to help this colleague by giving him some of the best people from his own team. "Now you put yourself in my shoes. And I am telling you, 'Give me the best people which you are managing.' What will you do, right? So I said no," he recounted (although the "no" was likely something he told himself rather than his boss). He felt caught between trying to follow orders and watching his own back. He decided at the end to sabotage his colleague and so gave him his weakest team members. The colleague found out and in turn, launched a grievance with HR, and Colin was eventually reprimanded and denied a promotion. While he regrets his decision now, Colin felt at the time he could not do anything else but protect himself. He said that his faith was "not so strong" that he could do the right thing when it came to many situations in which he found himself in the workplace. But it was not because he tried to integrate his faith and failed; rather, he did not think it possible to even try to do so. I asked Colin if his prayer group provided him any help in making decisions in the workplace. He replied that such topics would be out of place; the group's focus, as he saw it, was on improving one's personal prayer life, not dealing with workplace issues.

People also learn to draw boundaries when their attempts at integration fail. Mona, who worked several administrative jobs in Dubai, said that during her early years at work, she was quite brazen in her attempts to witness her faith in her workplace, in ways that she regrets now. In a previous job, for instance, she would loudly sing Christian hymns or play them on her computer. This was perceived as overbearing by most of her colleagues, who were not Christian. But at the time, she saw it as something she needed to do in order not to compromise her identity; in fact, she saw the responses of her colleagues as "spiritual attacks" that she had to resist. In another job, she would avoid colleagues at lunch time in order to spend time with her devotional practices and escape their "corrupting" influences. Now she realizes that she should have been spending time with them and trying to be a good witness instead. In hindsight, she looks back at her various attempts at failed integration as reflecting a lack of maturity on her part. She has opted for more implicit and subtle forms of witnessing and has drawn a boundary that keeps out some of the more easily misunderstood aspects of her spiritual practice. Thus elements of practice, skill, and discernment are involved as these professionals figure out how to navigate the workplace as a mission field.

Success and Failure at the Mercenary Game

Having examined the various modes in which ECC group members try to navigate the workplace as a mission field, let us now summarize the implications of faith for their working lives. To what extent can the character of the Missionary shape these professionals' choices in workplaces governed by the Mercenary norm? And to what extent does religion contribute to their success in the workplace?

Robert Wuthnow's findings from nationally representative research conducted in the 1990s in the United States suggested that religion's role in the workplace was mostly "a way of making ourselves feel better." Speaking for Americans, he argued that "we have largely abandoned the idea that religion can guide our behavior, except to discourage activities considered blatantly immoral. . . . We look to religion . . . to make us happy about our preferences, not to channel them in specific directions."[36] My findings echo this perspective to some degree in the contexts I studied, but it is not the whole picture.

On the one hand, the beliefs of the Missionary come into play more in *justifying* their career choices than in motivating them from the outset.[37] Their decisions to pursue corporate careers are governed largely by the factors that attract other professionals: money, modernity, status, and professionalism. To them, work is mainly a means to other ends, such as supporting their family. Once these choices have been made, religion shapes their interpretation by recasting the workplace as a mission field. In addition, indicators of worth in the Mercenary ideal—raises, promotions, and even switching jobs to a reputed company—are described in ECC groups as "gifts" and "blessings" from God and are subjects of prayer and testimony. Religion can also justify the mistrust people feel toward colleagues. The idea that one's trust should be put solely in God and not in people is present both in Scripture (see for instance Psalms 118:8 and 146:3) and in popular devotional manuals used in some ECC groups, such as the *Imitation of Christ*. My respondents used these references, along with the belief that a believer ought to be "set apart" from others and should associate primarily with other believers, to justify their wariness toward colleagues. Religion (usually coupled with ethnicity and language) can also become a basis for cliques or alliances that form in the workplace. In these ways, the Missionary can bolster the Mercenary norm.

On the other hand, religion does play a role in "channeling" professionals in particular directions. First, it can guide them toward situations of greater compatibility with their beliefs and values, directing them away from situations in which they would compromise their faith. This channeling includes not only avoiding activities they consider immoral, such as lying or cheating, but also moving to other functions or teams within their firms where they would feel less compromised. Second, and perhaps more commonly, religion can guide professionals into contexts in which they can maintain greater continuity of the skills and dispositions cultivated in religious settings. As Ann Swidler has argued, culture provides people with a "tool kit" or repertoire of skills, dispositions, and habits that shape their "strategies of action."[38] Professionals who belong to ECC groups seem drawn to roles in which they can use (and be rewarded for) practical skills cultivated in their church settings. As I discuss later, when such skills are valued in the workplace, they can provide an alternative path to workplace success than some of the typical means of the Mercenary (e.g., sycophancy and lying).

Such capacities may not simply provide alternative means but can also challenge the aims of the Mercenary. Religion can occasionally enable organizational commitment, in spite of the Mercenary norm, by providing alternative criteria against which people weigh their choices. In such cases, religion can challenge corporate logics of mistrust and apprehension, and instead facilitate a commitment to the organization that is lacking among professionals who prioritize mobility. Through mentors and guides who privilege goals other than careerist ladder climbing, religious communities can enable a reflexivity that enables professionals to break out of taken-for-granted Mercenary goals and to scrutinize their decision-making criteria. Any loyalty to companies mediated in this manner, however, is always subject to reassessment. People like Vinay and Donnie may decide, as a result of religious considerations, not to quit their jobs; yet their narratives suggest that this discernment is always provisional—"for now"—and subject to reevaluation. In such cases, their chief criterion is not whether the position serves to maximize their career mobility, but whether it serves the will of God, especially in relation to their ability to serve their faith communities. It is important to note, however, that invoking this criterion was quite rare in my data, even among professionals who were the most active leaders in their faith communities. Not everybody has a spiritual guide, and most groups do not prompt reflexivity on these questions. There is no institutionalized mechanism in ECC groups to interrogate Mercenary aims.

To what extent do ECC groups contribute to people's success in the workplace? My data cannot adequately address religion's effect on people's actual workplace performance: that would require a larger, quantitative study, as well as data beyond individual self-reports. But the mechanisms I find here reveal a fundamental tension. On the one hand, modes of cultural capital learned in church settings—organizing and presentation skills, for instance—can contribute to workplace success (I write more in chapter 5 about how these skills are cultivated in churches). The therapeutic individualism cultivated in ECC groups can provide professionals with a means of rejuvenation and release from the forms of existential insecurity cultivated in workplaces. Like people who "live for the weekend," Missionaries eagerly look forward to weekly church meetings where they can unload their burdens, spend time with friends, participate in powerful emotional experiences, find moral orientation and a sense of worth, and thus return equipped with a new sense of strength and purpose with which to navigate their work environments.

Yet, religion may impede professional success. ECC groups can pose ethical constraints on members' behaviors in the workplace when they perceive a conflict between their religious identities and workplace demands. At times, people may be able to justify an initially perceived conflict as being trivial (and hence, ultimately inconsequential to their faith) or may eventually recast it as compatible by drawing boundaries on what counts as appropriate integration. But at other times, the religious "challenge" may eat away at them, like the voice of their conscience that grows louder until they eventually give in and change the offensive behavior. Such "invasion" of religion may cost the firm if employees reject typically accepted means of profitability (e.g., when they involve lying to customers) and can lead to detrimental outcomes for the employees in question, including demotion, transfer, or termination. In other cases, the effect may be primarily psychological; for instance, when ECC group members start avoiding colleagues or office events because they do not want to be tempted to gossip or drink or "backslide" in other ways. This avoidance can heighten the ECC member's sense of isolation and alienation. Limits posed by religion may thus not only constrain the corporate machine but also adversely affect the workplace success of believers. Such impediments, however, can also become occasions for the further strengthening of faith, as when their alienation intensifies the need for a religious refuge or for a miracle that would prevent them from being fired.

The ability of ECC groups to cultivate perseverance may enable survival, but does not contribute to the ambitious pursuit of career mobility. Some professionals rejected job offers with higher salaries and positions, because their current work situation allowed them to maintain their commitments to church, which would not be possible with the more financially lucrative offers. Others shared how their religious beliefs and commitments prevented them from moving to certain locations that would offer higher wages (such as Saudi Arabia, where they would be unable to practice their faith). Religion thus provides both assets and liabilities for the corporate professional.

Conclusion

The stories and mechanisms examined in this chapter have a number of implications for how we should understand and study the role of religion in the workplace. First, we can see that the integration of religion into the workplace involves a great deal more than simply applying a set of religious principles and moral values to work settings, which is the focus of much of the practitioner literature on this topic. We need to look beyond religious beliefs and values to examine "nondeclarative" forms of culture, such as skills, habits, and dispositions cultivated in religious settings, which can spill over into the workplace.[39] Different contextual conditions can facilitate the extension of such nondeclarative forms from religious settings into the workplace and yield different workplace outcomes—some of which are conducive to workplace success, while others are not.

It is also important to look beyond people's typical preferences for integration and segmentation, which are the focus in the scholarly literature on religion and work. The same person can participate in multiple forms of overlap or separation of work and religion in a given day. As Berger argues, modern individuals need to become adept at managing religious and secular discourses and definitions of reality, depending on their relevance to the situation at hand.[40] Religious identities and interpretations can be triggered by the context in spite of one's preferences to maintain boundaries. This is evident in people's experiences of a "pricking of conscience" when they experienced workplace norms as conflicting with aspects of their faith. To deliberately conceal their religious identity—even though they might *prefer* to do so—became unbearable. For instance, Gemima in Dubai told me how she was extremely uncomfortable bringing up religion with her "hardcore atheist" colleagues; yet, despite her desire to avoid conflict, she felt "compelled" not to be "ashamed" of her religious commitments and endured "awkward" situations when she felt she had to correct colleagues who insulted her beliefs. Similarly, when people start to perceive routine workplace practices as violating key elements of their religious identity, they may even be led to quit their jobs, as we saw in Roland's case. My interviews suggest that this process is gradual: they initially participated in the practice, following their workplace norms; it was simply "part of the game" entailed by their role. Yet, over time, they increasingly felt unable to bear the tension created by the demands of faith and felt forced either to change their behaviors or remove themselves from these situations, at a personal cost they would have preferred not to bear.

The boundary work entailed in attempts at integration also requires skill and practice.[41] It can be strengthened by repeated success and weakened by experiences of failure. As various scholars have pointed out, the interpretation and experience of one's workplace context as either friendly or hostile to expressions of faith play an important role in determining what aspects are integrated.[42] We also need to consider that factors beyond the workplace play a significant role here. In my cases, the political restrictions in Dubai and the cultural restrictions in BJP-dominated India certainly impose limitations on Christians who may aspire to fuller forms of integration. I discuss these macrolevel factors in more detail in chapter 5.

But it is not just that the workplace limits integration; it is also that the kind of religion one adheres to affects the scope of what counts as integration. For ECC group members, integration means symbolic witnessing: putting up Bible-verse screensavers, wearing subtle crosses, making the sign of the cross before meals, disclosing that one is part of a church group, and avoiding certain kinds of behavior (e.g., cheating, lying, and gossiping). Other possible modes of integrating Christianity—understanding work as a vocation, as an occasion of creative co-creation, as a pursuit of excellence or craftsmanship, as something intrinsically valuable, or as a means of cultivating solidarity, contributing to justice, and serving the common good—are rendered out of scope in this context. Resources for such interpretation, which are available and deployed in other contexts of Catholicism, have not been made accessible to these professionals in their ECC groups or parishes. Again, sociopolitical factors in these cities, along with the minority position of Christianity, play a role in shaping individualist sensibilities here: other social conditions would activate other resources, yielding different outcomes.

Since the intentional pursuit of integration is a function of what one is habitually attuned to, it comes with blind spots. ECC groups have no systematic theology of work, and their groups are not seen as spaces for honest deliberation about workplace dilemmas. As a result, members' styles of witnessing reflect themes that stand out to them in their respective groups. The wide range of possibilities for witnessing according to their criteria allows them to check the box and feel they have done their job of integrating faith at work. This can lead to a form of "moral licensing," a well-documented phenomenon in which committing an act we consider morally praiseworthy boosts our self-image, to the point that we grant ourselves license to be morally lax in other areas.[43] Many professionals who gave me examples of witnessing as evidence of their ability to integrate faith and work also admitted to treating subordinates poorly or neglecting their families. They overlooked structural consequences of their working environments, in which they were often expected to work twelve- to fourteen-hour days. Clergy and counselors I talked to in both cities complained that in families where both spouses worked corporate jobs, infidelity and divorce were increasingly common, even among Catholics; also common were adverse effects on children, such as feelings of neglect and behavioral problems.

Thus far we have examined the relationship between the characters of the Mercenary and the Missionary in the workplace. But professionals' lives, as well as the reach of these representative characters, extend beyond these realms. To better understand the relationship between capitalism and Catholicism in Bangalore and Dubai, we need to look outside workplaces and churches to examine the lifestyles of Catholic professionals.

FINDING ESCAPE VELOCITY

Just as the acquisition of money plays a prominent role in the Mercenary professional's occupational choices, the *use* of money is a central component of their lifestyles. But how do these professionals spend their money and evaluate its use? And to what extent does religion shape their lifestyle choices, habits, and aspirations?

The notion of lifestyle does not simply indicate a person's way of life at a particular point in time; rather, as Roland Benedikter notes, it also encompasses how, over time, "a 'good life' is conceived on the basis of changing convictions, values and imaginations in a given context, and how it is projected as a perspective into the future."[1] One's use of money is greatly shaped by one's vision of a good life. And the good life, in contexts of rapid economic development, is often tied to increasing one's material standard of living. This linkage is a lingering trait of the recent past in which making ends meet was a constant struggle. Of course, participating in many of the activities that members of the new middle classes consider key to a good life—buying a comfortable home, spending time with family, being able to travel, and even making charitable contributions—requires a certain level of financial resources. These ideals of the good life are not idiosyncratic, but are shaped by commonly shared narrative scripts of what counts as a worthwhile life in these contexts. In this chapter, I show how once again—even in the realm of lifestyles—narrative scripts, mimetic processes, and habituation generate self-sustaining routines that are often difficult to overcome.

In rapidly developing cities like Bangalore and Dubai, consumerism becomes central to the identity of the new middle classes, such that those with habits of thrift and frugality see themselves as a minority. Such consumerism, as many have argued, has a corrosive influence on social institutions and civic life. Religion is hardly immune to these negative impacts. Zygmunt Bauman argues that consumerist pleasures "substitute for both the uplifting solidarity of work-mates and the glowing warmth of caring-for-and-being-cared-by the near and dear inside the family home and its immediate neighborhood."[2] Others point to the commodification of religion and its co-optation by consumerism.[3] Many insist on the fundamental irreconcilability of consumerism with Christianity in particular.[4] Burt Fulmer, for instance, argues that the call of a Christian is to "a life of poverty, suffering, and martyrdom" in self-service to God and neighbor, whereas the lifestyles promoted by consumer advertising "promise nothing but comfort, pleasure, and self-glorification."[5] Vincent Miller contends that "when the desire for God is assimilated to the workings of consumer desire, . . . its demand for something more than the status quo is harnessed into service of a system that provides only more of the same."[6] Popes John Paul II and Francis have, on numerous occasions, denounced consumerism.[7] What happens then to Christianity in consumer societies? Can religious communities offer adherents the possibility of resisting and perhaps even exiting consumer lifestyles? Or are they co-opted by consumerism?

In examining the lives of Catholic professionals in Bangalore and Dubai, this chapter shows that the church has little *direct* influence on professionals' lifestyles in these contexts. Indeed its silence inadvertently enables consumerism even among those professing Missionary ideals. Most of the Catholic professionals I interviewed in Bangalore and Dubai, such as Menezes from chapter 1, instantiate the dominant middle-class pattern that sociologist Leslie Sklair calls the "culture-ideology of consumerism." Their lifestyle habits, choices, and aspirations, couched in terms of consuming material goods and experiences that signal upward mobility, reflect the "belief that human worth is best ensured and happiness is best achieved in terms of our consumption and possessions."[8] At the same time, they remain firmly committed to their churches and religious groups. Religion does not have much direct influence on their use of money; money, in turn, does not have much effect on their religious commitment. However, even though religion may not be in the driver's seat when it comes to shaping Catholic professionals' use of money, there are conditions under which its influence becomes more prominent. This chapter identifies such conditions and explains why they are so difficult to obtain.

Consumerism and the New Middle Classes

Consumerism, as historian Peter Stearns defines it, "describes a society in which many people formulate their goals in life partly through acquiring goods that they clearly do not need for subsistence or for traditional display. They become enmeshed in the process of acquisition—shopping—and take some of their identity from a procession of new items that they buy and exhibit."[9] It is not a phenomenon unique to modernity. Historical research shows, for instance, that well-developed consumer outlets and interests in various urban centers in Asia pre-date the industrial revolution. What is new is "full-blown consumerism, in terms of intensity, commitment to novelty, and application to numerous social groups": it is a phenomenon primarily of the past three centuries.[10]

As a result of globalization, consumerism, "especially of consumer and luxury goods," has become a highly visible phenomenon around the world and has become central to the self-definition of the "new middle classes."[11] Like transnational capitalism and professionalism, consumerism has become a driver of global convergence, with scholars predicting "increasing similarities not only in social structures and socio-economic performance, but also in lifestyles, which will become more consumerist wherever poverty is diminished and mass wealth becomes a reality."[12] Contemporary urban centers in these new economies, such as Bangalore and Dubai, can readily be characterized as consumer societies, widely endorsing a "distinctive cultural standard associated with a hegemonic lifestyle of a liberalizing middle-class."[13] In such contexts of rapid economic development, as sociologist Carol Upadhya observes, people come to "define their new social and economic status in terms of their ability and willingness to consume more than their parents could."[14] These new forms of consumerism—like new forms of work in global corporations—cannot adequately be understood as passive colonization by neo-imperialist forces. Rather, consumerism offers a vision that is attractive to its pursuers: an identity quest that is, in Bauman's analysis, "a liberation from the inertia of traditional ways, from immutable authorities, from preordained routines and unquestionable truths."[15] Further, it is not simply seen as a form of individualistic or hedonistic liberation, but is claimed as a way of fulfilling one's responsibility to provide for one's family and progeny.[16]

Consumer societies, however, are not merely clusters of individuals aspiring to betterment. Rather, they constitute emergent realities that, as sociologist John Meyer might say, provide a new model of "actorhood" in the form of the consumer, which becomes a distinctive mode of selfhood.[17] As a result, Bauman notes, "consumerist performance [becomes] the paramount stratifying factor and the principal criterion of inclusion and exclusion," which also governs "the distribution of social esteem and stigma, and shares in public attention."[18] Leslie Sklair similarly identifies consumerism as a "culture-ideology," which denotes "the institutionalization of consumerism through the commodification of culture." This institutionalization refers to cultural norms that are taken for granted. Their effect "is to increase the range of consumption expectations and aspirations without necessarily ensuring the income to buy," and they contain an implicit promise of "a better life for everyone."[19] Consumerism thus comprises both ideology and habitual practices, which reinforce one another.[20]

My research demonstrates the dominant pattern of pervasive middle-class consumerism that other studies in such contexts have documented. It was pervasive across respondents: those who were religiously disengaged expressed similar lifestyle ideals and practices to those who were highly involved in church groups. Girish and Nikhila, a nonreligious couple in Bangalore, exemplify this theme.

Consumerism: The Dominant Pattern

I first met Girish and Nikhila while conducting research on call centers in Bangalore in 2007 and interviewed them several times during my many visits to the city. It was always easy to find them. During the day they regularly hung out at the Coffee Day café on MG Road, a branch of an Indian coffee chain with a large outdoor space on one of the busiest streets in the heart of the city; in the evenings, they could be found at the Hard Rock Café down the street. When I first interviewed them, they both worked at call centers, having already had several such jobs and making incrementally higher salaries with each move. Eventually they made their way out of the sector altogether. The last time I met them, in mid-2012, both their fortunes had soared, contrary to the predictions of many about how call center employees without college degrees were doomed to stagnancy. Both now worked in the event-management sector and claimed to love their jobs for the autonomy, creativity, challenge, and remuneration they provided. In 2012 Girish headed the India office of a global event management firm, and Nikhila was a senior analyst at a competitor. They had changed little over the years; they were still full of laughter, aggressively confident in demeanor, cynical about Indian politics—and heavy spenders. Buying several packs of cigarettes and pints of alcohol a week continued to devour a large proportion of their salaries, thanks to India's heavy taxes on these goods.

For Girish and Nikhila, the fat paycheck is what initially made call center work worthwhile, despite its numerous pitfalls and their persistent distaste for these jobs. Nikhila talked about how the money in these jobs was a source of "newfound independence" from her parents: "I'm earning my own money and you don't get to ask me what I'm doing with it. So I do with it whatever I want; I'm shopping, I'm having more cups of coffee than I normally would, I'm going for more movies," and so on.[21] Girish echoed similar sentiments. "When I was in college I used to get pocket money, and there was a limit for everything," he recalled. "But once I started working, like we said, the lifestyle changes, and you start drinking and getting bills of 3–4 grand in one weekend." And as you stay on in the industry, "you step up in your lifestyle" with every promotion and salary hike, from beer to Chivas Regal, from "a cheap pair of pants at Pepe Jeans" to Levi's, with a view that "I can afford it, so I'll get it." The sorry consequence of all this is that "there's no way you can save up money!" After they had been working for more than four years in call centers, Nikhila lamented, "We've not saved a buck till date! And it's like we've earned lakhs and lakhs of rupees—I'm talking about lakhs, not thousands, I'm talking about *lakhs*—there's not a single rupee I've saved, till date! Not even a single rupee!" After they left the call centers for higher-paying jobs, their spending increased in proportion to their earnings, continuing to constrain their ability to save for the future.

FAST MONEY

A consistent theme among the Mercenary professionals I spoke to, regardless of their religious tradition or degree of involvement in it, was that their relatively high earnings in comparison to others around them prompted a greater propensity to spend impulsively. As many of sociologist Reena Patel's respondents in Indian call centers described it, it was "fast money."[22] The high starting salaries, often far exceeding their parents' income and the lifestyles they were used to, gave many of them a new and unexpected sense of power and freedom. Once they started working, and especially once they started getting used to a new lifestyle with new modes of regular consumption, it was hard to put the brakes on spending.

Many Filipinos I talked to in Dubai expressed similar sentiments about being seduced by the greater capacity for consumption that Dubai offered them. Maryann, a sales manager in Dubai, noted that back in the Philippines, "you're quite conscious on how to spend. But here, because you have all the money, and here your salary is way, way better than what you were earning in the Philippines, right? So you're like blinded by it, so to speak." Many Filipinos who move to Dubai see the new higher income level as an occasion to indulge. Some expressed that such spending was a form of "therapy," given the difficult and often unjust situations that many of them faced in their workplaces. Maryann explained,

> It's a common problem, especially for us—I can speak for our nationality, for our countrymen—because we tend to be blinded. Once we have the money, we want to spend-spend-spend; we want to pamper-pamper ourselves. Because in the Philippines we cannot do that. You don't have

that leverage to do spending that much; you have your family to deal with. But here, once you send that portion of your money [i.e., remittances], then all your money will be yours. But then, the more you spend, the more—you want to have more of everything. After spending all your money, you will get in a rut, and even go to jail! And people will sometimes do things you cannot believe to avoid that.[23]

This inclination to spend lavishly seems somewhat less pronounced among Indians who come to Dubai. The reason for this—at least, the impression I gained in speaking to counselors and financial planners—is that the Indians who move to Dubai tend to be comparatively older and are accustomed to a culture of austerity and thrift, which imposes social stigma against self-indulgence. But an additional contributing factor neglected in these accounts is that the period of accelerating migration of Filipinos to Dubai coincided with the increasingly widespread access to credit cards.[24] Indians, in contrast, already had long-established communities in Dubai, within which frugality was more common, and so were better able to resist the lure of easy credit.

Among corporate professionals, however, frugality is not the norm even among Indians. For instance, Jason Edwards, a talented second-generation Indian expat in Dubai, who at the age of thirty became managing director of a multinational advertising firm, expressed a commonly voiced desire to maintain a "great lifestyle" as long as one could afford it:

> I'm a fan of "work hard, earn well, play hard, party hard, spend hard." . . . And even then, it's all about value. If I see something, if I see its value, I'll pick it up. Doesn't matter whether I need it or not. On an average, if you look at my wardrobe, you'll find six–seven brand new shirts, not opened, or four–five ties, not opened also. It's just because I'd have gone shopping wanting a blue shirt, and saw a white shirt that's nice, on a sale, or a deal or something, [and] just pick it up. That's my saving pattern I guess.

Jason was not exaggerating about his wardrobe. Certainly he has not put to regular use many of the twenty or so pairs of Nike sneakers I saw lined up in his apartment. Jason was especially insistent that money earned through one's hard work deserves to be spent well and in ways that are adequately self-expressive. "If you work hard for money, take care of it, but also spend it hard," he counseled. He gave me an example:

> So I felt like a couple of years back I needed to have a watch that said something about me. I found the watch—bam! The guy was selling it for whatever. I went and badgered him for four days continuously, and

he gave it to me for 45 percent discount. I'm still wearing the watch, so I'm happy about it.

Such forms of consumption simultaneously entail self-expression, class-based distinction, and conceptions of value-for-money that I found pervasive among second-generation Indian expats in Dubai. Unlike some other respondents who see some of their spending as frivolous and impulsive, for Jason, spending money on quality goods was a well-earned right, reflecting the hard work that he put into earning that money. He talked about it in universalistic terms: "Whether it's Sheikh Mohammed or myself or the laborer in Sheikh Zayed Road—each and every one of us has a degree of difficulty, we're working hard. We're not sitting and money is just rolling in. It's work! You're working hard for your money. Maximize your dollar!"

But consumerism among these professionals is not always self-expressive or self-centered. Some professionals justified their splurging as a sign of commitment to their families: an effort to ensure that their children and families will not go without things they were deprived of in their own childhoods.

MONEY AND FAMILY LIFE

Colin Perera in Bangalore talked about how he was brought up "in an environment where we did not have all the luxuries in life." The financial struggles experienced by his brothers and him very much shaped their "outlook to life." He remembers them growing up with a persistent sense of deprivation: "things could not be got so easily," and they "had to struggle through school, struggle through college." By the time they graduated, they "were rearing to get on to a good job, because we felt we did not get what we wanted at that age." Their main priority was to start earning money as quickly and as much as possible: "I wanted to get things that I did not have, like a vehicle for myself, getting some fancy clothes and those kind of things."

The memories of his past deprivations are still fresh to Colin and shape his own child-rearing practices, particularly his generosity toward his children: "I don't want them to go through what I went through, right?" He continued,

> We did not have that much in terms of toys or those kinds of things which kids now would have. So I used to look at my neighbor, the guy who used to study in my same school, and he used to have things which I used to desire for. Things like a Lego set, right? I did not have that, so I had to go to his place and play. We did not have a television at least for a long, long time. We grew up without it. So I used to go to his house and watch television. We did not have access to cable or access to a VCD [Video Compact Disc] or something like that, so I had to go to his house

and watch it. So most of the time I spent there at his place, and so that's how I grew up.

This widely shared and expressed belief that one needs to provide sufficiently for family members so that they do not experience deprivation explains why the heavy spending that characterizes professionals' lifestyles cannot always be seen as simply self-centered or hedonistic.

Some professionals I talked to not only wanted to prevent their children from experiencing something similar to their own past deprivations but also wanted to make it up to them for not being able to spend enough time with them; they claimed they felt guilty denying their children consumer goods they wanted. As Arlie Hochschild notes, employees are thus caught in a vicious cycle, working longer hours so they can afford to buy more things and then, to appease their guilt for being away from their family, needing to buy even more things, thus "materializ[ing] love."[25] Schoolteachers and counselors I spoke to in Dubai and Bangalore identified this substitution of parental time with money and gifts as one of the leading complaints among troubled children. "These kids are just brought up by their nannies," said one family counselor I spoke to in Dubai who worked with expat families.[26] "Their parents have no time for them, because they both need to work full-time jobs to maintain their residence visas in Dubai. And so they feel they have to make up for it by buying their children whatever they want." Vinod Prabhu in Bangalore, who quit his corporate job to become a "full-timer" for the church, working as a counselor and retreat director, made a similar observation:

> You have parents who are working multiple jobs sometimes. Usually both parents are working. And if they're working in the I.T. sector, you know work times—it's not a 9 to 5 job. So the mom is as busy as the father. And they have nannies, they have *ayahs* to take care of the kids. Through my counseling sessions, we found the kids telling us that our parents are replacing their time with things. So, gadgets or gizmos or, you know, most of them [i.e., parents] say, "Just go out somewhere, here's some money, just have some fun." . . . Because dad sometimes works from home, most of them. I have seen parents who come and say sometimes, "I have no time—for myself, forget about family!" [*laughs*]. It's stupid actually to say that. Because it's you who are actually putting yourself in that position. Because the job doesn't own you—you own the job, no? And if you don't realize that, then you are the slave of something that actually you just want to be. . . . But you can't help it. The kind of environment we are in, I don't think that parents want to choose anything else, no? So difficult!

In addition to spending on one's immediate family, first-generation migrants supporting families in other towns and cities keenly feel the expectation to spend money on friends and extended family through gifts and remittances. Grace Princesa, the Philippine ambassador to the UAE, identified this as a common problem: "The family back home often thinks the migrant is earning a lot and raises its expectations. . . . The poor migrant goes deeper into debt just to answer. It's a vicious cycle."[27] Terence, a Filipino manager in Dubai, explained his inability to save during his initial years in Dubai this way: "I am generous. So I wasn't able to save money. Because my friends, classmates, relatives will call and ask for money."

Spending a large amount of money in general seems unavoidable for day-to-day survival in rapidly developing cities such as Bangalore and Dubai, where costs of living are on a steady rise, quickly surpassing the ability of most residents to manage even basic expenses such as rent. In addition to housing, maintaining a family in general is expensive. In Dubai and other Gulf cities, even qualifying for a family visa requires a fairly high salary. Foreign residents are denied access to public school, which requires them to pay for expensive private schooling, another hefty financial requirement. Government regulations require proof that one's residence has a certain number of rooms and is not shared with nonfamily members. This adds to the difficulties of lower-income families in Dubai. As a result, many of those who work in lower-wage positions—not only cab drivers or housemaids but even those in lower-tier white-collar jobs—leave their families behind in their home countries. Consider how Francis, a Nigerian manager working for a global shipping firm, explained the financial difficulties faced by members of his church group:

> The main challenge we face is the high cost of living in Dubai, especially in terms of accommodation. For example, a lot of folks are married. Some are here with their family; some are not here with their family. The reason they are not with their family is not that they cannot afford their family to come. It is not just paying for the house or getting a visa for the family, but at the same time they have to make sure they live comfortable. So when you feel you cannot be able to afford it—maybe the salary cannot be able to solve all those problems—you need to allow them to stay back home. Normally we see them every six months.

SHOPPING

Shopping is a central feature of consumer lifestyles. Many professionals I talked to enjoyed shopping as an activity and could not pass up a sale. Carol, for instance, laughed about how her friends knew that an easy place to find her would be at a discount sale at major retailers. Shopping for brand-name clothing and high-tech goods was a common pastime for Conrad, a software engineer in Bangalore. "I've been really bad at managing my finances so far," he admitted when I asked about his use of money. "Currently I just buy by impulse. Like, if I want something, I just go get it. I think I have a lot of reading up to do on managing finance" [*laughs*].

Many admitted that they regularly indulged in such impulsive spending. I got to witness this behavior on several occasions. One such instance occurred when I visited Natalie, a second-generation Indian expat in Dubai and HR manager at a global technology firm, who is also one of the leaders of a prayer group. That evening, she had returned home with her sister, giddily excited, with a large box. She explained that she had just driven to the other end of the city and back because she heard about a sale at a major department store. The box contained an assortment of items, including china, perfumes, toys, and various trinkets. Natalie expressed her incredulity at how cheap some of these items were; in response, her sister rolled her eyes. As Natalie pulled the items out and placed them onto the table one by one, her sister asked her what she was planning to do with them, since she obviously did not need them. Natalie agreed and replied distractedly that she might use them as gifts; she would figure it out later. Her priority at the moment was to sort through them and get them out of the way before her husband returned home.

Others, such as Charmaine, a former finance professional who was unemployed at the time of our interview, noted explicitly that the process of shopping mattered more than the purchases themselves. Several times a week, she would take her toddler window-shopping in some of Dubai's massive shopping malls. In Dubai and other Gulf cities, the intolerable weather makes large, air-conditioned shopping malls an ideal venue in which to kill time. While I was interviewing Melanie, a French expat at a café at the Dubai Mall, her mother-in-law was getting her exercise by walking around the six million square feet of internal space, which would have been impossible in anything but a mall in the 40-degree Celsius heat.

Cities such as Bangalore and Dubai have seen a proliferation of new, super-sized shopping malls. Such commercial spaces house not only retail outlets but also restaurants, food stalls, children's activities, and various forms of spectacle. They are not merely places to buy things, but serve as something like piazzas—common spaces in which people can gather and meet—and thus cultivate what anthropologist Neha Vora calls "consumer citizenship."[28] They thus become an almost unavoidable aspect of a middle-class lifestyle. In both Dubai and Bangalore, however, these spaces are also restricted, policed by guards and security staff, granting access only to select populations who are deemed fit to belong there (i.e., those with the assumed spending power).

FIGURE 4.1.   A shopping mall in Dubai. Photo by Mika Aarensberg.

SAVING AND INVESTING

In spite of professionals' consumer lifestyles and spending habits, many of them make some effort to save for the future. For instance, despite Jason's injunctions to "spend hard," he also claimed that saving and investing had become increasingly important to him, especially once it started to dawn on him that he was being irresponsible:

> I worked for two–three years, I had nothing to show; I had nothing in the bank! I didn't have a new car, I hadn't gone on any holidays, I wasn't paying for rent, I wasn't paying for food; I was living with my parents. What was I doing with all that money? So that, to me, was like a wake-up call, to say hey, you need to have a backup plan. . . . So I started saving. I made sure that I wasn't cheap, but if I didn't need to spend on something, I wouldn't. Simple as that.

His high salary allowed him to hire a personal financial planner to manage his money for him, so that he would not need to worry about saving and investing. His own habitual pattern, however, continued to lean toward impulsive spending.

Only a handful of my respondents were committed to being thrifty and saw themselves as different from their colleagues in this respect. For instance, Noel, the management consultant whom we met in chapter 3, talked about how one of the main reasons he decided to come to Dubai was "to get some savings":

When I came here, I set an extremely high savings rate for myself. Ridiculously high. And actually I achieved it in the first year. And then I thought, if I can do it then—and I've continued to maintain it till now. For me I don't get any joy by buying something nice or spending money, but rather by saving it.

Noel saw his approach, which was cultivated early on by his parents, as highly unusual in comparison to his peers, especially so because his parents did not depend on his financial support. He saw himself as going against the current. Most people around him, he claimed, were not careful with their money, and he looked disparagingly on the tendency of his fellow consultants to "live it up." Noel also insisted that his sense of thrift was purely a result of his family upbringing:

For me, I think almost 100 percent of my financial discipline is from my parents; my faith has nothing to do with it. My parents were extremely conservative, and for quite a part of my childhood, I was brought up on less than a dollar a day. So I'm very sensitive to money matters and how it should be managed and all of that.

"Faith has nothing to do with it," he insisted. "In fact, the money-spending principle comes above faith in some matters for me. So if somebody is strong in faith and doesn't know how to spend his money, I keep away from him as well." Similarly, Dianne in Bangalore, who grew up in the Gulf before returning to India for college, saw her sense of thrift as unusual in comparison to her work colleagues, and she attributed it to her parents' influence:

I grew up in a family where they taught us the value of money. Even if we had extra money, we wouldn't give in to our whims and fancies. You'd get it only if you need it, but not if you only want it, or "somebody else has it," blah blah blah. So that was pretty frustrating, because we knew we weren't, like, really destitute, and we didn't really get why we couldn't have what everybody else had. But I think it taught us . . . the value of money. It's something that you need to give its due respect, but not make it a god. So if you ask how I manage my finances, I'd probably say I'm a conservative person. I tend to save more than I spend, and I don't spend unless I really need something. I rarely come to a state where I go into a shop and really like something and just pick it up on an impulse. Even if it's a toothbrush! . . . So I've learned self-restraint.

Not everyone who grew up in thrifty families ended up embracing practices of frugality. Indeed for some, their impulsive spending seemed to be a reaction to having begrudgingly endured a thrifty upbringing. For instance, Preethi, a PR executive in Dubai, claimed that it was her frustration with her parents' miserly attitude that led her to become carefree with her money once she started earning it. Several others told me that their parents did not teach them anything at all about financial matters, and they felt they had to figure it out by themselves. "I think nowadays guys like me are pretty much left on their own to do what they want to do," said Conrad. "Parents don't really ask you to do anything. My dad did ask to help with getting an apartment, like an investment. But other than that, he didn't really tell me anything about my financial life."

A handful of my respondents, usually those in more senior management positions or in the financial sector, regularly invested their income, especially in real estate. Some gained financial leverage from their parents. Comparing investments, particularly in real estate, seemed to be a common mode of status signaling in many workplaces. Many of those who invested in property in Dubai before the 2008 financial crisis expressed regret for doing so. Sameer, a senior manager at a global security firm based in Dubai, lost more than a million dirhams that he and his father had invested in a new building, when its construction came to a sudden halt in 2010 and the developers fled the country. While the majority of professionals I spoke to did not earn enough to make property investments in Dubai, many Indians and Filipinos managed to buy, or at least contribute significantly toward the buying of, property in their home countries.

All in all, most professionals I talked to, even those who saved and invested some of their money, admitted that they were not as fiscally responsible as they would like to be. On the one hand, many, like Jason and Alonso, believed that one should not be "cheap" and that people should be free to spend their hard-earned money however they pleased. On the other hand, most of them were also reluctant to wholeheartedly justify their own spending as laudable. Most professionals I talked to in both cities, regardless of religious affiliation or involvement, exhibited some regret about their "immature" spending habits. Credit card debt was an important source of such regret.

DEBT

What enabled Girish and Nikhila in Bangalore to "have a lifestyle"—one comparable to that of older professionals who frequented trendy restaurants, bars, retail outlets, and so on—while working in their very first jobs out of high school was access to credit cards. "I was nineteen when I got two credit cards," said Nikhila. For Girish and her, possessing those cards provided unprecedented access to power. Their sentiments echo that of a Filipina nurse in Dubai who was imprisoned for defaulting on credit card debt, when she described to a reporter her first experience of having access to a credit card: "It's a feeling of excitement, power—greatness even."[29] As Nikhila elaborated,

And you go, "Oh, I'm earning," so, swipe-swipe-swipe, and then you go, "Aaah, I'm in debt!" And then you need to work more to be able to pay off your debt. And trust me, they [i.e., other call centers] call you and go like, "Are you working for a call center?" And you get a pre-approved card!

Within their first year of working in call centers for American firms, both of them found themselves mired in credit card debt. They had to shelve their initial plans of completing their college education and to keep working to clear up new debts. As a result, said Girish, "you get trapped in call centers." It was not long before he had collectors knocking on his door: "I was really screwed over 'cause I had two credit cards which I'd just swiped it out, hadn't paid for it. So finally, these guys [i.e., debt collectors] came home. And I somehow managed with that."

According to financial analysts I spoke to in Bangalore, delinquent credit card debts among young professionals became so sizable a problem that banks stopped being so lenient with this demographic, at least when it came to issuing credit cards. I was told, however, that it remains relatively easy to acquire a personal loan to purchase a vehicle or a home. In Dubai, easy access to credit was an attractive feature of life in the years immediately preceding the recession. By the time the recession hit, there were four million credit cards in operation, a five-fold increase from 2003.[30] Just as in Bangalore, credit card salespeople in Dubai before the crisis would target populations with new money, such as Filipina nurses, accosting them outside hospitals or even after crowded masses at the Catholic Church. By the end of 2008, many banks drastically lowered their customers' credit card spending limits, at times by as much as 80 percent.[31] Many residents, however, did not realize until it was too late that defaulting on debts— indeed, even a single bounced check—could result in imprisonment.[32] Many Western expatriates with large debts who could afford to flee the country early in the recession did so, and the sight of their abandoned luxury cars gathering dust gained much global media attention.[33] Many others, however, found themselves in prison, even those who were ignorant of the law and those who attempted to leave after losing their jobs. Still others, including several prominent wealthy foreign developers who had made substantial earnings in real estate, were taken by surprise when their checks bounced and were sentenced to long prison terms, with a single bounced check garnering up to a three-year sentence. One British developer, Peter Margetts, was given a twenty-year sentence.[34] During the crisis, an estimated 20 percent of Dubai's prison inmates were serving sentences for bounced checks.[35]

Despite widely circulating horror stories recounted in newspapers of children and families deprived of their earning members who were in prison, or tales of personal encounters during charitable prison visits with debt-prisoners, many professionals I talked to in Dubai did not seem afraid of debt. For some such as Carol, accruing debt was essential in enabling them to move to Dubai in the first place. For others like Maryann, debt enabled her to help to her family:

> I took loans from the bank; I'm still paying for it. I'll be finishing hopefully by next year. But that money, I know, was a good thing. It went—I paid for my family for a house, for relatives who got sick, you know these emergency things that you have no control over? I was there for all of it basically.

Of course, the beneficial usage of borrowed money does not prevent people from getting into trouble with the law. Others I talked to, like Alonso, claimed to have learned from their mistakes. "I don't use credit cards. I used to have credit cards and I kind of misused it," he confessed. "Because it is really tempting if you have the card. Buy small things, 100 dirhams, 100 dirhams, and it accumulates. At the end of the month, it's too much." Eventually, he said, "after paying it, I cut it and I didn't get any card after." But not everyone I talked to was so fortunate. For one Filipino couple, whose story I recount later in the chapter, the pursuit of the "Dubai dream" turned into a nightmare—until it gained them the "escape velocity" to break free from the centripetal force of consumerism. But what makes consumerism so powerful, and how is it sustained?

Sustaining Consumerism

These examples suggest that consumer lifestyles are in part supported by widely shared narrative scripts about what constitutes a good lifestyle. Such scripts are building blocks of people's narratives and orient their behavior in particular realms. They structure people's internal conversations and guide their trajectories in specifying the kind of person one should or should not become. Through injunctions, imperatives, and orientations for reflexivity, these scripts, which are echoed by peers, relatives, and advertising media, shape people's lifestyle pursuits. Some of the scripts that emerged in my research, either explicitly voiced by respondents or implicitly suggested in their statements, were as follows:

> "It's essential to have a good lifestyle."
> "Why settle for less?"
> "I need a watch and car that say something about myself."
> "You shouldn't be cheap."
> "Where you eat makes a statement about who you are."

"I'm a senior manager now; I can't afford to be seen with that crowd."

"Our kids deserve only the very best."

"Now that we have money, we pamper ourselves."

"If you can afford it, buy it!"

Not every middle-class professional aspires to such ideals, but even those who resist them—those who follow traditional injunctions toward thrift—usually see themselves as deviations from the norm. The narrative scripts of consumerism imply a trajectory of purchasing goods that promise greater luxury and comfort and signal higher status. Pursuing this trajectory requires ever more disposable income and purchasing power. "Worth" here is signaled not only by the objects possessed but also by the kinds of experiences one has access to (e.g., shopping in high-end malls; frequenting trendy bars, clubs, salons, and spas; and vacationing in luxury resorts). This pursuit is facilitated by constant comparisons to colleagues, family members, and even acquaintances from the past; for instance, without my prompting, respondents would mention that they are doing "better" (materially) than their old schoolmates or work colleagues. These narrative scripts are reinforced by people, such as peers, and discourses like advertising that targets members of the new middle classes, which always surround the professionals. Workplaces and even church groups become channels for transmitting and cultivating consumerist criteria of worth.

Central to the shared ideal of the good lifestyle, despite the variation in how people conceive and express it, are the high status and quality of material goods and experiences, the acquisition of which requires disposable income. Mercenary professionals, while pursuing career mobility, reflect status changes by purchasing higher-end goods that promise greater luxury and comfort and signal higher status. Yet "moving up" in one's lifestyle means not only purchasing higher-status objects but also moving to higher-status neighborhoods.

Consumerism cannot be explained as simply reflecting inherent desires of human nature or the inherent desirability of objects. Rather, it is sustained by implicit interactional processes, which can be explained by René Girard's theory of mimetic desire. In this view, our propensity to consume stems from our tendency to imitate the desires of a "model." "Once their natural needs are satisfied, humans desire intensely, but they don't know exactly what they desire, for no instinct guides them," he argues. "The essence of desire is to have no essential goal. Truly to desire, we must have recourse to people about us; we have to borrow their desires."[36] As Burt Fulmer explains, much of what counts as consumerism "promotes the purchasing of goods not by appealing to any desire inherent to the consumer or any desirability inherent to the product but rather by appealing to the desirability and desire of a model": a model that is provided by real people such as peers and colleagues, as well as vicariously through advertisements.[37] For middle-class professionals, these models are colleagues and superiors in the workplace, particularly those of higher status, thus reinforcing their distinction from the working classes.

These models exert powerful influences of which people are seldom conscious. Mimetic desire constitutes "a motivating force in our behavior as consumers," argues Arthur Asa Berger. It "helps explain our consumer lust: we desire what others have desired and have purchased, especially those we look up to—such as celebrities, movie stars, and sports heroes."[38] In consumer societies, it is through consumption rather than production that many people seek to acquire identities, and work becomes simply a means of producing the money required to consume what one needs for one's identity.[39]

Yet consumer lifestyles are sustained by more than narrative scripts and mimetic mechanisms. Sustained practices of work and consumption generate a centripetal force: one earns in order to spend and goes to work in order to afford to continue to spend. In our interviews, professionals often suggested that their lifestyle practices seemed to be sustained by a force of their own. They would talk about how, once they started their professional careers, they simply fell into a certain routine of spending time and money, which came to constitute their lifestyle. Greater disposable income and access to credit enabled them to begin their consumerist adventure: as they developed new tastes, got used to certain comforts, and became habituated to a certain way of being, they developed the habitus of a neoliberal consumer. These shared tastes and dispositions, as Pierre Bourdieu argues, become for members of a particular social class a key mode of distinction from others.[40] It becomes second nature to know, for instance, what restaurants or golf clubs or nightspots to frequent: that knowledge is all part of learning to play the game well, because it determines where one can be seen or should not be seen by important others. Signals of taste, including what one is wearing, what one is driving, and so on, become increasingly important. By and large, people attribute their consumerism and spending habits to what they consider idiosyncratic preferences. "I don't know why I do it" is the best many can do in offering explanations for their consumption choices.

Escape Velocity

To what extent and under what conditions can religion facilitate an exit from consumerist lifestyles? In the rest of this chapter, I offer three distinct modes through which religion moves from having a marginal status to becoming dominant in shaping one's lifestyle. In so doing, religion can pull professionals out of their consumerist routines and even, in some cases, out of the corporate jobs that sustain them. Under rare conditions religion becomes an alternative to the neoliberal order; it is not instrumentalized in the service of neoliberal ends, but conversely becomes one's dominant commitment, to which everything else is subordinated.

Forced Exit: Finding Escape Velocity in Prison

Therese and Bernie Ocampo moved to Dubai from the Philippines in 2007. Therese arrived first, securing a job as an accountant in a multinational IT firm. Three months later, she sponsored Bernie on her visa. He was a real estate salesman, and the housing boom in Dubai at that time meant he had no trouble finding a job in a leading real estate firm. Moving to Dubai provided them with a significant lifestyle boost from their lives in the Philippines. Over time, they admitted, they became reckless with their expenses, particularly in what they spent on their children and families: "In order for us to show our love for them, we were giving everything to them," admitted Therese. "So we didn't control our finances." Month after month, they began to spend more than their joint salaries brought in.

Through all this, they remained hopeful that their wages would surely increase soon and they would be able to repay their debts. But by the time they were due for promotions, the recession struck Dubai, and people all around them were being laid off. They decided to send their kids back home to the Philippines and hoped to be able to join them soon. But that plan did not materialize. Instead, after a couple of their checks bounced, they were arrested and sentenced to nine months in prison.

Neither Bernie nor Therese was particularly religious before going to prison. For Bernie, the sudden humiliation, as well as all the time he had to himself, generated a deep sense of remorse. In prison, he realized he had become selfish and immature and regretted most of all that his recklessness with money was responsible for his family's difficult situation. He blamed himself for having separated his children from their parents and for his wife being in prison.

The growing sense of desperation that was building up within him came to a head when a number of inmates started a fire in the prison by burning mattresses. He described the event as follows:

> There was a cloud of smoke. It was dark. The thing is, mattresses don't burn. If you light it up, you will see only a burning rubber, but it produces a lot of smoke. Then we were sent out. The worst thing was we were taken out to a long garage, totally isolated, the roof was covered. There's no air coming in and the smoke was not coming out. The worst

thing the policemen did was the exhaust fan: instead of letting it out on the compounds of the police station, they shifted the direction toward the garage. So all the smoke went to us.

So imagine 275 of us, they were slamming the door. They [i.e., the guards] cannot open [the door], because obviously if they open, [the prisoners] will run. It's a big headache for the government of Dubai. So I think it lasted for about 45 minutes, all the smoke. There were loud noise especially from the big guys, the African guys, the black guys, they were smashing doors. But as the time, when the time is going farther, the noise is getting lesser and lesser. Most of them have collapsed already. Since I was sick, I was just clinging on the bar. I was just holding there. Just like, I would say maybe fifteen more minutes I was losing my breath, I would be able to fall down. I decided not to hold on, because I am too weak to stand, my knees are buckling, so I need to sit.

Then, he said, when he had just about completely given up hope, the first miracle, "where God came in," occurred. He saw a flash of light shine out from amidst the darkness. Everything slowed down considerably. Then he saw a policeman "flashing the lights, calling us out." Soon they were ushered out by guards into the open air, and they could breathe again.

Bernie saw his close rescue from the fire as a miracle. He was on the verge of suffocating to death just before the prisoners were ushered out. As he sat recovering, he saw his wife, for the first time in months, among a crowd of female prisoners. When his wife saw him and smiled, he told me, "It's like God saying to me, I found you among the sinners. When our eyes met, she told me, I love you. . . . I could read her lips saying 'I love you.'" This moment was for him a divine revelation:

> It's like God saying, "Despite you have sinned, I love you. Despite you've been unfaithful to me, despite the fact that you've hurt me many times." As if he was saying it to me. God can also say it through her words, through her mouth. . . . So that's where my tears started to fall. Then I cried on that moment. Because it was a message that "Despite you've sinned, despite the sinner you are, sitting among those bunch of quote-unquote criminals, I've seen you, I've found you, I still love you, and I'll wait for you."

Bernie claimed this experience completely changed his life. During the rest of his prison stay, he developed new habits of prayer and scripture reading. In addition, the excessive heat and the restrictions of Ramadan (not being allowed to drink water in public) kept him indoors. He started writing regularly in a journal, and this new habit, in turn, prompted him to write an appeal to reduce his and Therese's prison sentences. He considered it a miracle that they were both granted an early release.

After their release from prison, they joined a Filipino Catholic Charismatic group to which one of Therese's close friends had invited them. There they felt welcomed unconditionally and were offered friendship, support, belonging, and even opportunities for leadership. Bernie was chosen by the leaders of the prayer group to receive a special "anointing" to a leadership role and thereafter regularly led their praise and worship and teaching sessions. The group also helped find them odd jobs and provided financial support, since they had overstayed their visas and were ineligible to take up formal employment. Their new lifestyle was drastically different, because they had to share a small apartment with two other families. Yet Bernie and Therese insisted that they had a greater sense of hopefulness and certainty in God's providence. "I'm so proud of him. You will never believe him, from the past life," said Therese, beaming at Bernie. He shared her enthusiasm in this transformation that he said they had both undergone from "selfish," consumerist professionals to "anointed" missionaries serving the church.

But their situation remained precarious. At the time of the interview, they owed more than AED 60,000 (USD 16,000) to various creditors, including the fines Bernie owed the government for overstaying his visa. They were constantly hounded on the phone by collection agencies. "That is why we're not answering the phone. Sorry for that," he laughed, apologizing to me for not answering my call when I was trying to set up the interview. "We can't speak to them," Therese added. "Their mindset is different. It's their job to collect. They don't believe [us]. They basically throw every insult in the book." Unable to settle these debts, they remained in the country illegally.[41]

Their situation seemed utterly bleak: how could they possibly manage to pay off an ever-growing debt that already exceeded their annual income? Yet, throughout the interview, even after recounting these challenges, they seemed calm and relaxed; they smiled and laughed readily. When I said that it must be extremely difficult for them to be in their situation, Therese smiled and said yes, it was, but they still felt incredibly blessed and grateful. Even though they did not know when they would be reunited with their children, she said, "It's really a miracle that our three children are studying. They didn't stop their studies, and somebody provided them financial support." She told me that faith encourages them to persevere with hope and confidence: "We just surrender to God and we just tell him that 'Whatever your will, we'll just follow.' What we did is, instead of crying or staying in the corner sentimenting, we looked for God. We searched for him. Because we repented, we want a new life. It's like we're born again after that imprisonment. We started a new life."

I stayed in touch with Bernie and Therese through Facebook. On January 1, 2013, Bernie announced, in the middle of a very long post with a litany of praises to God for the blessings of the past year, that he would be turning himself in. This statement was embedded among many one-liners from American televangelist Joyce Meyer. But this line announcing that he would be turning himself in the next day, in the hopes that he could return home, jumped out at me. I wrote to him at once to ask what he expected to happen. Would the government pardon his debt? Did he know for certain that he could return home? He replied promptly, informing me that an amnesty program had recently been announced by the UAE government, and he was confident that since there was absolutely no way he could pay off his debts, they would have to let him go. In fact, the Philippine embassy and consulate were urging their citizens who were staying illegally in Dubai to take advantage of the two-month amnesty window to safely exit the country without having to face prison terms.[42]

Over the next month, I heard no news from Bernie, but saw a number of posts from Therese expressing her love and prayers. Finally in mid-February on my Facebook newsfeed there appeared a number of photos of Bernie, back home in Manila with his children. He was one of more than 2,600 Philippines to return home during the amnesty period.[43] Therese remained on in Dubai for another year until, with the help of her employers, she too was able to return home to her family.

The Ocampos's story illustrates the perils of identity construction in consumerist societies, which place a heavy burden on those who cannot afford to buy high-status commodities to express the forms of selfhood they desire to imitate.[44] Members of the new middle classes thus become what Bauman calls "collateral casualties" of neoliberalism.[45] Three aspects of this story are noteworthy.

First, the economic crisis and its consequences, including the prison sentence for bounced checks, shattered the Ocampos's dominant consumerist scripts. Their pursuit of a good life, characterized in materialistic terms by a good income, impulsive spending, and easy access to credit, was not simply an individualistic or hedonistic quest, since they were trying to provide for their family. Nevertheless, the promises of the "Dubai dream" failed them; the "culture ideology" permitted them to sustain the illusion that they could attain and maintain an upper-middle-class identity and lifestyle while being unable to materially support it. Their imprisonment and subsequent illegal status brought about a structural collapse of their taken-for-granted narrative scripts. Without this collapse, it is unlikely that religion would have gained the prominence it did in their lives, nor would they have been placed in a structural position to exit.

Second, prison in and of itself would not have been a sufficient condition for exit in the manner in which the Ocampos achieved it. Many could plausibly be released from jail only to immerse themselves in pursuits that got them into trouble in the first place. For Bernie and Therese, religion took on new significance in prison, once their normal routines and patterns were severely disrupted. Subsequently, it was nurtured in the Charismatic community in which they not only felt a sense of acceptance and belonging but their status as "redeemed" prisoners was also seen as valuable.[46]

Third, it was in this context of a prayer group that they found the escape velocity through which religion was able to become a decisive factor in their lives, enabling them to cultivate new friendships, models, ideals, habits, and narrative trajectories. They were able to cultivate alternative identities and lifestyles in which religion played a dominant role.

While this mode of exit is forced in the sense that structural changes play a stronger role than agentic choices, it is also possible for people embedded in relatively stable narratives and structural positions to choose to put themselves in contexts that facilitate a departure from consumerist lifestyles.

Initiated Exit: Escape Velocity through Religious Immersion

"For most of my life, my faith has been very weak," admitted Anil Thomas, sipping his lemon soda at the prestigious Catholic Club in Bangalore, where he invited me to meet him. While his wife was active in church, Anil did not have much need for religion himself. "When things are going good for you in corporate life—the money's coming in—religion's a luxury," he explained. "It's more of a by-product of your existence. It's not the reason for your existence." He viewed religion as just "a framework for mankind to conform to rules," a way "to keep things in place" in society.

Anil spent many years of his career climbing steadily up the corporate ranks. He was out-competing colleagues, earning more money than he had initially envisioned, and was enjoying a "good lifestyle" by his peers' standards. He spent impulsively on food, clothing, gadgets, entertainment, and the usual trappings of wealth. The pinnacle of his success was being transferred to Australia, fulfilling the dominant script that encouraged he and his wife to "settle abroad" where they could pursue a better life. There they were, "two people earning, with no expenditure, pretty much. No kids." The company covered all their basic expenses, leaving them with plenty of disposable income. "We could have bought fancy cars if we wanted to; we had great cash flow," he said. "Happiness was at the end of the month when you saw your salary. It became, 'Oh wow, we can spend a lot!' And then you go out and you're like, 'Okay, what do we buy?'" But it did not take them long to realize that "the things we really cared about were back home. The food, the culture, the friends. So we had this money but we didn't have friends to spend it with." They keenly felt that something was missing. "Work is something you do to sustain your lifestyle. But then we found that we were sustaining nothing!"

Somehow, for Anil and his wife, their guiding scripts failed them, just when they had achieved great success. They were pursuing everything they thought they wanted and had "arrived," only to discover that their "hearts were not in it." They had money and status and purchasing power, but "it was pretty lonely." They had put in their paperwork for immigration, but began to seriously reconsider their decision to stay in Australia. "Even if you were a citizen of that place, what are the things that you are doing it for?" Other people would give them reasons such as, "Hey, there's no pollution here; the roads are so clean; the infrastructure is crumbling back home; I'm doing it for my kids." None appealed to them. They eventually decided to return to Bangalore.

Still feeling restless, Anil began to give religion a try, inspired by the devotion of his mother and wife. But it was difficult to find what he was looking for. He attended several weekend retreats and day-long courses, but would always find that any "progress" he made during these events would quickly dissipate once he returned to the corporate grind. He felt he needed a sustained break in order to develop new habits and routines:

> In my head, I needed the escape velocity to make a jump from the intellectual-connect to a concept to a faith-connect. And to do that kind of switch, you need the velocity to jump out of situation A and get into situation B. And I could never find that with the short retreats and short courses. I would just filter it out from my brain and pass it through.

A couple of years later, "by chance," he came across an ad in church for a "Discipleship Camp" run by the Navjyothi group. He was immediately drawn by the prospect of a three-month break from work where he could seriously explore his questions about religion, meaning, and happiness. Participants in the Discipleship Camp need to live in community for the duration of the three-month course, during which they spend a considerable amount of time in spiritual practices of prayer, as well as studying various aspects of theology and spirituality, with the eventual aim of becoming "disciples" who could proclaim the gospel effectively. It attracted a variety of middle-class Catholics with diverse motivations. "The kind of people who were there, many were discerning [a call to] full-time missionary work, marriage, priesthood; [there were] many problems they needed healing from," Anil observed. "They were in a place where they needed to get fixed or make decisions. And I just showed up to say, 'Hey, I just need to get my hands dirty with religion and get some faith-formation, the whole God-thing and religious concept,' which was quite different from other people there."

This residential program was an immersion experience in a language he was only minimally familiar with. It gave him the chance to "lead a different lifestyle, without the tension of having to get back into work or anything." This lifestyle was worlds apart from what he was used to. "Coming out of corporate life, which is, you're traveling to different parts of the globe, you're staying in good hotels, your travel needs are taken care of." In the camp, by contrast, there was "basic, frugal accommodation." Difficult though it was to get used to these changes, he very much appreciated the experience. "It showed me the difference between what one wants and how much one actually needs. And that changes your perspective of things a lot." He was especially struck by the Catholic priests he met, particularly their life commitments of celibacy and poverty. Anil claimed that the Discipleship Camp was exactly the sort of thing he needed to address his main problem, which was not one of motivation—he had become increasingly motivated to understand his religious tradition better—but rather, of follow through.

> And when I did the three-month course, there was plenty of time to follow through. Because you have the runway to build a momentum. So it's not like you're doing a one-week thing and a two-day thing and then you're in-and-out. . . . So [the Discipleship Camp] gave me the escape velocity. And that brought me back to balance. You find peace with who you are.

Anil, on his return to work, decided to switch from his senior role in the sales division to a lower-profile consulting position. It was a form of downward mobility, bringing lower pay and status, but it benefited him in other ways. "I always did aspire to really just go up the corporate ladder. But now I'm happy just being in a middle-level kind of role." In addition to having an impact on his work, his experience in the camp also shaped the way he has come to see and use money. "I think before a lot of my decisions were around money itself," he explained. "And now we've found that money comes and goes . . . and certainly not everything is about the money." He also claimed that the camp motivated him to considerably curb his spending: he and his wife have started saving more, as well as contributing to religious charities. They also spend more time in religious activities. Anil admitted, however, that maintaining this commitment remains a daily struggle.

The most extreme examples of the escape velocity generated by the Discipleship Camp were those of professionals who abandoned corporate life altogether. One such professional, Vinod Prabhu, was a successful IT manager who found himself unable to readjust to his corporate job after his experience at the camp:

I was in the corporate industry, working big money, enjoying, [having] fun. I had everything actually. And somehow after the [Camp], when I went back to the same industry, I found it very suffocating. And I really could not manage. Some reason, I did not know. Monies were still good. I had a good position as a senior manager, handling this, doing that. And for some reason I could not, so in June I just threw my papers and walked out.

He soon became what these groups call a "full-timer," working for the church as a lay missionary. His move also entailed a form of downward mobility, since his family now has to manage on his wife's income and any money he receives in donations from benefactors.

Anil's metaphor of "getting on the runway" is an apt description of the conditions of possibility for exit. What it took for him and many others was a script failure in their dominant narratives of careerism and consumerism. But unlike the case of Bernie and Therese, there was no structural collapse such as a layoff or imprisonment. Rather, Anil and Vinod, and others like them, were highly successful and thoroughly embedded in the routines of corporate life and consumer lifestyles. What occurred was a collapse in the taken-for-granted meanings of these goals, trajectories, and routines. These people were surprised to find themselves disillusioned, burned out, or unhappy—consequences that they did not foresee or expect.

In addition, they had to be in a position for religion to offer them a plausible alternative: new scripts, models, and routines that could plausibly offer a solution to these problems. They also needed sustained immersion in a closed environment to generate escape velocity, as Anil called it. At the Discipleship Camp, people are immersed not only in religious teachings and discourses but also in a new lifestyle: regular routines of prayer, several times a day; a complete disconnect from practices of buying and shopping; and having to live in frugal quarters, eat simple meals, and put up with the inevitable challenges of community life. There are certainly positive elements that make the experience appealing, such as moments of celebration, a climate of trust and warmth, and the absence of stress and anxiety about meeting performance criteria—all conditions that are difficult to achieve. In addition, the Discipleship Camp is a unique setup, held once a year, and is the only such program in Bangalore, according to my respondents. Dubai has no such equivalent program. But as Anil recognizes, even after such an immersive experiences changes one's habits, it is still a struggle to maintain that change after returning to everyday life. Thus, this mode of exit is an enormously difficult option.

There is, nevertheless, another means by which religion can take on a prominent role in shaping people's lifestyles, but in a more gradual manner: the practice of tithing.

Gradual Exit: Finding Escape Velocity through the Practice of Tithing

A less dramatic mode of resistance to consumerism is the practice of tithing. Many ECC groups encourage their members to tithe: to contribute 10 percent of their income either to the group or to other spiritual and charitable causes. Such encouragement, however, is never conveyed in the group's regular meetings and sessions, but instead only in private conversations with elders and long-term members. Nor is the practice of tithing mandated. For instance, Joel, an ECC prayer group leader in Dubai, said, "It's not a mandatory amount or something like that, but it's like something voluntarily which you commit for the programs and expenses of the movement." He insisted that the movement otherwise "does not talk about money," certainly not people's practical use of money.

Adopting the practice of tithing is a gradual process for many and is an especially difficult challenge for people immersed in consumerist lifestyles. Maryann in Dubai, whom I cited earlier, talked about the role of tithing in her life:

> When I started [working in Dubai], when I landed a job, I told myself that I will religiously give tithe, 10 percent of my total earnings. I was doing that for the first three months, I was doing it religiously. But then there came a point in my life when I said, "What the heck, why not pamper myself? Indulge, so to speak." So if there's a sale in my favorite store, I'll be there, you'll see me there. Then I forgot the tithing. I still gave love offering [i.e., spontaneously donating at religious services]. . . . But when I stopped tithing, [thinking] "I can do it anyways whenever I want to," then suddenly I felt my finances were going haywire.

Maryann admitted that she got carried away by her appetite for shopping and began regularly spending nearly as much if not more than she earned every month. "I believed in the power of tithing," she insisted. But she could not bring herself to make the necessary sacrifices. "When I wanted to go back to tithing, there was never enough for me, not even for myself, so how can I give?" Her spending habits began to affect her ability not only to tithe but also to send home remittances.

Things changed after she took a course offered by the movement's founder on "how to manage your finances." This course gave her new ways of looking at money as not simply a means to self-indulgence, but as a resource that could help people around her in need. She learned to become more aware and reflexive about her day-to-day use of money and developed strategies to handle her finances better. "Before I used to think, 'How can I pay my credit card?' I always paid the minimum, sometimes with the late payment fee; it really drains you out, you know?" She was able to engage in tithing again, despite the fact that her income remained the same. As a result, she claimed, "I felt my finances were becoming under control. I can say for a fact that after this year I'm gonna be debt-free."

Francesca, a leader in another Filipino Charismatic movement, talked about how her religious group "makes you habituated to tithing. Even when I haven't had a job, I would give 10 percent of what I had." What influenced her to begin tithing was not so much the formal encouragement of the practice within the group, but the influence of "models" in the group whom she looked up to, particularly a generous couple who were leaders in the group and whom she grew to love as second parents.

Some individuals in ECC groups were proponents of "word of faith" theologies and followed American Pentecostal/Charismatic "prophets" with large global followings, such as Kim Clement, Kenneth Copeland, Joyce Meyer, Benny Hinn, and Joel Osteen. These members expressed their beliefs and shared their methods in prayer groups, such as by "praying blessings" on people, interpreting financial difficulties as demonic attacks or as caused by a lack of faith, and so on. One such prophet devotee, Peter, was a senior manager in a major global bank in Dubai and an active member of the parish benevolence committee that distributed funds to the needy. I had to interview him three times, because he would seldom respond to my actual questions, but instead insisted on sharing details of prophecies that he had either personally received or seen on YouTube. In each interview he indicated a specific imminent date when the price of a stock he had invested in would skyrocket, making him abundantly wealthy and financially independent and allowing him to dedicate his life to hosting these American prophets in Dubai and India; in each subsequent interview, he informed me that the prophetic date had been mysteriously postponed by a few weeks.[47] As it was, he was contributing his 10 percent tithe to their "ministries" on a regular basis. Some other consumers of such "prophets" I talked to, like Peter, believed that wealth was a univocal blessing and did not see a problem with displays of prosperity among believers, since they could only be indicators of blessings. This sort of prosperity-based approach, I was told by leaders of Charismatic prayer groups in both cities, was influential among some members, but not among prayer group leaders; indeed, the leaders actively discouraged it. Members who insisted on these approaches tended to eventually leave the Catholic Church and join other churches that were more hospitable to it.

While other Charismatic groups encouraged tithing, they did not promote any particular view of money and were silent on how money should be spent or whether wealth or poverty had any theological meanings. "I don't remember any teaching on money as such," said Ashwin, for example, when I asked whether his prayer group in Bangalore addressed issues of finances. "Tithing, yes, but not how to prudently use cash and all. It's never been taught us. In hindsight I think it's a good thing to teach. But I don't remember anyone in [my prayer group] teaching that." This lack of teaching he said, led to his ambivalence about the impact of religion on his lifestyle. When I asked if he would say that his faith shaped his use of money, he replied,

> In a way, yes, because the tithing part has helped me to have some perspective on cash. But in a way no too, because my spending is totally un-Christian. Because I buy stuff, random stuff, that I don't need. I just spend for no reason. Many of the things I buy I never use it. Like clothes I buy I don't use, after wearing it once. Books I buy that I don't read. Keep on collecting stuff. Stuff like that.

Over time, tithing if practiced can become second nature. Cherian, a Dubai-based leader of an Indian Catholic Charismatic movement, talked about how his financial contributions to the movement increased gradually over the past couple of decades, allowing him to cultivate the habit slowly. By the time of our interview he was contributing well over 10 percent of his income, which paid for expenses incurred by the movement, in addition to his tithe. For instance, when he had to fly to another city or country for the purposes of the movement, he paid for the airfare himself. Similarly, when hosting events of the movement at his home, he covered the cost of meals and refreshments. He also readily contributed to additional charitable initiatives of the movement. He told me that he participated in this manner because he did not see the movement as extraneous to his life: rather, it is his home and family.

Lijo in Dubai talked about how contributing a specific amount every month "helps to cultivate a habit of giving." Tithing has also reinforced his belief in "the biblical principle of 'the more you give, the more you receive.'" He explained, "When you are really in need, you receive the money what you need, even though you give for charity, even though there is a clear need for yourself. But because you have made that commitment, you honor it, and there are other ways which this money comes back to you." He gave an example from the previous year, when his car was involved in an accident, and he had to take a loan to cover the damages until his insurance kicked in. Initially, he and his wife stopped tithing, but found that the insurance reimbursement kept getting delayed. Later, they felt guilty for having stopped tithing and decided to start again, despite being in debt. "And once we started doing that, all this changes started happening," Lijo declared. "Like, I got that insurance amount so I was able to clear the loan. . . . I got the bonus from my workplace. I got an increment today as well. So using all that money which came in, I have sorted out my debts now. So these are not expected things, but once we make that decision and start giving, it happens."

As a result of their renewed commitment to tithing, Lijo and his wife Gemima found that they learned to live with less. For instance, Gemima claimed that their tithing changed their response to their car situation: "Now we've made a decision not to buy a car now; we're just going to survive with [one] car for another six months until I find a new job. Whereas earlier we would have been like, 'Oh we're going to die without another car' kind of a thing." They admitted that not having two cars made life inconvenient for them and created occasional difficulties, such as having to ask friends for rides. In addition to tithing regularly to their prayer group, they also regularly contribute money to an orphanage in India. In these ways, their religious commitments shape and provide some constraints on their use of money.

In contrast to the more sudden modes of acquiring escape velocity that I discussed earlier, tithing constitutes a more gradual means by which religious groups can lead professionals to cultivate practices that constrain consumerism. Adopting such a practice requires the support of alternative motivations and justifications than the ones available in either the neoliberal consumerist script or the more traditional scripts of thrift and financial responsibility. While people often appealed to more pragmatic benefits of tithing—it made them feel good that they were contributing their money to good causes, or it gave them more control over their spending—there was also an appeal to a transcendental factor: God would somehow "bless them" for this. This becomes part of a new narrative through which money (and in turn, the corporate jobs that generate this money) becomes sacralized.

In addition to going against entrenched habits of spending and mainstream views about the use of money, tithing is also challenging to adopt and maintain in these contexts because it is not a requirement or mandate of ECC groups. People do not feel forced to tithe; they are "encouraged" to do so, if they want and are able to. And not everyone in the group is thus encouraged: it is mainly the long-term members and those involved in leadership who are advised to tithe. Even some of those who were encouraged to tithe expressed a reluctance to do so, because the groups did not account for how the funds collected were being used. So in most groups, the practice of tithing is prevalent mainly among leaders and a few active members for whom the group is already a home or family, and their investment simply expresses and reinforces their existing commitment.

Tithing is not thrift; people could, in theory, dutifully contribute their tithe and indulge in consumerist pursuits with the rest of their money. However, in the accounts of people I spoke to, it does seem to have the effect of encouraging thrift and constraining consumerism. The impact of tithing may be comparable to that of the practice of fasting. While it is not a bodily practice, tithing, like fasting, is what sociologist Daniel Winchester calls a "morally constitutive" practice that involves a "fundamental reorganization" of one's patterns, making what is otherwise backgrounded "a focal point of one's . . . experience."[48] Having to part with money that could otherwise be spent elsewhere may force people to become less impulsive in their spending and to consciously make different choices. Similar to fasting, tithing can also be seen as "a disciplinary sensibility" that contributes to "developing the spiritual strength and moral discipline necessary" for overcoming day-to-day temptations.[49] In addition to the effects of habituation, mimesis also likely plays a role here: people in these groups who tithe are trying to become like other more "holy" or committed members of these groups, who are likely older members living more frugal ways of life. This was acknowledged at least by one respondent, Cherian, who explicitly credited these role models for his present practices not only of tithing but also of opening his house and wallet freely to the causes of the movement.

ECC groups, however, do not always foster a responsible use of money; indeed, they can at times be exploited by predatory members. Several respondents in both cities talked about how some members of their prayer groups would borrow money from group members, only to vanish from the group. In some cases, the financial need was the result of a genuine emergency: family members fell ill or people were laid out. But it was not uncommon for borrowers to use this money to fund consumerist habits or the consequences of overspending: paying off credit card debt, putting money in the bank before a check bounced, and so on. In many cases, respondents said that they had learned to simply "write off" this borrowed money as an offering to God or a charitable act; however, for others, it turned them off from contributing money to church at all, since they felt their money was being distributed to "irresponsible" people. Overall, the general lack of discussion and transparency about financial matters in these religious groups is conducive to various dysfunctional practices that adversely affect groups and members alike.

Generating Escape Velocity

What can provide professionals with the escape velocity needed to break free from consumerist lifestyles? The examples presented in this chapter suggest it requires interruptions and changes to one's narrative scripts, models, and habitual routines. Because all three elements—scripts, models, and habits—are involved in sustaining consumer lifestyles, it takes some breakdown of these elements for a serious reordering to take place.

Narrative scripts can break down when they fail to deliver on their promises or when some of the assumptions underlying them are violated and thus rendered transparent, leading people to become conscious of and call into question aspects that were previously taken for granted. This collapse of "cultural scaffolding" reduces people's ability to continue on autopilot.[50] For instance, Martina, an HR executive in Bangalore, talked about her narrative script that collapsed, enabling her to make the decision to take a break from corporate life:

> From the time we're born, our parents have already decided, if you're a girl, that is, they will educate us all this time, that they will save up money to get us married by this time, and then their responsibility is over. These are the exact words that they use. . . . all our parents, my parents, probably yours, and parents of my friends. And for guys: you study by this time, and you finish and you do either your BE [Bachelor of Engineering] or your CA [Chartered Accountancy]. . . . So you finish by this time, then you get a good job, you work for three–four years, then you start looking out for a bride, and then you get married. That is the way.

Martina, like her parents, expected that she would marry by her mid-twenties. But when she was still single in her mid-thirties and still unsure of the larger trajectory of her life, she felt she could no longer sustain the old script. A "good job" meant little in the absence of the larger narrative it was supposed to be embedded in, which, for her, included a family. This led her to take a long hiatus to reassess her priorities and reorient herself in a different direction.

For Bernie and Therese, the script was something as simple as "Go to Dubai, make good money, and life will be great." When they found themselves in prison for defaulting on credit card payments, they could retain neither their old scripts nor habits. For Anil, the expectation was that making good money at a corporate job and migrating to Australia would mean having "arrived." He found himself at the pinnacle of success, having achieved his goals for career and consumption, but was still unhappy. There was a mismatch between the trajectory he was pursuing and what he was implicitly expecting to gain from this pursuit: an elusive something that he called "happiness," which he could see among religiously active people. He thus began to reassess his taken-for-granted narrative and to consider what it would take to seriously adopt an alternative. As Anil explained, his own process of exit from his entrenched routines required the provision of a "runway" on which people can gain "escape velocity" from the centripetal forces of consumerism and upward career mobility.

As religion gains prominence in people's lives, it can constrain consumer lifestyles. ECC groups can provide alternative scripts, with alternative models of mimesis, and alternative habits that enable the possibility of an exit from consumer lifestyles. Professionals like Donnie in Bangalore, who aspired one day to join the seminary, or Francesca in Dubai, who wanted to become a lay missionary, were content in their corporate jobs, living comfortable lifestyles, and yet actively made decisions to curtail their consumption because they were afraid of becoming habituated to a way of life that would be very difficult to forsake. "There's one thing at the back of my mind—that one day I will live as a missionary," said Francesca. "And I don't want to get a lifestyle now that I can't support then." Such commitments, bolstered by regular practices such as tithing, can enable Missionaries to resist the snares of consumerism.

Conclusion

This chapter makes two key points. First, religion has little *direct* influence on the lifestyles of professionals in these rapidly globalizing contexts, particularly when it comes to spending, saving, or investing their money. This is the case even among those who aspire to the ideals of the Missionary. Other, stronger factors such as parents, peers, and advertising, mediated through the centripetal force generated by habituation as most professionals engage in routines of work and consumption, together propel the pervasive practices of neoliberal consumerism. Religion in this context is mostly silent on economic issues, offering neither resistance to consumerism nor encouragement of saving or thrift. My data support Fulmer's contention that "the Church has abdicated any authority to speak to the consumer. . . . The Christian is addressed as worker, spouse, parent, friend, and benefactor, but not as consumer. This silence reinforces consumerism, and the economic system depends on this reinforcement."[51] By not directly addressing people's use of money—despite religious leaders' recognition of the problems consumerism poses for individuals and societies—churches help enable these practices. Mimetic sustenance of consumerism happens even among members of religious groups; for example, socializing after group meetings becomes an occasion to informally communicate consumer information, such as which new cell phones are worth buying or which department stores are having exciting sales. Religious groups also sustain consumerism through the performance of "consumer citizenship," unquestioningly legitimizing consumer spaces and practices, as I describe in the next chapter. Professionals who are active in ECC groups see little conflict between their religious commitments and lifestyle practices; the dissonance pointed out by theologians and popes that I discussed earlier remains for them an ethical blind spot.

Yet I also argue in this chapter that there are conditions under which religion can become a dominant influence in people's lifestyles. These conditions include interruptions or breakdowns in one's narrative scripts, models of mimesis, and habitual patterns, as well as the opportunity for re-habituation with alternative narrative scripts, models, and habits. Under such conditions, religion can facilitate an exit from consumerist lifestyles. Structures like the Discipleship Camp can enable people, through sustained immersion, to acquire escape velocity. (An alternative I examined in Dubai—prison—can hardly be embraced intentionally for this purpose.) Religion can also constrain consumerism through the practice of tithing. Regularly sacrificing a significant proportion of one's income can induce new reflexivity among professionals about their use of money. Religious communities can provide alternative mimetic models who can inspire members through their generosity or ability to make do with less, thus constraining consumerist routines.

The most extreme form of exit is to become a "full-timer" or lay missionary, exiting not only consumerism but also corporate life. However, because lay missionaries must raise funds to support themselves, this option is not a complete exit from capitalism. Prabhu and others in this position depend for their sustenance on friends who are well-to-do corporate employees: those who are firmly entrenched within the system but who regularly tithe at least 10 percent of their income to religious causes, including support for full-timers. Even sustaining annual events such as the Discipleship Camp requires the support of donors, many of whom are professionals. Those people who have access to such incomes enable the very viability of the full-timer option.

Additional factors shape the possibilities of exit. Anil mentioned toward the end of our interview that what allowed him to sustain his "downward mobility" was that he owned his house, had no debts, and had no pressing financial obligations or needs. Vinod struggled considerably with his transition from corporate life, but could always fall back on his wife's income. Many who have escaped thus remain dependent on the system. In essence, for professionals trying to live out religious commitments in rapidly globalizing contexts, as Simon During puts it, "neither an exit from, nor an alternative to, capitalism is imaginable."[52] Religion's role in consumer societies is thus paradoxical: while it can offer conditions that enable an exit from consumerism, not only are these conditions difficult to achieve but they also remain dependent on capitalism for their sustenance.

This chapter also shows that religiously active people can participate to a great extent in consumerist practices, with (at least on an externally observable level) no seemingly adverse effect on their religious commitments. They pursue self-denial and transcendence in some ways while in other ways engaging regularly in impulsive practices of self-gratification. Whether on a deeper level the net result is morally or spiritually corrosive is not something I can assess. Among those who are less religiously committed, consumerism may contribute more to religious decline because of their lack of immersion in the religious realm. Certainly for some, the new opportunities opened up by wealth and status make religious activities less attractive. Consumerist pursuits of comfort and self-gratification are more appealing than cultivating self-denial; the shopping mall is a more pleasant alternative to the religious service.[53] My respondents from the Arabic CP group, for instance, suggested that if some of their members had more money, they would probably spend their weekends going to high-end entertainment venues rather than coming to their church meeting. People can certainly sustain seemingly contradictory commitments, but perhaps this is only feasible in the short run: the long-term consequences of this dissonance remain to be seen.

Having examined the role of religion in corporate workplaces and in the lifestyles of these professionals, let us now examine how the relationship between the Mercenary and the Missionary is played out in churches. How are these interactions shaped by local sociopolitical contexts? And what are the consequences not only for church communities but also for civic life in these neoliberal cities more generally?

BELONGING AND CIVIC COMMITMENT IN THE NEOLIBERAL CITY

Rapid economic development can have a disorienting effect on people's lives. It affects their ability to feel at home in their cities and their willingness to contribute to serving and improving these environments. This alienation is not simply the result of a changing environment. Rather, as I argue in this chapter, rapidly developing cities also impose distinctive conceptions of worth on their residents, based on ethnicity, social class, and the ability to produce and consume. This process in turn generates new forms of exclusion.

In the disorienting neoliberal metropolis, many who feel ambivalent about these cities find in religious institutions a locus of belonging and a civic space. ECC groups provide members with a sense of home and moral community: they are a vital source of belonging that they find neither in their workplaces nor in their cities more generally. These communities, however, both shape and are shaped by their broader environments. In fact, as I argue, they reproduce the modes of stratified belonging and consumer citizenship that characterizes civic worth in these cities. And in this respect, important differences between Bangalore and Dubai—both in the role of corporate professionals in these church groups and in the impact these groups can have on their societies—come to the fore.

The Ambivalence of Belonging in Neoliberal Cities

"Fake," "plastic," "artificial," "superficial," "an illusion," "shallow," "a mirage," and "ridiculous": such words were widely used to describe Dubai when I asked professionals what they thought about the city. These terms were used by short-term and long-term residents alike, and even second-generation residents who were born and raised there and called it "home." Most expats I talked to in Dubai vacillated between detachment and attachment to the city: much like one of sociologist Syed Ali's respondents, who considered Dubai a "pitstop" despite never having left the UAE in his life.[1]

On the one hand, many claimed that they "loved" the city. They boasted about the "tremendous progress" it had made over the years and praised its "visionary leaders" for their dedication to developing the city from a barren desert into a major "global" and "cosmopolitan" hub in a matter of decades. Dubai was nowhere as crowded and polluted as other major cities they had lived in, such as Mumbai or Manila. Most of all, they enjoyed its comforts and conveniences: with air conditioning available everywhere, they barely noticed the vicious heat of the natural environment; they could simply call the supermarket next door and have groceries delivered; they could afford domestic help; and so on.

On the other hand, they complained that the city, with its iconic architecture and grandiose ambitions—indoor ski resorts and all—was very much a façade. Francesca, born and raised in Dubai, voiced this ambivalence well. On the one hand, she was very critical of Dubai:

> [Dubai is] hollow; it's plastic. And it tries and tries to create a personality for itself but it's not there. The whole obsession with being superlative—widest, tallest, whatever. And I also saw Dubai fall flat on its face, and that wasn't fun at all. Saw enough people suffer to learn a few lessons, about being grounded and not being carried away by the world around you. . . . I hope and pray that this is not the place that God wants me to settle down in, because I really wouldn't want to raise kids here.

And yet, she told me that there is no other place else she could call home: "I go away for a few weeks and then it's like, 'I wanna go back to Dubai, 'cause that's home.'" Expat professionals—even those like Francesca who call Dubai home—know well that they cannot honestly say that they belong there. Excluded from the possibility of citizenship, they remain in perpetual anxiety about maintaining jobs and visas. In my interviews, I came across many who had been terminated from previous jobs without notice and had to scramble quickly to make arrangements to return home with their families, while applying for new jobs in the city so that they could return as soon as possible. Indeed my own experience growing up was similar: every time my father was terminated or was transferred to a new city in the Gulf, we had to return to India for several weeks to wait for new visas. Capricious rules and laws that could change unpredictably from day to day and perceptions of mistreatment from the police and from "locals" (i.e., Emirati citizens) are additional sources of fear and worry. I experienced this stress throughout the years I lived in the Gulf and on a number of occasions while conducting research for this project, as I discuss in the appendix.

Women, Filipinas in particular, face additional challenges in a city with a predominantly male population. Nearly all my Filipina respondents said that, while walking or waiting for taxis, Arab men driving by would regularly drive up to them, roll down their car windows, and proposition them for sex. Such factors reinforce the sense that they do not belong there. Many, as a result, try to justify their stay in Dubai as a temporary nuisance to put up with until they can save up enough money to build a better life elsewhere. They are keenly aware that home is elsewhere: either "back" where they came from or someplace "ahead" to where they hope to migrate, such as Australia or Canada.

Despite being aware of these difficulties, many admitted that they had become so habituated to Dubai that they could not live elsewhere. Some who tried to return to their home countries, or even to migrate to the West, eventually returned to Dubai. Many Indians and Filipinos talked about how difficult they found it to adjust to the pollution and poverty back home, after living for years in a place as "comfortable" and "convenient" as Dubai. They complained about the difficulty of doing something as simple as crossing the street in busy Indian cities and of the regular power outages caused by rolling blackouts. Others returned from North America, complaining about how they had to manage everything on their own without domestic help. One French couple with five children told me how it would be impossible for them to return to Paris and find an affordable place to live with a family their size; in Dubai, they had grown accustomed to a large villa close to the beach. Their children, additionally, were now more adept in English than French. Indians, too, often lamented the fact that their children were not fluent in their mother tongues and, as a result, would find it nearly impossible to assimilate back home.

Second-generation Indians claimed they often felt treated as something between a traitor and a foreigner whenever they visited India. Their formal status as "NRI"—Non-Resident Indian, the legal term used by the government—has become a pejorative for someone "spoiled" by comfortable living. "People shun you because you are NRI—it's kind of like you don't belong either place," said Preethi, expressing a sentiment that I had often felt myself. "Being an expat anywhere else is different, but being an expat in the Middle East—you're not accepted here, and you don't feel like you fit in in India either, you know?" she added. "My parents are never gonna understand that." Church communities such as ECC groups in Dubai provide a deep sense of home and belonging for many like Preethi and enable them not only to feel welcomed but also to give back to others, as I discuss later in this chapter.

Bangalore residents also expressed ambivalence about their sense of belonging to their cities, but their evaluations were made along different registers. Their chief complaints included frustration at the Indian bureaucracy: the red tape, long queues, and unreliable wait times to get basic things done. Many complained that, in spite of its economic development, the city was deteriorating. Those who had grown up in the city lamented the transformation of what was once the "garden city" into a "garbage city," because of the ubiquity of trash and pollution. People regularly complained about its poor infrastructure: bad roads, excessive traffic, inadequate public transportation, and perpetual delays on projects such as the metro rail. Other complaints included the lack of sufficient "comfort" in lifestyles due to regular power cuts and air and noise pollution. Another common complaint by professionals at the time of this study was the legal "curfew," which required all establishments selling liquor to shut down by 11:30 p.m.[2] Such complaints exemplify what anthropologist Neha Vora calls "consumer citizenship," which I discuss shortly.

Despite some long-term residents' complaints about rising rents, pollution, and traffic that were forcing them out of their neighborhoods, Indian professionals living in Bangalore had no comparable fear or anxiety to that expressed by their counterparts in Dubai, who as Indians rank low in the "ethnocracy" of the Gulf. As Indian citizens, they had no anxieties about visas or fears of being expelled. Even the sorts of horror stories I heard from people in both cities differed. In Dubai and other Gulf cities, people regularly expressed fear of the police and of being unjustly and capriciously punished by the legal system; middle-class respondents in Bangalore are in a relatively greater position of power than their counterparts in Dubai and typically have nothing to fear from the police, whom many claim are easily bribed. The stories and warnings that circulated usually had to do with harm befalling people while traveling at night, often caused by reckless drivers. Many female respondents, while claiming that Bangalore was safer for women than other parts of India,[3] recounted experiences of harassment and molestation. "So I was walking in a group and this guy on a bike comes along and grabs [i.e., gropes] me and rides off. So that's one incident," recalled Jennifer. "And when I was with a friend on one of those streets, we were walking down to catch an auto, again one guy on a bike comes and grabs her. This happened quite a few times."

In many cases, respondents blamed this rise in "random" crime on "migrants" from outside the city, especially people from the northern states of India, who were supposedly "uneducated" and "uncultured."[4] Those who had grown up in the city complained that this new migration influx had contributed to a widespread disregard for the welfare of the city. As Michelle recounted, "There was one college student who was walking on Commercial Street; she threw something and so I said, 'Please pick it up and don't throw things' or something like that, and she's like, 'Why should I? Everyone else is throwing. Anyway, it's such a dirty city, so I might as well throw too!'"

Many middle-class professionals in Bangalore, whether they were born and raised in the city or had moved in from elsewhere, felt that locals who were not working in corporate industries did not fully appreciate their success and were always trying to take advantage of them. However, they did suspect that locals probably felt cheated or left out of the global economy. Eric, who had grown up in Bangalore, expressed this sentiment well:

> My [landlords], just because I work for an IT company, they think they can keep increasing the rent, or that I have crores [1 crore equals 10 million rupees, around $200,000 at the time] stashed away in the bank, and so on. And they start thinking like that. . . . The auto [rickshaw] driver . . . will shout at you when you get out of a pub and don't want to pay an extra fare [at night]: "You spend thousands on drink and can't spend a little extra?" They feel cheated. For them, it's a negative. For them, everybody is in IT and everybody is earning a lot. Earlier they could relate to someone who was in a bank or a teacher, but they can't understand IT. You go there, you sit in front of a computer, and you earn a lot of money, and sometimes you work from home, sometimes you don't go at all! So they don't understand it. All they do is drop you off in these shiny buildings which is steel and glass and they don't understand what goes on inside over there. They can understand factories and lifting and so on. But they can't understand [IT]. So there's alienation; they are angry that they are being displaced and their salaries are not going up and so on.

Many Bangalore professionals shared the uncomfortable recognition that local residents, particularly those of lower socioeconomic status, are often seriously disadvantaged by recent changes. They acknowledged that "outsiders," especially elites working in multinational corporations and enjoying consumerist lifestyles, have become the main beneficiaries of "progress." In Dubai too, some locals expressed similar sentiments. For instance, one young Emirati college student I spoke to expressed a great sense of pride in his identity as Bedouin and Emirati and complained that his family felt forced out from the center of their city by foreigners. But in spite of these symbolic losses, the economic benefits of global capitalism accrue very differently to them in comparison to locals in Bangalore. There is no denying that the extremely generous welfare state that the UAE offers its citizens—housing, education, health care, and generous stipends—would be impossible if not for the foreign labor force that is deprived of such benefits.[5]

Dubai and Bangalore thus differ in important ways in the evaluations of the professionals who live there. The complexities that come with navigating life as a long-term or second- or third-generation expat in Dubai are simply not found in Bangalore. A sense of belonging to the city is certainly more fraught in Dubai, particularly for those who are second- or third-generation residents. As much as Indian professionals claim to be at home there, they also keenly feel that they do not belong anywhere. This sense of dislocation, a kind of existential uncertainty, is far more intense than what Indian professionals in Bangalore express when they complain about changing neighborhoods or growing pollution or have aspirations to migrate elsewhere.

Yet there are also similarities in the narratives of the professionals in Dubai and Bangalore. The ways in which people evaluated gains and losses entailed by the rapid economic development of the past couple of decades were virtually indistinguishable in the two cities. There were also remarkably similar evaluations of how much more "modern" each city had become and of how each was now a "global" or "cosmopolitan" city, as evident in similar forms of employment and consumption: jobs in transnational corporations, branded retail outlets, and cuisines from all over the world. Such signs indicated that their cities had "really developed," "really come up"; they were now "on the map." Also similar were the narratives of loss—the loss of familiarity, of community, of simplicity: *When I grew up we used to know our neighbors. Now we don't even see the people next door; People used to know each other well, and we would regularly have dinners together. Now everyone's a stranger; We could walk around safely at night and now we can't.* The narratives in both cities also included the professionals' inability to adjust to their places of origin after migrating to new global cities.

Underlying these similarities and differences between Bangalore and Dubai are criteria particular to each city for what it means to be a worthwhile resident or citizen. These criteria, refracted through distinct modes of stratification in the two cities, shape not only the relationship between the city and the individual but also affect dynamics within churches in these cities and, in turn, how churches interact with their cities.

Civic Worth in the Neoliberal City

Those of us who live in Western democracies are accustomed to thinking of the notion of the civic in terms of the imagined social order of a democratic republic. As Luc Boltanski and Laurent Thévenot describe the logic of the civic realm, its reigning principle is the good of the collectivity, expressed in relations of solidarity and collective mobilization.[6] This civic logic is embodied in practices such as political voting, writing to representatives, joining demonstrations, signing petitions, participating in neighborhood and community groups and associations, taking on responsibilities in these groups, and becoming involved in initiatives to help the less fortunate or to defend universal rights. But the cities I study reveal a different set of "authorizing" principles that provide criteria for worth and moral orientation in the civic realm.

Dubai, like the rest of the UAE and Gulf states, is a "civic ethnocracy," as anthropologist Ahn Longva argues. The primary basis of governance is "not race, language or religion but citizenship conceived in terms of shared descent."[7] And the primary basis of civic worth is formal citizenship; those lacking it are rendered inferior and consigned to their respective rungs on an ethnic hierarchy. Unlike exclusion on the basis of race, the form of exclusion in civic ethnocracies, because it is based on legal citizenship, "strikes most observers as a 'normal' state of affairs . . . [and] appears rational and justifiable in our world of nation-states."[8]

In contrast, in Bangalore, where nearly everyone is a citizen, formal citizenship makes little difference to the majority of the participants in the civic realm, compared to other criteria such as class, language, ethnicity, caste, and religion. That is why, even if political structures posit formal equality between most residents, there still exist forms of stratification that shape civic worth. As Christophe Jaffrelot argues, the widespread civic and political disengagement of the Indian middle classes has very much to do with caste: even if members of the urban middle classes would be loath to admit that caste shapes their outlook in the slightest way (especially since the law forbids caste-based discrimination), their demographic is predominantly composed of upper castes, and thus their structural position makes it easy to understand why they would have little interest in policies catering to interests of lower castes.[9] Civic worth, therefore, is not simply accorded by formal membership in the polity (i.e., legal citizenship), but is refracted through various bases of stratification. I discuss such "stratified belonging" and its consequences in the next section.

Neoliberalism pretends to offer leveling mechanisms that cut across these criteria. The worth of neoliberal citizens, based on the criteria regularly articulated in official and popular discourses alike, comes both from their being economically productive (and thus contributing in a privileged way to the polity) and being a good consumer (by spending money to sustain the economy). Making such contributions by holding a job in a transnational corporation is especially valuable, since that position enables one not only to participate in a key engine of the economy but is also seen as helping put the city on the map and to make it a global player. Of course, in practice, any purported leveling is frustrated by structures that sustain unequal access to employment and consumption alike. But the overall ideal of the good citizen is effectively an individual who makes little to no demands of the government, but rather conforms to the neoliberal development agenda by being a "good player" in the market-driven strategies promoted by the state. It is a laissez-faire model in which the citizen effectively says to the state, "Leave me alone, and I'll leave you alone."[10]

The two bases of civic worth—being economically productive and being a good consumer—touch on vital ways in which citizenship is enacted in practice. As Neha Vora argues, they violate assumptions in the literature that equate citizenship with formal juridico-legal belonging.[11] These assumptions are so widely held because the terms of discourse and agendas for discussion have been set by Western scholars drawing on Western polities and models of statehood and citizenship. They also serve, in international discourse, as a means of justifying the neglect of those who do not meet this formal citizenship criterion, such as foreign residents of Arab Gulf states who are citizens of developing economies.

In light of the complexities identified earlier, juridico-legal belonging becomes a narrow and inadequate basis for understanding civic belonging in the contexts I study. Vora discusses mechanisms of enacted citizenship similar to the ones I identified, which she calls "racial consciousness" and "consumer citizenship." I modify and extend these concepts, arguing that these processes shape people's modes of belonging not only to the city at large but also to associations such as religious institutions.

Stratified Belonging

Professionals working in these neoliberal cities are very aware that their worth in the social hierarchy depends on their nationality, race/ethnicity, and social class. They experience and express their sense of belonging to their city through stratified lenses of nationality, ethnicity, and class, and it is on these bases that they experience the worth accorded to them by their cities. (As I argued in chapter 2, ECC groups propose a counter-narrative: that one's worth does not depend on these criteria, but comes from a personal relationship with God.)

Such ethno-racial differentiation in Dubai rose to prominence only with the population influx of the past four decades. As anthropologists have observed, the previously acknowledged sense of similarity between Arabs and South Asians has been erased, and a new "pure" ethnicity has emerged as the key basis of worth for the "local" citizen.[12] Anthropologists such as Ahmed Kanna have described how the construction of "Brand Dubai" is built on an orientalist model of the "Arab heritage," adopted to secure the interests of the ruling family by concealing the hybridity and diversity of their past and legitimizing this narrative on an international plane with the help of Western tourism, media, and "starchitects."[13] In Bangalore, while the influence of colonial rule was crucial in shaping the status enjoyed by the English language, recent economic development, migration, and ethnolinguistic politics (as well as caste influences hidden under the surface) play a role in shaping class and ethnic distinctions. Such stratified belonging in both cities shapes the Catholic Church in these cities as well.

STRATIFIED BELONGING IN DUBAI

Ethnoracial stratification in Dubai generates new modes of identification with one's nationality. People have to continually deal with stereotypes assumed by other groups, especially the locals; such assumptions are even embedded into legal procedures such as applications for and renewals of visas, drivers licenses, and other government documents. Not only do foreign residents feel "victimized" in this manner—for example, Indians complain that they are perceived of and treated as a lower class, and Filipina women complain that they are seen as chattel—but foreigners also in turn perpetuate stereotypes and distinctions against others: both those of different nationalities and less "worthy" members of their own nationality and ethnicity.

By virtue of living in such an environment, all of my respondents exhibited what Neha Vora calls a "racial consciousness": an awareness of one's nationality and ethnicity relative to those of others in their surroundings that they would not have developed in their own countries. For instance, Indian residents in Dubai are keenly aware of their being "Indian" in ways that would not occur to them while living in India, because there they experience no such "othering" on this basis. This awareness of being perceived as Indian (or Pakistani, Filipino, etc.) includes a recognition of stereotypes imposed on them as a result of perceptions of their co-ethnics living in the city. Like Vora, I found that "middle-class Indians . . . blamed [lower-class] migrants for the racism they experienced in their own lives, arguing that because uneducated and unskilled workers constitute the majority of South Asians in the Gulf, people assume all Indians are uneducated and unskilled."[14] This consciousness is not only of race or ethnicity but also of social class.

This stratified belonging is perpetuated through structural arrangements that are common across Gulf countries and that reflect and reinforce the same hierarchy. Locals and other GCC citizens come first; then citizens of developed countries (western Europeans, Americans, Australians, Japanese); then the non-Gulf

Arabs (e.g., Egyptians, Lebanese, Syrians); and at the bottom are South Asians, Southeast Asians, and Africans. This stratification of the ethnocracy is reinforced in numerous ways, beginning with one's entry into the country. To visit the UAE, citizens of GCC countries do not need a passport; citizens of developed countries can get a free visa on arrival[15]; and citizens of developing countries require visas, which can be expensive (e.g., US$100 for Indians), and also have to endure being herded through a long line for "iris scanning."

Second, as I mentioned in chapter 1, the labor market is ethnically segmented, and nearly everyone I interviewed described the pattern similarly.[16] CxOs and managing directors are typically local Arab or white American/Australian/Western European. Middle-to-senior managers and high-skilled engineers are predominantly non-Gulf Arabs (e.g., Egyptians, Lebanese). There is a preponderance of Indians in accounting, finance, and HR roles, mostly in junior and mid-level positions, rather than at the senior level. Cargo and shipping jobs are where most West Africans (mainly from Nigeria, Ghana, and Cote D'Ivoire) are employed. Service-sector and clerical work (e.g., wait staff, receptionists, etc.) are associated with Filipinos. Taxi drivers are predominantly assumed to be Pakistani. The domestic sector is dominated by Filipinos, Sri Lankans, and Indonesians. Manual laborers are typically from Pakistan, Bangladesh, and India.

Third, even among professionals there is a racialized hierarchy of pay. South Asian and Filipino respondents complained about an explicit pay scale hierarchy in most companies (including multinationals) that was determined by one's passport: a South Asian would get paid significantly less than a white European or local citizen.[17] Those who were unaware of this wage disparity before moving to Dubai felt there was nothing they could do about it, after they discovered it. This arrangement exemplifies the neoliberal logic. After all, why should migrants complain if their pay is comparable to what others of their nationality would make back home; the fact that they are in Dubai in this job at all reflects that they are "better off," and surely, if they did not like the arrangement, they could just vote with their feet.

A fourth layer of ethnic segregation in the city is spatial. Unlike many older metropolises in which development occurred in concentric circles expanding radially outward from an older downtown, Dubai developed in a linear fashion along a single highway. Older parts of town—near the Creek, the primary commercial center of old Dubai—have cheaper and older housing and are populated by the lower and working classes. Newer parts of town that are closer to the free trade zone, which once used to only house poorly maintained labor camps, now also cater to upper- and upper-middle-class expats in luxury housing areas.

How does all this stratification shape the Catholic Church in Dubai? Reflecting the broader ethnoracial segmentation of society, church groups congregate along ethnic and national groups, with little meaningful contact across nationalities. Until recently, the Catholic population in Dubai, as in the rest of the Arabian Gulf outside Saudi Arabia, was made up predominantly of Indians, mainly of Goan, Mangalorean, and Keralite ethnicities. In the past decade, however, the Filipino population increased rapidly and by now likely constitutes the majority of Catholics in Dubai. In addition, there are smaller numbers of non-Gulf Arabs (mainly Lebanese, Syrians, and Jordanians) and Europeans (mainly French). Dubai also has a sizable community of Nigerians, perhaps as large as the French community, who are very active in the African Charismatic community; there may now be as many Nigerians as French living in the city. This diversity of ethnicities and languages structures Catholic parishes into distinct language groups; Protestant churches are divided into smaller language-based churches as well. As I discuss presently, these ethnolinguistic communities cultivate strong internal bonds and ties and contribute in numerous ways to their members' ability to survive in the city; however, ties across ethnolinguistic groups are weak, reflecting the broader pattern of segregation and mistrust. Common complaints directed at priests and bishops in the region reflect such ethnically stratified belonging; for instance, complaints that one particular language group or other consistently reserves a meeting hall at "prime" hours, or that members of other nationalities did not dress appropriately in church,[18] or, at the most racist level, that members of some ethnicity they did not like should not be educating their children.

A final reflection of this stratified belonging is religion's attempt to cast itself as relevant to the neoliberal polity. Catholic leaders in the Gulf justify their presence in these cities, especially in their discussions with local political leaders, as a means of moral and social control. As one Indian priest who worked for many decades in the Gulf told me, "When people are morally weak, then there are problems for the country. The government knows this, and that is why they support us. They appreciate us. When people have space to pray, to turn to God, there is moral support, less frustration, less risk of agitation." In other words, if people have churches, they will have a moral community and will not engage in protests. The counterpart justification in Bangalore is provided by church-run institutions that partner with corporations to provide training and skill development offerings, both MBA programs and community college courses, which generate not only well-trained but also "ethical" employees. Because they offer people "values" in addition to training, leaders of some of these religious institutions assume they have fulfilled their responsibility by equipping people spiritually for the workplace.

STRATIFIED BELONGING IN BANGALORE

As in Dubai, Catholic parishes in Bangalore are segmented into different language communities. The two main language groups are Kannada (the official state language, but the mother tongue of only a minority of Catholics) and Tamil (the language of a neighboring state, but the mother tongue of the majority of Catholics). Two other widely used languages are Konkani (another prominent language in the state of Karnataka in which Bangalore is located) and Malayalam (the state language of Kerala). A good proportion of the Catholic population—mainly the educated middle and upper classes, to which corporate professionals belong—is more at home in English. Hence, most parishes in the city have English-language liturgies, choirs, and prayer groups. Because of the diverse language groups, even the parish councils in many of these churches operate in English. Unlike their counterparts in Dubai, therefore, Catholic professionals in Bangalore see themselves not primarily as members of particular ethnolinguistic communities, but as middle-class English speakers, in contrast to members of lower classes whose allegiance is primarily to their linguistic identity. To understand why this distinction matters so much to these professionals, we need to briefly consider the historical factors that generated it.

Bangalore is the capital of the state of Karnataka, where the official language is Kannada. The majority of Catholics, however, are of Tamil origin and maintain their mother tongue. Tensions between members of these languages, in the city of Bangalore and in Karnataka more generally, simmered during the twentieth century as their respective nationalist movements grew. Kannada nationalism, as historian Janaki Nair argues, was driven by both fear and envy of Tamil nationalism. For instance, Tamil films became considerably more popular in the city than Kannada movies; after Tamil films were accused of depicting the Kannada people unfavorably, demands arose for cinemas showing them to be shut down.[19] In the following decades, tensions worsened with disputes such as the sharing of the waters of the Cauvery River between the states of Karnataka and Tamil Nadu.

Within the Catholic Church, these tensions erupted shortly after the Second Vatican Council (1962–1965). The council's proclamations signified an *aggiornamento* or updating of the church to the modern world, bringing about changes in teachings, structures, and practices of the church around the globe. Key among these changes was the shift in the liturgical language from Latin to local vernaculars. A key question that implementers of these changes did not adequately consider, however, was whose vernacular.[20]

When these proclamations were issued, the Catholic population of the archdiocese was nearly 70 percent Tamil. The archbishop, a Tamilian, then decreed that the language of the liturgy should reflect that of the people and that priests should be assigned to parishes that best reflected their linguistic competence. Tamil-speaking priests thus began to enjoy coveted postings in comfortable urban parishes, while Kannada-speaking priests were relegated to underdeveloped rural areas. The combination of economic disparity and linguistic nationalism generated a vocal minority of activist priests, who stoked the anger of some of the laity and joined hands with Hindu nationalists to demand that primacy be accorded to Kannada (i.e., that it should be the chief language used in Catholic services across the city). Protests ensued, at times turning violent even during masses, leaving bishops afraid for their lives. The language issue still remains a source of tension, with conflicts extending to involve the Konkani and Malayalam languages as well and sometimes becoming violent. As recently as April 2013, the rector of the Bangalore seminary was murdered by priests over the language issue. Many complain about how language politics has been a considerable drain on the energy and focus in the church in Bangalore. Corporate professionals I spoke to were especially disparaging in their critiques, often distancing themselves from linguistic-based forms of identification within the church (defaulting, therefore, to English). Such boundary work plays a role in their disengagement from the clergy and their priorities, as I discuss later in this chapter.

Efforts to generate an indigenous expression of the liturgy have also distanced middle-class English speakers. After the Second Vatican Council, theologians attempted to "inculturate" or "Indianize" the Catholic liturgy through practices such as removing footwear, sitting on the floor, and incorporating Sanskrit language and Hindu scriptures. These changes were not well received by many middle-class English speakers, who were upset by what they saw as a "paganization" or "Hinduization" of the church. As one of the leaders of the Catholic Charismatic Renewal in Bangalore put it, Charismatics in particular were "up in arms against it," because they "felt strongly it was just Hinduism." These attempts at Indianization did not gain traction, and so the Catholic liturgy in India thus largely retains European forms.[21]

At the same time that efforts to adapt to local language and "Indian culture" were generating heated conflict among Catholics, Bangalore was increasingly becoming a cosmopolitan hub. By the late 1990s, it was India's high-tech capital, drawing skilled migrants from around the country. "Global" competencies such as familiarity with Western culture and the English language became key assets for success. These changes would not leave the church untouched, particularly because they tapped into capacities it had inherited from its colonial past. But the growing educated, English-speaking middle class in Bangalore was not the audience envisaged by proponents of enculturation, either of language or liturgical expression. Hence, this demographic became increasingly disconnected from those concerns. My interviews with these English-speaking professionals supported the idea that they were beyond these "petty" concerns of ethnic/regional language and identity.

Another contributor to stratification is the violence perpetrated against Christians in recent decades, supported by proponents of the Hindutva nationalist ideology that conceives of India as a Hindu nation and sees Christianity and Islam as foreign bodies that do not belong. Conversions to Christianity are interpreted in this ideology as being a result of force and deception. Catholics, mainly because of the visibility of the clergy and their institutions, are regularly accused of proselytism and have been the target of violent attacks in Karnataka and other states. However, the Catholic professionals I interviewed in Bangalore claim to have never been subjected to either violence or overt discrimination; they see these phenomena as affecting people in smaller towns and villages and do not seem greatly concerned by them. Even though such violence reinforces the sense of being seen as undesirable by dominant powers in their country, few Catholic professionals participate in protests or other collective action organized by the archbishop and clergy in Bangalore. They espouse a sense of pride in their Indian nationality and religious affiliation as Catholics, but do little to affirm this nexus in the context of political tension between both. They do not overtly claim to feel like second-class citizens, but in practice are politically disengaged, without offering a voice that might benefit lower-class and lower-caste Christians: they thus allow political marginalization of their own religious community to be perpetuated.

Civic Worth as Consumers and Professionals

In the neoliberal polity, the main criteria of worth are, first, access to meritocratic work that produces economic benefits and, second, an abundance of opportunities for consumption. Professionals use these criteria, which circulate in these cities, to evaluate the worth of these cities in which they live. Dubai does not satisfy the first criterion because of its strong ethnonational stratification; Bangalore does not meet the second criterion, despite its shopping malls and opportunities for consumption, because it is by this standard still "undeveloped," with its weak infrastructure, power cuts and rolling blackouts, pervasive pollution, and lack of "comfort." Both are, in this sense, seen as instances of "market failure." Jason, a second-generation Indian expat in Dubai, expressed his ambivalence at the prospect of having to return to India in these terms:

> Being Indian, I'm extremely proud. I would not change the passport for any other passport in the world. Because in about ten years' time, the Indian passport is gonna be gold. Just because we have a billion plus people, we're not gonna accept any other entries for the ones who wanna become Indian. There was a story of 45 percent repatriation of CEOs

from Silicon Valley back to India because they are getting so much money. People are making so much money in India! But it's just so difficult: the standards that people are willing to accept. Like a white shirt is more like brown; it's not white! There's bad B.O. [body odor] everywhere. I mean if you don't have electricity, you're just screwed! Doesn't matter who you are, unless you have some serious connections. Life is more difficult. I mean it's congested!

Dubai, in comparison to these inconveniences, is experienced "as a space of luxury and comfort" and generates a distinctive form of belonging that Neha Vora calls "consumer citizenship." This mode of belonging, she argues, is "integral to shifting identities among Indians in Dubai, and [leads] to affective and political stakes in the city that [a]re in fact irreducible to the economic terms through which they [a]re often framed."[22] This is not confined to Indians, but even applies to members of other nationalities who, as I discussed earlier, found it similarly difficult to return to their home countries.

Yet, consumer citizenship is about not only luxury and comfort but also the centrality of a consumerist orientation to the way in which people inhabit and relate to the city. In both Bangalore and Dubai, professionals' main mode of involvement in the city is through participation in consumer practices, rather than, for instance, collective or political action. Urban anthropologists nevertheless call this a form of citizenship because these are modes of "inhabiting" and "staking claims to" the city: it is through consumer spaces that people express and reinforce a sense of belonging to the city.[23] Consumer citizenship requires neither juridico-legal rights to citizenship nor does it demand political engagement. All it requires is for the denizen to contribute to the economy by consuming. Yet many are highly constrained in their ability to consume. It is thus a segmented mode of citizenship, mediated by the market and the potential for access to it.[24] In such contexts—which are not exclusive to my cases, but include, for instance, the case of marginalized African Americans in the United States, as many American sociologists have shown—minority groups look to consumption as a means "of affirming [their] insertion in mainstream society."[25]

RELIGIOUS BELONGING AND CONSUMER CITIZENSHIP

How does such consumer citizenship shape religion? First, at the level of the parish, numerous key events in churches are inflected by consumerism. Major parish events, such as feasts and festivals, are sponsored by corporations and smaller businesses, becoming for them a means of advertising to a ready audience. Church group leaders expend considerable energy finding corporate sponsors for events, developing means of advertising, coming up with ways to entice consumerist-minded people to participate (e.g., by offering free gimmicks, discounted meals, coupons, and t-shirts). In the Gulf, every parish festival involves a raffle. Volunteers and religious group members are goaded to sell as many tickets as possible, and various consumer and luxury goods, such as SUVs, watches, and electronic goods, are the coveted prizes awarded to lucky winners. The presence of these "generous corporate sponsors" is keenly felt at these events, with their pervasive banners that line the parish boundaries and the long litanies of thanks given by emcees at these events. Leaders acknowledged complaints from some "conservative" parishioners that such raffles were simply turning the church into a marketplace, but justify it by saying that the money they generate sustains the church's charitable activities.

Second, in both cities, church groups, not simply individuals, define their belonging to the city through consumer practices. Religious groups spend time in shared practices of consumption; for instance, going out to malls, dinners, movies, and even sometimes nightclubs. But there are some important differences in these religious groups' expectations of their members that either enable or constrain consumer citizenship. These differences reflect two ideal-typical tendencies, which I call exclusivist and integrative orientations.

Exclusivist orientation. In many ECC groups, particularly in Indian ones, commitment to the religious group was seen as something that competed with, but needed to be prioritized over, other nonchurch activities. Such competition was imposed structurally, since the group meetings would usually be scheduled on evenings and weekends at prime times when most members were not working—which also meant that they conflicted with other lifestyle commitments they could cultivate during their free time.

Freddie, the leader of a long-standing Charismatic prayer group in Dubai, talked about how "[f]or more than twenty years we have been faithfully meeting here every single Friday. And every Friday, for three–four hours, we are here. Even the children come. We could have easily said, 'Let's go for a movie,' 'Let's just stay in and take a nap,' or 'Let's go to the beach or have a barbecue.' But no, we have never missed one Friday. Forty-fifty families have been faithfully coming, even with the small children in tow." Leaders of Charismatic prayer groups in both cities would similarly talk to members about how "the first thing has to be the commitment" to regularly attending group events and that this meant making sacrifices.

Such groups had an implicit expectation that members would dedicate their spare time to the group, because it was the primary means through which to sustain their personal relationships with God. There was no expectation for people to sacrifice work; when someone could not attend a prayer group meeting because of work obligations, it was perfectly understandable. Spending time with family, however, or in non-urgent or leisure activities, was seen as a lack of seriousness in one's commitment to the group.

The ECC group is thus presented as an exclusive commitment that has to be sacred, reflecting the theological view that the believer or disciple has to be "set apart" for God and that the state of discipleship entails regular sacrifice. Just as tithing a proportion of one's income to the group makes an exclusive claim on people's money, commitment to attending the group regularly makes such a claim on people's time. Just as people believe that they would be "blessed" for giving away their money, they believe that God blessed them for their regular commitment of time to attending the group. Through such exclusive commitments, religion takes on a primacy in the lives of Missionaries. By competing with secular alternatives, it can pose constraints on participation in consumerist lifestyles. However, this constraint is largely implicit, and as we saw in the previous chapter, its power remains limited.

Integrative orientation. In contrast to the exclusivist tendency, some groups do not put religious and secular commitments in competition with one another, but rather try to integrate them. One such example is the Arabic-speaking group that is part of a European Catholic lay movement.

Unlike exclusivist ECC groups, this group intentionally integrates "nonspiritual" activities into weekly sessions. While their group meetings include prayer and readings and reflections on religious topics, they also include regular time for "physical," "professional," and "recreational" activities. These activities are provided through "clubs," smaller subgroups that offer courses on topics such as photography to improve members' skills; sports activities before or after the group meeting; and regular group outings to parks, malls, restaurants, bars, or nightclubs that group members want to visit. The group offers these activities in an effort to continue to be "relevant" to professionals, for whom "just spiritual activities would be boring," as Nadia put it. She continued:

> Sometimes, I find the life in Dubai very distracting. So you have a choice between going to [the prayer group] on a Thursday evening or going shopping on a Thursday evening. And I kind of drift toward shopping on a Thursday evening [*laughs*]. I find that sometimes you think, "Ahh, I've got to sit there for two and a half hours, listening to something, maybe it's boring." And you know it's boring! And there are times when we've fallen asleep at the back of the hall after a long day at work [*laughs*]. And everyone's waiting; at the end of the meeting, everyone's like, "Okay so where's dinner after this?" You know? So sometimes you just want to skip the spiritual part and just be there because all your friends are there.

So you kind of lose track of why you're actually there to start with. You lose focus sometimes.

Khaled noted that "to make [the prayer group] more interesting," he and fellow members have made it a regular practice to go out to dinner after meetings, usually at a trendy new restaurant. During the week they email each other with a list of options for dinner venues, and people "get to vote where they actually want to have dinner. So it becomes fun." After dinner, some of them go out to a nightclub or pub. They also regularly try to go out to movies as a group after mass. "So [the group] has become a circle of very close friends." In addition to weekly activities, they have monthly events. "Like next weekend we're going to a full day at a chalet on the beach," Nadia informed me. "So in that sense, if people say they don't want to commit to something at church because they want to have a social life, we've tackled that. We've given them a social life as well."

"The meeting is not a routine," explained Khaled. "It is not just a spiritual meeting every single week. Every week there is something different. And in the month where we have a fifth week we do a team-building activity, where people break that routine of coming and sitting and listening to someone. They just get up and try to use your brains and brawns." Rachid noted that the social context in Dubai required a movement like theirs to change its mode of operation to appeal to its sophisticated professionals and compete with their many "distractions":

> This is the difference between here and Syria. In Syria when I used to go to any youth meeting or something, we finish the meeting and then would go for a walk, or go to somebody's house and drink coffee or something. And that was, okay, we're having fun. But here, because there are so many distractions you have to do something very special, to make people not regret coming to [the group meeting]. You will have to organize some very good activities to just get people to come here. Keep the suspense going [laughs]. Whereas in other places like Syria, anything was okay. Over here, if you go to a restaurant, it's the minimum they expect every week! And the committees have been very helpful here. The activities they introduce every month—from desert safaris to beach activities.

In the integrative logic, various lifestyle activities that could compete with commitment to church groups are rendered compatible when these groups embrace them in the pursuit of being "relevant" to members. This strategy, they believe, allows them to draw and retain members. But part of the reason an exclusivist approach works for Indian groups is that they have a large population in both cities, and adopting a "strict" model of belonging becomes one way to keep the commitment level of the group strong. It may also be the case that a "purity" injunction matters more to them, especially to those in Charismatic groups, and thus any "diluting" of the spiritual core of the group would be unacceptable. The accommodationist, integrative model is seen as necessary in the Arabic community in the church in Dubai because it has a smaller pool of members. It is interested in casting a wider net and drawing more people in through these various activities, even if these people may not be interested primarily in the spiritual content of the group.

The exclusivist model of most ECC groups constrains consumer citizenship to some degree by prioritizing the church group as a primary locus of belonging. Missionaries are "set apart" in this separate realm and feel called to "sacrifice" alternative pursuits to some degree. The integrative model, in contrast, encourages consumer citizenship and fosters a sense of home through a fusion of realms, where one can attend a spiritual workshop, a photography class, and go to a trendy nightclub as part of the same prayer group meeting.

Most prayer groups in these cities fall somewhere in between these two tendencies. Many Charismatic groups, while focusing exclusively on spiritual content within group meetings, also have additional "ministries" for "social activities," which are responsible for planning activities such as movie nights, picnics, or sports. In cities like Dubai, where the weather for much of the year is unbearably hot, shopping malls and fast-food outlets are often the only available spaces for these groups to carry out their social activities. Thus, while the groups may impose constraints on the time that members could otherwise spend on consumerist pursuits, they also inadvertently support modes of consumer citizenship.

PROFESSIONAL LOGICS IN CHURCH

The Mercenary's pursuit of mobility finds little expression in church settings, although at times, as I discuss later, political struggles in churches can foster mistrust and even acts of sabotage. However, professionals do carry other aspects of their workplace orientations into church settings.

One way in which logics of professionalism seep into church settings is the criticism of church leaders. For instance, Menezes in Bangalore complained about the inefficiency and unwilling of the priests he knew to seek guidance in running an organization from professionals such as himself:

> The problem with [the] church is that priests want to do it all themselves. And priests are not aware of the corporate environment. . . . Of course, there are some very good priests who run some very good institutions. But in terms of banking on knowledge from professionals in the industry, I don't think—not many [priests] are taking professional[s'] help

[or] putting us into [roles] to guide them or to give input. . . . I think priests are very closed. They behave like they know everything.

Other corporate professionals active in the church raised similar criticisms. They see themselves as having much to offer their parishes in helping them run more efficiently, but do not see clergy as willing to grant them sufficient leadership responsibility to make a difference. Alonso in Dubai expressed similar sentiments to those of Menezes:

> I would say my work outside, I'm just trying to implement it here in the church, so it would be more professional and everything. Because, before I joined here, I noticed that everything is like, you work by trust, here in church. So it doesn't matter if you leave your money there, or you don't do inventory. Or you don't do auditing. Because the mindset is that, hey, this is the church, nobody will cheat us here. But it's not always like that. They don't have records, like what materials they have.

I asked if he had encountered any resistance in his attempts to "professionalize" things. "Oh yeah," he replied. "Because they don't want any changes. Because it's been here for thirty years I think. And some other parishioners have been here from the start. And this is the way they have started doing it." Yet, in contrast to Menezes's criticism, the barriers that Alonso identified were put up not by clergy but by other lay leaders in dominant positions of church leadership, who did not want either to relinquish their power or to change the way they did things. While younger professionals in parish committees complained, for instance, that the parish's registries were not yet digitized and "modernized," older members did not see implementing such changes as being worth the hassle.

Another instance in which integrating professional logics might conflict with church practice is the way in which it deals with its members. Many professionals claimed that the "traditional" way of treating people in church was rude and patronizing, in contrast to the more "Christian" ways in which they learned to communicate in their companies. Dianne in Bangalore claimed that "putting people before tasks" was something she learned at the workplace from a non-Christian manager: "I saw it very clearly there, because she was very empathetic. . . . She gave me time to settle in. You know, most people, they just expect you to perform on the job. So it's good to see human beings around." She claimed that her non-Christian manager taught her to treat colleagues in ways that were more in keeping with Christian ideals than the way some church leaders were treating one another. "And it also fell in line with what Christ teaches, you know? . . . I think you realize that your so-called tasks come and go, but the people, the way you have influenced them, and the wounds you give them or the assurances you give them, they last a lifetime." One might thus occasionally find the therapeutic ideals of the Missionary being lived out more fully by secular managers than by church leaders.

Some professionals found that their practical skills from the corporate world were useful in church. Francesca in Dubai, for instance, claimed that "definitely there has been a spillover" from her corporate life into her leadership role in her church group:

> A lot of things in [the group] involves communications, like social media or whatever. And [my company] does a lot of it too. Like Facebook, Twitter, communicating to young people in the channels they use. . . . Videos, PowerPoint, all this stuff. Apart from media, I've had three–four years of experience of organizing events, and that's of course very helpful in [the group] because we have lots of events. So I have been able to use a lot of my professional experience in working for [the church group].

Yet some also argued that corporate logics were not altogether appropriate or helpful in church settings. Menezes, again, in speaking about his own parish, said, "The church I am part of is very poor with lot of illiterate people, semi-literate and all. So you can't go and talk your [corporate] language there. You need to temper your language as per the requirement. You can't go do a corporate presentation there . . . you have to explain in simple Tamil or Kannada."

Dianne in Bangalore similarly talked about how corporate approaches would not always work with people in church groups. Professional logics of rational organization were out of place in an environment where emotion and spontaneity reigned:

> You need to realize that the church group is a very emotional bunch of people. You have people from different workplaces, from different walks of life. So you can't get a single mission statement and work toward it and—it doesn't happen that way, if at all. Working in church groups that are so disorganized, so spontaneous, I've learned not to take things personally when things don't go my way. Because I used to be this slave to routine and organization and scheduling and I had these people who were very spontaneous. . . . So, you know, you learn to relax. And in a way it's good because you realize that not everything can go as per your plan. And there's parts of it where you just surrender to God and you actually look back and say, "It couldn't have been done better."

Dianne also talked about how she had to learn that the spillover from her workplace professionalism into her church groups was at times counterproductive, because what mattered at church was not so much efficiency in running its events, but how she treated people.

> The organizing helps, but it generally puts people off, you tend to rub people on the wrong side. . . . And it doesn't really help when you upset people around you when you're rude and you're like, "Why aren't you on time?" You're beating the very purpose. Because you're here to serve God, and here you're snapping at your neighbor, being impatient. Uhh— it's not the way!

Francesca also talked about how one's experience of dealing with office politics can impede relationships in church if one allows corporate logics to spill over into that context:

> I think there's always this kind of tension where you have a structure and you have leadership and, in a sense, management, for it to get political. Because it's people at the end of it. And sometimes, because you are so used to working in a corporate situation, you assess things according to that. And you match your experience at work with your experience in [the church group]. And there is a tendency to think of things politically, because that's the way you think it is. But here it's not political. . . . Because you know that the people who are doing this first of all, they don't get anything out of it, to be honest. And I've been blessed actually to experience and get to know a lot of these leaders personally. And I know the kind of sacrifices they make and the situations they go through. And yet they do what they do.

These quotations suggest, therefore, that there are situations when church groups constrain consumer citizenship or members segment their professional sensibilities from their interactions in their parishes, recognizing that it is not always appropriate to be "professional" in church. Yet, churches also constitute another mode of belonging for these professionals: as civic spaces.

The Church as Civic Space

In addition to having a sense of belonging to church groups, professionals can experience in these contexts a feeling of solidarity through voluntary participation in activities that contribute to the common good and ameliorate issues of public concern. While one might expect that as citizens in a democratic country, Catholic professionals in India would be engaged in more opportunities through the church to help the poor, surprisingly, it is in nondemocratic Dubai that they are more actively involved.

In Bangalore, the Catholic Church runs numerous schools and hospitals, many of which make provisions to assist people seeking these services who are in financial need. As of this writing, it also runs twelve dispensaries; twelve community health centers; six care facilities for people with cancer, HIV/AIDS, and leprosy; twenty-one charities; twenty-five orphanages; twenty-eight counseling and rehabilitation centers; and sixteen homes for the aged.[26] All of these, however, are run and staffed almost entirely by religious (i.e., priests, nuns, and brothers). Corporate professionals have little involvement in these institutions, at least, on any sustained basis. Most who are actively involved in church in Bangalore have a primarily spiritualized mode of involvement, restricted to ECC prayer groups that met in churches.

In Dubai, by contrast, even though ECC groups are just as dominant in church settings, professionals are more involved in poverty-alleviation activities, particularly in transmitting various forms of economic, social, and cultural capital. While the Catholic Church in Dubai cannot legally form organizations that operate outside the premises of the church campus, corporate professionals are highly involved in less formal attempts to help people in need.

Social, Human, and Cultural Capital

Because of the steady flow of migrants and the impossibility of their assimilation as citizens, Gulf parishes over the years have developed into robust ethnolinguistic communities with strong internal cohesion and in-group loyalty, which are manifested particularly by long-term residents. Robert Putnam refers to such intragroup cohesiveness as a kind of "sociological superglue" and terms it "bonding social capital."[27] These communities become like an immediate home for new visitors, many of whom soon become plugged into social networks of people who share their language, ethnicity, cuisine, and other cultural practices; this involvement enables them to feel a sense of belonging. It is not uncommon for people to come on visit visas to Dubai or other Gulf cities and to find a job and even housing through contacts they make at church. Bulletin boards at church in Dubai, for instance, routinely post advertisements by people looking for roommates or accommodations, always specifying language, ethnicity, and gender. In contrast, none of the Bangalore parishes use parish bulletin boards in this manner. Rather, that space is used only to advertise religious events.

As in Dubai, Catholic parishes in Bangalore are segmented into different language communities, with Kannada, Tamil, Konkani, and Malayalam being the most prominent. But as I mentioned earlier in this chapter, the majority of members from the educated classes, including corporate professionals, are more at home in English. Just as in Dubai, these language- and ethnicity-based groups in Bangalore enable new members to adjust to life in the new city, reinforce cultural values and practices central to their ethnic traditions, organize events such as celebrations and festivals, and provide opportunities for participation and leadership.

While the internal cohesion or the "bonding" capital within these groups tends to be strong, what Putnam calls the "bridging" social capital or the trust and cohesion *across* these language groups is relatively weak. Parish priests I interviewed in the Gulf complained that the parish seems to function like a large umbrella, sustaining autonomous ethnic groups, rather than a unified parish community. As one priest complained to me: "[The parishioners] say, 'We belong to the Tamil community' or 'We belong to the Malayalam community' or 'We belong to the Arabic community,' instead of saying, 'We belong to St. Mary's Church.'" By contrast, because of the large number of parishes in Bangalore, some of which have been around for more than a century, people can choose a parish that is predominantly composed of members of their ethno-linguistic group, and can develop a greater sense of affiliation with the parish. However, religiously committed corporate professionals often identify with one of the several ECC groups that do not cater to members of any one parish, but instead, draw people together from across different parishes. Many priests in Bangalore, just as in the Gulf, see these new forms of belonging as weakening their members' commitment to the parish.

In the Gulf, church leaders (i.e., priests and parish council members) regularly make attempts to cultivate in their members a sense of belonging to the larger parish and organize activities that build such bridging capital. Economic activity looms large in such events, which range from classes that cultivate skills and thereby enhance economic opportunities to raffles and fundraisers for various charitable causes internal to the church. Although bridging events, such as parish fairs, family festivals, and sports festivals, aim to bring together the different communities in church, each individual event also serves as an occasion to collect money that can be made available to needy parishioners. Such parish-level and community-level events, especially those with economic components aimed at helping members, are much more prevalent in Dubai than in Bangalore. The relatively large size of each ethnic community and the perpetual economic need among members of these communities in Dubai (not to mention the legal ramifications if these needs are not met, such as imprisonment or deportation) are among key contributors to sustaining the regularity of these events.

MEETING ECONOMIC NEEDS

Churches distribute funds in several different ways to needy people (who are not always members or even Christians, though they are given priority). In both cities, parishes have committees in charge of the disbursement of these funds. These groups meet with individuals in need who contact them, and they distribute funds after assessing their situations. Corporate professionals belonging to ECC groups, however, play more of a role in such committees in Dubai than their counterparts do in Bangalore.

From my observations and conversations with church leaders in Dubai, key recurring needs were medical (either for individuals who were uninsured or who were unable to afford to pay for the urgent medical needs of family members back home); educational (e.g., an inability to afford school fees for their children); immediate survival (for people who were either unemployed, whose spouses were in prison, or whose employers had not paid them on time and could not meet day-to-day needs); legal (particularly, those who had overstayed their visas and had to pay substantial fines to exit the country or to take up a new job without being imprisoned); and paying for return tickets home. Although for a while churches helped people pay off their credit card debts,[28] many have stopped doing so because of the pervasiveness of the problem. Funds for these various financial needs are often collected within ethnic or language communities, although parishes also centrally distribute a pool of funds through their benevolence committees that meet with applicants once a week over several hours.

Needy parishioners first fill out a form available from the church office. This request for financial aid is several pages long and requires people to submit both color and passport photos of themselves and to be able to write out their needs clearly. The form is in English, but I noticed that the writing, in most cases, was either in very broken English or in other languages such as Tagalog or Urdu or Malayalam. Committee members either understood these languages or could easily find someone to translate if needed. As I read through the forms filled out by various applicants, it felt as though this process was an extension of the same oppressive regime outside the church in which people have to provide considerable documentation for anything they request: a process that itself takes money and time (to make photocopies, take photos, etc.), resources that many of these applicants lacked. But apparently this amount of documentation was needed to reduce the massive number of requests for financial help, especially after the recession.

Based on my observations of several benevolence committee meetings, the following applicants who applied at one meeting were typical. The first applicant was a Filipino sailor who had been in jail for several months, serving a sentence for having unpaid debts; he had five children. His wife had already approached the church and been financially helped several times. This latest request was for AED 4,000 for rent money (around USD 1,100); the committee gave him only AED 500 because his family had already received a lot of aid and church funds needed to be available for others. The sailor was followed by an Indian woman with thyroid issues. The doctor on the committee examined her, said she did not need immediate attention, and prescribed a drug she could obtain cheaply. Next a young Pakistani man wearing a bandana came before the committee. He was an artist and carpenter by trade and was looking for work. He did not ask for money, so it is not clear if he expected to receive some or just wanted encouragement. The committee members who knew Urdu spoke to him in that language and encouraged him to keep trying to find a job. The fourth applicant was an Indian woman requesting help with rent, electricity bills, and overdue school fees for her children. She said her family had relocated from Dubai to Sharjah (a neighboring city, where rent is much cheaper), but was still struggling. She was unemployed, her husband had been laid off three months ago, and they were paying off a substantial loan. The committee asked her to produce supporting documents before it could help her and told her that church funds were typically reserved for health-related and urgent cases. In every case, the committee members, all middle-class professionals of Indian and Filipino origin, encouraged each applicant to persevere through what was "a time of trial." Those committee members who were more involved in Charismatic worship prayed with each applicant for "prosperity," "blessing," and "command[ed] healing"; told the person to "believe that you are healed"; prayed to "break the curse" that they believed was binding the person; and urged him or her to read the Bible daily. At each meeting, they would usually distribute around USD 3,000 in cash to select applicants.

My perusal of stacks of applications for charitable assistance and my conversations with benevolence committee members indicated that nearly every applicant was from the Philippines or the Indian subcontinent. Members of the African and Arabic communities seemed to take care of their needs within their communities. French and other European residents of Dubai usually held high-paying jobs, and when some were laid off and had to struggle financially, they would usually either leave the country or rely on friends or savings rather than request financial assistance from the parish.

Church groups in Dubai also make regular visits to hospitals, prisons, and labor camps, although often in small groups and not under church auspices, to avoid giving the impression of proselytism or of "meddling" in public affairs.[29] Getting permission from government authorities to make such visits was apparently easier when only a small number of people were involved. During hospital visits, members did not attempt to pray with non-Christians, but would talk to them and offer comfort, praying for them after they had left.

Participating in prison ministries and other social welfare activities is another means of cultivating bridging social capital, since some of these groups incorporate members from different ethnic backgrounds. However, it is important to note that only a minority of ECC members participate in these activities. This may be partly because such participation involves a significant time commitment and is emotionally taxing. Some even feared that participation might get them into trouble with the law.

An active but small contingent of professionals in Dubai engage in outreach as part of these subgroups or "ministries."[30] In many cases, group members who make such visits to prisons, hospitals, or labor camps return to the larger group to share their experiences, initiate prayers, and plan fundraisers involving the larger group to help individuals in need (e.g., paying someone's medical bill or buying someone an airplane ticket) and to fund the ministries' initiatives (e.g., buying paper supplies used in helping teach English to laborers).

While groups of parishioners in Bangalore also visit prisons and hospitals, corporate professionals are seldom found among them. ECC groups in which corporate professionals are involved visit orphanages or homes for the elderly two or three times a year at most. Fundraisers for the needy are also relatively infrequent. One parish priest who runs an orphanage told me that he would encourage parishioners occasionally during church services to donate to his organization, but was afraid that any more frequent and targeted appeals would upset them. Others in Bangalore suggested that such reticence may occur because priests there have a reputation for pestering people for money, particularly by asking applicants to schools and colleges to make "voluntary donations" before they could be admitted. The mistrust among people in Bangalore as to how donations are being spent or distributed by church leaders reflects a broader concern in India about political corruption.

SOCIAL CAPITAL AND EMPLOYMENT

The church in Dubai also generates a second type of social capital that differs from Putnam's concept of bridging capital, which produces a sense of cohesion between groups. This type involves the networks and ties through which members can find employment or other opportunities for social mobility.[31] Bulletin boards at church regularly display job postings in Dubai, but never in Bangalore. Priests encourage parishioners who become aware of opportunities in their companies to post these notices in church first before advertising them in newspapers. Direct contact with fellow members at church can also lead to jobs: a number of my respondents claimed to have found employment through contacts at church. In Bangalore, by contrast, church groups and priests seemed reluctant to directly promote employment opportunities in any way. Some expressed the belief that using spiritual settings for secular purposes was inappropriate. Underlying their reluctance were concerns about nepotism as a form of corruption and the idealization of meritocracy. The implicit expectation was that it would be better for people to turn to God alone and pray for employment to come about through "proper" means (i.e., applying to positions advertised in papers), rather than using the church or parishioners as a source of networks.

HUMAN CAPITAL

Professionals volunteering in churches in Dubai are directly involved in providing training in various skills—what some refer to as "human capital"—to enable people to make more money or improve their employment prospects.[32] Local laws seem to permit religious institutions to conduct such activities on their premises. Courses on "survival English," for instance, teach people how to better navigate job interviews or various interactions from making small talk to buying a car. During the planning meetings for a course teaching English-language skills, the committee felt that housemaids would benefit most from it. The committee members believed that most housemaids preferred working for European or American families, because in general they paid and treated maids better than did employers of other nationalities.[33] Other courses offered were on assembling and repairing computers, using software such as Microsoft Excel, and effective salesmanship (see Figure 5.1). These courses were well attended, sometimes drawing in several hundred participants, some of whom were neither parishioners nor Catholic. The parish priest told me he hoped to hold courses on "haircutting, nail-polishing, and massaging" in the future. Such skills could enable struggling members to gain additional income as well as switch careers.

Because of the shortage of clergy in Dubai, the task of organizing and running these activities falls mainly to skilled professionals: managers, accountants, engineers, lawyers, doctors, teachers, and so on. Organizing these activities allows professionals to use skills developed from their corporate positions to serve people in ways that they find meaningful: from organizing events to teaching people English or computer skills or sales techniques. As one professional told me, volunteering for these activities allowed him to do something beyond "just charity," by helping to "teach people to fish" rather than just feeding them.

While some of these classes taught basic survival skills, other groups more directly emphasized entrepreneurship. Though involvement in the informal economy was not actively or explicitly promoted in most churches, many members of those groups were engaged in that sector in several ways, generating revenue either to supplement their formal income or to help them survive if they had no formal employment (e.g., if they had overstayed their visas and were unable to renew them because they could not afford to pay the fines). The activities they were engaged in and the range of income generated varied considerably and included house cleaning, carpentry and interior decoration, electrical work, bookkeeping, playing music at private events, informal catering, tutoring, web-based businesses catering to local clientele such as housewives and mothers, and private consultancy.

FIGURE 5.1. Ads for job vacancies and skills training on church bulletin board, Dubai.

In contrast to the situation in Dubai, the Catholic Church in Bangalore itself is involved in promoting such forms of human capital through skills training and other classes: these programs are planned and organized primarily by clergy-run institutions and not lay professionals. One parish runs a computer training institute. Another institute run by a prominent religious order helps internal migrants who move to Bangalore find jobs in the service sector as well as entry-level jobs in multinationals. The priest who directs it told me he has minimal support staff and does all the fundraising and much of the teaching himself. While he collaborates with corporate professionals, most are not Catholic members of ECC groups, but instead are secular professionals who stand to benefit from the pool of labor the institute can offer.

CULTURAL CAPITAL

Cultural capital has to do with skills cultivated for purposes intrinsic to religious institutions that can be transposed into work settings to yield economic benefits. Unlike the aforementioned forms of social, economic, and human capital, the skills and habits I describe in this section were cultivated in ECC groups in both Dubai and Bangalore. Transmitting such cultural capital is not intentionally aimed at improving the economic conditions of the lower classes, but in many cases it does facilitate economic mobility among less privileged members who belong to such church groups.

Many who are involved in church groups in both cities said that their participation was instrumental in helping them develop what they described as "soft skills" in the areas of communications, teamwork, and handing conflict. Others claimed to have learned event management, organizational skills, and presentation skills from their church groups, which they said gave them an advantage in their workplaces and also motivated them to pursue careers in new fields, such as training, coaching, or human resources.[34] Church groups thus provided them with skills that were not only helpful for the running of the groups but also were valuable for their career development.

Often, the training that people receive in these church groups is provided by professionals who rely both on their experience in the workplace and on management texts such as Stephen Covey's *Seven Habits of Highly Effective People*, which was used in several English-language groups I observed in both cities. Many church group leaders believed there is a strong symbiotic relationship between religious faith and "effective management." As Cherian, a senior manager and prayer group leader, stated, "Basically, I think all the management principles came from the Bible." Often ideas about "relationship skills," "team-building," and "servant leadership" were imported from "management wisdom" and supplemented by Bible quotes to underscore their intrinsic compatibility.

Some Indian respondents described learning skills during their upbringing in Catholic households, which they said were generally more "westernized"; their greater familiarity with English and with Western customs later proved advantageous in their workplaces. Floyd, a motivational speaker and entrepreneur, provided an example: he was giving a talk in Dubai to a group of Indian senior executives from major corporations when, during one of the meals, it came to his attention that they were unsure of "basic [Western] table manners." This etiquette was an elementary aspect of his upbringing in a middle-class Catholic household in Bombay, in contrast to the experience of the managers he was addressing, who had grown up in more traditional Indian households. Hesitant to do something that could possibly humiliate them, he asked, "Would you mind if I demonstrate [Western manners] and use you as an example and do a correction on it?"

> They said, "Yes, certainly!" I said, "You will not hold that against me, that I am correcting you in front of so many people?" They said, "Our parents didn't teach us, our schools didn't teach us, our universities didn't teach us, our present employees don't teach us. So if you teach us, do you think that we will be angry with you?" So I was a little taken aback to think that they would accept. I mean senior, well-educated managers!

He credited this incident for having improved his professional reputation and relationships with his clients. At the time of our interview, he was organizing a seminar on etiquette to be sponsored by the church, which he believed could help many people in their professional lives. This was an example of how ECC groups in both cities contribute to cultivating not only job skills but also the *habitus* of a middle-class professional and the concomitant cultural capital that can improve social mobility. However, in Bangalore, these ECC groups do not actively participate in the church's other activities such as charitable work or human capital building, whereas their counterparts in Dubai do. Why?

Engaged Expats and Disengaged Citizens

Let me suggest three main reasons for the greater civic engagement of professionals in ECC groups in Dubai compared to Bangalore: differences in (1) organizational structures, (2) legal restrictions, and (3) institutional priorities. All these differences are shaped by the forms of stratification and neoliberal belonging in these cities that I discussed earlier in this chapter.

Differences in Organizational Structures

There are important differences across cities in the organizational structure of the church and, concomitantly, the relationship between clergy and laity. In Dubai, there are 10 priests for some 300,000 Catholics, in contrast to Bangalore, where there are around 1,600 priests for 400,000 Catholics. This difference had a great impact on laypeople's attitudes toward religious professionals. In Bangalore, many actively involved laypeople felt that they only had a peripheral role, which amounted to little more than tokenism. They complained that priests nominated only "yes-men and -women" to their councils and that the input of such people ultimately made little difference to the priests' decisions. For instance, a long-time member of the parish council of a large parish in the heart of the city told me,

> Parish council [*laughs*] is meant for: which hymn to sing, which door to enter, which candle to light, and which way to go. Whatever the parish council can suggest or recommend, the parish priest has the veto power to take it up or let it go. It is a paper tiger without teeth. It's just a cover-up. Because whenever you corner the man responsible, . . . he will say, "Finance we can never disclose; this is not the prerogative of the laity." No transparency, no accountability. And if you talk, you'll not be allowed to enter the room next time!

One priest I talked to sympathized considerably with the laity in Bangalore after having heard their complaints for years: "I don't think the laity feel good enough—even those who are there in the committees don't feel good enough from what I have seen and heard. They don't feel . . . that they count, really. They are there in committees but they don't really count."

Professionals in Bangalore who were actively involved in ECC groups felt that the church already was capably running several organizations to serve the poor. When I asked Thomas, one of the leaders of a Charismatic prayer group in Bangalore who works for a global human rights NGO, why corporate professionals were so disengaged from the church's social mission, he surmised,

> They just feel like there's a group of people that is meant to be doing it. So religious work is for priests and nuns—that's for them, lay people don't do stuff like that, that's not normal. The same kind of opinion when it comes down to social service as well: it feels like people are there, meant to be doing it.

Another respondent, Shereen, who manages an American fitness franchise in Bangalore, similarly thought that it had to do with the "caste system mentality" in India. Certain tasks are seen as the prerogative of certain groups of people, and those who wanted to do social work would dedicate themselves to that, rather than work for a for-profit corporation.[35] I asked Rajesh, the leader of another professionals' prayer group and a senior HR executive, whether his group participated in any of the church's various poverty-alleviation or social service commitments. He replied,

> No. I'll tell you why we don't do social service. Because [the] Church has been doing that a lot. We don't need another social service [organization]. What we can do in fact is touch people's lives positively. So what we say in [our group] is that let's build people's lives in such a way

that they become a blessing to others, encouraging people to lead a life that is positive. I mean that's really what is needed today.

He echoed the widespread sentiment that the church's social service functions were already well taken care of and that corporate professionals were meant to contribute in different ways. "If you think God has called you to build people's lives, connect to that. That's more important. . . . My calling is very clear, that I am not called to go into social service or community development. That's not my cup of tea."

Many Bangalore prayer groups in which professionals were involved certainly did volunteer and serve the poor, but these activities were held only a handful of times during the year. For that very reason, Thomas, the prayer group leader I quoted earlier who works for an NGO, has actively stopped his group from engaging in such efforts unless they are willing to commit to them more regularly:

> I feel our social awareness is very stunted by these sporadic one-off events that we do once a year: Christmastime mainly. These things somehow become like some sort of remedy for guilt that you might possibly feel for not doing enough, so Christmastime you go to the home for the aged, you do something, sing carols. But you vaporize throughout the year [i.e., they only visit them once a year]. Which is why [in our group] . . . I tell them, you're not going anywhere Christmastime, Eastertime, festive time, you're not doing anything! If you're not doing it during the year, you're not doing it especially during their festive times. Maybe it's because I'm with an NGO and I get to see the need for human compassion all year long and then you have this thrusted [sic] down your throat somehow, this love and compassion overflowing from such kind hearts, suddenly, in this miraculous season of Christmas or Easter, you know? So I think that stunts us.

Thus even though the church's social initiatives and poverty-alleviation efforts are objectively larger in Bangalore, group members play a minimal role in these efforts. By contrast, in Dubai, most people who were involved in church, across nationalities and ethnicities, clearly understood that there was a dearth of clergy and religious, which meant a greater need for lay involvement.

Differences in Legal Restrictions

In Dubai all Catholics (indeed, all foreigners) are required to possess a visa, for which they need to be employed (or, in the case of women and children, tied to the visas of family members who are employed). Other legal restrictions have rendered NGOs virtually nonexistent in Dubai. At the same time corporate professionals in Dubai have more flexibility in their work lives and use that freedom to become involved in church activities. In Bangalore, by contrast, nearly every Catholic is an Indian citizen and is free to leave corporate life and take up employment in either the public sector or in the vast number of NGOs or even to work for the church. As a result, it is possible that most Catholics who are strongly committed to alleviating poverty either avoid or self-select out of corporate jobs. This path was taken by some of my respondents who quit corporate jobs because they believed God was calling them to serve the poor more directly. Such options for "exit" are largely unavailable in Dubai.

These different political contexts generate different spatial arrangements and restrictions in both cities. In Dubai, all Catholics have to share the same space of the single church compound (or the two compounds if we count the church on the outskirts of the city), because of legal restrictions on foreign religions, whereas in Bangalore they are distributed in numerous churches across the city. While churches in both cities are divided into linguistic communities, in Bangalore, members of the English-speaking middle class (most of whom are professionals) form their own church groups and have little contact with others. Non-English-language groups in Bangalore churches are mostly made up of lower-class members, with whom English-speaking professionals do not identify. In Dubai, ethnic church groups incorporate English speakers because they are nationality based. Take, for instance, a Malayalee (an Indian from the state of Kerala) who has moved to Bangalore: if she were a corporate professional, she would likely join a professionals' group of English speakers from different parts of India rather than a nonprofessionals' group of Malayalam speakers. If she were in Dubai and wanted to join a church group with professionals in it, she would find herself in an Indian group of English speakers, which would include both lower-level and senior executives, families as well as singles. Therefore the composition of these ethnolinguistic communities differs: in Dubai, they are more heterogeneous in terms of class, and professionals come into more contact with lower classes (who share their ethnic-based identification) in their church groups than do professionals in Bangalore. This might help explain why Catholic professionals in Dubai are more willing to commit time, energy, and money to helping poorer members of their communities.

Differences in Institutional Priorities

There are also important differences in the priorities of the Catholic Church in the two cities, which have very much to do with historical factors that have shaped the church in each context. In Dubai, the primary challenge faced by church members is economic survival, which becomes the key priority for church leaders as well. This is not simply because all Catholics in Dubai are foreigners. Rather, Dubai was more severely affected by the financial crisis of 2008 than was Bangalore. Its negative impact was particularly felt by the church when a growing number of members in its ethnic communities and various groups began to turn to it for support. Many of the aforementioned initiatives to provide members with skills to improve their job prospects (e.g., computer training and financial management classes) were only put into place after the crisis.

In Bangalore, even though the number of migrants and the poverty rate have been rising steadily, the church has different challenges to contend with. The most pressing concern is religious violence, in the form of attacks on churches by state-sponsored Hindu fundamentalists, who want to expel Christianity from India or to have Christians "return home" to Hinduism. Church leaders have been preoccupied in recent years with demanding fair treatment from the government and a response to this violence, by staging protests and demonstrations. Since urban corporate professionals have not been personally affected by this violence, they are mostly uninvolved with these concerns of the church (with the exception that they usually vote against the fundamentalist party in elections). Priests in Bangalore are also preoccupied with nationalist language politics around whether the state language (Kannada) or the language of the majority of Catholics (Tamil) should be given more priority. This issue affects priests' lifestyles, livelihood, and identities. However, as I discussed earlier, urban corporate professionals, who mostly function in English, see themselves as above what they characterize as the seemingly petty concern of language and have become further distanced from their clergy. While migration and poverty are certainly recognized as important concerns by church leaders in Bangalore, they are less of a priority than religious violence and language and are handled primarily by religious professionals who do not seem to see any need to get corporate professionals involved.

Institutional priorities also are shaped by leadership and agency. The advent of the financial crisis in Dubai coincided (inadvertently) with the installation of a new parish priest. Fr. Jerry was a younger man than his predecessor. He was equipped with an MBA and also had recently supervised the successful opening of a new parish in another Gulf city. Frustrated by the fragmentation of the Dubai parish into ethnic enclaves and by the long-standing fiefdoms that constituted the parish council, he undertook a major overhaul of the parish structure. He dismissed the existing parish council and installed a new one headed by a young corporate manager who shared his vision. As part of the restructuring, various initiatives that were once contained within ethnic communities or prayer groups were centralized at the parish level, including the benevolence committee (newly headed by several corporate professionals). Such efforts also made the economic concerns of members a central priority of the parish.[36] It would be difficult to imagine such changes being instituted in any of the Bangalore parishes I studied, because professionals there seem more distanced from poorer members of their parishes, as well as from clergy, and there is no similar sense of pressing economic need. It would also be difficult to see such changes in other Gulf cities, because Dubai tries to present itself as a fairly liberal city; it is also in the global limelight and under more international scrutiny. I found the church to be much less activist in Muscat, Doha, and Kuwait.

In these ways, a convergence of political, historical, economic, and organizational factors have resulted in middle-class Catholic professionals in Dubai being much more actively involved in addressing poverty than their counterparts in Bangalore. This diversity in outcomes reveals how the same global religious form can exhibit significant variation in how it participates in the broader church and society.

The Dark Side of Neoliberal Civic Engagement

Despite the seemingly greater civic engagement of Catholic corporate professionals in Dubai, various factors serve to undercut and impede the flourishing of these modes of solidarity.

First, because of the diverse workforce and the legal framework that binds foreign religions—they are allowed to exist in the country only as long as their activity remains contained within confined spaces—churches function as umbrellas for a multitude of ethnic communities. The parish's spatial limitations, together with the large numbers of church members and of ethnic communities, turn religious spaces into contested spaces. At any given time, a number of groups are vying for prime-time slots in the few meeting rooms available. Much of the internal politics of the parish, therefore, involves competing efforts of ethnic groups to maximize limited resources—not only rooms but also priests—for their own activities. Representatives of ethnic groups continually petition the parish priests and bishop for the use of resources that they allege other ethnic groups have unfairly obtained. They voice complaints within group meetings and then to church leaders via their representatives, who tend to be financially and socially powerful: most are prominent and well-established businessmen. Ethnic groups that take offense at some action of the parish priest may even resort to forms of sabotage. The most common form is withdrawing financial sponsorship of church events. On one occasion during my fieldwork, members of one Indian ethnic community, upset by the parish priests' censure of their fundraising activities conducted without his permission, complained to government authorities that the church was sponsoring illegal activities. If government officials viewed these complaints as serious, they could close down the church altogether—at least, that is the belief of church leaders, which has been strengthened by recent calls from incendiary Saudi clerics to destroy all foreign religions in the Gulf region.[37]

Thus, while the existence of these ethnic enclaves draws people to church in large numbers, since it constitutes their primary social space, this arrangement privileges the needs and interests of the ethnic community over and above the collective needs of the parish. Strong bonding capital thus becomes an inhibitor of bridging capital. Even collective events such as parish festivals or sporting tournaments, which are meant to bring the parish together, tend to be organized in ways that reinforce ethnic segregation. For instance, sports teams are made up of members of the same ethnic community, and various events and stalls at parish festivals are managed separately by distinct ethnic communities. This ethnic segregation characterizes churches through the Gulf region, and church leaders find it difficult to manage. Some expressed to me that they wished they could abolish language groups altogether, but recognize that it is precisely the existence of these niches that draws people of those communities in such numbers to religious institutions. For instance, many Filipinos I spoke to said that they only started attending church after moving to the Gulf: church did not mean much to them back home, but in Dubai it gave them a sense of belonging and home.

A second downside of stratified belonging in churches is that only the wealthier communities (e.g., Europeans) are able to raise funds, but do not use them to benefit the Sri Lankan or Pakistani groups, whose class positions and incomes are much lower and whose survival needs are more dire. As Lisette, one of my French respondents, admitted, "We are the wealthiest community in the parish, but also the least generous. We contribute the least in comparison to other groups." It was only during the course of our interview, she said, that it occurred to her that perhaps the lack of contact with other groups and the subsequent lack of knowledge of their needs might be contributing factors to their unwillingness to share their resources.

Third, the present stratified arrangement privileges the first generation of migrants and drives away many members of the second or third generation from participation in the church; those who attend schools that have a diversity of nationalities are particularly alienated from the church. Many second-generation Catholics I spoke to who no longer participate in church said that they found church groups too focused on the first generation of migrants (their influx continues to be steady), and those who did not strongly identify with their ethnic or linguistic group identity did not feel they fit anywhere in the structures available to them in the church.[38] Thus the very processes that enable many people to find a home in church (i.e., the strong bonds within ethnolinguistically based community groups, their common sense of identity against other ethnic groups) alienate others.

Fourth, while the strong bonding capital in churches provides many with a new sense of responsibility and leadership, an inadvertent side effect is the abuse of authority. This is evident in the curious case of what many called volunteer "thugs." Like an extension of the famous Stanford prison experiment,[39] we see in the Dubai church a tendency among some volunteers to get carried away with a newfound sense of their power. Donning their uniforms (white shirt, black tie, black trousers, and red badge), many of them can be seen rudely shouting at parishioners on a regular basis, while trying to herd crowds of ten thousand or more in and out of a space meant for only two thousand. One parish priest told me that he had just seen one of these volunteers beating a woman on her head with a rolled-up newspaper because she was talking on her cell phone as she came into the church compound. Some non-practicing Catholics I interviewed in Dubai claimed that these "pushers" (rather than ushers) were among the main reasons they stopped going to church. As Judy, an Indian who identified herself as "spiritual but not religious," expressed it, "These people are so rude! What is the point of going to try and pray there if you are not welcome? They treat you like animals!" Some parishioners surmised that these volunteers perpetrated this abusive behavior because, in their work lives, they were treated badly by superiors and now were simply passing on the lessons they had learned about how to treat others.

Fifth, for some volunteers and ECC leaders, involvement in church goes hand in hand with a neglect of their own families. The issue of balancing work, family, and church commitments is seldom discussed in the church groups. There is an expectation in some groups that, aside from one's job, one's primary commitment has to be to the church group, even if it means sacrificing family activities and time. Some of the high levels of commitment to church may thus be motivated by guilt (that one is not sacrificing enough for the church) and constitute a form of escapism from family responsibilities. The tension between home and church surfaced both explicitly—as when religiously disengaged professionals shared examples of close relatives whom they considered to be hypocrites for neglecting their families—and implicitly in my interviews with active members. For instance, Floyd is an entrepreneur who volunteered for a couple of hours every day in church despite his busy work schedule. When I asked him whether he was able to balance work and family, he immediately looked away and, in a hesitant voice, which differed from his characteristically confident demeanor, said, "See, when you have a business, sometimes you have to make sacrifices, and for that, sometimes family times suffers." Even the parish priest, Fr. Jerry, mentioned that he was worried that many of the volunteers at the parish were neglecting their families (in Dubai) and escaping from their responsibilities.

This brings me to the sixth point. Religious institutions in these contexts, despite functioning under strict legal constraints and a lack of staff, are able to do a

considerable amount to meet members' needs by providing various forms of economic, social, human, and cultural capital; making regular visits to prisons and
hospitals, and so on. In leading and participating in such activities, professionals
gain a deep sense of fulfillment and purpose. Certainly the magnitude of need in
cities like Dubai is immense: exploited laborers who have not been paid their
wages for months, battered housemaids, people trapped in debtor prisons, and
those who are unable to leave the country because of an inability to pay fines lev-
ied for exceeding their stay are only some of those who need support. And this
need has certainly heightened in the aftermath of the financial crisis. But amid
the fundraising efforts and appeals for volunteers, there is no suggestion that the
problem may have structural causes, or that the state needs to take more responsibility in addressing the roots of these problems.

This lack of attention to structural causes is by no means exclusive to Christians. For instance, a devout Muslim expatriate woman I interviewed, who used to
work as an investment banker for many years, but now runs a prominent charity
that supports laborers in need, spoke with great respect and fondness for the
laborers she had come to know and the severity of their need; her dedication of time
and energy to helping them was unwavering. But at the same time, she did not
think the government needed to take any responsibility for ameliorating the plight
of these people; instead, concerned individuals—but not citizens (even though
they are the primary beneficiaries!)—should come together to meet those needs.

Catholics in church groups who provided direct service to laborers, teaching
them English and helping them obtain clothing, also saw such action as needing
to be the prerogative of individuals (here, churchgoers) and did not voice any critique of the state or of citizens in neglecting their responsibility to those on
whose backs progress is being built. As I mentioned earlier, voicing such a critique publicly could lead to deportation. But even in private, their response was
not one of resignation or cynicism; rather, they seemed to have internalized an
individualistic response to this situation. This may owe in part to a genuine sense
of gratitude for the state that grants them freedom to worship as Christians. Such
gratitude has likely only increased with the Crown Prince's decision in 2017 to
rename a mosque in Abu Dhabi "Mary, Mother of Jesus."[40]

In any case, satisfying one's needs for belonging and generosity in a depersonalized, materialistic, and consumerist society goes hand in hand with absolving the
state of its duties to those who sustain it. Excusing the neoliberal state reinforces its
ability to perpetuate its "fend for yourselves" model of dealing with social ills. As
Pardis Mahdavi notes, the ethnocratic state formally discourages the involvement
of informal organizations that do the "dirty work" of dealing with the collateral
damage of neoliberalism, but turns a blind eye to them in practice.[41] This allows the
state to wash its hands clean of the matter if and when such groups fail.

Conclusion

"Who in society needs me?" This, argues Richard Sennett, is the key question of character that modern capitalism is unable to answer.[42] Drawing on Paul Ricoeur, Sennett argues that human beings need loci of belonging—people to whom they feel accountable and by whom they feel needed—and not in the trivial ways that "shallow" corporate goals and environments purport to cultivate. Sennett suggests that global capitalism deprives people of such modes of belonging. But that is not the case if we look at the lives of professionals outside their workplaces.

I examined in this chapter how the Catholic Church in Bangalore and Dubai provides many with a locus of belonging and a civic space. Through their churches, Missionaries find a sense of home, meaning, power, solidarity, and moral community. Professionals, who operate as Mercenaries during the week, feel they are able to give back to their communities by transmitting various forms of economic, social, and cultural capital. Yet these churches are embedded in the larger environments of neoliberal cities and thus are profoundly shaped by those environments. While providing for many a civic space in which to enact commitments to solidarity and community, religious institutions also reproduce the broader city's stratified modes of belonging and sustain modes of consumer citizenship. Religion, in this manner, becomes largely symbiotic with neoliberalism: it gains the commitment of politically alienated members and plays an important social role by taking care of some of the "dirty work" neglected by the state, without offering any direct critique.

This chapter also contributes to our understanding of civic engagement and citizenship in the context of transnational migration. U.S.-based research on this topic has focused on the role of religion in cultural and political assimilation, as well as how congregations provide social services for immigrant members.[43] But there are important gaps and omissions in this work. Many of these have been identified by Neha Vora in her study of Indian residents of Dubai, which I echo and build on here.[44]

First, existing studies focus almost entirely on democratic host countries in the Global North, to the neglect of South–South migrations, which I have examined in both Bangalore and Dubai. Second, as Vora argues, the assumed model of migration is assimilationist: there is a teleology of naturalization or permanence in the assumption that "migrants" are moving in order to permanently be assimilated into the host society. What is overlooked are various modes of "permanent impermanence" that in the present global context are no longer rare, particularly with the rise of guest-worker programs.[45] Finally, the model of citizenship is typically assumed to be formal and juridico-legal, which renders unimportant and illegible other practices and modes of lived citizenship. As Vora notes, the dominant understandings of the civic realm "lead us to believe that politics is based in the relationship between state and citizen, and that it is through participation in this relationship or by contesting its parameters that individuals become political subjects."[46] This understanding assumes migrants to be tied to their home countries and writes off noncitizens as essentially marginal to the workings of these countries. My study builds on Vora's work, examining how citizenship is not only a juridico-legal category but can also manifest itself in diverse scales and forms. My work also questions dominant understandings of citizenship by examining a case in which members of the same demographic exhibit greater civic consciousness and engagement in a nondemocratic ethnocracy than their counterparts in a democracy. By examining ways in which religious institutions constitute a civic space for otherwise politically disengaged people, it strengthens the argument for looking beyond formal citizenship to understand the civic realm as pertaining to practically enacted modes of belonging.[47]

Does the Catholic Church play any unique role here in terms of civic engagement? While Catholicism in many ways provides resources such as benevolence committees, meeting spaces, and so on, as we have seen in this chapter, there does not appear to be anything uniquely Catholic in the content of these approaches that would preclude their accessibility to non-Catholics. Beliefs about trusting in God, concepts such as servant leadership, or the belief that God wants someone to use his or her talents to make the world a better place—all may be found among people of diverse religious and spiritual backgrounds. Similar beliefs about trust and perseverance were expressed by some Hindu and Muslim businessmen I interviewed. Furthermore, even in Dubai, nonreligious organizations (or at least, those not formally tied to any religion) exist that provide similar services to those offered by the church, such as independent shelters for women, informal Filipino networks of workers, and secular volunteer organizations that engage professionals.[48] In Bangalore, many corporations have their own employee volunteer programs that partner with NGOs and community organizations. But members of ECC groups were seldom involved in these efforts; many of them would prefer to dedicate their spare time to their prayer groups. The Catholic Church, however, does enjoy a particular visibility and institutional legitimacy in the eyes of the state as well as the general public, which allows it to provide a key institutional locus for the cultivation of various forms of human, cultural, and social capital without facing some of the challenges of smaller organizations. The downside of this visibility, however, is that the church can be monitored easily. As a result, it becomes more difficult to cultivate modes of resistance to the various abuses of human dignity in these cities, or even to collectively imagine and promote constructive solutions that serve the common good.[49]

Conclusion

During one of my many visits to Bangalore, which I made after completing the bulk of my data collection for this project, Mark, one of the leaders of a professionals' prayer group, invited me to a workshop. The facilitators were flying in all the way from the United States: they were five highly successful franchise owners in one of America's most renowned fast-food chains. They had no franchises in India and so did not travel for business, but instead to fulfill their new mission: to "build up" Christian businesspeople around the world.

Over the simple South Indian breakfast of *uppama* and tea that was being served outside the meeting room, Rajesh, an HR manager and one of the prayer group's founders, told me he was elated that these businessmen were speaking to his group. Their presence there was able to draw in a number of Protestant executives, which reinforced Rajesh's vision for his group as a rare space for ecumenism that was "taking the church forward." While the Catholic Church on the ground complained about "sheep stealing" by new "born-again" churches and Pentecostals, in this setting, instead of fighting about apologetics, Catholics and Protestants were coming together united under a common goal: developing executive leadership skills.

After the praise-and-worship session, Rajesh introduced the speakers and their company to the audience of seventy-five executives, most of whom worked in global corporations. He talked about how in India, "leadership is not familiar in the Christian world." He expressed his conviction that the leadership wisdom of American executives was something that could vitally rejuvenate churches in India. It was, he insisted, "a gift of the Holy Spirit."

During the workshop, the American franchisees asked the audience of corporate managers, all of whom saw themselves as leaders, for their definitions of leadership. They responded with rosy terms: influencing others, service, putting people first, and so on. Using well-rehearsed PowerPoint presentations, the speakers emphasized the importance of alignment between "vision, values, and character," and of "engaging and developing others," rather than treating them as "dispensable parts in a machine." Success was not simply a matter of being nice to people; it also required "continual reinvention": the willingness to risk unsettling the familiar. People were their "key asset," and leadership was fundamentally about the uncompromising fidelity to core values and principles. The Americans insisted that such fidelity may at times inhibit profit maximization; indeed, working in a company led by a devout and conservative Christian, they had to make decisions at times that privileged principles over profit. Nevertheless, they believed that God had blessed them for their fidelity by making their franchises highly profitable. Thus, they insisted, business and religion are perfectly compatible.

The workshop was very well received, judging by the enthusiastic standing ovation the visitors received. But having heard the stories of some of the professionals in that room during the last several years, I suspected many of them may have been unwilling to voice any reservations. I went up to Mark at the end and asked if he planned to implement any changes as a result of this workshop; he was, after all, a senior HR manager for a major global IT giant. With a nervous laugh, he said, "See, the leadership at my company doesn't care about its people." Navigating the challenges in his day job was already a constant uphill battle. He could not imagine how he could convince senior executives to implement a greater commitment to employees in their policies or, for that matter, to get employees to trust the company after repeated experiences of betrayal. Indeed, a year after that conversation, he quit, going out on his own as a consultant instead.

The tension between the Mercenary norms and expectations of the corporate workplace and the Missionary ideals of Evangelical-Charismatic Christianity is felt much more keenly by corporate middle managers like Mark than by the confident American franchisees. The view from the top within privately owned firms is very different from that in the publicly traded firms in which people like Mark worked, especially in emerging markets in the Global South; facing the sorts of pressures I discussed earlier in the book, the managers of public firms have much less discretion and control. Think of Colin Perera, the middle manager who tried to foster collaboration and commitment among his team throughout the year, only to have to rank them at the end of the year on a scale in which the person at the bottom risks getting fired. In such settings, many of the norms of corporate life are implicit: they operate "under the radar," unlike the explicit leadership values proclaimed by the speakers at the workshop.

David Menezes, the HR director we met in chapter 1, would have been quite at home in this workshop; like many of its participants, he would have offered abundant examples of ways in which he integrated faith and work through fidelity to principles. But he would likely remain oblivious to the tension between his complaints about employee attrition and his own readiness to jump to the next higher-paying position, thereby perpetuating the Mercenary model. And like most others I talked to, he would also give little thought to the constraints on the relationship between faith and work beyond the workplace, in professionals' lifestyles and civic commitments. These blind spots, as I tried to show in this book, cannot be reduced to individual flaws: they are patterned and systemic, sustained by structural and cultural factors, including globally diffusing norms of individualism and constraints exerted by local sociopolitical regulations. Social structures thus shape the conditions of possibility for an integrated life: not only its expression but also its very meaning.

Capitalism and Catholicism in Bangalore and Dubai

In this book I told a tale of two characters—the Mercenary and the Missionary—to answer two questions: *How and why do global professionals in emerging economies sustain starkly opposing moral orientations in the realms of work and religion? And what consequences—both personal and social—does straddling these conflicting orientations produce in different sociopolitical contexts?*

I showed that both corporate workplaces and ECC churches are powerful sites of cultural and moral formation. They cultivate normative orientations in the realms of work and religion that are distinct, but that are sustained by the same key mechanisms: narrative scripts, mimesis, and habituation. Such processes operate under the radar and generate a centripetal force that is difficult to overcome. But the same person inhabits both characters, thus fostering their interaction.

The character of the Mercenary orients professionals to the relentless pursuit of mobility in corporate workplaces, cultivating an apprehensive individualism in which learned mistrust is a sign of maturity. Other possible meanings of work—whether a calling or vocation in the religious sense, or a pursuit of passion as in the popular "do what you love" mantra in the West—are alien to this logic. Meanwhile, the character of the Missionary, cultivated in communities of Evangelical-Charismatic Catholicism, prioritizes the believer's personal relationship with Jesus as healer, fostering a therapeutic individualism bereft of a discourse of justice, solidarity, or the common good.

The workplace, interpreted by the ECC group member as a mission field, affords multiple modes of accommodating religious beliefs, symbols, and practices. Faith provides both assets and liabilities for corporate success, as well as occasional resistance to the Mercenary norm. Overall, the therapeutic individualism generated in church communities rejuvenates professionals, enabling them to better endure the apprehensive individualism they experience in their workplaces, which then fuels again their need for healing. Professional logics and skills spill over into church settings, allowing professionals a means to give back to their communities and to find a sense of home and belonging. In doing so, they inadvertently reproduce the consumer citizenship and neoliberal conceptions of civic worth that alienate them from their cities, although such alienation again can reorient them to the healing power of faith. This symbiosis enables professionals to straddle these distinct moral orientations. However, their doing so comes with important personal and social consequences, which I discuss in more detail after first highlighting the crucial role of local contexts in sustaining such a symbiosis.

Varying sociopolitical factors specific to the cities of Bangalore and Dubai shape how these links between religion and capitalism are forged and yield important differences in the hybrids or "multiple modernities" that result from the global diffusion of new forms of capitalism and Catholicism. What explains the particular hybrid forms that we see in this study?

Consider first that the relationship between Catholicism and modern capitalism looks very different in other sociohistoric contexts. For instance, among the bourgeois middle class of eighteenth-century France, we see the emergence of a particular way of negotiating their religious and economic lives. They adopted a watered-down version of Catholicism, which was compatible with new standards of respectability and which also allowed them to justify their commercial ambitions that were being denounced by Catholic preachers of the time.[1] This mode of integrating faith and work was a stark contrast from that of Weber's anxiety-ridden Puritanism, which was essentially a form of segmentation and secularization. In a different context, such as Latin America in the late twentieth century, Catholicism was a source of activism and resistance against capitalism.[2] In still other contexts, such as in the American neoconservative movement, Catholicism serves as the basis for a theological defense of capitalism.[3] In Bangalore and Dubai, in contrast, Catholicism has a weakly symbiotic relationship with corporate capitalism, neither actively encouraging nor resisting it. A conjunction of several factors contributes to this outcome.

First, because of its minority status, Catholicism is either dependent on the state or unable to sufficiently challenge it. In Dubai, any perceived challenge to or criticism of the state can result in serious sanctions, including deportations or even the closing down of the church. People do not think that the latter possibility is likely to occur, given Dubai's aversion to bad publicity and its position in the global spotlight; nevertheless, there is still a sense of fear among religious leaders because of the visibility of the church (and hence its susceptibility to monitoring) and the occasional visits by government officials to ensure things are in order. Things have certainly changed over the past few decades. In my interview with the previous bishop of the region, now retired to a small convent in Florence, he seemed visibly perturbed and would not let me record our conversation or even take notes. He refused even to speak in English; I had to conduct the interview in my broken Italian. When I asked him to describe his experience as a bishop in the region, he looked to his left and right and, then gripping the table, told me in a whisper, "*Tutto era controllato!*" (everything was monitored). The current bishop, by contrast, feels free to speak more openly because of the global media attention Dubai has received, such as news coverage on violence against Filipina domestic workers. Nevertheless, he said that his biggest struggle was "how to help my people without being a total liar." Yet, recent years have also seen developments such as the UAE crown prince's growing public commitment to religious tolerance, evident in the recent naming of one of the mosques in the city's capital "Mary, Mother of Jesus."

In Bangalore, the church's opposition to the state focuses on the government's lack of response to religious violence. Attacks on churches are sponsored by fundamentalist political groups who see Christians as a foreign presence to be expunged from Hindu India. Middle-class professionals feel largely removed from these attacks, since the violence does not occur in their well-to-do neighborhoods, but church leaders in general remain preoccupied with the matter. Meanwhile, the elite business schools and colleges run by the Catholic Church serve as a significant source of revenue for the church and, in turn, are seen an important contributor to the economy. The church is thus incentivized to maintain the status quo.

The transience of church members is also an important factor. Both Dubai and Bangalore have high levels of migration and economic need. Churches in both cities try to address the problems of lower-class migrants, who have basic survival needs and are looking for housing, employment, and job training. The focus on these immediate, overwhelming, and practical needs leaves little room to think about systemic critique or reform—much less, the situation of elite professional workers. Only one of my respondents, a priest in Dubai, offered a strong systemic critique of capitalism; he denounced consumerism as a "dictatorial heresy" and insisted that it would "destroy everything." Claiming to be an ardent socialist, he nevertheless felt completely powerless and believed that, as a religious leader in Dubai, to help his people most effectively, he had to remain silent and do the best he could to provide for their bodies and souls. Similarly, in Bangalore, a

Jesuit priest who ran an institute that trains people for lower-level corporate jobs admitted having serious misgivings about the reigning economic system. "But what to do? Someone has to help these people find jobs and to survive!" He saw collaborations with corporations and up-and-coming fast-food and retail chains as his best bet to help his people survive.

In contexts where there is direct symbiosis between religion and capitalism, religious groups align with nationalist parties to promote loyalty to neoliberal development as key to being both a good citizen and a good member of the religious community.[4] Because of its minority status in Dubai and Bangalore, however, Catholicism does not buy into such nationalist projects: one cannot as easily equate being a good Indian (or Bangalorean or Dubaian) with being a good Christian. When one is effectively rendered second class by the state, it is difficult to cheerfully assent to its ideological commitments.

Consequences

Straddling the relationship between the Mercenary and the Missionary comes with personal and social consequences that involve both gains and losses. Undoubtedly, corporate jobs give these professionals a higher standard of living than their parents enjoyed. Having those positions has made it possible for many professionals to move from the lower to the upper middle classes and enabled them to provide for their parents and even buy them homes. In the religious realm, many of them express a deeper sense of commitment to their faith and relationship with God than their counterparts who are not in ECC groups. In their own estimation, both professionally and spiritually, many of them are flourishing. But there are costs too, for their professional and personal lives.

Workplaces

In the workplace, religion can offer both assets and liabilities for corporate success. Skills cultivated in church settings may transfer over into the workplace to yield career rewards. But religion can at times challenge workplace norms and logics, and it does not always win out in such conflicts. People who experience such dissonance, or want to preemptively avoid its occurrence, may draw strict boundaries between work and faith. Some find themselves incapable of integration, either because they are faced with structural constraints they do not know how to overcome or because that is an ability they have been unable to develop. As Berger argues, navigating religious and secular realms is a particular skill that the modern individual has to learn, especially in emerging economies, where there is a heightened sense of individuation as one is forced to make new kinds of choices in rapidly changing environments.[5]

Yet religion can be invasive, demanding that people make sacrifices and challenging the aims of the Mercenary ideal. This was the message of the American franchisees: be willing to take short-term losses in order to be faithful to your principles, and then God will bless you in the long term. This was, after all, their own experience. But for professionals in Dubai and Bangalore, there is no guarantee of material "blessing." The professionals I interviewed who made difficult compromises in favor of their faith did not become financially successful, though they are at peace with their consciences.

Many business leaders who aspire to integrate faith and work do not adequately recognize the severe structural hurdles that constrain the possibility of integration. This blindness to structure leaves professionals feeling that their failure to integrate the two realms is a result of flaws in their attitudes, efforts, or faith. Yet, my study findings challenge the pervasive idea that a coherent integration of work and religion in the workplace is simply a matter of espousing the same set of principles or values in both realms, or that integration in Mercenary environments can be accomplished simply by mustering up a little more willpower in sticking to one's principles. As noted even by passionate advocates of corporate capitalism such as Michael Novak, corporations have the ability to "injure dignity, cooperation, inventiveness, and personal development"; they can harm the consciences of employees and frustrate the common good.[6] Because of the power they wield in society, they ought to be held to high ethical standards.

Constraints to integration are also broadly systemic, as revealed in the consistency of complaints expressed not only by professionals across industries and positions but also by church leaders, teachers, and counselors, who had a keener sense of the widespread toll exacted by the new economy: workdays lasting twelve hours or more, stress caused by intensely competitive workplaces, the breakdown of relationships among dual-income couples with little time for each other or their children, and the subsequent distress felt by children. Yet often, even parents and teachers who recognize the systemic nature of the problem continue to perpetuate among their children a vision of success defined by increased mobility and purchasing power. Meanwhile, people's inability to leave their stressful jobs or to make time for their children or to prevent their marriages from breaking down is largely seen as their own fault. "Because it's you who are actually putting yourself in that position," as Vinod Prabhu, the full-time Missionary, explained. Even while admitting that to some extent the fault lay in "the kind of environment we are in," Vinod and others did not want to absolve people of any personal responsibility. This mindset might be part of the reason why many professionals do not think their ECC groups are appropriate (or safe enough) spaces to discuss workplace challenges.

Structural issues pose a particular challenge for an individualist theology. Similar to what research on American evangelicals has revealed,[7] therapeutic individualism neglects systemic and structural causes for social problems, for fear that acknowledging them would undermine personal responsibility. Sunil, an architect I talked to in Bangalore, became defensive when I presented him with Colin's situation of structural irony: of having to cultivate teamwork and then rank the employees for the purpose of firing one of them. "Do you mean to tell me that God is powerless in this situation?" he demanded. For Sunil and many others, Colin's inability to come up with an optimal response meant that he was either not praying hard enough or it was his fault that God chose not to exercise power in that situation. The primacy of psychological tools and mantras among such executives is therefore not surprising: "The only disability in life is a bad attitude," as a poster in one workplace declared.[8] One Christian businessman, with whom I shared some of the challenges to integration that I came across in my interviews, also became defensive and retorted that God was present even in Nazi concentration camps. This mode of thinking puts the onus on the individual to find God in the concentration camp; in good neoliberal fashion, it leaves the individual to shoulder the blame for failure, while avoiding the question of whether we should be setting up concentration camps in the first place or whether a concentration camp should be a model for how we structure our working lives.

Another implication of this study is that workplace problems such as widespread attrition are not going to be resolved by giving professionals more extrinsic rewards. Organizations need to pay more attention to what implicit cultural messages are being communicated in the workplace. In particular, they need to attend to the widespread ideal of mobility that orients the Mercenary. If even senior executives such as Menezes are always ready to switch jobs, why should the average employee stay? Clearly, simplistic attempts to cultivate normative control will not work. This is especially the case when organizational structures and reward systems are set up in ways that are inherently inimical to trust and collaboration. Managers need to understand that one cannot sustain productivity in toxic work environments. They need to build structures that communicate genuine commitment to the well-being of employees and society; create a culture of safety and trust; and cultivate alternative standards and models of worth to those of the Mercenary.[9] These issues should also be of relevance to researchers and managers concerned with fostering business ethics. In addition to focusing on codes of ethics and individuals' application of ethical principles, cultivating more ethical work environments will likely require generating communities of sustained ethical reflection and models of exemplary practices. Churches and other faith communities might serve as sources of such communities.

Churches

In examining the role of professionals in churches, I highlighted how churches can serve as a space for community and solidarity for Mercenaries who, when studied in isolation in the workplace, seem incapable of commitment and devoid of coherent identities, narratives, and communities.[10] But many of them are indeed capable of finding community elsewhere, in another realm to which belonging and meaningfulness are relegated. Many situate their primary commitments within this realm and see work simply as something they need to do as a means to other ends: to earn an income with which to support their family or even to maintain legal immigration status in order that they may serve their church community. Work as such is not seen as a vocation, but is only instrumental to living out one's vocation to families and church communities. The workplace becomes a mission field in which to reinforce their faith commitments. This is how several ECC leaders articulated their identities in reference to the Missionary ideal, even if once they were in the workplace, they often became unwittingly subject to its inner logic.

The Missionary model has no theology of work: there is no professed aspiration for work as such to be meaningful, or to be a calling, or to contribute to human flourishing. The Missionary articulates no theology of the common good, nor recognizes how reigning structures systemically undermine such ideals as articulated in both Catholic and Protestant theology: those resources have not been transmitted to these contexts. That may be due to the Pentecostal inclination toward "supernatural" solutions to problems. God, in this view, operates primarily through extraordinary interruptions and interventions in the course of reality—as in Randall's conversion in chapter 2—rather than as a "non-competitive transcendence" working in and through the human will and inclinations.[11]

Outside church walls, the narratives and dispositions that Missionaries cultivate in church settings have little effect on their economic lives. Many are trapped within routines of consumerism, which seem to have a centripetal force of their own that people admit they are unable to overcome. But the weak grasp of religion over people's economic lives is not simply a result of consumerism, because even those who are thrifty claim that religion has little to do with their frugal practices. As I showed in chapter 4, it is very difficult to achieve the conditions required for religion to have a dominating influence on people's lifestyles. Church leaders seldom overtly discuss consumerism either in sermons or prayer group meetings; that may be because many do not recognize the systemic nature of the problem. The solutions offered from the pulpit or in counseling sessions are mainly individualistic and voluntaristic, focused on helping individuals strengthen their faith and make choices that could help them cope better.

In addition to cultivating the distinctive normative ideal of the Missionary, Evangelical-Charismatic Catholic groups in churches can enable corporate professionals to cultivate civic engagement and solidarity. But this civic capacity of religion is not always activated. As we saw in chapter 5, in Bangalore, church leaders do little to involve professionals in social and charitable works. There, professionals' prayer groups seem to fulfill a primarily spiritual or psychological role, becoming largely disconnected from the needs of the poor. In Dubai, many Indian and Filipino groups are able to bring together people across different social classes, and church leaders actively structure the environment to assist the needy. But because of the parish's weak bridging capital and inadvertent reproduction of the city's ethnic stratification, wealthier nationalities seldom come into meaningful contact with less advantaged groups, who are therefore unable to benefit from the former's resources. While churches cultivate bonding capital within ethnic communities in places like Dubai, this very strength contributes to the alienation of younger generations from what they see as ethnic cliques. As succeeding generations become more and more economically successful, upwardly mobile, and disconnected from the concerns (and even languages) of first-generation migrants, church groups and parishes that are experienced primarily as ethnolinguistic hubs may become less important and less influential in their lives.

Considering the systemic aspects of their economic problems could provide opportunities for people to recognize that their burdens are not entirely due to personal failings. It could help them see that it takes more than effort or willpower on the part of the individual to solve structural problems. Rather than simply seeing corporate jobs and higher status and salaries as univocal "blessings"—while criticizing people for being unable to maintain family commitments or falling into consumerist patterns—faith communities could provide strategies and mechanisms to help members overcome potential pitfalls and traps. Churches could help professionals understand the pervasive difficulties and patterns that others in their contexts face, especially those of lower socioeconomic status. A more accurate diagnosis of problems might help clergy, lay leaders, and professionals to work together toward more creative solutions, in forms of community that are less complicit in reproducing systemic problems and that can imagine what *could be*.[12]

I recognize that moving in this direction will not be easy. Church leaders in both cities are overwhelmed by the myriad challenges of rapid economic globalization. In spite of the ambivalence some of them may personally feel toward the new economy, it would not be helpful for them to simply complain about the system when they need to meet the practical needs of struggling people. It is difficult for the church to address systemic issues, not simply in Dubai, where doing so could meet with swift sanctions, but even in Bangalore where church leaders are overwhelmed by the steady influx of migrants and by local ethnopolitical tensions. Among lay leaders, the widespread ignorance of the body of Catholic Social Teaching—which could provide resources to help Catholics think differently about their participation in and commitments to society—together with the individualistic nature of evangelical-Pentecostal influences, inhibit the potential to recognize systemic and structural issues.

Implications

Both capitalism and religion are social structures with characteristic powers and properties that are differently activated by different contextual factors. If we want to meaningfully address either capitalism or religion, we cannot expect them to function the same at all times and places.

By looking at particular types of capitalism and religion, this study uncovers a number of mechanisms that characterize the mutual relationship between global religion and global capitalism in these contexts. Religion enables capitalism by providing forms of cultural capital, social capital, a rejuvenating refuge, apprehensive individualism, organizational loyalty, institutional support for corporations, and consumer citizenship. Capitalism, in turn, enables religion by provoking existential insecurity that strengthens the need for religion and providing new spaces for enacting religious commitment, increased scope and relevance for religious institutions, and resources to sustain possibilities of "exit" from corporate jobs and consumerist lifestyles.

While symbiosis is dominant, there are secondary constraints in both directions. As we have seen, religion can constrain capitalism by providing moral constraints in workplace decisions, alternative goals and commitments in the workplace, and alternative lifestyle commitments to consumerism. These constraints at best weaken rather than seriously obstruct or challenge capitalism. Capitalism, in turn, can constrain religion by encouraging normative segmentation of realms, challenging religious ideals and commitments, imposing constraints on people's time and energy, and providing alternative forms of existential security in the form of consumerism. Further, drawing on Albert Hirschman's metaphors of exit, voice, and loyalty,[13] we can see religion's marked absence of voice or systemic critique (or overt systemic support, for that matter), though symbiosis can be weakened by discouraging loyalty to the system or encouraging exit from it to some degree.

It is important to note that religions contain diverse elements (beliefs, practices, dispositions, and communities) that can serve as resources to both support and challenge different aspects of corporate life and consumerism, which themselves are only two aspects of capitalism. One could also consider other aspects of capitalism—entrepreneurship or the global financial system, for example—and come to different conclusions. A study of other "varieties of capitalism," such as coordinated market economies, would also likely yield different results.[14] Which properties of religion and capitalism are activated and come into interaction and whether those interactions enable symbiosis or constraint depend on a host of contextual factors. We may likely find comparable processes of symbiosis happening with other minority religions, for instance. But the configuration of the religion-capitalism relationship will always be highly contingent and will depend on what properties of these entities are activated by different contexts, resulting in "multiple modernities" or diverse hybridized forms of global-local and religious-secular linkages. No universal law or formula can determine this relationship or its consequences. The global diffusion of such new hybrids provides a new challenge for the sociology of religion: to better understand how different populations in different contexts negotiate the relationship between religious and secular spheres and what consequences these actions have for their lives and their societies.

This project raises a final question about the cultural consequences of modernity more generally, across its multiplicity of hybrid forms. As Berger argues, modernity necessitates not so much religious decline as a pluralism of multiple religious and secular choices and discourses.[15] In a highly pluralistic, differentiated world, what does it mean to live an integrated, coherent life? Is such integration or coherence possible or even desirable? I don't mean a kind of integration in which there are no boundaries around our roles—certainly it is crucial to be able to unplug and disconnect from work, to maintain a sense of professional distance, privacy, and so on. What I mean, rather, is the possibility of living out a coherent life-project, across the different roles and domains into which our lives are often fragmented.

Some, certainly, appear to have cultivated the skills to thrive in drastically different environments, weaving together their commitments to disparate realms of life: David Brooks calls them "amphibians."[16] People like Ashwin Mathews, whom we met at the beginning of this book, embody something like that quality: Ashwin is at once the Missionary and the Mercenary. Like most professionals I interviewed, he sees himself as living a largely integrated life, and certainly aspires to it.

But this mode of integration is also highly privatized. I do not mean this in the sense that Ashwin keeps his religion to himself: he is able to express his faith at work in many ways and can avoid compromising his principles. Rather, this mode of integration is only concerned with the actions of the private, individuated self, who is trying to coherently follow certain principles or signal certain commitments. It does not integrate one's personal good with the common good. That sort of integration would require resources that are not just ideological, but political. The individualism of the Mercenary-Missionaries results not simply from rapid economic development or from the cultures of corporations and churches. It also results from the social and political restrictions in these cities on migrants and minorities, which limit the extent to which they can fully participate in their societies. Such restrictions, in spite of the differences between democratic India and ethnocratic UAE, similarly limit how these professionals can even imagine integration. They constrain the extent to which people can harness their imaginations and creative contributions toward a shared collective future. That sort of integration would require civic inclusion in a community that encourages meaningful participation: where one's voice can matter and one's actions can contribute to the common good and to a flourishing society for all. But in a world of weakening democracies, proliferating guest worker regimes, and growing nationalist and populist movements, ever more people may be denied the possibility of such integration.

Appendix

METHODOLOGY

This study is based on twelve months of participant observation and 200 interviews I conducted from 2010 to 2012. While the bulk of the research was done in Bangalore and Dubai, I also conducted interviews and observations in other Arabian Gulf cities—Abu Dhabi, Al Ain, Doha, Muscat, Sharjah, and Kuwait—as well as in Mumbai in India. I also interviewed a number of officials at the Vatican concerned with issues of migration, economic justice, culture, and church affairs in India and the Middle East.

I recruited respondents from church groups and through snowball sampling from prior contacts in companies and educational institutions in these cities, in an effort to generate a sample that varied sufficiently along the following criteria: occupation, religion, gender, length of residence in city, and church involvement. My primary sample consisted of 122 corporate professionals in Bangalore and Dubai, 103 of whom were Catholic (56 in Dubai and 47 in Bangalore); the remaining 19 were of Hindu, Muslim, or Protestant backgrounds. Sixty-six were male and fifty-six female. Most of these professionals (N = 85) were long-term residents who had lived more than ten years in these cities, and all participants had lived in these cities for a minimum of three years. Most respondents were mid-level professionals who either currently or recently worked in publicly traded Fortune 500 companies. Respondents had at least three years of work experience and ranged in age from twenty-five to fifty-five. Of the Catholic professionals I interviewed, twenty respondents (ten in each city) could be categorized as religiously disengaged (i.e., they did not participate in church activities more than a few times a year), nine (five in Dubai, four in Bangalore) attended church weekly, and the remaining seventy-four were involved more than once a week in church activities that went beyond religious service attendance.

In addition, the sample comprised twenty-six lay leaders in church groups who were not corporate professionals (e.g., entrepreneurs, homemakers, etc.), thirty-three clergy and professed religious (including priests, nuns, bishops, and cardinals), and nineteen others who provided additional contextual data (including counselors, journalists, academics, college students about to embark on professional careers, and parents of some respondents).

In Dubai, the respondents had the following nationalities: Indians (forty-five), Filipinos (eighteen), non-Gulf Arabs (Lebanese, Syrians, Jordanians, Egyptians: twelve), Europeans (French, Italians, Spanish, Swiss: eleven), Gulf Arabs (Emiratis, Kuwaitis, Qataris, Saudis: ten), Nigerians (four), and other nationalities (Sri Lanka, Pakistan, United States: four). Thirty-three of my Dubai respondents were second-generation residents (i.e., were born and raised in the Gulf). In India, I interviewed eighty Indian citizens and two U.S. expats who were corporate professionals involved in Catholic church groups. Not included in this count are additional informants such as friends, acquaintances, and people with whom I had conversations that I did not formally record.

I conducted participant observation in both religious settings (e.g., church groups, services, committee meetings, retreats) and secular settings (e.g., shopping malls, entertainment venues, workplaces, and industry association conferences). I also gathered relevant historical and statistical documents on churches in both cities.

The interviews lasted ninety minutes on average and were digitally recorded. Nearly all were conducted in English, with the exception of three in French and one in Italian. Some respondents (N = 29) were interviewed multiple times as my research progressed over the years. Throughout the process, I also systematically recorded and coded fieldnotes. Data were analyzed iteratively. I developed initial coding categories during preliminary fieldwork conducted in 2010 in both cities, using NVivo software. These categories formed the bases for subsequent interviews I conducted in 2011 and 2012. I transcribed and analyzed these data for emergent themes within categories.

Because I visited nearly every Catholic group in each city in which corporate professionals are involved, my sample can be considered sufficiently representative of this category of Catholic professionals with high church participation. My sample, however, is not meant to be statistically generalizable to all corporate professionals or to all Catholics in these cities. Instead, my aim was to highlight the workings of processes and mechanisms that characterize the relationship between religion and capitalism in these contexts, as well as the contextual conditions that shape these mechanisms. The generalizability here is analytical, rather than statistical.

Groups Studied
Bangalore

In Bangalore, my observations were mostly among English-speaking Catholic Charismatic groups. The Catholic Charismatic Revival (CCR) originally took root and spread among middle-class English speakers. While over time it gained a considerable vernacular following, English remains the predominant language used in CCR groups across India. The names of groups here are all pseudonyms in order to protect confidentiality.

Living Word was the first Catholic Charismatic prayer group to be established in Bangalore. The group meets weekly at a Catholic school and draws more than one hundred members from across parishes in Bangalore to each meeting. Regulars range in age from the very young to the very old and include people who are active members of other prayer groups in the city as well.

A second group, Navjyothi, is run by a Catholic lay missionary. With about one hundred active members, Navjyothi is the Indian branch of an international Catholic Charismatic organization of lay missionaries focused on evangelization. About a dozen individuals and families live together in community and depend on benefactors (many of whom are professionals) for financial support while they work as "full-timers," conducting retreats and other religious events around the country. In Bangalore, in addition to retreats and conferences, Navjyothi runs weekly meetings for two groups, one for single young adults and one for married couples; both groups are populated by a number of corporate professionals. They also run an annual three-month immersion program that involves living in community and participating in various spiritual and educational activities. I describe this experience and its effects on participants in chapter 4.

A third local group, which I call the Alleluia Youth Group (AYG), was founded in the 1980s by a college professor who was part of the Living Word group and was designed to reach its younger members. Its membership today consists primarily of single college students and young professionals, and its weekly meetings are attended by about fifty participants who come regularly.

A fourth group I studied is a professionals' prayer group that is part of Youth Alive (YA), a Catholic Charismatic movement that originated in the state of Kerala in the 1980s and has now spread to nearly twenty countries. While the movement's original constituents were college students and it still has an active presence in colleges in India, many of the initial members, now upwardly mobile professionals located around the world, continue to remain involved in leadership positions in the movement and support it financially. In Bangalore, the movement has several chapters across the city catering to students, married couples, and those who prefer to speak Malayalam (the regional language of Kerala). Its initial members in Bangalore were primarily AYG members; in about 2001 the IT boom brought in a large influx of members from Kerala. The chapter I attended comprises fifteen English-speaking corporate professionals, both singles and couples without children, who meet in the foyer of a convent.

I also interviewed members of another transnational lay Catholic Charismatic community based in the United States. Several of its members of this group are "full-timers" who depend on benefactors for financial support and who conduct educational, counseling, and leadership programs aimed at families. Unlike other groups in my study, this particular community inculcates strong patriarchal gender norms, particularly around male headship.

While these are all English-speaking Catholic Charismatic groups, there are differences in their ethnolinguistic composition. Members of Navjyothi, particularly the singles group, are predominantly of Goan and Mangalorean Konkani-speaking origin, as indicated by their Portuguese-origin last names. AYG is made up mostly of Tamil speakers, reflecting the majority language of Catholics in Bangalore. The composition of YA seems to be predominantly people from Kerala. "Somehow when you say Youth Alive, it almost has a Malayalee tag on it," the leader of AYG explained. "Not that they keep it that way; it has just become that way."

Another local group I visited is led by a feminist Catholic theologian who became a lay evangelist and currently runs a charitable organization that provides education, food, and vocational training for destitute children. About two dozen young professionals come together to pray, find guidance about how to live better lives, and participate regularly in acts of service. While not formally connected to the Charismatic Renewal, this group does participate in forms of Charismatic intercessory prayer. It is also the only group of Catholic professionals I came across in Bangalore with an active commitment to social service.

A final group whose regular monthly meetings I attended is Divine Work, an interdenominational group (though attended mostly by Catholics) that is aimed exclusively at corporate professionals. Between fifty to seventy-five participants regularly attend its meetings, which are neither explicitly Catholic nor Charismatic; however, some elements are similar to the features of the aforementioned Charismatic groups, such as the format of guitar-and-keyboards "praise and worship" music followed by a lecture-style "teaching." These "teachings" are given by corporate managers and trainers who integrate biblical ideas with pop-psychological materials on emotional intelligence, positive thinking, and relationship management. Some members of this group also participate in an ecumenical effort aimed at providing entrepreneurship training to working-class Christians, supported by an evangelical college in the United States. These latter groups (Divine Work and the smaller ecumenical entrepreneurs circle) were formed very recently and include members of other nationalities (mainly Americans).

In addition to these groups, I also interviewed corporate professionals involved in three other groups: a nondenominational corporate prayer group in a U.S.-based IT firm, an interdenominational church that meets at a downtown hotel, and the Art of Living movement, based on Hindu spirituality, which conducts meditation workshops in corporations to improve productivity and facilitate stress management.

Dubai

In contrast to Bangalore, where these various groups operate out of different parishes and institutional centers, the restrictions on foreign religions in Dubai limit the meeting spaces available to Catholic groups. Most groups are organized into ethnolinguistic communities and subgroups within each community that meet in the handful of rooms available in churches. A few groups met in hotels or homes, but acknowledged this was probably not legal. Most of my observations were of the main parish, St. Mary's, located close to the old downtown area, and secondarily of the new, smaller parish, St. Francis, located on the outskirts of the city. As in Bangalore, many of the groups I studied in Dubai are English-speaking groups affiliated with the CCR. I also attended parish-level committee meetings and meetings of non-Charismatic groups.

Indians comprise the largest ethnic population in Dubai and also constitute the majority of Catholics who are active in parish groups. While the Filipino influx since 2003 may have displaced Indians from their position as the majority of the Catholic population in Dubai, various Indian communities of diverse ethnic origins are well entrenched in churches. Corporate professionals are more prominent in the various English-speaking Indian groups than in vernacular-language groups. At the downtown parish, St. Mary's, I attended meetings of the oldest Catholic Charismatic group in the city, which has more than one hundred regular members who attend weekly. I also attended weekly meetings of the YA movement at St. Mary's, which draw fifty to seventy-five members weekly. I also observed a local parish-based group at St. Mary's that I will call Salt and Light (SL), which was founded by an Indian evangelist in the 1990s; its activities and discourses are in many ways identical to those of YA.

There are some noteworthy differences between these groups. Members of the English-language Charismatic group tend to be older on average and are mostly long-standing members of the CCR, which they first encountered in India. The religious expression in this group is noticeably louder than in other groups. Its meetings, held in a large auditorium, involve sustained periods of praying in tongues, with members clapping, jumping, shouting "Alleluia," and "prophesying." SL, in contrast, whose meetings are in a small room, about 20' × 20' in size, has a much more contemplative style. The music is more subdued; it is still mostly of the contemporary worship music genre, but also includes contemplative forms of prayer such as that developed in the Taizé community in France, consisting of repetitive, meditative chants punctuated by periods of silence. Unlike the English-speaking Catholic Charismatic group, its members are mostly second-generation Arabian Gulf residents (i.e., who have spent most of their lives either in Dubai or neighboring cities), who do not explicitly identify with the CCR (even though the influence is palpable). The YA group falls somewhere in between: it meets in a small room, but has a vibrant musical expression, with members standing, raising hands, clapping (in comparison to SL where members are mostly seated), and also praying in tongues, albeit in a more subdued manner than in the older group.

In addition to observing these groups at St. Mary's and speaking to many of their leaders and members, I also interviewed professionals who were members of (predominantly Indian) English-language Charismatic groups and a young adults' group at the suburban parish. Additionally, while these groups tend to be pan-Indian (although YA still predominantly comprises Malayalees), the parish also has Indian ethnic associations of groups such as Goans, Mangaloreans, Bengalis, and Tamils. I spoke with members of some of these groups.

I also observed meetings of two Filipino Charismatic movements in Dubai, both of which began in Manila in the early 1980s. The first, which I call Christian Families International, started as a movement to evangelize married couples, but eventually expanded to include a singles' wing. Unlike the other groups I studied, all members of this group are required to complete a three-month Christian initiation course to become members. The second movement, the New Life Community, has an influential leader, a renowned Filipino author and entrepreneur. The central weekly event of this group is a meeting that involves, in addition to usual charismatic practices such as praise and worship, a video broadcast of the founder giving a motivational talk to large audiences. The talks are punctuated by short reflection questions on topics such as leadership, improving health, and how to find fulfillment and success. Both these movements run various social service and charitable organizations in the Philippines, as well as participate in charitable initiatives in Dubai. I also spoke to professionals who belong to a non-charismatic parish-based Filipino group.

The Arabic-speaking community is composed of non-Gulf Arabs, predominantly Lebanese and Syrians, with smaller numbers of Jordanians, Palestinians, and Iraqis. The community is based primarily in St. Mary's church and has only one Arabic-speaking priest, whom they share with the French-speaking community. This priest serves these communities not only in Dubai but also in three neighboring emirates, which involves a considerable amount of travel, leaving him with very little time to attend to members' needs. Members of the Arabic community tend to be relatively isolated from others in the parish. Some told me that they felt demeaned because even in an Arabic-speaking country, they are forced to have to communicate in English at church, because most priests and parishioners do not speak Arabic. The exception is one group that belongs to an international movement, Christian Professionals (CP); many of its members are engineers, and I spent time with several of them. While all the previously mentioned groups are predominantly focused on spiritual activities, the CP group aims to draw in professionals by providing clubs through which people can develop various skills and hobbies, such as photography, sports, and business presentations.

The French-speaking community consists predominantly of upper-middle-class French families, most of whom are married with children, with the men employed in senior management positions in global firms; most of the women are homemakers or self-employed. There are a smaller number of lower-middle-class Africans from French-speaking countries such as Cameroon, but they do not seem well integrated either into the French community or the African one. In the French community, women play a much more prominent leadership role than in other ethnic communities. Much of the activity of the community revolves around religious education and catechesis of its 200-plus children, as well as running the weekly liturgy. Many active leaders in the community are involved in a prominent French Charismatic movement or at least grew up as part of this movement in France. Many members of the community attend both parishes, St. Mary's and St. Francis, so they can participate in activities that are held in either location. For much of the year, the community does not have a French priest and shares the trilingual Lebanese priest with the Arabic-speaking community.

The final group I studied was the African community, which is based at St. Mary's and is composed predominantly of Nigerians. Many of them work in the shipping industry, either running their own businesses or working at global shipping firms. Most members consider themselves Charismatic and, in addition to attending weekly liturgical services, meet for a large weekly gathering in St. Mary's auditorium. Similar to the English Charismatics, this group is strongly influenced by Pentecostalism, particularly its preaching styles, but is not as influenced by American evangelical literature or music. The group also has a more vibrant form of religious expression than any of the other groups, with loud singing and drumming that can be heard in meeting rooms above the auditorium.

Doing Fieldwork: Between Insider and Outsider

The many months of fieldwork I undertook for this study often entailed navigating a challenging tension between being an "insider" and an "outsider." I constantly found myself occupying a space between a number of roles and identities, some of which had to do simply with my appearance, others with how I presented myself, and still others with assumptions that were made about me: Indian, Tamilian, American, local, foreigner, Westerner, Catholic, visitor, new member, old-timer, male, student, researcher. Often, people's responses to me varied according to which of these roles became salient in particular situations.

In Dubai, I seemed to have no special status as a convert to Catholicism in that parish; most respondents did not know or care about this. Nobody asked me about it, nor did I bring it up. (In fact, the only person to whom I mentioned it explicitly was the former bishop of the region when I was interviewing him in Italy. I told him this in an attempt to win his trust, since he was very reluctant to talk about his experience. However, he did not seem interested, but instead repeatedly insisted that the church never proselytized.) So I do not think my status either gained me any advantage nor proved to be a disadvantage in conducting my research.

Much of my insider status came from simply having spent my childhood in both India and the Arabian Gulf; as a result I was intimately familiar with the environments and experiences of most respondents. On a practical level, the familiarity I had as an insider was an asset simply in being able to navigate these cities on a daily basis. With my parents residing in Bangalore, it became easy to pass for a local, and my brother, who had graduated from a business school there, was an invaluable help in connecting me to professionals in the city across a range of global companies. My work in Dubai was helped greatly by old schoolmates and friends. During some of my research visits to Dubai, I stayed with friends who became key informants; through them I was able not only to think through my ideas but also to gain access to other respondents in ways I could not have done on my own. I also spoke to group leaders early on to let them know I was conducting research. I obtained the permission of bishops in both cities to do this work, and they were very supportive.

In some situations, being an insider had to do with my ascribed status of nationality and ethnicity, which presented different challenges and opportunities.

For instance, when I started studying Indian groups in Dubai, just as in Banga-lore, it was easy for me to join and sit in on a group since they assumed I was another transient visitor. When I visited a Filipino or African group, in contrast, I could not just be an inconspicuous observer. This was not always a handicap, since most members of these groups were very friendly and would come up and talk to me, though I was clearly a newcomer. The advantage of being an ethnic in-sider among Indians in Dubai was that they could express to me their misgivings about other ethnic groups. Non-Indian groups may not have felt particularly comfortable expressing to me their problems with Indians if I had not first introduced myself as an American researcher. I was able to hear some honest frustrations and misgivings about Indians in Dubai from Filipino and French re-spondents, for example.

During my research in India, my ethnicity was not always an asset. It posed a challenge when it came to studying some of the language politics between ethnic groups. My last name is Tamil, which automatically positioned me in the eyes of some people I was observing, even though I did not have a dog in the fight. Some respondents told me explicitly that certain people I wanted to talk to would not talk to me if they knew my last name. So I contacted them by phone; my Ameri-can accent and first name were enough to gain me a phone interview.

In some cases, my perceived insider-outsider status had to do with experience: it was a sort of achieved status. For instance, being an Indian citizen in Dubai, I was subject to the same forms of discrimination that many of my interviewees experienced. My (Caucasian) wife and two daughters accompanied me for five months of my research in Dubai, which gave me a number of opportunities to better understand the nature of stratified belonging in the city. For instance, two Emirati transportation inspectors came up to me in the metro when I was sitting next to my wife and children and asked her, without looking at me, if I was with them. On another occasion, a Spanish neighbor told my wife in all innocence, "Your husband is not like other Indians," explaining that what she meant was "he doesn't just stand there and stare at me." The only Indians she had come into con-tact with were gardeners at her housing complex, who were prone to gawking at foreigners.

A third instance occurred when a friend lent us her car for a few months. The Dubai police website stated at the time that holding a U.S. license in combina-tion with an international driver's permit would allow my wife, a U.S. passport holder, to drive (I had an Indian passport, so was not permitted to drive). We also confirmed this through the public relations officer of the university that spon-sored my visa. My wife once accidentally ran a red light at a roundabout, and was stopped by a nearby police officer. After looking at our documents, he told us it was illegal for us to drive the car. I happened to have the printout from the

Dubai police website, but he dismissed it and said that the law had changed. Apparently, we were now only allowed to drive rental cars. He then threatened to impound our vehicle and charge us a fine of AED 2000. We pleaded our ignorance repeatedly. He looked again at my wife and our children in the back seat and finally dismissed us with a stern warning to return the car and not to drive it again. The university official, an Emirati citizen, was quite surprised when I told him about this incident. He called a friend in the police department and was informed that the law had indeed changed and apparently applied only to the emirate of Dubai. Immediately, however, he assured us that the police would do nothing to us if my wife, a white American, was driving. He admitted, by extension, that if it had been me at the wheel and she had not been in the car, it would have been confiscated.[1] We decided not to risk our racial "advantage" and stuck to cabs and the metro for the rest of our stay.

A crucial aspect of such "achieved" insider status that many respondents were concerned about was whether I had the relevant religious experience necessary to take seriously what they had to say. Did I understand the nature and importance of these religious experiences, which they could not adequately express in words in an interview? Would I misunderstand or misrepresent them? Consider the following example.

At St. Mary's in Dubai, I was once introduced to a group of five young adults, all of Indian origin, who were organizing a parish event: designing posters, figuring out the details of the setup, and so on. I was introduced as a PhD student from the United States who was conducting research on the parish. The young man closest to the door looked somewhat older than the others, and I assumed he had some position of responsibility in the church. Because of his hairstyle and white shirt, I will call him Elvis. "So why are you doing research on the church?" he asked me soon after I was introduced to the group. I told him I was trying to understand whether religion played any role in people's lives in rapidly developing cities like Dubai. "Are you a Catholic?" he asked. I said yes. "But practicing? Are you a *practicing-practicing* Catholic?" he asked sternly, attempting to scrutinize my soul through his dark-rimmed glasses.

It was not simply paranoia on my part to think that giving the "wrong" answer could jeopardize the study. Not long before this conversation, I was conducting preliminary research at an evangelical outfit in Dubai, when the pastor's wife asked me where in the United States I was studying. When I said Notre Dame, her expression changed to something between concern and annoyance, as she asked, "So are you Catholic?" I replied yes, after which she grunted and excused herself. Not long after, the pastor, who earlier in the day seemed quite willing to talk to me, said he had to cancel our interview; it was impossible to get in contact with him after that conversation.

I tried to dodge Elvis's question and said I was not sure what exactly he meant by "practicing-practicing." He was honest enough to admit that he had the impression that I was there to do a write-up on why people are wasting their time with religion. (There was, I discovered, a pervasive view among many I spoke to that people in the West are materialistic and lack spiritual sensibilities because they are spoiled by comfort and luxury. This seemed ironic coming from people living in Dubai, of all places!) Elvis was concerned that my stance as a "Western" researcher—he picked up this marker first, rather than the commonality that I was an Indian or Catholic—was one that disrespected and belittled the faith of the people of his church. Like many others, he wanted to gauge where I stood and whether I could be trusted.

This is just one example of a particular challenge that frequently recurred as I was conducting my research: balancing the tension between not putting off potential participants and not misleading them. How does one address their expectation for you to be an insider of sorts before they are willing to share things of importance to them, but not to be so much of an insider that you are unable to get them to articulate what they expect should be as obvious to you as it is to them? Being too much of an insider poses the danger of overfamiliarity; it prevents you from observing and inquiring into things as an outsider could. Being too much of an outsider poses the problem of unfamiliarity, in which everything you observe might be equally striking and weird or where it becomes too easy to jump to facile conclusions independent of how the people studied actually experience them.

Being positioned in multiple ways as both insider and outsider allowed me to at least partially overcome what some identify as an incommensurability between the two positions: between being able, on the one hand, to understand the meanings of people's actions from their own points of view and, on the other, to access, as an outsider, insights and explanations for these actions that insiders may be unable to reach.[2] This entailed a constant process of transition and translation. It also required that I constantly ask myself these questions: How can I adequately make sense of this (insider) experience through the categories of the outsider, through the lenses of theories in which I had been immersed? And conversely, how can I adequately translate the understandings and categories of the insider to those of the outsider?

For instance, both the terms "Mercenary" and "Missionary" were generated by my respondents, as part of their self-descriptions. However, I did not simply render them to the reader intact; I refined them through engagement with other respondents as well as "outsider" interlocutors. The resultant conceptual hybrids, I would argue, are modified but not distorted: my informants, with whom I have discussed the work as it developed, can recognize themselves in these descriptions.

Throughout my fieldwork, I thus found myself reshaping categories on both sides: modifying existing theories (whether of Bourdieu or Girard or Nippert-Eng or Taylor) to better account for what I was studying and also constantly reinterpreting what I was observing in light of these different modified lenses, all the while trying not to distort or damage either. I do not claim I have succeeded perfectly. *Omnis traductor traditor,* after all. Yet I think the overall goal of our striving in such efforts is more modest than perfection. It is, as Clifford Geertz argued, "to produce an interpretation of the way people live which is neither imprisoned within their mental horizons, an ethnography of witchcraft as written by a witch, nor systematically deaf to the distinctive tonalities of witchcraft as written by a geometer."[3]

As a sociologist writing primarily for interlocutors in my field, my temptation is admittedly to privilege the outsider perspective, which often runs the danger of reducing people's actions to some "real" external cause inaccessible to them. This can turn into smug, self-serving attempts to explain away the phenomenon observed as "nothing but" the result of certain macrolevel social forces. Yet neither did I want to reject "outsider" explanations at this level: people who inhabit a particular social context are often incapable of seeing the contingent macrolevel factors that crucially shape what appears to them as natural or commonsensical. Nevertheless, as Boltanski and Thévenot insist, ordinary people also have considerable "critical capacity" of their own to evaluate their own actions; it is not that they are utterly incapable of reflection without the help of the sociologist.[4] It has been a challenge to keep this tension in mind. As someone who has lived these experiences, who is in many ways an insider, I found myself constantly asking whether these "outsider" explanations allowed me to better understand my experience, without denigrating it or explaining it away. Inasmuch as they seemed helpful and illuminative, rather than seeming alien or grossly inadequate, I retained them.

I want to add a final point about doing this sort of research. The idea of a stranger who shows up at your door and asks questions without revealing anything at all about him- or herself, in the name of something like science or professionalism or objectivity, is a very strange phenomenon outside North America. And the attitudes that respondents may have toward this "stranger" certainly pose challenge for social-scientific research.[5] Very often among my respondents in India and the Middle East there seemed to be some implicit expectation of a sort of quid pro quo: they wanted me to tell them not only how the research would be used and so on but also where I stood personally, both in my stance toward them and how I myself would respond to some of the questions that I asked them. (In contrast, I have never experienced this expectation when doing research on Americans.) In part, they wanted to know whether I was an insider or not, in the sense of whether I would understand, on the basis of common experience and commitments, the things that mattered to them or whether, on the contrary, I had already dismissed these matters out of hand, and so they might need to be on the defensive. There was also often a desire for reciprocity, especially since I was a sort-of insider. This was often framed as an expression of friendship: *I have just told you a lot of confidential things that I haven't told anyone else before. So now we are friends. And now it's your turn.* (But in some cases, this also took on a certain instrumentality: *Ah, you are in America, so you can help me make some connections with people in America, so I can expand my business or my ministry.*)

These demands challenge assumptions that we often take for granted in qualitative research. The professionalism required of a researcher—the widely accepted norm in the West that makes mutually understandable the situations in which we strangers sit and observe and interrogate people and then fly away—excuses the researcher from being the subject of the other's interrogations. Often I was not granted this luxury. I am grateful for the friendships that have come about as a result.

Notes

INTRODUCTION

1. See Blair-Loy (2003) on the "competing devotions" of women professionals; also see Nippert-Eng (1996) on the integration and segmentation of distinct experiential realms.

2. Weber 1958b.

3. Appadurai (1990) identifies five global cultural flows that characterize a "disorganized" capitalism: flows of finance (financescapes), people (ethnoscapes), images (mediascapes), ideas (ideoscapes), and technology (technoscapes)

4. I anonymized the names of people and organizations in this book to protect confidentiality. There are some exceptions. I retained the names of parishes in Dubai because they are so easily identifiable that it would be pointless to disguise them. Some respondents, such as the founder of the Charismatic Renewal in Bangalore and local bishops, are also not disguisable.

5. On the use of such "representative characters," see Bellah et al. (1985) and MacIntyre (1984).

6. Boltanski and Chiapello 2005, 433.

7. My use of the word "moral" here is formal, rather than substantive (Tavory 2011; Hitlin and Vaisey 2013, 55). In other words, I am not making judgments about what is moral versus immoral, but rather am describing and analyzing how different groups of people understand what is right/wrong, worthy/unworthy: what Charles Taylor (1989) calls "strong evaluations." I am also less interested in what people consider morally justifiable or permissible in particular situations: what Abend (2011) calls "thin" understandings of morality. Instead my interest is in "thicker" understandings of identities, orientations, and visions of the good. This should become clear as I develop my two central "characters" in chapters 1 and 2. For more on the incipient field of the sociology of morality, see Hitlin and Vaisey (2010, 2013).

8. Berger 2014.

9. Berger 2014, 14.

10. For example, Ali 2010a, 2010b; Kanna 2011; Nadeem 2009, 2011; Upadhya 2008; Vora 2008, 2013. Mahdavi (2011) and Radhakrishnan (2011) examine religion, but not in sufficient depth.

11. See Chakrabarty (2000) on the tension between dominant Western analytical categories and the postcolonial experience, and on the need to "provincialize" or recognize the parochial nature of the former.

12. On continued support for the decline thesis, see, e.g., Bruce (2013) and Norris and Inglehart (2004).

13. Norris and Inglehart 2004.

14. Marx appropriated Feuerbach's critique of religion, but rejected the idea that a mere change in consciousness was sufficient to do away with religion (Tucker 1976, 144, 85, 53; cf. Feuerbach 2004, 71).

15. Brown 2010, 91.

16. Brown 2010, 96; Tucker 1976, 476.

17. Brown 2010, 95.

18. Weber 2011 [1920].

19. Luthy 1968; Marshall 1982, 56.

20. Weber 2011 [1920], 123, emphasis original. The only prospect he considers is the faint possibility of the rise of new "prophets."

21. Gorski 2000, 140. However, as Lough (2004, 14) argues, while Weber's argument might mean that "one should no longer anticipate finding ultimate and sublime values lurking behind the practices, structures, processes or dispositions that shaped or mediated action in the public sphere . . . it did not mean that people in large numbers would cease to be religious."

22. Berger 1967; Casanova 1994, 18; Gorski 2000, 141; Weber 1958b.

23. Weber 1958c, 355, 152.

24. Brubaker 1984, 74.

25. Turner 1992, 63.

26. Casanova 1994.

27. Smith 1996.

28. Budde 1992.

29. Ashmos and Duchon 2000; Miller 2007; Gotsis and Kortesi 2008.

30. Ngunjiri and Miller 2013; Green 2016.

31. Butt 1973; Miller 2007; Novak 1996.

32. Grant, O'Neil, and Stephens (2004) is a rare exception.

33. See Bruun 2008; Oakes 2003.

34. Casanova 1994; Toft, Shah and Philpott. 2011.

35. Berger 1997; Berger 2014.

36. Pope 1942.

37. Gusfield 1967; Fowler 1989.

38. Berger 2002, 2; Jameson 1998, 58; Tomlinson 1999, 10.

39. "Multiple modernities" is an orienting framework that sensitizes us to recognize modernity (including its components, such as capitalism) as a cultural program that is not monolithic, but is internally conflicted and therefore prone to multiplicity in expression; see Eisenstadt 2000; Taylor 2007; Smith 2008; Smith and Vaidyanathan 2010; Casanova 2011. On the concept of hybridization, see Holton 2000; Berger and Huntington 2002; Robertson 1995.

40. Gusfield 1967.

41. Harvey 2006; Tanner 2018.

42. Hodgson 2015.

43. Hall and Soskice 2001.

44. Harvey 2005, 2. See also Mudge (2008).

45. Harvey 2006, 24

46. Harvey 2005; Ong 2006; Sklair 1994.

47. Sklair 2000, 2001, 2010. Sklair's concept of the transnational capitalist class includes CEOs and owners of transnational corporations, globalizing bureaucrats, consumerist elites, and globalizing professionals. My focus is only on the last category of transnational actors, who can be said to constitute the transnational professional class; see Radhakrishnan 2011.

48. Bennett 2015; Irwin 2015.

49. Berger 1991; Novak 1991. By contrast, others, such as Hadas (2017) and Tanner (2018), argue that the actual system of finance-dominated capitalism is fundamentally incompatible with Christianity.

50. Kanna 2011; Radhakrishnan 2011; Rudnyckyj 2009; cf. Foucault 2008, 318.

51. See the debate in Eriksen et al. 2015.

52. Eriksen 2015, 915–917.

53. Stone 2000; Cullinane and Dundon 2006.

54. Vaidyanathan 2012.

55. It is not only that they cannot participate because of a lack of resources; in many cases they are also physically prevented from entering (Voyce 2007; Vora 2013).

56. Kanna 2010; Friedman 2005.

57. See, e.g., Martikainen and Gauthier 2013.

58. Radhakrishnan 2011, 17; italics in the original.

59. It is not simply the prospect of global travel but also the ability to work in spaces and structures that transcend local and national boundaries (i.e., the prospect of "virtual migration"; see Aneesh 2006) that define these actors as transnational.

60. Lange and Meier 2009. As Zhou (2008, 170–171) describes members of this class in China, "like young, urban middle classes anywhere in the world, they are sophisticated, lead sophisticated lifestyles and want sophisticated products and services."

61. As a result I also include in this category workers in sectors such as business process outsourcing who work in transnational firms, participating in similar career trajectories as their counterparts in more skilled occupations, rising similarly to occupy managerial roles or similarly switching occupational sectors, and for whom being a "global professional" is similarly a central marker of status and identity. Thus the scope of my category of transnational professionals is wider than that given by Radhakrishnan (2011).

62. These professionals may not be elite architects of global capitalism in the sense in which owners of transnational corporations or globalizing bureaucrats and politicians are. Nevertheless, they are powerful constituents of neoliberalism, with roles that are both technical and ideological. As Leslie Sklair (2010) explains, their technical roles stem from their expertise in creating and managing modes of global benchmarking (i.e., the practices and outcomes of transnational corporations), and their ideological role is to sell these systems as ultimate indices of competitiveness and therefore of national success.

63. Boli and Thomas 1997; Meyer, Boli, and Thomas 1987; Meyer et al. 1997. However, it is also important to note that such global flows do not originate exclusively from the West. For instance, consider the isomorphism generated in the West by the Japanese total quality management (TQM) approach.

64. Fernandes 2006; Davidson 2008.

65. Ali 2010a, 2010b; Vora 2008, 2013; Nadeem 2009, 2011; Radhakrishnan 2011.

66. The state government changed the city's official name to its Kannada pronunciation in October 2014 (BBC 2014). Consistent with most English-language media and scholarly publications, I retain the use of "Bangalore." The Roman Catholic archdiocese also retains "Bangalore" as of this writing in spite of the change at the state level.

67. Reddy and Lakshmikantha 2012.

68. On this tendency in globalizing cities, see Sassen (1988, 2007).

69. Patnaik 2007; Adebayo 2018.

70. Lange, Meier, and Anuradha 2009; Upadhya 2008.

71. Beblawi 1990.

72. Pradhan 2010, 65; Davidson 2008; Krane 2009.

73. Vora 2013.

74. Harmassi 2009; Longva 1999; Motaparthy 2015.

75. Ali 2010b.

76. Longva 2005, 119.

77. See Kanna 2011.

78. Krane 2009, 267; Associated Press 2014.

79. Kanna 2011.

80. Ali 2010a, 2010b; Kanna 2011; Vora 2008.

81. Jaffrelot and Van der veer 2008; Upadhya and Vasavi 2006.

82. Hari 2009; Human Rights Watch 2006; Krane 2009; Mahdavi 2011.

83. Vora 2013, 11.

84. Vora 2013, 12.

85. Krane 2009; Davis and Monk 2008.

86. Mahdavi (2011) is an exception, although her treatment of religion is rather limited.

87. See, e.g., Radhakrishnan 2011.

88. See, e.g., Asad 1993. My approach of studying a "Western" religious institution should also help overcome some objections of such critics with regard to extending methods used in studies in the West to non-Western contexts.

89. Riesebrodt 2010, 75.

90. Smith 2017.

91. Chaves 2010.

92. Smith 2017, 99–118. See also Schilbrack (2010).

93. A "covering law" is the dominant positivist understanding of causality that conflates causation with mere empirical regularity and entails lawlike generalization predicting that, if event B always follows event A, we can predict B whenever A occurs (Elder-Vass 2010, 40–41).

94. Marx 1972; Smith 1998.

95. See Guhin (2014) on the advantages of using religion as a "site" rather than an analytical category.

96. Levitt 2007, 120.

97. Upadhya and Vasavi 2006.

98. Nair 2005.

99. Katju 2015

100. Mohammad-Arif 2011; Mondal 2012; *Times of India* 2015.

101. *Times of India* 2008; *Deccan Herald* 2011.

102. *The National* 2010.

1. THE MERCENARY

1. Friedman 1970.

2. Bellah et al. 1985, 45. They elaborate, "[The manager's] role is to persuade, inspire, manipulate, cajole and intimidate those he manages so that his organization measures up to criteria of effectiveness shaped ultimately by the market but specifically by the expectations of those in control of his organization . . . . The manager's view of things is akin to that of the technician of industrial society par excellence, the engineer, except that the manager must admit interpersonal responses and personalities, including his own, into the calculation of effectiveness" (1985, 45).

3. See MacIntyre 1984, 29.

4. Note that these shared goals and bases for evaluating oneself and others include not only criteria restricted to the workplace but also things such as houses, cars, and other lifestyle elements outside work.

5. Jepperson 1991, 149.

6. Taylor 1989.

7. Boltanski and Thévenot 2006.

8. Sennett 1998, 44.

9. Senge 1990.

10. These are the title and subtitle of Bridges's (1998) career management guide

11. See Jackall 1988, 68–69 on the centrality of promotability in the lives of managers.

12. Sennett 1998, 87.

13. Sennett 1998, 87.

14. Jackall (1988, 71) describes the "mobility panic" that sets in when middle managers experience stagnation.

15. As Sennett observes, "Detachment and superficial cooperativeness are better armor for dealing with current realities than behavior based on values of loyalty and service" (1998, 25)

16. Sennett 1998, 87.

17. Sennett 1998, 91. As Sennett argues, the earlier capitalist model of the "organization man" is now replaced by the "ironic man" (1998, 116). This mode of selfhood is ironic in the sense that people are keenly aware that their self-definitions and vocabularies are fragile, contingent, and always subject to change.

18. Cavanaugh 2008.

19. Cavanaugh 2008; Lipovetsky 2005.

20. Cox 2002, 1.

21. Beck, Giddens, and Lash 1994; Bell 1973; Touraine 1971.

22. Castells 1996; Boltanski and Chiapello 2005; Powell 1990.

23. Touraine (1995) contrasts "rationalization" to a different kind of "subjectivation," one that refers to the birth of "the subject," which is capable of critique and dissent. But I use a different term to refer to the emphasis on subjectivity in the practice of neoliberal capitalism and how it is marshaled in the service of rationalization. The aspects of subjectivity Touraine focuses on might have some bearing on expressions of "voice" in the capacity to critique and resist rationalization, but these, as I argue, seldom occur in my cases.

24. Giddens 1990.

25. Friedman 2005.

26. Boltanski and Chiapello 2005.

27. Taylor 2001.

28. This is true despite figures showing that, for instance, IT managers in India are among the lowest paid in their profession globally (Economic Times 2012).

29. Chinmay 2011; Patel 2010; Rahman 2013; Vora 2008.

30. Boltanski and Thévenot 2006.

31. Abbott 1988, 8; Friedson 2001.

32. Larson 1977; Spillman 2012.

33. Marks and Scholarios 2007, 113.

34. "The refusal of trust and discretion is itself an indignity," notes sociologist Andrew Sayer (2011, 201), and employees at times use the word "professionalism" to refer to the dignity denied here.

35. See Vaidyanathan 2012 for an analysis of such professionalism in Indian call centers.

36. See Spillman 2012.

37. Wagner (2001) argues that the central tension of modernity is between autonomy and mastery or control.

38. Weber 1958b, 139; Touraine 1995. The term "rationalization" in Weber's corpus has multiple referents pointing to qualitatively distinct and independent "processes that variously conflict and coalesce with one another at all societal and civilizational levels" (Kalberg 1980, 1147), whether in realms of knowledge in general, in societal spheres such as law and economics, or in "internal" spheres such as religion, ethics, or even the aesthetic and erotic realms (1150). Kalberg notes that the process in Weber's view is radically perspectival: "the existence of a rationalization process depends on an individual's implied or stated, unconscious or conscious, preference for certain ultimate values and the systematization of his or her action to conform to these values. These values acquire

'rationality' merely from their status as consistent value postulate" (1156). My use of the term "rationalization" here refers specifically to the dominance of instrumental rationality in complex systems in the economic sphere.

39. Schumpeter 1975 [1942], 82–85.

40. Morris 2006.

41. Morris 2006, 84.

42. Meyer and Rowan 1977; Meyer et al. 1997, 154–155.

43. Morris 2006, 74.

44. Richard Sennett calls this "concentration without centralization" (1998, 51).

45. Castells 1996; Powell 1990.

46. Sennett 1998, 57.

47. Weber 2011 [1920]; Baehr 2001.

48. I credit Rouleau (2000) for the use of the term "flexibilization" as a polar contrast to "rationalization." However, I use the term differently, to reflect Peter Wagner's (2001) insistence on the dual commitments to mastery and autonomy being the central tension of modernity. For a broader treatment of flexibilization, see Taplin 2012.

49. In using this term, my focus is primarily on the relationship between the organization and its employees; I am not referring to "flexible specialization" or modes of "just in time" production that organizations need to adopt to respond to volatile demand. The origins of "flexibilization" as I see it are not new either. If rationalization was epitomized in the mechanistic, "scientific management" approach of Frederick Taylor (1911), the opposite polarity was evident in the "human relations" school of Chester Barnard (1938). In addition, processes such as "lean production" and "networked" structures, as well as the increased malleability in the workforce through practices such as variable hours, are included in Boltanski and Thévenot's notion of "external flexibility" (2005, 218), whereas I would categorize the former as aspects of rationalization.

50. Certainly industry is also a factor here: firms in the finance sector insist on formal attire, whereas technology firms tend to encourage informal attire.

51. Jeffcoat and Gibson 2006.

52. Bell 1976, 71–72.

53. This term was even used by Filipinos and Gulf-raised Indians working under older Indian managers in Dubai. They referred to "Indian management" in a derogatory manner similar to that of younger professionals in Bangalore.

54. His claim here also echoes the findings of recent survey data in India on the preference exhibited by women and married couples for flextime options at work; see DNA 2011.

55. Harrison 1997, 45.

56. Sennett 1998, 59.

57. Goudreau 2013.

58. J. Martin 2002; Morrill 2008.

59. Kanter 1996 [1988], 95.

60. Deal and Kennedy 1982; Peters and Waterman 1982.

61. Bate 1997.

62. Van Maanen and Kunda 1989.

63. Etzioni 1961; Kunda 1992, 11.

64. Kunda 1992, 10.

65. Kunda 1992, 218.

66. Whyte 1956.

67. This sentiment is exemplified in the following quotation from an employee: "I feel like putting a lot of time in. There is a real kind of loyalty here. We are all working this together . . . I'm not a workaholic—it's just the place. I love the place." (Deal and Kennedy 1982, 9, cited in Kunda 1992, 10).

68. Kunda 1992, 64.

69. A number of newspaper reports address soaring attrition in both these cities; see AME Info 2008; IBM Live 2009; Kapur 2010, 2013b; Saleem 2012.

70. Kunda 1992, 21.

71. There is a notable difference among my cases, however, which also might be more pronounced in developing economies: while "losers" in the corporation might be blamed for a lack of individual initiative and hard work and so on, *the poor* in society are not similarly blamed for their plight. A likely contributor to this fact is the absence of a social safety net. It is difficult to see the poor in places such as India and the Philippines as being "lazy" or living off handouts; at least, this notion was not supported by people I studied.

72. MacLeod 2009, 264, 200.

73. As Sennett observes, "For all the psychological heavy breathing which modern management does about office and factory teamwork, it is an ethos of work which remains on the surface of experience. Teamwork is the group practice of demeaning superficiality" (1998, 99).

74. Sennett 2006, 66.

75. There is an important distinction to make between *calculative* and *normative* trust: the former is more instrumental and has to do with competence, whereas the latter has to do with a sense of belonging, home, and family (Mizrachi, Drori, and Anspach 2007; see also Lewicki and Bunker 1996; Rousseau et al. 1998). I am not saying that people are incapable of trust as such and do not engage at all in practices and forms of trust. There need to be banal forms of trust even for one to be able to take for granted that, when a colleague tells you, for example, where the bathroom is, that he is not deceiving you. Calculative trust is also necessary for coalitions and alliances that form in these settings, which help people achieve their goals of survival and success. But I am not going to focus on this form of trust; my concern here is with normative trust and how its absence in these contexts contributes to the inability of people to feel the sense of home or belonging that proponents of normative control strategies aspire to generate.

76. On such segmentation between "work" and "personal" friends in the west, see Nippert-Eng 1996, 244–245. In my cases, these descriptions are strongly inflected with a pervasive sense of suspicion, wariness, and distrust that do not similarly characterize Nippert-Eng's "segmenting" respondents.

77. Sennett 1998, 84.

78. Kunda 1992, 178, 181.

79. As MacIntyre argues, "A *character* is an object of regard by the members of the culture generally or by some significant segment of them. He furnishes them with a cultural and moral ideal. Hence the demand is that in this type of case role and personality be fused. Social type and psychological type are required to coincide" (MacIntyre 1984, 29, emphasis original).

80. For examples of such socialization of subjectivities in medical schools, see Vaidyanathan 2015.

81. Knapp 2012, 79.

82. Girard 1979, 2007. My goal here is not to provide a detailed application of Girard's oeuvre to the setting of professional organizations (for this, see Desmond and Kavanagh 2003; St. Pierre and Holmes 2010). I am mainly drawing on it to shed light on processes of mimesis and rivalry that sustain mercenary professionalism.

83. Girard 1979, 146.

84. Girard explains: "Two desires converging on the same object are bound to clash. Thus, mimesis coupled with desire leads automatically to conflict. However, [people] always seem half blind to this conjunction, unable to perceive it as a cause of rivalry. In human relationships words like *sameness* and *similarity* evoke an image of harmony. If we

have the same tastes and like the same things, surely we are bound to get along. But what will happen when we share the same desires?" (1979, 146; emphasis in original).

85. Girard 1986, 16.

86. Desmond and Kavanagh 2003, 246–247.

87. Courpasson 2000.

88. On the concept of habitus, see Bourdieu 1990.

89. Solomon 1997, 139.

90. See, e.g., Kanna 2010, Vora 2008; 2013.

91. Anthropologist Neha Vora (2008; 2013) provides several similar examples from her ethnographic research in Dubai on wage discrimination encountered by Indians due to their nationality.

92. See http://gulfbusiness.com/revealed-average-asian-expatriate-salaries-in-the-gulf -2017/ and http://gulfbusiness.com/revealed-average-western-expatriate-salaries-in-the -gulf-2017/.

93. This is akin to the "self-determining" individualism that Bellah et al. talk about—"a belief in the inherent dignity and . . . sacredness of the human person," bearing concomitant rights "to think for ourselves, judge for ourselves, make our own decisions, live our lives as we see fit" (1985, 334, 142).

94. BBC News 2006.

95. A recent report from the General Secretary of the International Trade Union Confederation stated, "As well as denying workers their rights, the [UAE] government has used its power to restrict any unwanted actions taken by professional associations, which have sprung up in an attempt to circumvent the restrictive labour laws" (ITUC 2012).

96. Scholars have argued that Indian IT professionals find unionization abhorrent because of their class distinction from blue-collar workers: these professionals cannot imagine themselves "slogan shouting and picketing on the streets" (Noronha and D'Cruz 2006, 2119). But this argument is insufficient to explain the lack of solidarity. Consider, for instance, that the central union in the industry, precisely to cater to middle-class professionals, strategically calls itself an "association of professionals" rather than a union and yet still is unable to retain member commitment. As its secretary told me, professionals use the organization as an "agony aunt" whose shoulders they can cry on in difficult situations, but disappear as soon as they find a new employment opportunity.

97. Taylor 1989.

98. On utilitarian individualism, see Bellah et al. 1985, 336.

99. Wuthnow 2005, 618.

100. Novak 1991, 123.

101. Whyte 1956, 3; emphasis in original.

102. Whyte 1956, 11.

103. Coyle 2018; Lencioni 2012; Novak 1981, 1991.

2. THE MISSIONARY

1. In the Gulf, the term tends to be used as slang, usually pejoratively, to refer to any man wearing their style of clothing: long-sleeved cotton shirts, sleeveless vest, and baggy trousers.

2. Smith 1998, 189; Emerson and Smith 2000, 76–77; Hunter 2001, 145; Robbins 2004, 136; Martin 1990, 266.

3. Berger 2014, 62.

4. Emerson and Smith 2000, 76–77.

5. Other scholarship on the Pentecostal/Charismatic movement makes a similar argument about relief from the anxieties of turbulent political/economic changes; see Brenneman (2011); Comaroff and Comaroff (2000); Chesnut (1997); Smilde (2007).

6. Smith and Denton 2005; Hunter 2001.

7. For the relativistic conception, see Smith and Denton (2005, 173).

8. Smith and Denton 2005, 175.

9. See, for instance, Prov. 4:20–22; Ps. 107:19–21; Ps. 30:2; Ps. 41:2–3; Is. 53:4–5; Mt. 8:5–17; Mt. 9:35; Mk. 5:34; Lk. 8:43–56; Rev. 21:4.

10. Davis and Robinson 2006.

11. Hefner 2013, 2

12. Jenkins 2002; Millerm, Sargeant, and Flory 2013.

13. Anderson 2013; Hefner 2013.

14. Berger 2014, 24.

15. Hefner 2013, 13.

16. Jacobsen, cited in Anderson (2013, 5).

17. "Classical Pentecostalism" originated in early-twentieth-century revival movements. These include groups such as the Holiness Pentecostals, Oneness Pentecostals, and Apostolic Pentecostals. "Older Church Charismatics" are Charismatic movements within Anglican, Catholic, Orthodox, and other Mainline Protestant churches. "Older Independent Churches" include churches in India and China that are largely independent from classical Pentecostalism. They may not see themselves as "Pentecostal," but have similar beliefs and practices focused on healing, spiritual gifts, and Charismatic prayer. "Neopentecostal" or "Neocharismatic" churches include "Word of faith" churches, "Third wave churches," New Apostolic churches," and numerous independent churches and megachurches with overlapping theologies (Anderson 2013).

18. Miller 2013, 7.

19. Robbins 2009.

20. Miller 2013, 7

21. Martin 1990, 108; Miller 2013, 12.

22. Miller 2013, 13; Hill 2017.

23. Martin 1990, 33–34.

24. Martin 1990, 228–229.

25. Martin 2002, 71

26. Attanasi and Yong 2012.

27. Chesnut 1997, 166,116; Martin 1995.

28. On the application of the Protestant Ethic thesis to Pentecostalism, see Berger (2010). Robbins (2004, 136) summarizes some of the ambivalence around this view.

29. Martin 2002, 165.

30. Martin 2002, 75; Burdick 1996; Brenneman 2011.

31. Hefner 2013, 9.

32. Hefner 2013, 10.

33. Robbins 2009, 63

34. Gifford 1991, 65–66.

35. Martin 1990, 266

36. Miller 2013, 13.

37. Miller and Yamamori 2007

38. Hefner 2013, 6.

39. Klandermans and Oegema 1987.

40. Miller 2013, 8; Weber 1947.

41. Miller 2013, 6–7.

42. For scholarship that examines Pentecostalism as offering existential security in the face of neoliberalism, see e.g., Comaroff and Comaroff 2000; Chesnut 1997; Smilde 2007.

43. Miller 2013, 17–18.

44. Riesebrodt 2010, 89.

45. Burdick 1996; Miller 2013, 17.

46. Collins 2004; Brenneman 2011; Robbins 2009.

47. Collins 2004, 49.

48. Robbins 2009, 61.

49. Robbins 2009, 62.

50. For a firsthand account of this event, see Mansfield 1992.

51. Clark 1976; Ghezzi 1976.

52. Catechism of the Catholic Church (paragraphs 1299, 1831).

53. The CCR's views on these phenomena are not an innovation of the twentieth century, but were discussed in earlier theological commentaries on the role of Charismatic authority in the early church; see, e.g., de Dunin-Borkowski 1913, 331–334. What is new is the emphasis on how these manifestations are not simply the prerogative of virtuosi, but accessible to ordinary laypeople today.

54. *Bangalore Archdiocese Directory* 2012.

55. The director of the International Catholic Charismatic Renewal Services, the CCR's Vatican office, insisted in an interview that these two events are central to membership in the CCR. But members of CCR groups I interviewed thought that the experience of God traditionally communicated through the Life in the Spirit Seminars can occur outside such ritualized means.

56. Nearly all the songs used in these groups can be found on the list of the top CWM songs of the past couple of decades as reported by Christian Copyright Licensing International (CCLI), compiled in Woods and Walrath (2007, 24–27).

57. Riesebrodt 2010.

58. Snow and Machalek 1984, 176.

59. Yamane 2000.

60. This retreat center, run by a Charismatic order of priests in Kerala, was referred to by several of the respondents. Attending a retreat there constituted a pivotal moment in their religious journeys. Only one other respondent mentioned undergoing a conversion from a different religious background (also Hinduism). Several others who grew up Catholic but were uninvolved mentioned developing a relationship with God for the first time when they visited this retreat center.

61. For a summary of research on sudden and gradual conversions, see Hood, Hill, and Spilka (2009, 206–243).

62. Copyright Hillsong United.

63. The idea that existential security comes from simply economic development and having material needs met (Norris and Inglehart 2004) ignores the universality of matters like heartbreak, failed relationships, and so on. The claims of a relational God that bestows eternal worth, guarantee of intimacy, promise of transformation and fulfillment can certainly be appealing in this context.

64. Smith 2007, 167, 169–176.

65. On how members of such communities learn to "listen" to God, see Luhrmann 2012.

66. On the whole, emotional and psychological healing were given more attention in the groups I studied than physical healing, so I pay less attention to the latter. For an extensive treatment of the dynamics of Charismatic healing in Catholic Charismatic groups, see Csordas (1994). See also McGuire (1982) and Neitz (1987).

67. Collins 2004, 181.

68. Collins 2004, 51.

69. Carney, Cuddy, and Yap 2010; Cuddy, Wilmuth, and Carney 2012. This research remains the subject of ongoing debate at the time of this writing. See https://ideas.ted.com/inside-the-debate-about-power-posing-a-q-a-with-amy-cuddy/.

70. Bellah et al. 1985, 221.

71. I should be clear that my argument is not that the type of neoliberal regime determines the type of religiosity one finds here. Rather, it is simply that we do find such contextual influences, which coexist with considerable homogeneity, across the groups in these cities.

3. MISSIONARIES IN A MERCENARY WORLD

1. On works aimed at practitioners and professionals, see Benefiel (2008); Butt (1973); Gunther (2001); Jones (1996); Marques, Dhaman, and King (2007); Metcalf and Hateley (2001); Nash (1994); Nash and McLennan (2001); Pierce (2005). On literature by theologians and religious leaders, see Dalai Lama and Cutler (2004); Stevens (2006); Naughton and Alford (2012); Novak 1993. Scholarly publications on the topic include books such as Hicks (2003) and Mitroff and Denton (1999), handbooks such as Giacalone and Jurkiewicz (2010) and Neal (2013), and journals such as the *Journal of Management, Spirituality, and Religion.* For reviews of the scholarly literature and history of the field, see Lund Dean and Fornaciari (2007); Miller (2007); Neal (2013).

2. Miller 2007.

3. See for a summary of this background, Ashmos and Duchon (2000); Miller (2007); Gotsis and Kortesi (2008).

4. Fombrun and Foss 2004.

5. Dalai Lama and Cutler 2004; Meir 2003.

6. Konrad, Prasad, and Pringle 2006.

7. Brown and Leledaki 2010; Goldberg 2010.

8. Leigh 1997.

9. Covey 1989; Senge 1990, 130; Mitroff and Denton 1999; Hicks 2003, 52; Marques et al. 2007, 214.

10. Conger 1994, 13; Ashmos and Duchon 2000.

11. Khasawneh 2011.

12. See, e.g., Nash 1994; Miller 2007; Lindsay 2008.

13. Lindsay and Smith 2010.

14. Miller 2007.

15. Chaves 2010.

16. See Giacalone and Jurkiewicz (2003, 6–12) for a review.

17. Mitroff and Denton 1999, xvii.

18. Fenwick and Lange 1998, 63.

19. Gotsis and Kortesi 2008; Tourish and Pinnington 2002; Ashforth and Vaidyanath 2002; Kamoche and Pinnington 2012.

20. See, e.g., Gregory (1989). Also, as José Casanova (2008) argues, the centrality of this concept of church-state separation is so taken for granted in Western thought, but is alien to contexts in which there is either no historical drama about the need for such separation or no centralized "church"-like entity that could be separated from the state.

21. On the history of construction of boundaries between home and work in the West, see Nippert-Eng (1996, 18–20), especially the extensive bibliography on p. 18 n3.

22. Langton and Dajani 2017.

23. See Gautier (2008) and Tøllefsen (2011) on its international expressions.

24. Websites for their corporate programs are http://www.artofliving.org/bangalore-ashram/corporate-programs-workshops and http://www.tlexprogram.com/tlex-approach/. More details on their ideas on linking meditation and corporate productivity are available at Nair, Pratika. (n.d.). "Just Do It with Meditation." Art of Living Foundation. http://www.artofliving.org/meditation/meditation-for-you/meditation-productivity. The founder of the movement, Sri Sri Ravi Shankar, also recently touted the importance of spirituality as a source of competitive advantage for corporations at an international conference held in Bangalore on corporate culture and spirituality in India (attended, surprisingly, by several Norwegian public officials): http://www.artofliving.org/spirituality-will-give-corporations-edge-over-others-sri-sri-ravi-shankar.

25. Pattanaik gave essentially the same talk at a TED conference, available online. Here he talks about his job, which involves trying to create rituals based on what he sees as essential features of Indian (i.e., Hindu) culture: "You see, Indian music, for example, does not have the concept of harmony . . . . The ground reality is based on a cyclical world view. So, it's rapidly changing, highly diverse, chaotic, ambiguous, unpredictable. And people are okay with it. And then globalization is taking place. The demands of modern institutional thinking is coming in. Which is rooted in one-life culture. And a clash is going to take place." Pattanaik also talks about a ritual he created to "align" beliefs of employees with that of the company: "After a leader completes his training and is about to take over the store, we blindfold him, we surround him with the stakeholders, the customer, his family, his team, his boss. You read out his KRA [Key Result Area], his KPI [Key Performance Indicator], you give him the keys, and then you remove the blindfold. And invariably, you see a tear, because the penny has dropped. He realizes that to succeed, he does not have to be a "professional"; he does not have to cut out his emotions. He has to include all these people in his world to succeed, to make them happy, to make the boss happy, to make everyone happy. The customer is happy, because the customer is God. That sensitivity is what we need. Once this belief enters, behavior will happen. Business will happen" (Pattanaik 2009).

26. See, e.g., Novak 1996, Grudem 2003, Keller 2014.

27. Such fusion is an extreme version of integration, reflecting a tendency to obliterate distinctions between the two categorical realms and to use the same logics, mental frameworks, emotional approaches, motivations, and even objects in both realms, with "a single, all-purpose mentality, one way of being, one amorphous self," regardless of context or role (Nippert-Eng 1996, 5).

28. See Nippert-Eng 1996, 36–38, 280.

29. On the difficulty with such "translation" of religious into secular discourse, see the debate between Charles Taylor and Jurgen Habermas in Mendieta and VanAntwerpen (2011).

30. Lips-Wiersma and Mills 2002; Lindsay and Smith 2010.

31. These findings resonate with research on self-discipline among Pentecostals and Charismatics (e.g., Berger 2010; D. Martin 1990; B. Martin 1995; Miller and Yamamori 2007).

32. Petchsawang and Duchon 2012.

33. Gould 1997.

34. Berger 2014, 73.

35. Berger 2014, 73–74.

36. Wuthnow 1994, 39.

37. On the distinction between motivation and justification, see Vaisey 2009.

38. Swidler 1986.

39. See Lizardo (2017) on declarative and nondeclarative forms of culture.

40. Berger 2014, 57.

41. Nippert-Eng 1996.

42. Lips-Wiersma and Mills 2002; Lindsay and Smith 2010.

43. Merritt, Effron and Monin 2010; Klotz and Bolino 2013.

4. FINDING ESCAPE VELOCITY

1. Benedikter 2012, 1076.

2. Bauman 2007, 121–122.

3. Stevenson 2007; Turner 2011.

4. Cavanaugh 2008; Fulmer 2006a.

5. Fulmer 2006b, 45.

6. Miller 2007, 130.

7. See, for instance, Pope John Paul II 1987 §28; Pope Francis 2013 §53–54.

8. Sklair 2010, 136.

9. Stearns 2001, vii. Zygmunt Bauman similarly argues that consumerism must be understood not as an individual-level attribute but as a collective one: "an attribute of *society*. For a society to acquire that attribute the thoroughly individual capacity for wanting, desiring and longing needs to be, just as labour capacity was in the producers' society, detached ('alienated') from individuals and recycled/reified into an extraneous force which sets the 'society of consumers' in motion and keeps it on course as a specific form of human togetherness, while by the same token setting specific parameters for effective individual life strategies and otherwise manipulating the probabilities of individual choices and conduct" (2007, 28, emphasis in original).

10. Stearns 2001, vii. Historically and across societies the types of material goals pursued as well as their meanings were very different from present-day consumerism (see Stearns 2001, 12). The advent of consumerism as we know it now was hardly "natural," but required a revolution that entailed a redefinition of people's needs and aspirations and changes in the interests and activities of the wealthy, as well as ordinary denizens (Campbell 1987).

11. Sheth 1999, 11; Fernandes 2006; Jaffrelot and van der Veer 2008; Upadhya 2008, 60. There is much in common here with Thorstein Veblen's (1899) classical analysis of "conspicuous consumption."

12. Schmidt 2009, 45.

13. Fernandes 2006, 59.

14. Upadhya 2008, 62. Nevertheless, as Upadhya notes, even among the "new middle classes" in India, there are differences that should prevent us from treating them as homogeneous. For instance, IT professionals in Bangalore tend to distinguish themselves "from the young and trendy call centre crowd, whose frivolous lifestyles and profligate consumption habits they tend to disparage" (63). Among my sample of Catholic respondents, however, I did not see such differences between IT and BPO professionals. Part of the reason may be that their status as a religious minority distinguishes them from the majority of Indian IT professionals who exhibit upper-caste Hindu nationalism and assert of modes of continuity with familial ideals and traditions (Upadhya 2008, 62–63; Radhakrishnan 2011).

15. Bauman 2004, 50.

16. Boltanski and Chiapello (2005) argue that this is a key property of any "spirit" of capitalism that renders it attractive to its proponents.

17. Meyer 2010.

18. Bauman 2007, 52–53.

19. Sklair 1994, 178.

20. Sklair argues, "Culture-ideology indicates that consumerism in the capitalist global system can only be fully understood as a culture-ideology practice where cultural practices reinforce the ideology and the ideology reinforces the cultural practices" (2010, 136).

21. See Patel 2010 for similar narratives of independence among female call center workers.

22. Patel 2010.

23. Here she is referring to women who feel forced to resort to sex work to pay off debts. On this topic, see Mahdavi 2011.

24. Between 2003 and 2008, the number of Filipinos living in Dubai shot up from 50,000 to nearly 200,000 (Agunias 2010, 6).

25. Hochschild 2003, 209.

26. A journalist I spoke to in Dubai who was making a documentary film on three generations of Emiratis said that she came across the same complaints among older-generation Emiratis. They expressed worry that the younger generations were no longer being raised to learn older traditions and could not even speak proper Arabic, because they were mostly being brought up by South Asian or Filipina housemaids.

27. DeParle 2011.

28. Vora 2008; 2013.

29. DeParle 2011.

30. DeParle 2011.

31. Swan 2008.

32. In 2013, the UAE government announced that it would be reforming its debt laws and that it was in the process of forming a credit bureau. UAE nationals were also decreed exempt from prosecution over bounced checks, and the pardon of seven thousand Emirati nationals with two billion dirhams in debt made local headlines. After conflicting media reports, the government clarified that these exemptions would apply only to nationals and not foreign residents, although other reports suggest that government officials hope that measures such as credit scores and credit bureaus will enable them to eventually decriminalize debt defaulting (Burggraf 2013).

33. Bond 2012; Hari 2009; Worth 2009.

34. In 2012, along with twenty other businessmen in Dubai, he staged a hunger strike and suffered a stroke (Hall and Kerr 2012).

35. Clancy 2013.

36. Girard 2001, 15.

37. Fulmer 2006b, 5.

38. A. Berger 2000, 30.

39. Fulmer 2006a, 60. See also Bocock 1993, 105.

40. Bourdieu 1984.

41. As he put it, "Technically I am stuck. I can go out, but [if I do so] I still have to land inside the jail. The policy here is that if you are in debt, they can stop you in the immigration [if you owe AED] 10,000 and above. It's useless to go to the immigration; they will just arrest you and then you will see all the litany of charges. But I am not fazed, because I have already endured it for 100 days, so I know what is like inside. It's like I already died. You can shoot me again, but I know the experience of it."

42. Kapur 2013a.

43. Medina 2013. They were luckier than thousands of others for whom the fate that would befall them if they were to return to their home countries would be worse than a prison sentence in Dubai (Kannan 2013). Many were fleeced by loan sharks, paid exorbitant amounts for their tickets and visas, had no job prospects at home but still had families to provide for, and therefore preferred to continue staying illegally in Dubai rather than return.

44. Bauman 2004, 38.

45. Bauman 2007.

46. See Brenneman 2011 on the cachet of a criminal past in such groups.

47. While I was transcribing the interview, a year after I had conducted it, I decided to check to see how the stock for Pacific Ethanol had done. Its price increased fivefold within three months of our first interview, but then declined quickly. Its performance over the past couple of years has been far from stellar. At the time of this writing, Peter is still working at his corporate job.

48. Winchester 2008, 1767, 1768.

49. Winchester 2008, 1769.

50. Lizardo and Strand 2010.

51. Fulmer 2006a, 251.

52. During 2010, 157.

53. Gruber and Hungerman 2008.

5. BELONGING AND CIVIC COMMITMENT IN THE NEOLIBERAL CITY

1. Ali 2010a, 154.

2. Between 2008 and2011, there was also a ban on dancing and live music, which was eventually lifted after a series of protests. This seems to be one of the few occasions when middle-class professionals participated in any collective action. See http://next.upi.com /archive/2012/03/11/From-nightlife-to-trite-life/2951331481641/.

3. The seriousness of violence against women in India garnered national as well as international outrage after a series of brutal gang rapes in December 2012 (George 2012; Mandhana and Trivedi 2012). It is difficult to assess the accuracy of data on how much safer Bangalore is than other cities. Statistics from the National Crime Records Bureau show a dramatic decline in the proportion of "stranger rapes" (i.e., proportion of rapes committed by men who were strangers to the victims) in Bangalore, from 77% to 0% from 2009–2010, raising questions about their reliability, although the police maintain that rapes committed by strangers amount to a very small percentage of the total (Shrinivasan 2013).

4. Vora (2013, 131–133) in her interviews with North Indians in Dubai found similar criticisms of South Indians. Such mutual judgments between Indians from northern and southern states based on claims about education and culture are common in India.

5. See http://www.dailymail.co.uk/wires/ap/article-2820598/A-lifetime-perks-UAE-help -cushion-wealth-gap.html.

6. Boltanski and Thévenot 2006, 185.

7. Longva 2005, 119.

8. Longva 2005, 119.

9. Jaffrelot 2008.

10. This describes to a great extent the attitude of Catholic professionals I studied in Bangalore. In the case of Dubai, however, this model is modified in an important way: it is a neoliberal realm of this sort for foreigners—the 90 percent or so of its population who are not citizens—but for its "locals" it is a welfare state. Citizens receive generous benefits simply for being citizens: their worth lies not in their neoliberal performance but in their formal-legal status (Davidson 2008; Kanna 2011; Vora 2013).

11. Here I echo Neha Vora's (2013) central argument.

12. Kanna 2011; Vora 2013.

13. Kanna 2011.

14. Vora 2013, 131.

15. In 2010, Canada became an exception after it insulted the country by violating an agreement with Emirates Airlines. Before 2013, Canadian citizens found themselves in the

long maze-like queue of citizens of the Global South waiting for an iris scan to collect their entry visas to the country.

16. Official statistics on labor market segmentation by nationality are not made available, so I can only report here the perceptions shared almost unanimously by my respondents.

17. Nobody could give me exact figures, so I am unable to confirm the extent to which this variation in pay exists. But because it emerged so regularly among nearly all my respondents from India and the Philippines—even the few who claimed that this arrangement was not the case in their companies seemed to think that their situation was exceptional rather than the rule—and from respondents across occupations and status (e.g., from bankers as well as IT workers, from junior employees as well as general managers), I believe that the practice is prevalent enough to generate feelings of injustice, resentment, and resignation in most foreign residents. Vora (2008; 2013) also confirms this perception.

18. Indians tended to complain that Filipino and Arab women in church were dressing "immodestly" because they revealed their shoulders; others in turn complained that South Indian women were exposing their midriffs by wearing Saris.

19. Nair 2005.

20. See Vaidyanathan (2018).

21. See Vaidyanathan (2018) for details on both the language politics and attempts at inculturation.

22. Vora 2013, 136.

23. See Srinivas (2004). They can, however, in certain cases even generate protest. For example, in Bangalore, the attempt of moral policing by banning drinking and dancing was protested primarily by the middle classes. Other scholars who have used the term "consumer citizenship" emphasize the centrality of consumerism to conceptions of "worthy" membership (Bauman 2007, 53; Turner 2011, 267–268).

24. Cohen 2003.

25. Lamont and Molnar 2001, 42.

26. *Bangalore Archdiocesan Directory* 2012.

27. Putnam 2000, 23.

28. Because the penalty for bounced checks or unpaid credit card debt is imprisonment, it becomes imperative for people to be able to clear their debts as soon as possible.

29. Both these activities, charitable contributions and visits, are also found among certain Protestant, Hindu and Muslim communities here. In addition, some secular volunteer organizations also organize events to benefit laborers. For all groups, however, aiding domestic workers is much more challenging because the labor law treats them as members of their sponsors' families rather than as contracted workers, and there are restrictions against interfering in "family matters" (see Mahdavi 2011).

30. These forms are not restricted to Catholic parishes. Protestant churches in the region have similar contingents.

31. Bourdieu 1986; Granovetter 1985.

32. Farkas 1996; Rank 2004.

33. Church groups that work with runaway maids, as well as studies on the topic (e.g., Mahdavi 2011; Human Rights Watch 2014), suggest that many domestic workers throughout the Gulf are abused in households of local citizens and believe they will be better treated by Western expat employers.

34. This supports Swidler's (1986, 2003) argument that people will gravitate toward contexts in which their habits, skills, and capacities can be perpetuated. On the importance of cultural capital and the distinction from social capital, see Bourdieu (1986). See also Rivera (2012) on the importance of "cultural matching" for hiring among corporate professionals.

35. This explanation does not seem to fit with the fact that numerous corporations encourage employees to volunteer in ways that promote social development, even in rural communities. Companies often see such volunteer programs as a means of fostering team building, as well as giving back to society.

36. Opposition from several factions within the parish, stemming primarily from people whose power had been displaced, eventually led Fr. Jerry to burn out and go on an extended leave of absence for several months. Randall and a few young professionals, in collaboration with a rookie priest, took charge in the interim. But the changes he implemented remain firmly in place as of this writing.

37. Broomhall 2012.

38. On similar tendencies in Indian-American churches, see Kurien (2017).

39. Haney, Banks, and Zimbardo 1973.

40. See http://gulfnews.com/news/uae/culture/mary-jesus-mother-is-new-name-for-uae-mosque-1.2043544.

41. Mahdavi 2011.

42. Sennett 1988, 146–147.

43. Cadge and Ecklund 2007; Levitt 2007; Mooney 2009.

44. Vora 2013.

45. Ali 2010b.

46. Vora 2013, 174.

47. Holston and Appadurai 1995; Levitt 2007; Srinivas 2004; Vora 2013.

48. Mahdavi 2011.

49. On what cultivating such an imagination might look like, see Block (2008).

CONCLUSION

1. Groethuysen [1927] 1968. However, I suspect that if a study were conducted of the Catholic middle class populations in Bangalore and Dubai more generally—not simply those who are most actively involved in church—the results might turn out very similar to Groethuysen's account.

2. Budde 1992; Smith 1996.

3. Novak 1991, 1993.

4. Anthropologists have recently shown how this happens in certain Islamic groups in Indonesia and Morocco, as well as in certain Hindu groups in the Indian diaspora (Rudnyckyj 2009; D'Iribarne 2003; Radhakrishnan 2011).

5. Berger 2014, 57.

6. Novak 1981, 51.

7. Emerson and Smith 2000.

8. The quote is attributed to American figure skater Scott Hamilton.

9. See, e.g., Coyle (2018) and Lencioni (2012) on the importance of creating cultures of safety, vulnerability, trust, and purpose.

10. Sennett 1998.

11. Barron 2015.

12. Block 2008. Naughton and Alford (2012) also provide a helpful summary of Catholic Social Teaching applied to the business world that can inform discussions in Catholic business schools, ECC groups, and other forums.

13. Hirschman 1970.

14. Hall and Soskice 2001.

15. Berger 2014. Others, like Simmel (1971, 23), seem to suggest that such fragmentation may not be unique to modernity; rather, as social selves, we are nothing but personas and fragments. But this view reduces the person to the persona, and cannot explain why

some people want to live a life in which the commitments of their various personas are more fully aligned. For other problems with this situationist view of the self, see Smith (2015, 110–118).

16. Brooks 2018.

APPENDIX

1. Pardis Mahdavi (2011), an American anthropologist of Iranian descent, was not as lucky. She narrates an incident from her research in Dubai in which someone hit her car, and because she did not speak Arabic, she was unable to defend herself and was charged as causing the accident.

2. MacIntyre (1970); McCutcheon (1999).

3. Geertz (1983, 57).

4. Boltanski and Thévenot (1999).

5. Weinreb (2006).

References

Abbott, Andrew. *The System of Professions: An Essay on the Division of Expert Labor*. Chicago: University of Chicago Press, 1988.

Abend, Gabriel. "Thick Concepts and the Moral Brain." *European Journal of Sociology* 52, no 1 (2011): 143–172.

Adebayo, Bukola. "Nigeria overtakes India in extreme poverty ranking." *CNN* June 26, 2018. https://www.cnn.com/2018/06/26/africa/nigeria-overtakes-india-extreme-poverty -intl/index.html.

Agunias, Dovelyn Ranneveig. *Migration's Middlemen: Regulating Recruitment Agencies in the Philippines-United Arab Emirates Corridor*. Washington, DC: Migration Policy Institute, 2010.

Ali, Syed. *Dubai: Gilded Cage*. New Haven, CT: Yale University Press, 2010a.

Ali, Syed. "Permanent Impermanence." *Contexts* 9, no. 2 (2010b): 26–31.

AME Info. "Employee Turnover Remains Regional Business's Invisible Enemy, despite Global Crisis, Says Management Expert." *AME Info*, December 13, 2008. https:// www.albawaba.com/news/employee-turnover-remains-regional-business%E2% 80%99s-invisible-enemy-despite-global-crisis-says-manage.

Anderson, Allan Heaton. *An Introduction to Pentecostalism: Global Charismatic Christianity*. Cambridge: Cambridge University Press, 2013.

Aneesh, Aneesh. *Virtual Migration: The Programming of Globalization*. Durham, NC: Duke University Press, 2006.

Appadurai, Arjun. "Disjuncture and Difference in the Global Cultural Economy." *Theory, Culture, and Society* 7 (1990): 295–310.

Asad, Talal. *Genealogies of Religion: Discipline and Reasons of Power in Christianity and Islam*. Baltimore: Johns Hopkins University Press, 1993.

Ashforth, Blake, and Deepa Vaidyanath. "Work Organizations as Secular Religions." *Journal of Management Inquiry* 11, no. 4 (2002): 359–370.

Ashmos, Donde P., and Dennis Duchon. "Spirituality at Work: A Conceptualization and Measure." *Journal of Management Inquiry* 9, no. 2 (2000): 134–145.

Associated Press. "A lifetime of perks in UAE help cushion wealth gap." *Daily Mail*, November 4, 2014. https://www.dailymail.co.uk/wires/ap/article-2820598/A-lifetime -perks-UAE-help-cushion-wealth-gap.html.

Attanasi, Katherine, and Amos Yong, eds. *Pentecostalism and Prosperity: The Socio Economics of the Global Charismatic Movement*. New York: Palgrave-Macmillan, 2012.

Baehr, Peter. "The 'Iron Cage' and the 'Shell as Hard as Steel': Parsons, Weber, and the Stahlhartes Gehäuse Metaphor in the Protestant Ethic and the Spirit of Capitalism." *History and Theory* 40, no. 2 (2001): 153–169.

Bangalore Archdiocesan Directory. Bangalore: Brilliant Printers, 2012.

Barnard, Chester I. *The Functions of the Executive*. Cambridge, MA: Harvard University Press, 1938.

Barron, Robert. *2 Samuel (Brazos Theological Commentary on the Bible)*. Grand Rapids, MI: Brazos.

Bate, S. Paul. "Whatever Happened to Organizational Anthropology? A Review of the Field of Organizational Ethnography and Anthropological Studies." *Human Relations*

50, no. 9 (1997): 1147–1175.Bauman, Zygmunt. *Identity: Conversations with Benedetto Vecchi*. Cambridge, MA: Polity, 2004.

Bauman, Zygmunt. *Consuming Life*. Cambridge, MA: Polity, 2007.BBC. "UAE to Allow Construction Unions." *BBC News*, March 30, 2006. http://news.bbc.co.uk/2/hi/business/4861540.stm.

BBC. "Bengaluru: India's Bangalore City Changes Name." *BBC News*, October 31, 2014. http://www.bbc.com/news/world-asia-india-29845215.

Beblawi, Hazem. "The Rentier State in the Arab World." In *The Arab State*, edited by Giacomo Luciani, 85–97. London: Routledge, 1990.

Beck, Ulrich, Anthony Giddens, and Scott Lash. *Reflexive Modernization: Politics, Tradition, and Aesthetics in the Modern Social Order*. Stanford, CA: Stanford University Press, 1994.

Bell, Daniel. *The Coming of Post-Industrial Society: A Venture in Social Forecasting*. New York: Basic Books, 1973.

Bell, Daniel. *The Cultural Contradictions of Capitalism*. New York: Basic Books, 1976.

Bellah, Robert, Richard Madsen, William M. Sullivan, Ann Swidler, and Steven M. Tipton. *Habits of the Heart: Individualism and Commitment in American Life*. Berkeley: University of California Press, 1985.

Benedikter, Ronald. "Lifestyles." In *The Encyclopedia of Global Studies*, edited by Helmut K. Anheier and Mark Juergensmeyer, vol. 3, 1076–1979. Thousand Oaks, CA: Sage, 2012.

Benefiel, Margaret. *The Soul of a Leader: Finding Your Path to Success and Fulfillment*. New York: Crossroad, 2008.

Berger, Arthur Asa. *Ads, Fads, and Consumer Culture: Advertising's Impact on American Character and Society*. Lanham, MD: Rowman & Littlefield, 2000.

Berger, Peter. 1967. *The Sacred Canopy*. Garden City, NY: Anchor.

Berger, Peter. "Epistemological Modesty: An Interview with Peter Berger." *Christian Century* 114 (October 29, 1997): 972–75.

Berger, Peter. "Introduction." In *Many Globalizations: Cultural Diversity in the Contemporary World*, edited by Peter Berger and Samuel Huntington, 1–16. New York: Oxford University Press, 2002.

Berger, Peter. "Max Weber Is Alive and Well, and Living in Guatemala: The Protestant Ethic Today." *Review of Faith and International Affairs* 8, no. 4 (2010): 3–9.

Berger, Peter. *The Many Altars of Modernity: Toward a Paradigm for Religion in a Pluralist Age*. Berlin: De Gruyter, 2014.

Berger, Peter, and Samuel Huntington, eds. *Many Globalizations: Cultural Diversity in the Contemporary World*. New York: Oxford University Press, 2002.

Blair-Loy, Marie. *Competing Devotions: Career and Family among Women Executives*. Cambridge, MA: Harvard University Press, 2003.

Block, Peter. *Community: The Structure of Belonging*. San Francisco: Berrett-Koehler, 2008.

Bocock, Robert. *Consumption*. London: Routledge, 1993.

Boli, John, and George M. Thomas. "World Culture in the World Polity: A Century of International Non-Governmental Organization." *American Sociological Review* 62, no. 2 (1997): 171–190.

Boltanski, Luc, and Eve Chiapello. *The New Spirit of Capitalism*. Translated by Gregory Eliott. London: Verso, 2005.

Boltanski, Luc, and Laurent Thévenot. "The Sociology of Critical Capacity." *European Journal of Social Theory* 2, no. 3 (1999): 359–377.

Boltanski, Luc, and Laurent Thévenot. *On Justification*. Translated by Catherine Porter. Princeton, NJ: Princeton University Press, 2006.

Bond, Anthony. "Dumped in Dubai: The Luxury High Performance Cars Left Abandoned." *Daily Mail*, August 28, 2012. http://www.dailymail.co.uk/news/article-2194633

/Luxury-high-performance-cars-left-abandoned-British-expats-fear-jailed-debts .html.

Bourdieu, Pierre. *Distinction: A Social Critique of the Judgment of Taste*. Translated by Richard Nice. Cambridge, MA: Harvard University Press, 1984.

Bourdieu, Pierre. "The Forms of Capital." In *Handbook of Theory and Research for the Sociology of Education*, edited by J. G. Richardson, 241–258. Westport, CT: Greenwood, 1986.

Bourdieu, Pierre. *The Logic of Practice*. Translated by Richard Nice. Stanford, CA: Stanford University Press, 1990.

Brenneman, Robert. *Homies and Hermanos: God and Gangs in Central America*. New York: Oxford University Press, 2011.

Bridges, William. *Creating You and Co: Learn to Think like the CEO of Your Own Career*. Cambridge, MA: Da Capo/Perseus, 1998.

Brooks, David. "The Rise of the Amphibians." *New York Times*, February 15, 2018. https://www.nytimes.com/2018/02/15/opinion/the-rise-of-the-amphibians.html.

Broomhall, Elizabeth. "Destroy all Churches in Gulf, Says Saudi Grand Mufti." *Arabian Business*, March 15, 2012. http://www.arabianbusiness.com/destroy-all-churches -in-gulf-says-saudi-grand-mufti-450002.html.

Brown, David, and Aspasia Leledaki. "Eastern Movement Forms as Body-Self Transforming Cultural Practices in the West: Towards a Sociological Perspective." *Cultural Sociology* 4, no. 1 (2010): 123–154.

Brown, Wendy. "The Sacred, the Secular, and the Profane: Charles Taylor and Karl Marx." In *Varieties of Secularism in a Secular Age*, edited by Michael Warner, Craig Calhoun, and Jonathan VanAntwerpen, 83–104. Cambridge, MA: Harvard University Press, 2010.

Bruce, Steve. *Secularization: In Defense of an Unfashionable Theory*. New York: Oxford University Press, 2013.

Budde, Michael L. *The Two Churches: Catholicism and Capitalism in the World System*. Durham, NC: Duke University Press, 1992.

Burggraf, Helen. "UAE Expats May Still Be Charged for Bad Checques, Gov't Clarifies." *International Adviser*, January 3, 2013. http://www.arabianbusiness.com/bad -cheques-still-criminal-offence-for-uae-expats-484353.html.

Burdick, John. *Looking for God in Brazil: The Progressive Catholic Church in Urban Brazil's Religious Arena*. Berkeley, CA: University of California Press, 1996.

Butt, Howard Edward. *The Velvet Covered Brick: Christian Leadership in an Age of Rebellion*. New York: Harper and Row, 1973.

Cadge, Wendy, and Elaine Howard Ecklund. "Immigration and Religion." *Annual Review of Sociology* 33 (2007): 359–379.

Campbell, Colin. *The Romantic Ethic and the Spirit of Modern Consumerism*. New York: Blackwell, 1987.

Carney, Dana R., Amy J. C. Cuddy, and Andy J. Yap. "Power Posing: Brief Nonverbal Displays Affect Neuroendocrine Levels and Risk Tolerance." *Psychological Science* 21, no. 10 (2010): 1363–1368.

Casanova, José. *Public Religion in the Modern World*. Chicago: University of Chicago Press, 1994.

Casanova, José. "Public Religion Revisited." In *Religion: Beyond a Concept*, edited by Hent de Vries, 101–119. New York: Fordham University Press, 2008.

Castells, Manuel. *The Rise of the Network Society, The Information Age: Economy, Society and Culture*. Vol. 1. London: Blackwell, 1996.

Cavanaugh, William T. *Being Consumed: Economics and Christian Desire*. Grand Rapids, MI: Eerdmans, 2008.

Chakrabarty, Dipesh. *Provincializing Europe: Postcolonial Thought and Historical Difference.* Princeton, NJ: Princeton University Press, 2000.

Chesnut, Andrew. *Born Again in Brazil: The Pentecostal Boom and Pathogens of Poverty.* New Brunswick, NJ: Rutgers University Press, 1997.

Chinmay, Tumbe. "Remittances in India: Facts and Issues." Indian Institute of Management Bangalore Working Paper 331, April 2011.

Clancy, Rebecca. "UAE Stops Jailing Expats for Bounced Cheques." *The Telegraph*, January 1, 2013. http://www.telegraph.co.uk/finance/financial-crime/9774247/UAE-stops-jailing-expats-for-bounced-cheques.html.

Clark, Steve. *Baptized in the Spirit and Spiritual Gifts.* Ann Arbor, MI: Servant, 1976.

Cohen, Lizabeth. *A Consumers' Republic: The Politics of Mass Consumption in Postwar America.* New York: Vintage, 2003.

Collins, Randall. *Interaction Ritual Chains.* Princeton, NJ: Princeton University Press, 2004.

Comaroff, Jean, and John Comaroff. "New Protestant Ethics and the Spirits of Capitalism in Africa and Elsewhere." *Afrika Spektrum* 35 (2000): 293–312.

Conger, Jay A. "Introduction: Our Search for Spiritual Community." In *Spirit at Work: Discovering the Spirituality in Leadership*, 1–18. San Francisco: Jossey-Bass, 1994.

Courpasson, David. "Managerial Strategies of Domination: Power in Soft Bureaucracies." *Organization Studies* 21, no. 1 (2000): 141–161.

Covey, Stephen. *The Seven Habits of Highly Effective People.* New York: Simon & Schuster, 1989.

Cox, Robert W. "Civilizations and the Twenty-First Century: Some Theoretical Considerations." In *Globalization and Civilizations*, edited by Mehdi Mozaffari, 1–23. New York: Routledge, 2002.

Coyle, Daniel. *The Culture Code: The Secrets of Highly Successful Groups.* New York: Bantam, 2018.

Csordas, Thomas. *The Sacred Self: A Cultural Phenomenology of Charismatic Healing.* Berkeley: University of California Press, 1994.

Cuddy, Amy J. C., Caroline A. Wilmuth, and Dana R. Carney. "The Benefit of Power Posing before a High-Stakes Social Evaluation." Harvard Business School Working Paper 13–027, September 2012.

Cullinane, Niall, and Tony Dundon. "The Psychological Contract: A Critical Review." *International Journal of Management Reviews* 8, no. 2 (2006): 113–129.

Dalai Lama, and Howard C. Cutler. *The Art of Happiness at Work.* New York: Riverhead, 2004.

Davidson, Christopher. *Dubai: The Vulnerability of Success.* New York: Columbia University Press, 2008.

Davis, Mike, and Daniel Bertrand Monk, eds. *Evil Paradises: Dreamworlds of Neoliberalism.* New York: New Press, 2008.

Davis, Nancy J., and Robert V. Robinson. "The Egalitarian Face of Islamic Orthodoxy: Support for Islamic Law and Economic Justice in Seven Muslim-Majority Nations." *American Sociological Review* 71, no. 2 (2006): 167–190.

Deal, Terrence E., and Allan A. Kennedy. *Corporate Cultures: The Rites and Rituals of Organizational Life.* New York: Basic Books, 1982.

Deccan Herald. "Karnataka Bishops to Protest Church Attacks." *Deccan Herald*, February 17, 2011. http://www.deccanherald.com/content/138635/karnataka-bishops-protest-church-attacks.html.

de Dunin-Borkowski, Stanislaus. "Hierarchy of the Early Church." In *The Catholic Encyclopedia.* New York: Encyclopedia Press, 1913. http://home.newadvent.org/cathen/07326a.htm.

DeParle, Jason. "Migrants in United Arab Emirates Get Stuck in Web of Debt." *New York Times*, August 20, 2011. http://www.nytimes.com/2011/08/21/world/middleeast /21debtors.html?_r=0&pagewanted=print.

Desmond, John, and Donncha Kavanagh. "Organization as Containment of Acquisitive Mimetic Rivalry: The Contribution of René Girard." *Culture and Organization* 9, no. 4 (2003): 239–251.

D'Iribarne, Philippe. *Le Tiers-Monde qui Réussit: Nouveaux Modèles*. Paris: O. Jacob, 2003.

DNA. "82% Indian working women prefer flexible office hours." *DNA*, May 30, 2011. https://www.dnaindia.com/india/report-82-indian-working-women-prefer -flexible-office-hours-1549231.

DNA. "Some Good News, for a Change: IT/BPO Sector Will Need 10mn People." *DNA*, March 5, 2013. http://www.dnaindia.com/bangalore/1807547/report-some-good -news-for-a-change-it-bpo-sector-will-need-10mn-people.

During, Simon. *Exit Capitalism: Literary Culture, Theory and Post-secular Modernity*. London: Routledge, 2009.

Economic Times. "Indian IT Companies among 10 Worst Paymasters in World: Study." *Press Trust of India*, September 9, 2012. http://articles.economictimes.indiatimes .com/2012-09-09/news/33713631_1_salaries-cash-compensation-paymasters.

Eisenstadt, Shmuel N. "Multiple Modernities." *Daedalus* 129, no. 1 (2000): 1–29.

Emerson, Michael, and Christian Smith. *Divided by Faith: Evangelical Religion and the Problem of Race in America*. New York: Oxford University Press, 2000.

Eriksen, Thomas Hylland, James Laidlaw, Jonathan Mair, Keir Martin, and Soumhya Venkatesan. "The Concept of Neoliberalism Has Become an Obstacle to the Anthropological Understanding of the Twenty-First Century." *Journal of the Royal Anthropological Institute* 21, no. 4 (2015): 911–923.

Etzioni, Amitai. *A Comparative Analysis of Complex Organizations: On Power, Involvement, and Their Correlates*. New York: Free Press, 1961.

Farkas, George. *Human Capital or Cultural Capital? Ethnicity and Poverty Groups in an Urban School District*. New York: Routledge, 1996.

Fenwick, Tara, and Elizabeth Lange. "Spirituality in the Workplace: The New Frontier of HRD." *Canadian Journal for the Study of Adult Education* 12, no. 1 (1988): 63–87.

Fernandes, Leela. *India's New Middle Class: Democratic Politics in an Era of Economic Reform*. Minneapolis: University of Minnesota Press, 2006.

Feuerbach, Ludwig. *Essence of Religion*. Translated by A. Loos. Amherst, NY: Prometheus, 2004.

Fombrun, Charles, and Christopher Foss. "Business Ethics: Corporate Responses to Scandal." *Corporate Reputation Review* 7, no. 3 (2004): 284–288.

Foucault, Michel. *The Birth of Biopolitics: Lectures at the Collège de France, 1978–1979*. Translated by Graham Burchell. New York: Palgrave Macmillan, 2008.

Fowler, Robert Booth. *Unconventional Partners: Religion and Liberal Culture in the United States*. Grand Rapids, MI: Eerdmans, 1989.

Friedman, Milton. "The Social Responsibility of Business Is to Increase Its Profits." *New York Times Magazine*, September 13, 1970.

Friedman, Thomas. *The World Is Flat: A Brief History of the Twenty-First Century*. New York: Farrar, Straus, and Giroux, 2005.

Friedson, Eliot. *Professionalism, the Third Logic: On the Practice of Knowledge*. Chicago: University of Chicago Press, 2001.

Fulmer, J. Burton. "René Girard and the Exorcism of the Possessed Consumer." MA thesis, Vanderbilt University, 2006a.

Fulmer, J. Burton. "Identities Bought and Sold, Identity Received as Grace: A Theological Criticism of and Alternative to Consumerist Understandings of the Self." PhD diss., Vanderbilt University, 2006b.

Gautier, François. *The Guru of Joy: Sri Sri Ravi Shankar and the Art of Living.* Santa Monica, CA: Hay House, 2008.

Geertz, Clifford. *Local Knowledge: Further Essays in Interpretive Anthropology.* New York: Basic Books, 1983.

George, Nirmala. "India Bus Gang Rape: Outrage Spreads over Public Sexual Assault." *Huffington Post*, December 19, 2012. http://www.huffingtonpost.com/2012/12/19/india-bus-gang-rape_n_2329002.html.

Ghezzi, Bert. *Build with the Lord.* Ann Arbor, MI: Servant, 1976.

Giacalone, Robert A., and Carole L. Jurkiewicz, eds. *Handbook of Workplace Spirituality and Organizational Performance.* 2nd ed. Armonk, NY: M. E. Sharpe, 2010.

Giddens, Anthony. *The Consequences of Modernity.* Cambridge: Polity, 1990.

Gifford, Paul. "Christian Fundamentalism and Development." *Review of African Political Economy* 18, no. 52 (1991): 9–20.

Girard, René. *Violence and the Sacred.* Translated by Patrick Gregory. Baltimore: Johns Hopkins University Press, 1979.

Girard, René. *The Scapegoat.* Translated by Yvonne Freccero. Baltimore: Johns Hopkins University Press, 1986.

Girard, René. *I See Satan Fall like Lightning.* New York: Orbis, 2001.

Girard, René, with Pierpaolo Antonello and João Cezar de Castro Rocha. *Evolution and Conversion: Dialogues on the Origins of Culture.* New York: Continuum, 2007.

Goldberg, Philip. *American Veda: From Emerson and the Beatles to Yoga and Meditation: How Indian Spirituality Changed the West.* New York: Crown Archetype, 2010.

Gorski, Philip S. "Historicizing the Secularization Debate: Church, State, and Society in Late Medieval and Early Modern Europe, ca. 1300–1700." *American Sociological Review* 65, no. 1 (2000): 138–167.

Gotsis, George, and Zoi Kortezi. "Philosophical Foundations of Workplace Spirituality: A Critical Approach." *Journal of Business Ethics* 78 (2008): 575–600.

Goudreau, Jenna. "Back To the Stone Age? New Yahoo CEO Marissa Mayer Bans Working from Home." *Forbes*, February 25, 2013. http://www.forbes.com/sites/jennagoudreau/2013/02/25/back-to-the-stone-age-new-yahoo-ceo-marissa-mayer-bans-working-from-home/.

Gould, Stephen Jay. "Nonoverlapping Magisteria." *Natural History* 106 (1997): 16–22.

Granovetter, Mark. *Getting a Job: A Study of Contacts and Careers.* Chicago: University of Chicago Press, 1985.

Grant, Don, Kathleen O'Neil, and Laura Stephens. "Spirituality in the Workplace: New Empirical Directions in the Study of the Sacred." *Sociology of Religion* 65, no. 3 (2004): 265–283.

Gregory, David L. "The Role of Religion in the Secular Workplace." *Notre Dame Journal of Ethics and Public Policy* 4 (1989): 749–763.

Groethuysen, Bernhard. *The Bourgeois: Catholicism versus Capitalism in Eighteenth-Century France.* London: Barrie & Rockliff, [1927] 1968.

Gruber, Jonathan, and Daniel Hungerman. "The Church vs. the Mall: What Happens When Religion Faces Increased Secular Competition?" *Quarterly Journal of Economics* 123 (2008): 831–862.

Grudem, Wayne. *Business for the Glory of God: The Bible's Teaching on the Moral Goodness of Business.* Wheaton, IL: Crossway, 2003.

Guhin, Jeffrey. "Religion as Site rather than Religion as Category: On the Sociology of Religion's Export Problem." *Sociology of Religion* 75, no. 4 (2014): 579–593.

Gunther, Marc. "God and Business: The Surprising Quest for Spiritual Renewal in the American Workplace." *Fortune* 144 (2001): 58–80.

Gusfield, Joseph R. "Tradition and Modernity: Misplaced Polarities in the Study of Social Change." *American Journal of Sociology* 72, no. 4 (1967): 351–362.

Hall, Camilla, and Simeon Kerr. "Foreigners on Hunger Strike in Dubai Jail." *Financial Times*, April 23, 2012. http://www.ft.com/intl/cms/s/0/e5d80cbe-8d47-11e1-9798 -00144feab49a.html#axzz2UWTgOwmI.

Hall, Peter A., and David Soskice, eds. *Varieties of Capitalism: The Institutional Foundations of Comparative Advantage.* Oxford: Oxford University Press, 2001.

Haney, Craig, Curtis Banks, and Philip Zimbardo. "Study of Prisoners and Guards in a Simulated Prison." *Naval Research Reviews* 9 (1973): 1–17.

Hari, Johann. "The Dark Side of Dubai." *The Independent*, April 7, 2009. http://www .independent.co.uk/voices/commentators/johann-hari/the-dark-side-of-dubai -1664368.html.

Harmassi, Mohammed. "Bahrain to End 'Slavery' System." *BBC News*, May 6, 2009. http://news.bbc.co.uk/2/hi/middle_east/8035972.stm.

Harrison, Bennett. *Lean and Mean: The Changing Landscape of Corporate Power in the Age of Flexibility.* New York: Guilford Press, 1997.

Harvey, David. *A Brief History of Neoliberalism.* New York: Oxford University Press, 2005.

Harvey, David. *Spaces of Global Capitalism: Towards a Theory of Uneven Geographic Development.* London: Verso, 2006.

Hefner, Robert, ed. *Global Pentecostalism in the 21st Century.* Bloomington: Indiana University Press, 2013.

Hicks, Douglas. *Religion and the Workplace: Pluralism, Spirituality, Leadership.* New York: Cambridge University Press, 2003.

Hill, Graham. "Enchanting Self-discipline: Methodical Reflexivity and the Search for the Supernatural in Charismatic Christian Testimonial Practice." *Sociological Theory* 35, no. 4 (2017): 288–311.

Hirschman, Albert O. *Exit, Voice, and Loyalty: Responses to Decline in Firms, Organizations, and States.* Cambridge, MA: Harvard University Press, 1970.

Hitlin, Steven, and Stephen Vaisey, eds. *Handbook of the Sociology of Morality.* New York: Springer, 2010.

Hitlin, Steven, and Stephen Vaisey. "The New Sociology of Morality." *Annual Review of Sociology* 39 (2013): 51–68.

Hochschild, Arlie Russell. *The Commercialization of Intimate Life.* Berkeley: University of California Press, 2003.

Hodgson, Geoffrey. *Conceptualizing Capitalism: Institutions, Evolution, Future.* Chicago: University of Chicago Press, 2015.

Holston, James, and Arjun Appadurai. "Cities and Citizenship." *Public Culture* 8, no. 2 (1995): 187–204.

Holton, Robert. "Globalization's Cultural Consequences." *Annals of the American Academy of Political and Social Science* 570, no. 1 (2000): 140–152.

Hood, Ralph W., Peter C. Hill, and Bernard Spilka. *The Psychology of Religion: An Empirical Approach.* 4th ed. New York: Guilford, 2009.

Human Rights Watch. "Building Towers, Cheating Workers: Exploitation of Migrant Construction Workers in the United Arab Emirates." Human Rights Watch Report, November 11, 2006. http://www.hrw.org/reports/2006/11/11/building-towers-cheating -workers.

Hunter, James Davison. *Death of Character: On the Moral Education of America's Children.* New York: Basic Books, 2001.

IBN Live. "Attrition Rate in Bangalore Highest: Study." *IBN Live*, July 25, 2009. http://ibnlive.in.com/news/attrition-rate-in-bangalore-highest-study/97856-7.html.

ITUC. "UAE Reports Shows Violation of All Labour Standards." *International Trade Union Confederation*, March 27, 2012. http://www.ituc-csi.org/teachers-jurists-maids-and?lang=en.

Jackall, Robert. *Moral Mazes: The World of Corporate Managers*. New York: Oxford University Press, 1988.

Jaffrelot, Christophe. "'Why Should We Vote?' The Indian Middle Class and the Functioning of the World's Largest Democracy." In *Patterns of Middle Class Consumption in India and China*, edited by Christophe Jaffrelot and Peter van der Veer, 35–54. New Delhi: Sage, 2008.

Jaffrelot, Christophe, and Peter van der Veer. "Introduction." In *Patterns of Middle Class Consumption in India and China*, edited by Christophe Jaffrelot and Peter van der Veer, 11–34. New Delhi: Sage, 2008.

Jameson, Frederic. "Notes on Globalization as a Philosophical Issue." In *The Cultures of Globalization*, edited by Frederic Jameson and Masao Miyoshi, 54–77. Durham, NC: Duke University Press, 1998.

Jeffcoat, Kellmeny, and Jane Whitney Gibson. "Fun as Serious Business: Creating a Fun Work Environment as an Effective Business Strategy." *Journal of Business and Economics Research* 4, no. 2 (2006): 29–34.

Jenkins, Philip. *The Next Christendom: The Coming of Global Christianity*. New York: Oxford University Press, 2002.

Jepperson, Ronald L. "Institutions, Institutional Effects, and Institutionalism." In *The New Institutionalism in Organizational Analysis,* edited by Walter W. Powell and Paul DiMaggio, 143–163. Chicago: University of Chicago Press, 1991.

Jones, Laurie Beth. *Jesus, CEO: Using Ancient Wisdom for Visionary Leadership*. New York: Hyperion, 1996.

Kalberg, Stephen. "Max Weber's Types of Rationality: Cornerstones for the Analysis of Rationalization Processes in History." *American Journal of Sociology* 85, no. 5 (1980): 1145–1179.

Kamoche, Ken, and Ashly Pinnington. "Managing People 'Spiritually': A Bourdieusian Critique." *Work, Employment, and Society* 26, no. 3 (2012): 497–513.

Kanna, Ahmed. "Flexible Citizenship in Dubai: Neoliberal Subjectivity in the Emerging 'City-Corporation.'" *Cultural Anthropology* 25, no. 1 (2010): 100–129.

Kanna, Ahmed. *Dubai: City as Corporation*. Minneapolis: University of Minnesota Press, 2011.

Kannan, Preeti. "'I Will Die if I Go Home:' UAE Visa Amnesty Is Not an Option for All." *The National*, January 8, 2013. http://www.thenational.ae/news/uae-news/i-will-die-if-i-go-home-uae-visa-amnesty-is-not-an-option-for-all.

Kanter, Rosabeth M. "When a Thousand Flowers Bloom: Structural, Collective, and Social Conditions for Innovation in Organizations." In *Knowledge Management and Organizational Design*, edited by Paul S. Myers, 93–132. 2nd ed. Boston: Butterworth-Heinemann, 1996.

Kapur, Shuchita. "Staff Attrition to Stir again among UAE Employers." *Emirates 24/7*, March 25, 2010. http://www.emirates247.com/eb247/economy/uae-economy/staff-attrition-to-stir-again-among-uae-employers-2010-03-25-1.72743.

Kapur, Shuchita. "Philippines Urges Overstaying or Absconding Filipinos to Avail of UAE Amnesty." *Emirates 24/7*, January 3, 2013a. http://www.emirates247.com/news/philippines/philippines-urges-overstaying-or-absconding-filipinos-to-avail-of-uae-amnesty-2013-01-03-1.489576.

Kapur, Shuchita. "Top 3 Reasons Why UAE Pros Quit Their Jobs." *Emirates 24/7*, February 24, 2013b. http://www.emirates247.com/news/emirates/top-3-reasons-why-uae-pros-quit-their-jobs-2013-02-24-1.496245.

Katju, Manjari. "The Politics of Ghar Wapsi." *Economic and Political Weekly*, 50, no. 1 (2015): 21–24.

Keller, Timothy, with Katherine Leary Alsdorf. *Every Good Endeavor: Connecting Your Work to God's Work*. New York: Penguin, 2014.

Khasawneh, Samer. "Cutting-Edge Panacea of the Twenty-First Century: Workplace Spirituality for Higher Education Human Resources." *International Journal of Educational Management* 25, no. 7 (2011): 687–700.

Klandermans, Bert, and Dirk Oegema. "Potentials, Networks, Motivations, and Barriers: Steps Towards Participation In Social Movements." *American Sociological Review* 52, no. 4 (1987): 519–531.

Klein, Naomi. *No Logo: Money, Marketing, and the Growing Anti-Corporate Movement*. New York: Alfred Knopf, 1999.

Klotz, Anthony C., and Mark C. Bolino. "Citizenship and Counterproductive Work Behavior: A Moral Licensing View." *Academy of Management Review* 38, no. 2 (2013): 292–306.

Knapp, John. *How the Church Fails Businesspeople (And What Can Be Done about It)*. Grand Rapids, MI: Eerdmans, 2012.

Konrad, Alison M., Pushkala Prasad, and Judith Pringle, eds. *Handbook of Workplace Diversity*. Beverly Hills, CA: Sage, 2006.

Krane, Jim. *City of Gold: Dubai and the Dream of Capitalism*. New York: St. Martin's Press, 2009.

Kunda, Gideon. *Engineering Culture: Control and Commitment in a High-Tech Corporation*. Philadelphia: Temple University Press, 1992.

Kurien, Prema A. *Ethnic Church Meets Megachurch: Indian American Christianity in Motion*. New York: New York University Press, 2017.

Lamont, Michele, and Virag Molnár. "How Blacks Use Consumption to Shape their Collective Identity Evidence from Marketing Specialists." *Journal of Consumer Culture* 1, no. 1 (2001): 31–45.

Lange, Hellmuth, and Lars Meier, eds. *The New Middle Classes: Globalizing Lifestyles, Consumerism, and Environmental Concern*. New York: Springer, 2009.

Lange, Hellmuth, Lars Meier, and N. S. Anuradha. "Highly Qualified Employees in Bangalore, India: Consumerist Predators?" In *The New Middle Classes: Globalizing Lifestyles, Consumerism, and Environmental Concern*, edited by Hellmuth Lange and Lars Meier, 281–298. New York: Springer, 2009.

Langton, James, and Haneen Dajani. "UAE Ambassador Explains What Secularism Means for Middle East Governance." *The National*, August 8, 2017. https://www.thenational.ae/uae/uae-ambassador-explains-what-secularism-means-for-middle-east-governance-1.618023.

Larson, Magali S. *The Rise of Professionalism*. Berkeley: University of California Press, 1977.

Leigh, Pamela. "The New Spirit at Work." *Training and Development* 5, no. 3 (1997): 26–33.

Lencioni, Patrick. *The Advantage: Why Organizational Health Trumps Everything Else in Business*. New York: John Wiley & Sons, 2012.

Levitt, Peggy. *God Needs No Passport: Immigrants and the Changing American Religious Landscape*. New York: New Press, 2007.

Lewicki, Roy J., and Barbara Bunker. "Developing and Maintaining Trust in Work Relationships." In *Trust in Organizations*, edited by R. M. Kramer and T. R. Tyler, 114–139. London: Sage, 1996.

Lindsay, Michael, and Bradley C. Smith. "Accounting by Faith: The Negotiated Logic of Elite Evangelicals' Workplace Decision-Making." *Journal of the American Academy of Religion* 78, no. 3 (2010): 721–749.

Lipovetsky, Gilles. *Hypermodern Times.* Cambridge: Polity, 2005.

Lips-Wiersma, Marjolein, and Colleen Mills. "Coming out of the Closet: Negotiating Spiritual Expression in the Workplace." *Journal of Managerial Psychology* 17, no. 3 (2002): 183–202.

Lizardo, Omar. "Improving Cultural Analysis: Considering Personal Culture in its Declarative and Nondeclarative Modes." *American Sociological Review* 82, no. 1 (2017): 88–115.

Lizardo, Omar, and Michael Strand. "Skills, Toolkits, Contexts, and Institutions: Clarifying the Relationship between Different Approaches to Cognition in Cultural Sociology." *Poetics* 38, no. 2 (2010): 205–228.

Longva, Anh Nga. "Keeping Migrant Workers in Check: The Kafala System in the Gulf." *Middle East Report* 29, no. 2 (1999): 20–22.

Longva, Anh Nga. "Neither Autocracy nor Democracy but Ethnocracy: Citizens, Expatriates, and the Socio-Political System in Kuwait." In *Monarchies and Nations: Globalisation and Identity in the Arab States of the Gulf*, edited by Paul Dresch and James Piscatori, 114–135. New York: I. B. Tauris, 2005.

Lough, Joseph W. H. *Weber and the Persistence of Religion: Social Theory, Capitalism, and the Sublime.* New York: Routledge, 2004.

Luhrmann, Tanya M. *When God Talks Back: Understanding the American Evangelical Relationship with God.* New York: Vintage, 2012.

Lund Dean, Kathy, and Charles J. Fornaciari. "Empirical Research in Management, Spirituality, and Religion during Its Founding Years." *Journal of Management, Spirituality, and Religion* 4, no. 1 (2007): 3–34.

Luthy, Herbert. "Once again: Calvinism and Capitalism." In *The Protestant Ethic and Modernization: A Comparative View*, edited by S. N. Eisenstadt, 87–108. New York: Basic Books, 1968.

MacIntyre, Alasdair. *After Virtue.* Notre Dame, IN: University of Notre Dame Press, 1984.

MacIntyre, Alasdair. "Is Understanding Religion Compatible with Believing?" *Rationality* 68 (1970): 110–113.

MacLeod, Jay. *Ain't No Makin It: Aspirations and Attainment in a Low-Income Neighborhood.* 3rd ed. Boulder, CO: Westview, 2009.

Mahdavi, Pardis. *Gridlock: Labor Migration and Human Trafficking in Dubai.* Stanford, CA: Stanford University Press, 2011.

Mandhana, Niharika, and Anjani Trivedi. "Indians Outraged over Rape on Moving Bus in New Delhi." *New York Times*, December 18, 2012. http://india.blogs.nytimes.com /2012/12/18/outrage-in-delhi-after-latest-gang-rape-case/.

Mansfield, Patti Gallagher. *As by a New Pentecost: The Dramatic Beginning of the Catholic Charismatic Renewal.* Steubenville, OH: Franciscan University Press, 1992.

Marks, Abigail, and Dora Scholarios. "Revisiting Technical Workers: Professional and Organizational Identities in the Software Industry." *New Technology, Work, and Employment* 22, no. 2 (2007): 98–117.

Marques, Joan, Satinder Dhaman, and Richard King. *Spirituality in the Workplace: What It Is, Why It Matters, How to Make It Work for You.* Fawnskin, CA: Personhood, 2007.

Marshall, Gordon. *In Search of the Spirit of Capitalism.* Aldershot, UK: Gregg Revivals, 1982.

Martikainen, Tuomas, and François Gauthier, eds. *Religion in a Neoliberal Age: Political Economy and Modes of Governance.* London: Ashgate, 2013.

Martin, Bernice. "New Mutations of the Protestant Ethic among Latin American Pentecostals." *Religion* 25 (1995): 101–117.

Martin, David. *Tongues of Fire: The Explosion of Pentecostalism in Latin America.* Oxford: Blackwell, 1990.

Martin, David. *Pentecostalism: The World their Parish.* Oxford: Blackwell, 2002.

McCutcheon, Russell. *The Insider/Outsider Problem in the Study of Religion: A Reader.* New York: Continuum, 1999.

McGuire, Meredith B. *Pentecostal Catholics: Power, Charisma, and Order in a Religious Movement.* Philadelphia: Temple University Press, 1982.

Medina, Andrei. "Over 2,600 Pinoy Amnesty Seekers in UAE back in PHL." *GMA News Online,* February 8, 2013. http://www.gmanetwork.com/news/story/294085/pinoyabroad/news/over-2-600-pinoy-amnesty-seekers-in-uae-back-in-phl-dfa.

Meir, Asher. *The Jewish Ethicist: Everyday Ethics for Business and Life.* Jersey City, NJ: Ktav, 2003.

Mendieta, Eduardo, and Jonathan VanAntwerpen, eds. *The Power of Religion in the Public Sphere.* New York: Columbia University Press, 2011.

Merritt, Anna C., Daniel A. Effron, and Benoît Monin. "Moral Self-Licensing: When Being Good Frees Us to Be Bad." *Social and Personality Psychology Compass* 4, no. 5 (2010): 344–357.

Metcalf, Franz, and B. J. Gallagher Hateley. *What Would Buddha Do at Work? 101 Answers to Workplace Dilemmas.* Berkeley: Ulysses, 2001.

Meyer, John W. "World Society, Institutional Theories, and the Actor." *Annual Review of Sociology* 36 (2010): 1–20.

Meyer, John W., and Brian Rowan. "Institutionalized Organizations: Formal Structure as Myth and Ceremony." *American Journal of Sociology* 83, no. 2 (1977): 340–360.

Meyer, John W., John Boli, and George M. Thomas. "Ontology and Rationalization in the Western Cultural Account." In *Institutional Structure: Constituting State, Society, and the Individual,* edited by George M. Thomas, John W. Meyer, Francisco O. Ramirez, and John Boli, 12–38. Newbury Park, CA: Sage, 1987.

Meyer, John W., John Boli, George Thomas, and Francisco Ramirez. "World Society and the Nation-State." *American Journal of Sociology* 103 (1997): 144–181.

Miller, David W. *God at Work: The History and Promise of the Faith at Work Movement.* Oxford University Press, 2007.

Miller, Donald E. "Introduction: Pentecostalism as a Global Phenomenon." In *Spirit and Power: The Growth and Global Impact of Pentecostalism,* edited by Donald E. Miller, Kimon H. Sargeant, and Richard Flory, 1–24. New York: Oxford University Press, 2013.

Miller, Donald E., Kimon H. Sargeant, and Richard Flory, eds. *Spirit and Power: The Growth and Global Impact of Pentecostalism.* New York: Oxford University Press, 2013.

Miller, Donald E., and Tetsunao Yamamori. *Global Pentecostalism: The New Face of Christian Social Engagement.* Berkeley: University of California Press, 2007.

Mitroff, Ian, and Elizabeth Denton. *A Spiritual Audit of Corporate America: A Hard Look at Spirituality, Religion, and Values in the Workplace.* San Francisco: Jossey-Bass, 1999.

Mizrachi, Nissim, Israel Drori, and Renee R. Anspach. "Repertoires of Trust: The Practice of Trust in a Multinational Organization amid Political Conflict." *American Sociological Review* 72, no. 1 (2007): 143–165.

Mohammad-Arif, Aminah. "Muslims in Bangalore: A Minority at Ease?" In *Muslims in Indian Cities: Trajectories of Marginalization,* edited by Laurent Gayer and Christophe Jaffrelot, 287–310. New York: Columbia University Press, 2011.

Mooney, Margarita A. *Faith Makes Us Live: Surviving and Thriving in the Haitian Diaspora*. Berkeley: University of California Press, 2009.

Morrill, Calvin. "Culture and Organization Theory." *Annals of the American Academy of the Political and Social Sciences* 619 (2008): 15–40.

Morris, Betsy. "The New Rules." *Fortune* 154, no. 2 (2006): 70–87.

Motaparthy, Priyanka. "Understanding Kafala: An Archaic Law at Cross Purposes with Modern Development." *MigrantRights.org*, March 11, 2015. http://www.migrant-rights.org/2015/03/understanding-kafala-an-archaic-law-at-cross-purposes-with-modern-development/.

Mudge, Stephanie Lee. "What is neo-liberalism?." *Socio-Economic Review* 6, no. 4 (2008): 703–731.

Nair, Janaki. *The Promise of the Metropolis: Bangalore's Twentieth Century*. New Delhi: Oxford University Press, 2005.

Nash, Laura L. *Believers in Business: Resolving the Tensions between Christian Faith, Business Ethics, Competition, and Our Definitions of Success*. Nashville: Thomas Nelson, 1994.

Nash, Laura L., and Scotty McLennan. *Church on Sunday, Work on Monday: The Challenge of Fusing Christian Values with Business Life*. San Francisco: Jossey-Bass, 2001.

Naughton, Michael J., and Helen Alford., eds. *Vocation of the Business Leader: A Reflection*. Vatican City: Pontifical Council for Justice and Peace, 2012.

Neal, Judi, ed. *Handbook of Faith and Spirituality in the Workplace: Emerging Research and Practice*. London: Springer, 2013.

Neitz, Mary Jo. *Charisma and Community: A Study of Religious Commitment within the Charismatic Renewal*. New Brunswick, NJ: Transaction, 1987.

Nippert-Eng, Christena. *Home and Work: Negotiating Boundaries through Everyday Life*. Chicago: University of Chicago Press, 1996.

Noronha, Ernesto, and Premilla D'Cruz. "Being Professional: Organizational Control in Indian Call Centers." *Social Science and Computer Review* 24, no. 3 (2006): 342–361.

Norris, Pippa, and Ronald Inglehart. *Sacred and Secular: Religion and Politics Worldwide*. Cambridge: Cambridge University Press, 2004.

Novak, Michael. *Toward a Theology of the Corporation*. Washington, D.C: The AEI Press, 1981.

Novak, Michael. *The Spirit of Democratic Capitalism*. New York: Rowman & Littlefield, 1991.

Novak, Michael. *The Catholic Ethic and the Spirit of Capitalism*. New York: Free Press, 1993.

Novak, Michael. *Business as a Calling: Work and the Examined Life*. New York: Free Press, 1996.

Oakes, Guy. "Max Weber on Value Rationality and Value Spheres." *Journal of Classical Sociology* 3, no. 1 (2003): 27–45.

Ong, Aihwa. *Neoliberalism as Exception: Mutations in Citizenship and Sovereignty*. Durham, NC: Duke University Press, 2006.

Patel, Reena. *Working the Night Shift: Women in India's Call Center Industry*. Stanford, CA: Stanford University Press, 2010.

Patnaik, Utsa. "Neoliberalism and Rural Poverty in India." *Economic and Political Weekly* 42, no. 30 (2007): 3132–3150.

Pattanaik, Devdutt. "East vs West: The Myths that Mystify." TED India, November, 2009. http://www.ted.com/talks/devdutt_pattanaik.html.

Petchsawang, Pawinee, and Dennis Duchon. "Workplace Spirituality, Meditation, and Work Performance." *Journal of Management, Spirituality, and Religion* 9, no. 2 (2012): 189–208.

Peters, Thomas, and Robert Waterman. *In Search of Excellence: Lessons from America's Best-Run Corporations*. New York: Warner, 1982.

Pierce, Gregory F. A. *Spirituality at Work: 10 Ways to Balance Your Life on the Job.* Chicago: Loyola Press, 2005.

Pope Francis. *Apostolic Exhortation Evangelii Gaudium (The Joy of the Gospel).* 2013. http://w2.vatican.va/content/francesco/en/apost_exhortations/documents/papa-francesco_esortazione-ap_20131124_evangelii-gaudium.html.

Pope John Paul II. *Encyclical Letter Socllicitudo Rei Socialis (Concern for the Social Order).* 1987. http://w2.vatican.va/content/john-paul-ii/en/encyclicals/documents/hf_jp-ii_enc_30121987_sollicitudo-rei-socialis.html.

Pope, Liston. *Millhands and Preachers: A Study of Gastonia.* New Haven, CT: Yale University Press, 1942.

Powell, Walter W. "Neither Market nor Hierarchy: Network Forms of Organization." In *Research in Organizational Behavior,* edited by Barry M. Staw and L. L. Cummings, vol. 12, 295–336. Greenwich, CT: JAI, 1990.

Pradhan, Samir. "Foreign Labor in the Gulf." In *On the Move: Migration Challenges in the Indian Ocean Littoral,* edited by Ellen Lapison and Amit Pandya 65–67. Washington, DC: Henry L. Stimson Center, 2010.

Putnam, Robert D. *Bowling Alone: The Collapse and Revival of American Community.* New York: Simon & Schuster, 2000.

Radhakrishnan, Smitha. *Appropriately Indian: Gender and Culture in a New Transnational Class.* Durham, NC: Duke University Press, 2011.

Rahman, Saifur. "Global Remittance Flow Grows 10.77% to $514 Billion in 2012: World Bank." *Gulf News,* April 20, 2013. http://gulfnews.com/business/economy/global-remittance-flow-grows-10-77-to-514-billion-in-2012-world-bank-1.1172693.

Rank, Mark Robert. *One Nation, Underprivileged: Why American Poverty Affects Us All.* New York: Oxford University Press, 2004.

Reddy, Y. Maheswara, and B. K. Lakshmikantha. "Bangalore trash woes: From Garden City to Garbage City." *DNA,* November 7, 2012. https://www.dnaindia.com/india/report-bangalore-trash-woes-from-garden-city-to-garbage-city-1761357.

Riesebrodt, M. *The Promise of Salvation: A Theory of Religion.* Chicago: University of Chicago Press, 2010.

Rivera, Lauren A. "Hiring as Cultural Matching: The Case of Elite Professional Service Firms." *American Sociological Review* 77, no. 6 (2012): 999–1022.

Robbins, Joel. "The Globalization of Pentecostal and Charismatic Christianity." *Annual Review of Anthropology* 33 (2004): 117–143.

Robbins, Joel. "Pentecostal Networks and the Spirit of Globalization: On the Social Productivity of Ritual Forms." *Social Analysis* 53, no. 1 (2009): 55–66.

Robertson, Roland. "Glocalization: Time-Space and Homogeneity-Heterogeneity." In *Global Modernities,* edited by Mike Featherstone, Scott Lash, and Roland Robertson, 25–44. London: Sage, 1995.

Rouleau, Linda. "Les restructurations d'entreprise: quelques points de repères." *Management International* 5, no. 1 (2000): 45–52.

Rousseau, Denise M., Sim Sitkin, Ronald Burt, and Colin Camerer. "Not So Different after All: A Cross-Disciplinary View of Trust." *Academy of Management Review* 23 (1998): 393–404.

Rudnyckyj, Daromir. "Spiritual Economies: Islam and Neoliberalism in Contemporary Indonesia." *Cultural Anthropology* 24, no. 1 (2009): 104–141.

Saleem, Shaikh Z. "Bangalore Has among Highest IT Attrition Rates Globally: Study." *Business Standard,* September 21, 2012.

Sassen, Saskia. *Globalization and Its Discontents: Essays on the New Mobility of People and Money.* New York: New Press, 1998.

Sassen, Saskia. *A Sociology of Globalization.* New York: W. W. Norton, 2007.

Sayer, Andrew. *Why Things Matter to People: Social Science, Values, and Ethical Life*. New York: Cambridge University Press, 2011.

Schilbrack, Kevin. "Religions: Are There Any?" *Journal of the American Academy of Religion* 78, no. 4 (2010): 1112–1138.

Schmidt, Volker H. "Convergence and Divergence in Societal Modernization: Global Trends, Regional Variations, and Some Implications for Sustainability." In *The New Middle Classes: Globalizing Lifestyles, Consumerism and Environmental Concern*, edited by Hellmuth Lange and Lars Meier, 29–48. New York: Springer, 2009.

Schumpeter, Joseph. *Capitalism, Socialism, and Democracy*. New York: Harper, [1942] 1975.

Senge, Peter. *The Fifth Discipline: The Art and Practice of the Learning Organization*. New York: Doubleday, 1990.

Sennett, Richard. *The Corrosion of Character: The Personal Consequences of Work in the New Capitalism*. New York: W. W. Norton, 1998.

Sennett, Richard. *The Culture of the New Capitalism*. New Haven, CT: Yale University Press, 2006.

Sheth, D. L. "Secularisation of Caste and Making of New Middle Class." *Economic and Political Weekly* 34 (1999): 2502–2510.

Shrinivasan, Rukmini. "'Stranger Rape' Rises over 10%." *Times of India*, June 15, 2013. http://articles.timesofindia.indiatimes.com/2013-06-15/delhi/39992572_1_rapes -delhi-police-ncrb.

Simmel, Georg. *On Individuality and Social Forms: Selected Writings*. Chicago: University of Chicago Press, 1971.

Sklair, Leslie. "Capitalism and Development in Global Perspective." In *Capitalism and Development*, 165–187. London: Routledge, 1994.

Sklair, Leslie. *The Transnational Capitalist Class*. Oxford: Blackwell, 2001.

Sklair, Leslie. "Iconic Architecture and the Culture-Ideology of Consumerism" *Theory, Culture, and Society* 27, no. 5 (2010): 135–159.

Smilde, David. *Reason to Believe: Cultural Agency in Latin American Evangelicalism*. Berkeley: University of California Press, 2007.

Smith, Christian. *The Emergence of Liberation Theology: Radical Religion and Social Movement Theory*. Chicago: University of Chicago Press, 1991.

Smith, Christian, ed. *Disruptive Religion: The Force of Faith in Social Movement Activism*. New York: Routledge, 1996.

Smith, Christian, with Michael Emerson, Sally Gallagher, Paul Kennedy, and David Sikkink. *American Evangelicalism: Embattled and Thriving*. Chicago: University of Chicago Press, 1998.

Smith, Christian. "Why Christianity works: An emotions-focused phenomenological account." *Sociology of Religion* 68, no. 2 (2007): 165–178.

Smith, Christian. "Future Directions in the Sociology of Religion." *Social Forces* 86, no. 4 (2008): 1–29.

Smith, Christian. *To Flourish or Destruct: A Personalist Theory of Human Goods, Motivations, Failure, and Evil*. Chicago: University of Chicago Press, 2015. Smith, Christian, and Brandon Vaidyanathan. "Multiple Modernities and Religion." In *The Oxford Handbook of Religious Diversity*, edited by Chad Meister, 250–265. New York: Oxford University Press, 2011.

Smith, Christian, and Melina Lundquist Denton. *Soul Searching: The Religious and Spiritual Lives of American Teenagers*. New York: Oxford University Press, 2005.

Snow, David, and Richard Machalek. "The Sociology of Conversion." *Annual Review of Sociology* 10 (1984): 167–190.

Solomon, Robert C. *It's Good Business: Ethics and Free Enterprise for the New Millennium.* Lanham, MD: Rowman & Littlefield, 1997.

Spillman, Lyn. *Solidarity in Strategy: Making Business Meaningful in American Trade Associations.* Chicago: University of Chicago Press, 2012.

Srinivas, Smriti. *Landscapes of Urban Memory: The Sacred and the Civic in India's High-Tech City.* Hyderabad, India: Orient Blackswan, 2004.

Stearns, Peter N. *Consumerism in World History: The Global Transformation of Desire.* New York: Routledge, 2001.

Stevens, R. Paul. *Doing God's Business: Meaning and Motivation for the Marketplace.* Grand Rapids, MI: Eerdmans, 2006.

St. Pierre, Isabelle, and David Holmes. "Mimetic Desire and Professional Closure: Toward a Theory of Intra/Inter-Professional Aggression." *Research and Theory for Nursing Practice* 24, no. 2 (2010): 128–143.

Stevenson, Tyler Wigg. *Brand Jesus: Christianity in a Consumerist Age.* New York: Church Publishing, Inc., 2007.

Swan, Melanie. "Authorities Prepare for Defaulters." *The National,* December 19, 2008. http://www.thenational.ae/news/uae-news/authorities-prepare-for-defaulters.

Swidler, Ann. "Culture in Action: Symbols and Strategies." *American Sociological Review* 51, no. 2 (1986): 273–286.

Swidler, Ann. *Talk of Love: How Culture Matters.* Chicago: University of Chicago Press, 2003.

Tanner, Kathryn. *Christianity and the New Spirit of Capitalism.* New Haven: Yale University Press, 2018.

Taplin, Ian M. "Flexibilization." In *The Wiley-Blackwell Encyclopedia of Globalization,* edited by George Ritzer. New York: Blackwell, 2012. DOI: 10.1002/9780470670590. wbeog207

Tavory, Iddo. "The Question of Moral Action: A Formalist Position." *Sociological Theory* 29, no. 4 (2011): 272–293.

Taylor, Charles. *Sources of the Self.* Cambridge, MA: Harvard University Press, 1989.

Taylor, Charles. *The Malaise of Modernity.* Toronto: Anansi, 1991.

Taylor, Charles. "Two Theories of Modernity." In *Alternative Modernities,* edited by Dilip Parameshwar Gaonkar, 172–196. Durham, NC: Duke University Press, 2001.

Taylor, Charles. *A Secular Age.* Cambridge, MA: Harvard University Press, 2007.

Times of India. "Archbishop Slams Karnataka CM over Church Attacks." *Times of India.* September 22, 2008. http://timesofindia.indiatimes.com/india/Archbishop-slams -Karnataka-CM-over-church-attacks/articleshow/3513469.cms.

Times of India. "A Chilling Reminder That All Is Not Well." *Times of India,* October 16, 2012. http://articles.timesofindia.indiatimes.com/2012-10-16/bangalore/34498037 _1_gang-rapes-men-over-three-days-electronic-city.

Times of India. "Bishops Express Concern over Church Attacks, 'Ghar Wapsi' in Bengaluru." *Times of India.* February 6, 2015. http://timesofindia.indiatimes.com/city/bengaluru /Bishops-express-concern-over-churchattacks-Ghar-Wapsi-in-Bengaluru/article show/46148179.cms.

Toft, Monica, Timothy Shah, and Daniel Philpott. *God's Century: Resurgent Religion and Global Politics.* New York: W. W. Norton, 2011.

Tøllefsen, Inga Bårdsen. "Art of Living: Religious Entrepreneurship and Legitimation Strategies." *International Journal for the Study of New Religions* 2, no. 2 (2011): 255–279.

Tomlinson, John. *Globalization and Culture.* Chicago: University of Chicago Press, 1999.

Touraine, Alain. *The Post-Industrial Society: Tomorrow's Social History; Classes, Conflicts, and Culture in the Programmed Society.* New York: Random House, 1971.

Touraine, Alain. *Critique of Modernity.* London: Wiley-Blackwell, 1995.

Tourish, Dennis, and Ashly Pinnington. "Transformational Leadership, Corporate Cultism, and the Spirituality Paradigm: An Unholy Trinity in the Workplace?" *Human Relations* 55, no. 2 (2002): 147–172.

Tucker, Robert C. *The Marx-Engels Reader.* 2nd ed. New York: Norton, 1976.

Turner, Bryan S. *Religion and Modern Society: Citizenship, Secularisation, and the State.* New York: Cambridge University Press, 2011.

Turner, Charles. *Modernity and Politics in the Work of Max Weber.* New York: Routledge, 1992.

Upadhya, Carol. "Rewriting the Code: Software Professionals and the Reconstitution of Indian Middle Class Identity." In *Patterns of Middle Class Consumption in India and China,* edited by Christophe Jaffrelot and Peter van der Veer, 55–87. New Delhi: Sage, 2008.

Upadhya, Carol, and A. R. Vasavi. *Work, Culture, and Sociality in the Indian IT Industry: A Sociological Study.* Bangalore: National Institute of Advanced Studies at Indian Institute of Science, 2006.

Vaidyanathan, Brandon. "Professionalism 'from Below': Mobilization Potential in Indian Call Centres." *Work, Employment, and Society* 26, no. 2 (2012): 211–227.

Vaidyanathan, Brandon. "Professional Socialization in Medicine." *American Medical Association Journal of Ethics* 17, no. 2 (2015), 160–166.

Vaidyanathan, Brandon. "The Politics of the Liturgy in the Archdiocese of Bangalore." In *Catholics in the Vatican II Era: Local Histories of a Global Event,* edited by Kathleen Sprows Cummings, Timothy Matovina, and Robert A. Orsi, 180–205. New York: Cambridge University Press, 2017.

Vaisey, Stephen. "Motivation and Justification: A Dual-Process Model of Culture in Action." *American Journal of Sociology* 114, no. 6 (2009): 1675–1715.

Van Maanen, John, and Gideon Kunda. "'Real Feelings': Emotional Expression and Organizational Culture." In *Research in Organizational Behavior,* edited by Barry M. Staw and L. L. Cummings, vol. 11, 43–103. Greenwich, CT: JAI Press, 1989.

Veblen, Thorstein. *The Theory of the Leisure Class: An Economic Study in the Evolution of Institutions.* New York: Macmillan, 1899.

Vora, Neha. "Producing Diasporas and Globalization: Indian Middle-Class Migrants in Dubai." *Anthropological Quarterly* 81, no. 2 (2008): 377–406.

Vora, Neha. *Impossible Citizens: Dubai's Indian Diaspora.* Durham, NC: Duke University Press, 2013.

Voyce, Malcolm. "Shopping Malls in India: New Social 'Dividing Practices.'" *Economic and Political Weekly* 42, no. 22 (2007): 2055–2062.

Wagner, Peter. *Theorizing Modernity: Inescapability and Attainability in Social Theory.* London: Sage, 2001.

Weber, Max. "The Routinization of Charisma." In *The Theory of Social and Economic Organization.* Translated by A. M. Henderson and Talcott Parsons, 363–386. New York: Free Press, 1947.

Weber, Max. "Science as a Vocation." In *From Max Weber: Essay in Sociology,* edited by Hans H. Gerth and C. Wright Mills, 129–156. New York: Oxford University Press, 1958b.

Weber, Max. "Religious Rejections of the World and Their Directions." In *From Max Weber: Essay in Sociology,* edited by Hans H. Gerth and C. Wright Mills, 323–362. New York: Oxford University Press, 1958c.

Weber, Max. *The Protestant Ethic and the Spirit of Capitalism.* Translated by Stephen Kalberg. New York: Oxford University Press, [1920] 2011.

Weinreb, Alexander A. "The Limitations of Stranger-Interviewers in Rural Kenya." *American Sociological Review* 71, no. 6 (2006): 1014–1039.

Whyte, William H. *The Organization Man.* Philadelphia: University of Pennsylvania Press, 1956.

Winchester, Daniel A. "Embodying the Faith: Religious Practice and the Making of a Muslim Moral Habitus." *Social Forces* 86, no. 4 (2008): 1753–1780.

Woods, Robert, and Brian Walrath, eds. *The Message in the Music: Studying Contemporary Praise and Worship.* Nashville: Abdington, 2007.

Worth, Robert F. "For a Bounced Check in Dubai, the Penalty Can Be Years Behind Bars." *New York Times*, September 11, 2009. http://www.nytimes.com/2009/09/12/world/middleeast/12dubai.html?_r=2&.

Wuthnow, Robert. *God and Mammon in America.* New York: Free Press, 1994.

Wuthnow, Robert. "New Directions in the Study of Religion and Economic Life." In *Handbook of Economic Sociology*, edited by Neil J. Smelser and Richard Swedberg, 603–626. Princeton, NJ: Princeton University Press, 2005.

Yamane, David. "Narrative and Religious Experience." *Sociology of Religion* 61, no. 2 (2000): 171–189.

Zhou, Xun. "Eat, Drink, and Sing, and Be Modern and Global: Food, Karaoke, and 'Middle Class' Consumers in China." In *Patterns of Middle Class Consumption in India and China*, edited by Christophe Jaffrelot and Peter van der Veer, 170–185. New Delhi: Sage, 2008.

Index

Abu Dhabi, 84–85, 206
Accenture, 33, 109
Al Maktoum, Sheikh Muhammad, 19
Ali, Syed, 169
Anderson, Allan, 78
Andhra Pradesh, 62–63
Apostolic Vicariate of Arabia, 84
Apple, 2, 43
apprehensive individualism, 4, 10, 17, 33–34,
    52–54, 57–61, 63–65, 73, 102–3, 211–12,
    219. *See also* global professionals
Arab Spring, 21
Art of Living (AOL) movement, 109–10, 118
Australia, 61, 104, 155–56, 164, 170, 176–77
Azusa Street revival, 77–78

Bahrain, 19
Bangalore
    attrition rates, 51, 54
    call centers, 5–6, 23, 38–39, 112, 137–38
    Catholic Charismatic Renewal (CCR)
        influence, 85–86
    civic stratification, 17, 19, 26, 171–75,
        178–81, 201, 204
    collectivism possibilities, 64, 181
    consumerism, 17–19, 135–36, 141–43, 147,
        181–82
    cost of living challenges, 142
    demographic patterns, 17–19, 23–25, 84–85,
        178–80, 218
    Discipleship Camp, 156–58, 166
    economic growth, 7, 17–19, 30, 39–40, 81,
        135–36, 142, 171, 173, 218
    educational institutions, 17
    Electronics City suburb, 28, 39
    Evangelical-Charismatic Catholicism (ECC)
        presence, 23–26, 76, 79, 83–89, 92–93, 95,
        102, 180, 190
    individualistic focus, 17, 64
    information technology (IT) industries, 2,
        18–19, 33, 40, 44, 63, 172, 180
    language groups, 17, 178–81, 190–92, 201–2
    management styles, 47, 62–63
    middle class identity, 18–19, 135, 171, 174,
        180

outsourcing, 5, 17–18
political environment, 17, 92
poverty-alleviation efforts, 9, 19, 200–203
racial discrimination, 62–63, 178–81
religious violence, 25–26, 111–12, 180, 213
shopping options, 142–43, 181
social regulations, 24–26, 137, 221
socioeconomic inequalities, 17, 25–26, 172
wage structures, 62–63, 142
Bangladesh, 177
baptism, 78, 83–86
Bauman, Zygmunt, 135–36, 154
Bell, Daniel, 47
Bellah, Robert, 32–33, 100
Benedikter, Ronald, 134
Berger, Arthur Asa, 150
Berger, Peter, 7, 9, 13, 72–73, 77, 126, 132,
    214–15, 220
Bible, 3, 26, 70, 72, 74–75, 87–88, 95, 104, 109,
    112, 114, 117, 132, 197
Boltanski, Luc, 5, 33, 37–38, 174
Bourdieu, Pierre, 60, 150
Brooks, David, 220
Budde, Michael, 12
business process outsourcing (BPO) industries,
    5, 17–18, 40, 43

call centers, 5–6, 23, 38–39, 112, 137–38, 147
Calvinism, 11, 79
Canada, 170
catechism, 71, 76, 87, 93
Catholic Answers, 26
Catholicism
    alcohol acceptance, 113
    catechism usage, 71, 76, 87, 93
    Catholic Charismatic Renewal (CCR), 26,
        82–83, 85–87, 180
    Catholic Social Teaching, 77
    discipline teachings, 116
    Eucharist adoration, 75, 88
    global appeal, 23, 84
    habituation, 73
    institutional hierarchies, 73
    liturgical services, 75–76, 85, 96, 179–80
    migrant appeal, 24–25, 84, 86, 212

Catholicism *(continued)*
  poverty-alleviation efforts, 9, 23
  Second Vatican Council, 82, 179–80
  social issue contributions, 23, 77, 213
  traditional tenets, 102
  See also Evangelical-Charismatic Catholicism
    (ECC)
Cauvery River, 179
Cavanaugh, William, 37
Chaves, Mark, 108
Chiapello, Ève, 5, 37–38
Christianity, 25–26, 70, 72–77, 84, 87, 95, 107,
    109–15, 125, 133, 135, 165, 181, 187, 202,
    209, 213–14
Christmas, 109
Clement, Kim, 160
Coca Cola, 109
collectivism, 15, 42, 48–53, 63–64, 95–96,
    99–101, 174, 181–82, 204, 208, 221
Collins, Randall, 82, 99
consumerism
  Bangalore, 17–19, 135–36, 141–43, 147,
    181–82
  debt accumulation, 146–48, 150–51, 153–54,
    159–60, 163
  Dubai, 17, 21, 23, 135–36, 138–43, 147, 182
  family obligations, 140–42, 151
  freedom connections, 138
  globalization, impact of, 136
  good life pursuit, 134, 139, 149, 166
  habituation, 144, 146, 150, 160–63, 165–66
  middle class identity, 135–37, 154
  mimetic process, 149–50, 163–65
  narrative scripts, 134, 148–50, 154–58, 162–66
  religion as escape mechanism, 151–66
  saving and investing efforts, 144–46, 165
  shopping experiences, 17, 23, 142–43, 167,
    181, 184, 186
  social stigma, 139
  sustainability, 148–50, 165–66
  tithing, impact of, 159–63, 165–66
coordinated market economies (CMEs), 14, 220
Copeland, Kenneth, 160
Covey, Stephen, 197

Davis, Nancy, 76
Dell, 2, 33
Denton, Elizabeth, 108
Denton, Melina Lundquist, 73
deportations, 26, 64, 111, 191, 206, 212
Discipleship Camp, 156–58, 166
Diwali, 109
Doha, 203

Dubai
  anti-conversion laws, 24
  attrition rates, 51, 54
  Catholic Charismatic Renewal (CCR)
    influence, 83, 85
  citizenship boundaries, 21, 169, 174–75
  collectivism, 63–64
  consumerism, 17, 21, 23, 135–36, 138–43,
    147, 182
  cost of living challenges, 142
  demographic patterns, 19, 21, 24–25, 61, 85,
    103, 177–78, 186
  economic growth, 7, 17, 19, 39, 81, 135–36,
    142, 151, 169, 173, 218
  ethnoracial stratification, 17, 21, 169–71,
    173–78, 181–82, 201, 204
  Evangelical-Charismatic Catholicism (ECC)
    presence, 23–24, 26, 76–77, 84–89, 92–96,
    102–5, 171, 177–78, 190–94, 197–98
  foreign labor force, 19, 21, 61–62
  free-trade zones, 16, 19, 21–22
  iconic architecture, 5, 16–17, 20–21, 23, 39,
    169
  individualistic focus, 17, 21
  Internet City suburb, 39
  Islamic Affairs and Charitable Activities
    Department, 26
  kafala system, 19
  management styles, 47, 61–62
  middle class identity, 22, 135, 143
  political environment, 17, 21, 132
  poverty-alleviation efforts, 9, 190, 200–203
  racial discrimination, 61–62, 103–4, 171
  religious regulations, 24, 26, 74, 81, 84, 94,
    111, 132, 190, 200–201, 212–13
  rentier state status, 19
  shopping options, 17, 23, 142–43, 184, 186
  social regulations, 25, 221
  socioeconomic inequalities, 17, 21, 176–78
  tax policies, 30
  visa requirements, 19, 74, 119, 142, 153–54,
    169–70, 176, 190, 200
  wage structures, 61–62, 142, 177, 193
  weather challenges, 40, 143, 169, 186
Duquesne University, 83
During, Simon, 166

Egypt, 61, 177
Electronics City, 28, 39
Enron, 106
entrepreneurship, 14–15, 35, 82, 107, 111, 195,
    205, 220
Eriksen, Thomas Hylland, 15

Eternal World Television Network (EWTN), 26, 72
Eucharist, 3, 75, 88, 98
Evangelical-Charismatic Catholicism (ECC)
  Bangalore, presence in, 23–26, 76, 79, 83–89, 92–93, 95, 102, 180, 190
  catechism usage, 71, 76, 87, 93
  commitment levels, 72–76, 94, 98, 112–14, 214
  community, sense of, 72, 94–95, 100–102, 168, 171, 190–91, 217
  conversion experiences, 72, 89–95
  diverse influences, 26, 72–74, 77
  Dubai, presence in, 23–24, 26, 76–77, 84–89, 92–96, 102–5, 171, 177–78, 190–94, 197–98
  Eucharist adoration, 75, 88, 98
  fitness qualifications, 72, 74, 87
  group orientations, 183–86
  growth techniques, 75–76
  habituation, 9, 73, 79, 87, 96–97, 105–6, 114–17, 122, 125–26, 131, 133, 160–63, 165–66, 198, 211
  healing function, 4, 26, 72–74, 78, 80, 88–93, 96–98
  leadership practices, 72, 87–89, 96–97, 99, 101, 186–87
  liturgical services, 26, 75–76, 86–87, 96, 98–99, 179–80
  media influence, 26–27, 72, 75–77, 87–88
  mimetic process, 96–97, 163–66, 211
  music, role of, 2, 26, 86–87, 94–95
  narrative scripts, 72, 74–77, 92, 95–96, 100, 165–66, 175, 211, 217
  organizational structures, 198–200
  Pentecostalism, influence of, 4, 26–27, 72, 74, 77–79, 88, 96, 102, 217
  personal relationship with Jesus, 26, 72–74, 78, 85, 96–97, 102, 112, 211
  prayer, role of, 72, 76, 85, 89–92, 95–99, 101, 155, 160–61, 190, 199–200
  professional logic integration, 186–89
  prophesying, 26, 78, 83
  religious activity levels, 72–75
  religious celebrities, 27, 72, 77, 88, 154, 160
  renouncements, 74
  rosary devotion, 88
  social issue contributions, 76–77, 94–95, 189–208, 213, 218
  speaking in tongues, 3, 26, 74, 78–79, 83, 87, 98
  therapeutic individualism, 4–5, 9–10, 37, 72–74, 95–100, 106, 130, 211–12, 216
  tithing, 72, 75, 159–63, 165–66
  traditional tenets, 26, 73, 76, 88

values compatibility, 115–16
voluntary service, 76, 189–90
witness experience, 26, 74–75, 104, 106, 111–15, 125–28, 132–33, 212
World Youth Day events, 89

Facebook, 76–77, 125, 154, 188
flexibilization, 36, 41–42, 46–48, 53, 57, 123, 125, 201
Fortune 500, 16, 43
Fowler, Robert Booth, 13
Francis, Pope, 89, 135
Fulmer, Burt, 135, 149, 165

General Electric (GE), 43
Ghana, 177
Gifford, Paul, 80
Girard, René, 58–59, 97, 149
global professionals
  ambition levels, 53–54, 131
  apprehensive individualism, 4, 10, 17, 33–34, 52–54, 57–61, 63–65, 73, 102–3, 211–12, 219
  attrition rates, 30–31, 51–55, 64, 211, 216
  career mobility, 2, 4, 16, 29, 33–36, 58–60, 64–65, 130–31, 149, 155, 186, 211, 216
  collectivism, 49–54, 57, 63–64
  competitive work environment, 2–5, 59–60, 215
  debt accumulation, 146–48
  faith instrumentality, 116–20
  flexibilization, 46–48, 53, 57, 201
  habituation, 8, 43, 57–60, 133, 144, 211
  informal trust development, 31, 54–57, 59, 64–66, 216
  mimetic process, 8, 57–60, 149–50, 211
  mission field role, 5, 9, 66, 106, 110–15, 125–28, 132–33, 212, 217
  moral conflicts, 120–25, 131
  narrative scripts, 8, 34–35, 37–38, 57–60, 65–66, 173, 211
  normative control, 51–52, 58, 64, 132, 216
  office politics, 31, 35–36, 189
  performance evaluations, 51, 53–54, 57–60, 116
  professional status, 40–42, 53, 58, 63, 116, 129, 214
  rationalization, 36–37, 43–50, 57, 188
  saving and investing efforts, 144–46
  values compatibility, 115–16
  wages, focus on, 2–4, 29–31, 33–34, 38, 53, 58, 123, 129, 137–38, 155, 214, 218
  workplace discrimination, 61–64, 103–4

Google, 39
Gould, Stephen Jay, 126
Gulf Business salary survey, 61
Gusfield, Joseph, 13–14

habituation, 8–9, 43, 57–60, 73, 79, 87, 105–6,
    114–17, 122, 125–26, 131, 133–34, 144–46,
    150, 160–63, 165–66, 211
Hahn, Scott, 88
Harrison, Bennett, 48
Harvard Business School, 109
Harvey, David, 14
Hefner, Robert, 77, 80–81
Hinduism, 25, 63, 80, 84, 92, 108–11, 114, 118,
    180–81, 202, 208, 213
Hinn, Benny, 88, 160
Hirschman, Albert, 219
Hochschild, Arlie, 141
Holy Spirit, 26, 73–74, 76, 78, 82–83, 85–88,
    90, 209
HP, 2, 33, 51

IBM, 2, 33, 51
Imitation of Christ, 129
Indian Institutes of Management (IIM), 103
Indonesia, 177
information technology (IT) industries, 2,
    18–19, 29–30, 33, 40, 44, 63, 104, 120, 172,
    180, 210
Infosys, 47
Internet City, 39
Iran, 12
Islam, 24, 26, 80, 84, 108, 181

Jaffrelot, Christophe, 174
Japan, 49, 85, 176
Jesuits, 84–86, 214
Jesus Christ, 26, 72–74, 78, 85, 93, 96–100, 102,
    105, 111–12
Jobs, Steve, 43
John Paul II, Pope, 83, 135
John XXIII, Pope, 82
Jordan, 178

kafala system, 19
Kanna, Ahmed, 16, 176
Kannada language, 17, 178–80, 188, 190, 202
Kanter, Rosabeth Moss, 49
Karnataka, 17, 179, 181
Knapp, John, 58
Konkani language, 179–80, 190
Kunda, Gideon, 49
Kuwait, 19, 203

labor unions, 63–64
laïcité, 108
layoffs, 44, 158
Lebanon, 177–78
Levitt, Peggy, 23
Life in the Spirit Seminar, 83, 86
Lindsay, Michael, 107
Longva, Ahn, 21, 174

Machalek, Richard, 92
MacIntyre, Alasdair, 32–33
Mahdavi, Pardis, 206
Malayalam language, 179–80, 190–92, 201
Mangalore, 29
Margetts, Peter, 147
Martin, David, 79
Marx, Karl, 10–11
Mary, 88, 93
Mascarenhas, Fritz, 85–86
Mathews, Ashwin, 2–4, 27, 36, 121, 160, 220–21
meditation, 12, 107, 109, 118
Mercenary. *See* global professionals
Meyer, John, 16, 136
Meyer, Joyce, 27, 72, 88, 154, 160
Microsoft, 39, 51
Miller, David, 106–7
Miller, Donald, 80–81
Miller, Vincent, 135
mimesis, 8, 57–60, 96–97, 149–50, 163–66, 211
miracles, 3, 26, 77, 83, 92–93, 98, 102, 119,
    152–53
Missionary. *See* Evangelical-Charismatic
    Catholicism (ECC)
Mitroff, Ian, 108
modernity, 1–2, 6–14, 38–40, 45, 79, 129, 136,
    173, 207, 212–214, 220
    multiple modernities, 14, 212, 220
Moen, Dan, 87
Muscat, 203
Muslims, 25, 108–10, 206, 208

Nair, Janaki, 179
narrative scripts, 8, 21–22, 34–35, 37–38,
    57–60, 65–66, 74–77, 92, 95–96, 100, 134,
    148–50, 154–58, 162–66, 173, 175, 211,
    217
National Association of Software and Services
    Companies (NASSCOM), 110
New Testament, 31, 73, 77–78, 83
Nigeria, 177–78
Nike, 139
non-governmental organizations (NGOs),
    199–201, 208

Non-Resident Indian (NRI), 170
Notre Dame, University of, 83
Novak, Michael, 215

office politics, 31, 35–36, 189
Old Testament, 73
Oman, 19
Oracle, 51
Osteen, Joel, 27, 72, 77, 88, 160

Pakistan, 177, 193, 204
Patel, Reena, 138
Pattanaik, Devdutt, 110
Paul VI, Pope, 83
Pentecostalism, 7, 26–27, 69, 72, 74, 77–83, 85,
        88, 96, 102, 209, 217
performance evaluations, 51, 53–54, 57–60, 116
Peters, Tom, 49
Pope, Liston, 13
poverty, 9–10, 19, 23, 39, 82, 135–36, 157, 160,
        170, 190, 199–203
prasad, 114
Princesa, Grace, 142
prophesying, 26, 78, 83
proselytism, 3, 26, 73, 106, 111–12, 193
Protestantism, 11, 70, 78, 88, 114, 209, 217
Puritanism, 11, 212
Putnam, Robert, 190–91, 194

Qatar, 19

Radhakrishnan, Smitha, 16
Ramadan, 152
rationalization, 36–37, 43–50, 57, 188
Ravi Shankar, Sri Sri, 109
Ray, Steve, 70, 88
Redman, Matt, 87
Ricoeur, Paul, 207
Riesebrodt, Martin, 22, 89
Robbins, Joel, 80, 82
Robinson, Robert, 76

Salt and Light, 96
Sanskrit, 180
Saudi Arabia, 19, 26, 84, 131, 178
Schumpeter, Joseph, 43
Second Vatican Council, 82, 179–80
Senge, Peter, 35
Sennett, Richard, 35–36, 57, 65–66, 207
Seven Habits of Highly Effective People, 197
Siemens, 39, 109
Sklair, Leslie, 14, 135–37

Smith, Bradley, 107
Smith, Christian, 22, 73, 95
Smith, Michael W., 87
Snow, David, 92
Solomon, Robert, 60
speaking in tongues, 3, 26, 74, 78–79, 83, 87, 98
Sri Lanka, 177, 204
Stearns, Peter, 136
Suenens, Leo, 83
Swidler, Ann, 129
Syria, 177–78, 185

Tagalog language, 192
Tamils, 84, 179, 188, 190–91, 202
Taylor, Charles, 8, 33, 64
Taylor, F. W., 43
Tesco, 33
therapeutic individualism, 4–5, 9–10, 37,
        72–74, 95–100, 106, 130, 211–12, 216. *See
        also* Evangelical-Charismatic Catholicism
        (ECC)
Thévenot, Laurent, 33, 174
tithing, 72, 75, 159–63, 165–66
Tomlin, Chris, 87
Twitter, 188

United Kingdom, 50, 104, 114
United States, 2, 12, 16, 70, 80, 83, 86, 88, 106,
        108, 129, 176, 182, 207, 209
Upadhya, Carol, 136
Urdu language, 192–93
Uruguay, 81

Vatican, 6, 82–83
Vora, Neha, 21, 143, 171, 175–76, 182, 207–8

Way of the Cross, 98
Weber, Max, 1, 11–13, 43, 45, 79, 212
Welch, Jack, 43
Whyte, William H., 65
Winchester, Daniel, 162–63
Wipro, 47
World Bank, 109
World Youth Day, 89
Wuthnow, Robert, 65, 129

Yahoo!, 48
Yamamori, Tetsunao, 80
Yamane, David, 92
Yemen, 84
yoga, 12, 50, 107, 109
YouTube, 75, 160

CPSIA information can be obtained
at www.ICGtesting.com
Printed in the USA
LVHW031723020419
612710LV00003B/498

9 781501 736230